Heinemann

Learning to Pass

ECDL Syllabus 4.0

Using Office XP

Angela Bessant

www.heinemann.co.uk

✓ Free online support
✓ Useful weblinks
✓ 24 hour online ordering

01865 888058

Heinemann

Inspiring generations

Heinemann Educational Publishers
Halley Court, Jordan Hill, Oxford OX2 8EJ
Part of Harcourt Education Ltd

Heinemann is the registered trademark of Harcourt Education Limited

First published 2004

07 06 05
10 9 8 7 6 5 4

British Library Cataloguing in Publication Data is available from the British Library on request.

ISBN 0 435 45580 X

Text design by Artistix

Typeset by TechType, Abingdon, Oxon

Cover design by Tony Richardson at the Wooden Ark Ltd

Printed and bound in the UK by Thomson Litho Ltd

Author's acknowledgements
This book would not have been written without the help and encouragement of a great many people and I would like to express my profound thanks to all of them. Thanks to staff at Heinemann, above all I would like to thank Julia Sandford and Anna Fabrizio for their professionalism and support in making the work easier and more pleasant. Many thanks to Margaret Berriman, also of Heinemann, for enabling publication of the 'Learning to' texts since 1997. Thanks to the ECDL Foundation and to Wilf Voss of the British Computer Society. A huge thank you to all learners, tutors and colleagues whose critical comments always add more clarity to the text. Finally I would like to thank my family, and in particular Gemma, for her shrewd eye over the exercises and Mike, for his help with module 1.

For my mother, Lily Hemsley.

Photo acknowledgements
Screen shots reprinted with permission from Microsoft Corporation, Yahoo! Inc and AltaVista. AltaVista is a registered trademark of AltaVista Company, and the AltaVista Logo is a trademark of AltaVista Company. The British National Space Centre website homepage on page 356 © Crown copyright. Reproduced under Class Licence Number CO1W0000141 with the permission of the Controller of HMSO and the Queen's Printer for Scotland.

Every effort has been made to contact copyright holders of material reproduced in this book. Any omissions will be rectified in subsequent printings if notice is given to the publishers.

Tel: 01865 888058 www.heinemann.co.uk

Contents

Introduction

In order to become proficient in using a computer, it is necessary to practise. This book enables you to do that, leading you through Microsoft Office XP applications step by step so that you can build up confidence. With the aid of the quick reference guides at the end of each chapter, and referring back through the sections for points you are unsure of, there is ample practice material for you to attempt. In this way, you will consolidate your understanding of the methods used. Sample answers to exercises (where appropriate) are provided. Other useful information appears in the Appendix.

This book assumes no prior computer knowledge. It covers all seven modules (listed below) for Version 4 of the European Computer Driving Licence (ECDL) syllabus. It also contains an additional section 'Using IT' which forms part of the BCS IT User qualification Level 2. See the following websites for more information on ECDL and the BCS IT User qualifications:

www.ecdl.co.uk
www.ecdl.com
www.bcsituser.org

Contact:

ECDL
The British Computer Society
1 Sandford Street
Swindon
Wiltshire SN1 1HJ

The book is so packed with information and advice that it would be equally suitable for anyone wanting to learn or brush up his or her skills in Office XP, regardless of whether he or she is working towards a particular qualification.

There are many ways of performing tasks in Windows and Office XP applications, for example via the keyboard, using the mouse or using the menus. For simplicity, the practical exercises demonstrated usually show one method. There are, however, instructions given for other methods at the end of the modules or in the Appendix. You will then be able to decide which is the best method for you.

ECDL modules

Module 1   Concepts of Information Technology
Module 2   Using the Computer and Managing Files (using Windows XP)
Module 3   Word Processing (using Word)
Module 4   Spreadsheets (using Excel)
Module 5   Database (using Access)
Module 6   Presentation (using PowerPoint)
Module 7   Information and Communication (using Internet Explorer and Outlook Express)

Angela Bessant website for updates and forum: **www.bessant.co.uk**
Heinemann website for errata, additional material and updates: **www.heinemann.co.uk**

About the CD-ROM

The CD-ROM contains files that are required as you progress through the practical work. You need to make copies of these files to your own storage medium, eg hard disk (see the Appendix for instructions on how to do this). The CD-ROM also contains sample answers to exercises. These are in PDF file format and can be accessed as shown below. Note: If you do not have Acrobat Reader on your computer, it can be downloaded for free from the Internet.

Accessing the answers to exercises

1　Load Acrobat Reader.
2　From the **File** menu, select: **Open**.
3　Select the location from where you want to open the file.
4　With the file selected, click on: **Open**.

Printing the answers to exercises

1　From the **File** menu, select: **Print**.
2　A Print dialogue box is displayed with a number of different options.
3　Make any changes to the printing options as required.
4　Check that the correct printer is selected and click on: **OK**.

What's on the CD-ROM

The CD-ROM contains the source files that are needed to complete the exercises in Module 3 (Word), Module 4 (Excel), Module 5 (Access) and Module 6 (PowerPoint), along with examples of model answers in PDF form. Modules 1 and 7 contain general information about using a computer and do not include exercises that require source files or model answers. This is why there are no files relating to these modules on the CD-ROM.

The CD-ROM does contain source files for Module 2 but no PDF model answers because the exercise requires moving and deleting files and folders rather than working with software documents.

Note

This book has been produced using Office XP. You will notice that many of the figures show dialogue boxes with round corners and white outlines on the buttons. However, your XP settings may be set up to look slightly different. For example, if your computer's appearance is set to Windows Classic, the buttons on the blue bar at the top of the dialogue boxes have square corners and black outlines. The content is exactly the same however your computer has been set up.

Type of software	Use
Spreadsheet	This program has some aspects of a filing system and some of a calculator. It consists of a large area, or grid, in which you enter data and text and work out sums. The program will do the calculations as instructed by you. When changes are made, the spreadsheet automatically recalculates new values. It is very fast, accurate and flexible. You can save the spreadsheets to disk and print them. Spreadsheets are used in accounting to produce budgets, balance sheets, payrolls and in scientific analysis and 'what if' scenarios. Microsoft *Excel* is a spreadsheet program.
Database	This type of program allows you to store data in an organised record format. It is sometimes known as an 'electronic filing system'. It is structured to search, retrieve and sort data rapidly and in many different ways. Databases can be saved to disk and printed. They are much faster than a manual paper card-index system and require less office space. Microsoft *Access* is a database program used by government and commerce.
Accounting	There are many specialised accounting packages available eg Sage Instant Accounts. Modern spreadsheet packages are capable of undertaking some accounting tasks required by small to medium-sized companies.
Presentation	Presentation software allows you to create, organise and design effective presentations. Options include transmitted overhead transparencies, 35 mm slides or material via a computer-compatible projector. Microsoft *PowerPoint* is a presentation program.
Desktop publishing	Desktop publishing (DTP) software allows you to create professional-looking manuals and brochures etc. It has more advanced capabilities than a word processing program. Microsoft *Publisher* is a DTP program.
Multimedia	There are many programs available to use with multimedia, ie combining graphics and images (for example, from digital cameras), text, sound, video editing and user interaction. *Paintshop Pro* is an example of an image manipulation program.
Web browser	A web browser is software that allows you easily to view, navigate and interact with the World Wide Web. Two commonly used browsers are *Internet Explorer* and *Netscape Navigator*.

Software versions

Developers are continually improving operating system and application software and periodically release new versions. Although the user normally benefits from the new features that have been added to the latest version of software, additions can lead to incompatibility problems. For example, a document previously saved using an early version of a word processor application may not always be read or edited correctly by a later version. It may also be necessary to upgrade your computer to cope with the increased demands of the new software.

1.3 How is a specialised system developed?

Imagine that you run a small company that produces and distributes greetings cards. You want to set up a computer system to monitor stock levels, track goods that have been despatched, maintain accounts, send invoices and keep a database of customers and suppliers.

The scenario above involves data to be input, processed, stored and output in a variety of ways. It would require specialised staff (eg systems analysts, programmers) to carry out this type of *systems development*. This team would probably work to a development cycle with the following basic stages:

Analysis

Agree with the user on the features and performance of the proposed computer system, together with cost and time constraints.

Design

Decide on the optimum hardware and software design to meet the user's specified requirements, within cost and time limits.

Programming

Write the program(s) required for the tasks. This may need new software or the customising of an existing applications program.

Testing

The system then needs to be tested to prove that it provides the specified features and performance. Any software and hardware modifications that result from these tests need to be well documented.

Implementation

This includes producing operating manuals, training staff and converting from an old system.

Monitoring and user acceptance

The system will be monitored so that any 'bugs' (problems with the system) can be sorted out. The user will only accept the system once it has been fully implemented and tested.

1.4   How does the computer system work?

The basic computer system outlined in Figure 1.1 works in the following way:

1 Instructions and data are input.
2 These instructions are stored so that they can be used when requested.
3 Data is processed and controlled according to instructions.
4 Results are output.

We will now look in more detail at how different components of the system carry out the above.

Input devices

There are many ways of feeding information into the computer using input devices. The most common types of input devices, with descriptions of what they do, are listed below.

Figure 1.2 The keyboard

Keyboard

A keyboard consists of input keys. In the UK, computer keyboards are based on the standard typewriter layout *QWERTY* (this refers to the first six letters on the top row). Foreign language keyboards are available. Computer keyboards have additional keys, such as function keys (programmed to perform frequently used tasks), arrow keys and the Control (Ctrl) key that is used, in conjunction with other keys, to perform specific tasks.

Mouse

The mouse is a hand-operated pointing device that enables you to interact with (eg select and move) items on the screen. A rotating ball and sensors mounted on the underside of the mouse track its movement over the desk. Optical mice (with sensors that directly track its movements without the need of a ball) are becoming increasingly common. When you move the mouse across your desk (or *mouse mat*) the mouse *pointer* moves on the screen in the same direction. The mouse pointer changes shape depending on where it is and what it is doing. Mice have two or more buttons on the top that are used to select and choose options. Newer mice have a wheel to help scroll up and down the screen display.

Figure 1.3 The mouse

Trackball

A trackball performs the same function as a mouse, but is a stationary unit with the rotating ball mounted on top. The ball is manipulated with the fingers or palm of the hand. Trackballs are often used where space is limited (eg on laptop computers).

Touchpad

A touchpad is another alternative to a mouse in that it is a device for interacting with a computer screen. A touchpad is also common on laptop computers for the same reasons as the trackball (it can be used where space is limited). A touchpad is a flat pad that works by sensing finger movement and downward pressure.

Scanner

A scanner can convert physical printed text or images into digital signals that the computer can understand. Scanners are normally of the flatbed type – capable of scanning a whole page of text or images at a time or can be hand-held for scanning portions of text.

Lightpen

This is a light-sensitive detector in the shape of a pen. It enables the user to draw and change pictures by moving the pen across the screen. Lightpens are now only used in specialised applications.

Joystick and games controller

Joysticks and games controllers are able to interact with a computer program. The user manipulates a lever and/or buttons to control the actions of an object on the screen. The majority of these devices are used for playing computer games.

Graphics tablet

A graphics tablet is a flat pad that detects the movement of a stylus (pen), often used in drawing and design.

Digital camera

Digital cameras are becoming very popular because they eliminate the need for films to be processed using chemical methods. Digital cameras store images in digital format. These images can be input directly to a computer. Having images in digital format can be really useful since, as well as being printed as many times as necessary, they can also be resized and edited, used on websites or in computer presentations and can be e-mailed to others.

Microphone

Some computer programs can recognise and interpret speech (a process known as *voice recognition*). When you speak into the microphone the speech can be translated into text on the screen.

Storing information

Memory is the place where the computer stores instructions and data. The computer could not even add two numbers together if it immediately forgot the first number! In order to make sense of the amount of memory a computer has, an understanding of how the computer handles information is helpful.

The principle behind all modern computers is the *binary* system. Binary means two and data can be represented by using only two digits, 0 and 1. The computer has a series of electronic switches that turn on and off (0 could represent off and 1 represent on). Signals in separate bits are called *digital signals*. Older computers used continually varying (*analogue*) signals. It might help to differentiate between analogue and digital by thinking of the two common forms of wristwatch. A digital display has digits that change in discrete steps (ie when each second has passed) but the hands of an analogue watch appear to change smoothly. Although the analogue display provides higher resolution (infinitely variable) the digital display has the advantage that it can be read more accurately.

Each digit of 0 or 1 (the smallest element of computer storage) contained in binary code is called a *bit*. A bit is short for *binary digit*. A string of eight bits make up one *byte*. Computer memory is measured in *bytes*. A byte can hold the equivalent of a single character: eg the letter A, the number 6, a full stop or space. Because a byte is such a small unit of storage, computer memory is more commonly measured in terms of thousands of bytes, *kilobyte* or *KB* (actually 1024 bytes); millions of bytes, *megabyte* or *MB* (1024 KB); thousands of millions of bytes, *gigabyte* or *GB*; and even millions of millions of bytes, *terabyte* or *TB*. A word processor *file* (a document is called a file when it is saved) of one thousand words will use approximately 20 KB. A full-screen colour picture file will take up approximately 300 KB. Computers have systems that allow related files to be stored in *folders* (also known as *directories*).

Memory Capacity

Unit	Representation	Description
b	Bit	Single binary digit of information, either 0 or 1
B	Byte	Group of 8 bits
KB	Kilobyte	Approximately a thousand (1,000) bytes
MB	Megabyte	Approximately a million (1,000,000) bytes
GB	Gigabyte	Approximately a billion (1,000,000,000) bytes
TB	Terabyte	Approximately a trillion (1,000,000,000,000) bytes

These terms for information storage are inherited from the familiar 'paper office' where a traditional filing cabinet would contain folders that each contained a number of smaller files. Individual folders and files are uniquely labelled to aid the storing and retrieval of items. However, unlike a traditional filing cabinet, if you want to store information safely in a computer, you need to place it on one of the *non-volatile* (holds content when the computer is switched off) storage devices described later.

A computer uses two types of memory, *RAM* (**R**andom **A**ccess **M**emory) and *ROM* (**R**ead **O**nly **M**emory).

RAM is used for the computer's *immediate access* memory. The larger the amount of this fast-access RAM, the less often the computer is forced to exchange information with its slower/cheaper memory devices when running demanding applications programs. This is also one of the reasons why applications may function more slowly when the number of applications running (and thus the demands on RAM) is increased. Therefore, in general the more RAM the computer has, the faster applications will run. Unfortunately, RAM needs electricity to retain information; any information stored will be lost when the power is turned off (its contents are said to be *volatile*). A typical basic PC might have 256 MB of RAM.

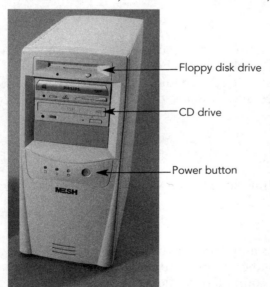

Floppy disk drive

CD drive

Power button

Figure 1.4 The system box

ROM permanently stores instructions and data (that cannot easily be altered) even when the power is turned off (its contents are said to be *non-volatile*). The computer's BIOS is stored in ROM. ROM is slower than RAM but both are much faster than disk memory devices described later. Access time to RAM and ROM is usually measured in nanoseconds (billionths of a second) whereas access time to disks is usually measured in milliseconds (thousandths of a second).

Hard disk

Most computers use one or more *hard disks*. A hard disk is used as the main permanent store of programs that have been loaded on to the computer so that they are always available (ie do not need to be loaded every time the computer is used). Hard disks are also used as the main storage location for folders and files that you have created.

A hard disk consists of magnetic storage plates permanently encased in a sealed drive unit, together with the electronics for reading and writing data. These units are normally fixed within the computer housing but have the option of being mounted externally or on a removable tray. Compared with internal units, access time to external hard disks can sometimes be slower because of the more complex way they are connected to the computer.

Hard disk capacity is currently measured in gigabytes (GB). Typical hard disk capacity is 20 GB to 120 GB. Cost can vary from around fifty to three hundred pounds. Because access may become slower as the disk fills with data, it is always a good idea to buy a large hard disk and regularly delete unwanted items to release storage space. Defragmentation (a process that ensures that files are not scattered around the disk) can be carried out to ensure that good use is made of hard disk space.

Floppy disk (diskette)

A *floppy disk* (sometimes known as a *diskette*) is a *removable* $3\frac{1}{2}''$ magnetic disk that you can easily insert and remove from a mechanical disk drive on the front of your computer (see Figure 1.4). Floppy disk access is slower compared with a hard disk but provides a convenient and cheap way of *backing up* (saving a copy of) or transferring relatively small amounts of data. However, floppy disks are gradually being phased out of new computer systems.

A floppy disk has a hard plastic case (protecting its floppy interior) with a metal cover that slides back to allow the contents to be read when the disk is in the drive. It also has a small tab in one corner that slides across to *write-protect* the contents. This stops accidental over-writing and corruption of data. The amount that can be stored on a floppy disk depends on whether it is single or double sided and whether it is single, double or high density. A double-density floppy disk stores approximately 720 KB and a high-density disk approximately 1.44 MB. Floppy disks can be purchased ready *formatted* to work with your particular type of system, but if unavailable you will have to *format* blank disks in your computer before storing data. Formatting is the process of organising the disk into a pattern of tracks and sectors, onto which the computer can write and read data. Floppy disks cost less than fifty pence each.

Zip disk

A *zip disk* is a removable magnetic disk similar to a floppy disk, but it can store 100 MB or 250 MB of information with much faster access. Zip disks are useful for storing applications programs or large amounts of data. Zip drives may be mounted internally or externally (the latter option may provide slower access depending on the method of connection used). The cost of a zip disk is approximately five to ten pounds.

Data cartridges

Data cartridges use magnetic tape technology and are really only used for backing up very large amounts of data cheaply. They commonly hold from 2 to 40 GB and cost from five to fifty pounds. Data cartridges are slower than other forms of removable storage and only provide *sequential access* (working along the tape until finding the required information). In contrast, disk technology provides *random* access (jumping directly to information required).

CD-ROM

Unlike the magnetic technology storage devices mentioned above, a *CD-ROM* (*Compact Disc Read-Only Memory*) disk is a flat optically read device with data, laser-etched on to its surface in the form of minute patterns. Laser technology is also used by internal or external CD-ROM drives that read the removable disk. CD-ROMs provide a cheap way of backing up or transferring large amounts of data. Single disks can hold in excess of 600 MB, equivalent to an entire encyclopedia or the content of five hundred floppy disks. As the size of operating systems and applications software has increased, these are now usually distributed on CD-ROMs instead of floppy disks.

A *CD-R* is a recordable CD that can be recorded on once only. A *WORM* (*Write-Once, Read-Many*) is an optical disk that allows the user to write data to it once only. A CD-RW is recordable and can be used many times and costs less than one pound.

DVD (digital versatile disk)

A DVD is a high-speed, ultra-high capacity (about 5 GB) flat optical storage medium. It can store full-length feature films on a single disk. Cost is significantly higher than for a CD-ROM.

Care of removable storage

1 Always label and store disks carefully.
2 Keep magnetic storage devices away from monitors, phones or anything else magnetic.
3 Keep disks away from direct heat, eg radiators or sunlight.

4 Never touch the recording surface of disks or tapes.

5 Write-protect important data to prevent overwriting or deleting.

6 Always keep disks and tapes safely packed whilst transporting them.

7 Be careful not to scratch CDs.

Output devices

There are many ways of getting information out of the computer. Some common output devices are listed below.

Monitor

A monitor (Figures 1.5 and 1.6) is the name given to the device that presents information on a display screen (*soft copy*, as opposed to *hard copy* when it is printed out) and is normally separate from other parts of the computer. It is sometimes called the *visual display unit* (*VDU*). Monitors can be monochrome or colour. Desktop computers traditionally used separate monitors based on the type of display found in most televisions. Portable *laptop* computers have lighter and thinner *LCD* (*liquid crystal display*) screens mounted in their lids. Although more expensive to purchase, LCD screens consume less power so cost less to run. LCD technology is now used to produce separate, space-saving, flat screen monitors for use with desktop PCs.

Figure 1.5 CRT monitor

Figure 1.6 Flat screen monitor

Printer

A printer provides printed (*hard copy*) output. There are two commonly used types of printer: *inkjet* and *laser* (Figures 1.7 and 1.8).

Figure 1.7 An inkjet printer

Figure 1.8 A laser printer

Both inkjets and lasers use non-impact technology that is quiet in operation. The inkjet sprays ink on to the paper from a cartridge. Laser printers use laser beams reflected from a mirror to attract ink (called toner) to selected paper areas when the paper is fed over a drum. Laser printers are generally quicker and produce the higher-quality output. All types have models available to print in black and white and/or colour. Printers come with a recommendation for types of paper since the quality of paper used has an effect on the quality of output produced. The resolution (sharpness) of the printout is usually measured in *dots per inch* (*dpi*). A typical laser printer offers a resolution of 1,200 dpi and a speed of ten pages per minute. Printers range greatly in price depending on the quality of output required and speed of print. Most printers now have embedded computers and memory that speed up the print process.

Plotter

A plotter controls pens to produce drawings. The computer gives the instructions so that the plotter knows which pen colour to use and where to draw. Plotters are normally used in engineering design applications.

Speakers

Speakers produce the audio output used for music, speech and games sound effects.

Speech synthesiser

Speech synthesisers turn text into spoken words and vice versa. They can be used by people who are sight impaired.

Input/output devices

Touch screen

This input/output device is normally used where it is not possible to operate a mouse or keyboard. A touch screen is a pressure-sensitive transparent layer that fits over the computer screen. To select an option, you just touch the relevant part of the screen.

Processing information and computer performance

The *central processing unit* (*CPU*) is the processing part of the computer that carries out calculations and logical operations. It is made up of the *arithmetic logic unit* (*ALU*) that carries out high-speed data manipulation. It also contains the *logic control unit* that controls the passage of data to and from the ALU by locating and carrying out instructions. In order to carry out these tasks, the CPU has a small amount of very fast immediate access memory. In a PC, these CPU functions are housed in a single *microchip* (a credit-card sized module with a large number of connections) known as a *microprocessor*. The Pentium, made by Intel Corporation, is an example of a popular microprocessor found in many PC designs. One of the main issues affecting overall computer performance is the speed of the microprocessor. This speed is called the *clock speed* or *clock rate* and is measured in *hertz* (*Hz*), the number of cycles per second: *megahertz* (*MHz*), one million cycles per second; or *gigahertz* (*GHz*) one billion cycles per second. Generally, for a given type of microprocessor design the higher the speed of operation of the microprocessor the better the performance. Clock rates are currently 1 GHz for a basic PC and 3 GHz for a top-range version.

Other factors that can have an impact on computer performance (some of these have been mentioned earlier in this section) are:

- amount of main RAM
- hard disk speed and capacity (defragmenting the disk can help free up space)
- the number of applications that are running.

In this section you will learn about different types of computers, computer networks and the Internet

2.1 / From the early days

There has always been a need for readily available, accurate and up-to-date information, but before the advent of computer technologies it used to be a time-consuming process to gather, store and process relevant information. In the 1950s the advent of *mainframe* computers brought a change in the way business and government handled information (eg insurance details and census returns). These early mainframes occupied large environmentally controlled rooms with many specialised support staff, but could only offer a similar performance to today's pocket calculators. However, rapid advances in technology vastly improved the performance and reliability of computers over the following decades. The current generation of mainframes is used by large commercial and government organisations that require the ultimate in processing power and storage capacity.

Advances in technology made possible the introduction of smaller and lower-cost computers for use by medium-sized businesses and research establishments (eg accounting, engineering design). Originally termed *'minicomputer'* in the 1960s, this class of computer evolved over the years into specialised categories (eg *workstations*, *mid-range servers*) that became increasingly used to form parts of interconnected *networks* (described later). The processing and storage capacity of this family of computer are midway between the mainframe and the PC described below.

By the 1980s it became possible to produce *desktop*-sized computers that were inexpensive enough to be purchased for use by an individual. This class of computer was termed personal computer. Of the two most commonly used *personal computers*, the most widespread in business and research are based on the original IBM *'PC'*. Less common is the Apple Macintosh (Mac), which has a niche in creative fields such as publishing and design. Today a basic PC costing approximately five hundred pounds might have a clock speed of 1 GHz, 128 MB RAM, 20 GB hard disk and a 15-inch monitor. A higher specification model, costing approximately one thousand pounds, might have a clock speed of 3 GHz, 512 MB RAM, 40 GB hard disk and a 17-inch flat screen (LCD) monitor. When purchasing a personal computer, choose a specification that best fits your requirements (eg trade monitor size for memory capacity).

Laptop computers are portable versions of desktop personal computers that can run the same applications software. People who need a computer whilst working away from the office, eg to deliver a presentation, or who work in a laboratory, often use laptops. If necessary, files created on a laptop can be transferred to a desktop PC and vice versa. The smaller and lighter laptops have lid-mounted LCD screens and can operate from internal batteries. These advanced hardware features make laptops more costly than desktop versions of equivalent performance. However, they are cheaper to run than desktops. There is a wide choice of price and performance to fit requirements with typical laptops costing approximately one thousand pounds.

Personal digital assistants (PDAs) are pocket-sized computers. They have lower performance and smaller LCD screens than laptops. They also differ from laptops by not using hard disk storage (in order to save space and battery power) and only run cut-down versions of popular PC applications software. PDAs are popular with business travellers who need to enter and access information (eg contacts database, diary entries and note taking) whilst on the move. Because there is little space for a keyboard, operation is normally via a touchscreen and stylus. The cost of a PDA is upwards of £150.

Computer type	Storage capacity	Processing speed	Unit cost (£UK)	Typical users
Mainframe	very large	very fast	100 K upwards	Large companies, government
Network	large	fast	3 K-to-10 K	Companies, hospital, university
Personal	medium	medium	0.5 K-to-2 K	Small business, school, factory
Laptop	medium	medium	1 K-to-2.5 K	As above, but portable applications
PDA	small	slow	less than 0.5 K	Sales representative, health visitor

2.2　Connecting computers

Computers can be used *standalone* (not connected to any other computer) or they can be connected together to form a *network*. The two main approaches to networking computers are as follows:

- *Client/server*, in which the *client* computers request and the *server* computer supplies. Servers are relatively high performance computers and clients are normally standard PCs. The role of the client is to perform local applications processing and communication tasks. The remote server processes requests from the many client PCs, for example, to extract data or to update a common database.
- *Peer-to-peer*. This alternative does not use a dedicated server computer because any client PCs on the network can also perform the roll of a server.

The size and performance of a computer network depend on the requirements of the users but the two main categories are as follows:

- *LAN* (*local area network*) that connects computers located within a confined geographical area, eg a single office, building or across a site.
- *WAN* (*wide area network*) that connects computers located nationwide or even around the world.

LANs are now common in medium to large-sized organisations, such as banks, schools and hospitals. There are many advantages in working on a network. It is easy to share files and resources, send messages to one another (*e-mails*, see below) and to group work on specific tasks. Software can be installed centrally from a server computer. Cost benefits include the ability to share resources (eg printers and scanners).

LANs are able to use simple wire cables to connect over the relatively short distances between computers. In contrast, WANs must rely on telecommunications links (eg fibre-optic cables, satellite links) to cover the potentially vast distances involved. The increased complexity is more than compensated for by the time and cost savings, compared with sending hard copy information by traditional routes. Probably the most familiar example of a WAN is the *Internet*, described below.

2.3　The Internet

Linking computer networks together to form the *Internet* has resulted in an explosion in the amount of data being exchanged worldwide every day. Originally developed for the military in the 1960s as a robust means of communication, the Internet became widely used as a research tool by academia and industry. However, with the later addition of the *World Wide Web* (*WWW* or *web*) service and the introduction of web browser software it became much easier for small organisations and individuals to use the Internet for business and pleasure.

From the earliest days of computer networking *electronic mail* (*e-mail*) proved very popular. It is a method of sending messages between connected computers. You can send and receive the electronic equivalent of letters, faxes, pictures, video and sound. It is a quick and efficient means of communication. It has the advantage that you can send and receive your messages when you choose (unlike 'live' telephone communication) and is cheaper because calls are charged at local rates (and sometimes even free!). (*Note*: If you have a web (see below) e-mail account, eg Hotmail, you can send and receive messages from most computers wherever they are, eg in a cybercafe in another country.) You may send these messages to many addresses at the same time. In addition, you will usually be informed if your message has failed to reach its destination(s). E-mail messages (and any files transmitted with them) can be saved and edited by the recipient, whether text or graphics.

The World Wide Web is one of the most popular services run on the Internet. It contains vast numbers of pages of words, pictures, video, sounds and graphics, stored on millions of computers located throughout the world that are connected to the Internet. The web provides information on almost every subject (from train timetables to scientific papers). Each document on the web is written in *HTML* (*Hypertext Markup Language*). This commonality of language makes it possible for *web browsers* to display *web pages* on many different types of computer. When looking for specific information on the web, if you do not know an address where you can find it, you can use a *search engine*. A search engine will look through its database of sites that contain the 'key word(s)' you are looking for and will return a list of possible suitable sites. There are also search directories that set out information in subject categories.

In order to send/receive e-mail or access information on the web you need the following:

- A telephone system to connect to, either dial-up (temporary) or a leased line (permanent) connection.
- A modem.

- Communications software.
- An account with an Internet service provider (ISP) who will register your unique Internet address.

Many home and small business users connect to the Internet over existing national and international telephone systems that rely on the voice telephone network (*Public Switched Telephone Network – PSTN*). The newer digital network *Integrated Services Digital Network* (*ISDN*) is an international communications standard for sending voice, video and data over digital telephone lines and normal telephone lines (digital technology is able to transfer data faster than analogue because the quality of the network connections is higher). Telecommunication standards ensure that people and computers can communicate over existing connection facilities using common *protocols*. (See section 1 for definitions of analogue and digital.)

When a computer wants to send information to another computer using the ordinary public telephone system it must have a means of converting the digital signals from the computer into analogue signals used by the phone line, and vice versa for incoming information. (It must **mo**dulate and **dem**odulate.) The hardware that performs this transfer of data is called a *modem*. The speed of data transmission is measured in *bits per second* (*bps*). The maximum *transfer rate* for commonly available modems, using the ordinary telephone lines, is currently 56 Kbps. The transfer rate of these modems is the same for data transmission and reception (symmetrical). However, the increasing demand of Internet users for large amounts of graphics, sound and video data has recently lead to the creation of the *Asymmetric Digital Subscriber Line* (*ADSL*) standard. This standard enables special modems to receive data at a much higher transfer rate than they are able to send requests.

Intranet

Some companies and organisations operate a type of internal website known as an *intranet*. This facility only serves staff members and is not directly accessible to the public. However, intranets normally use the same language as the web and can exchange information via the Internet when necessary.

Extranet

This type of site is normally used to provide specific information to selected Internet users. The public may only gain access to sensitive information by using a password or some other form of security check. The main operators of extranet sites are businesses involved in electronic commerce.

Section 3 / Computers and people

In this section you will learn about:

- the information society
- where computers are used
- what people use computers for
- health and safety aspects

3.1 The use of information technology in everyday life

Because the society we live in now relies heavily on computers and telecommunications to enable us to gather and disseminate information quickly and easily, this reliance on *information technology* (*IT*) (sometimes known as *information and communications technology* (*ICT*)) has led to the increased use of the term *information society*. Computers can be linked together using telecommunications technologies to transfer and process information across the globe. The Information Superhighway is another name given to the Internet – the telecommunications infrastructure that allows access to a rapidly growing source of information across the world and enables *electronic commerce* (*e-commerce*). If you advertise a service or product, buy a book, order your groceries or arrange a holiday using the Internet, you are participating in e-commerce.

The way we live and work is changing at an ever-increasing rate. Some people feel unease about our increasing reliance on technology and wonder where it is leading us. Some feel empowered by it, whilst others feel threatened. You will have your own views. How, for example, would a major breakdown in telecommunications disrupt your daily life? In situations where you see computers being used it is worth asking 'Is this a job for a computer or would a human still be better and why?' In some situations, person skills cannot be replaced, such as in the caring professions (eg nursing and counselling), and anywhere where innovation, thinking and verbal interaction are vital. Maintaining a record of vehicle registration numbers is best left to a computer. Unfortunately the answer may not always be as clear-cut and much then depends on your general values. Examples of computer use by different sections of modern society are included below.

3.2 Where and how computers are used

Computers are busy doing all sorts of things. Some common places you will find them include:

- Supermarkets, where bar codes are scanned and product and customer information is stored. This is known as *Electronic Point Of Sale* (*EPOS*). Using such methods, stock control and marketing can be improved. Bank cards are also swiped at the checkout and payment is taken directly for goods. This is termed *Electronic Funds Transfer At Point Of Sales* (*EFTPOS*).
- Libraries, where books and other items are tracked using database facilities and swiped when taken out and returned.
- Doctors' surgeries, where patient records are computerised.
- Garages, where specialised engine diagnostics equipment is used to test for faults and check that exhaust emission levels are within legal limits.
- Bank/building society cash machines (known as *Automated Teller Machines* or *ATMs*), where cards are used to identify the customer by reading the magnetic strip and checking the user's *PIN* (*Personal Identification Number*). *Smart cards* – credit cards with a built-in microprocessor and memory – are more secure and flexible than magnetic cards.

More detailed examples of how sections of society rely on computers and telecommunications are outlined below.

Home

Many households now have computers and have Internet access. They are used by all family members for various activities, including:

- sending e-mails
- accessing the Internet to find information for various activities (eg homework, projects, hobbies)
- keeping household accounts and income tax submissions
- processing and printing images from digital cameras
- shopping, banking, booking tickets
- playing games
- working from home.

Business

Large corporations were amongst the earliest users of computers and networks since they have a great deal of data that needs calculating and analysing. They may have special systems known as *Information Management Systems* (*IMS*) or *Database Management Systems* (*DMS*). For example, insurance companies need to keep policyholders' details so that when a claim arises they are able quickly to access the claimants' details and cover. Today even the smallest family-run business has come to rely on computer technology. A typical business would use computers for many of the following tasks:

- Online banking is available at any time at reduced cost.
- Keeping databases of names and addresses (database applications).
- Account information (spreadsheet and database applications).
- Marketing, including advertising and selling via websites, such as airline booking systems (using e-mail and the Internet and web browser software).
- Stock control and sales analysis (spreadsheet and database applications).
- Payroll (using spreadsheets or customised software) and *Electronic Funds Transfer* (*EFT*), ie transferring money from one account to another.
- Producing all paperwork, letters, memos, brochures etc using word processing, DTP and integrated office suites.
- Designing products (*Computer Aided Design* (*CAD*) software).
- Automating industrial processes and robotics (specialised technology).
- Airline booking systems offer rapid and up-to-date ticket sales and selection.

E-commerce

One of the fastest-growing areas of business during the past decade is *e-commerce*. New companies have been formed to market and sell goods and services exclusively via the Internet. Many long-established companies then introduced the option of *online purchasing* (insurance and banking companies quickly identified the advantages of doing business via the Internet). The public was, in general, already familiar with the process of giving credit card details over the telephone (to pay bills and purchase tickets etc), including the need for security procedures like password protection. However, there were concerns about security issues associated with online purchasing. How would you know if the website was a genuine one? Would others have access to your personal details, such as name and address, credit card/bank details? Although there is a risk of credit card fraud, most e-commerce websites now implement a range of secure purchasing procedures. When using a commercial site, you are usually advised when you are entering a secure site. Secure sites use encryption – all the details that you enter are turned into a code that is meaningless other than to the computers involved. You can also check for the *padlock* symbol at the bottom of your browser window. A closed padlock denotes that the page is secure. Basic consumer rights to return unsatisfactory goods (purchased in the UK) may be similar to when making a card purchase in person from a shop. You should always check what rights you have before making a purchase.

E-commerce can benefit business and consumers by reducing operating costs and improving accessibility. The introduction of *online catalogues* and *virtual store* websites means that customers can now access up-to-date information on goods and services including the latest prices and delivery dates. They can then make a purchase at any time of day or night on any day of the week without having to leave their home or office. However, a badly designed website can leave potential customers wishing that they could still 'ask a member of the sales staff' (eg it may be difficult to 'navigate' around the site to find a specific product and web pages may be slow to download).

Government

In addition to the general administrative examples already mentioned above, the roll of government involves keeping vast amounts of information about individuals, households and businesses. The many large computer systems used are able to exchange information between the different central and local government agencies (eg local police can access information from the central vehicle registration authority). Examples of government use of IT are listed below:

- Vehicle registration.
- Processing census information.
- Planning future housing, healthcare, education and transport needs.
- Public records.
- Monitoring agricultural and industry performance.
- Financial modelling to predict expenditure requirements.
- Revenue collection.
- Electronic voting.
- Civil and military research.

Healthcare

Hospitals, doctors surgeries and dental practices depend heavily on keeping up-to-date patient records on computers. In the case of accident and emergency departments, the ability to access medical information quickly could save lives. The use of computers in hospitals has spread from central administration, throughout wards, reception areas and laboratories. This data network even extends via wireless links to paramedics in the field. The role of computers in healthcare includes the following:

- General administration (eg stock control, accounting, staff rosters).
- Storing and accessing patients' medical records.
- Despatching ambulances via the quickest route.
- Controlling and processing information from specialised equipment (eg X-ray scanner).
- Analysing and storing results from laboratory tests.
- Specialist surgical equipment (eg heart rate and blood pressure monitors).

Education

Many education establishments and commercial training centres rely on computers to store student details and plan teaching timetables. In addition to these administrative tasks, computers are increasingly being used as educational tools that present information and assess student performance. Specialised *Computer-Based Training* (*CBT*) software is now available for a wide range of subjects and age groups. These packages can allow a more flexible approach to learning, including the ability to study at a distance via the Internet. The web is used by students as a valuable additional information source for their learning.

Teleworking

Working from home using telecommunications is known as *teleworking*. It has many advantages and disadvantages. Some are listed below:

Advantages
- Flexible working hours and potential for increased family contact.
- Less commuting saves money, time and can improve the environment.
- More choice in location of home.
- Fewer distractions can improve worker efficiency.
- Reduces employers' accommodation costs.

Disadvantages
- Lack of team motivation and support.
- Loss of social interaction.
- Reduced health and safety supervision.
- Potential for longer working hours and domestic distractions.
- Additional cost of providing suitable working environment at home.

3.3 Environmental considerations

The ability of computers to store, send and present information electronically can directly help the environment by reducing accommodation and transport requirements (eg documents distributed on CD-ROMs or via an extranet website, rather than printing it on paper). Even when such information is printed, people are now more aware of the need to recycle paper and toner cartridges. Environmental considerations have also led to the development of energy-saving computer hardware that automatically switches off when not in use.

Unfortunately, the production and eventual scrapping of computer hardware can be very harmful to the environment. Items such as electronic circuit boards, batteries and toner cartridges contain dangerous chemicals that should not simply be discarded. Environmental legislation dictates that such material must be professionally recycled or disposed of safely (always consult your local environmental agency if you are unsure how to dispose of computer hardware or consumables).

3.4 Health and safety

When you are using a computer for prolonged periods it is important that you make yourself comfortable otherwise you may become easily fatigued or ill. Computing environments in the workplace must conform to the *Health and Safety at Work* (*HASAW*) legislation. An employer is responsible for providing a safe and comfortable working environment. *Repetitive strain injury* (*RSI*), an injury arising from making awkward movements or the prolonged use of particular muscles, is a recognised condition. Eyestrain and headaches have also been linked with working with computers. You can minimise risks by being aware of the information given below.

Positioning of the screen	All screens should be adjustable so that you can set them up for your own requirements to avoid muscle strain in the neck and shoulders. The screen should be directly in front of you, roughly at arm's length. The top of the screen display should be just above eye level.
Positioning of documents	To prevent visual fatigue and muscle tension and to minimise refocusing and twisting the neck, documents should be near the screen, at the same height and distance. Document holders that clip on to the side of the monitor are useful.

Positioning of keyboard	If your keyboard is not comfortable (ie it is placed too near the edge of the desk or is too far away to be comfortable), you could put unnecessary strain on your wrists and cause repetitive strain injury (RSI). Keep your wrists straight and try not to bend them upwards when keying in. Wrist rests are available.
Using the mouse	Ensure that you are using the mouse correctly. Keep it in a comfortable position and rest your fingers lightly on the buttons. Do not grip it too tightly or for prolonged periods. Use a mouse mat to provide smoother and more precise mouse movement.
Type of chair	An adjustable chair is essential. Your back should be straight and your feet should rest on the floor. Your forearms should be roughly horizontal when using the keyboard.
Lighting	Screen glare should be avoided by adjusting background lighting and using window blinds or positioning the screen so that it is unaffected. Optional anti-glare filters for screens are available.
Ventilation	Ensure that there is adequate ventilation in your working area.
Frequent breaks	When working at the computer for prolonged periods, it is important to take frequent breaks (about ten minutes every hour) to stretch and walk around. Also give your eyes a rest so that they do not become tired and sore from staring intently at the small screen area. Focus them in the distance. Consider the possibility that spectacles may be helpful even if you do not normally wear them for reading.
Ensure equipment is safe	It is important to have equipment checked periodically to ensure that it is safe to use. Power cables should be secured so that they cannot be tripped over and power sockets should not be overloaded. Any cable damage should be professionally repaired. Surge protectors can be purchased to protect equipment (particularly modems) from damage during thunderstorms and other forms of power surge.
Look after your computer	Do not eat and drink while using your computer. Crumbs can become lodged in the keyboard and spilt drinks can cause quite serious damage. Do not pile things on top of the monitor, system box or printer as this could block air vents. Computers should not be moved when they are in use since this may cause damage to the hard disk.

In this section you will learn about:

- backing up
- limiting access
- computer viruses
- copyright concerns
- the Data Protection Act

4.1 Backing up

Computers occasionally *crash* (eg screen display may freeze, mouse/keyboard input ignored). This may happen because there is an error in the program you are running or because there is a problem with the hardware. In such circumstances, information may be lost or corrupted because you are unable to follow the correct shutdown procedure before restarting the computer. Power cuts and computer *viruses* (see below) can cause similar problems. It is therefore a good idea to produce a *backup* (exact copy) of your files on removable disks or tape at regular intervals. This allows you to revert to the backup (backup copies should be kept in a safe and separate place) versions and minimises the effort required in redoing lost work. Generally the more often files are updated, the more often you will make backups to maintain a recent copy. If you have a power cut or major crash between backups, you may still be able to retrieve the data from damaged files with the aid of a specialised hard disk recovery program.

4.2 Information security

Information is a valuable commodity and therefore access to it is often restricted. Computers can rapidly copy, alter and delete large amounts of information, so organisations that use them must take measures to minimise the risk of unauthorised data access (particularly when computers are networked). Taking precautions makes it difficult for *hackers* (unauthorised illegal users) to break into the system to steal or alter confidential information or plant *viruses* (see below). An organisation's *information security* policy should include educating staff about a responsible attitude towards security procedures and the need to report any problems quickly. A well-defined reporting and recording system should be in place, including a nominated member of staff to investigate incidents in a timely manner.

Typical security procedures include user IDs to gain access to rooms and computers where confidential information is stored. Password-protecting computers means that only an authorised user with the correct user ID number, and password to match the user ID, has the right to access files. Often in the case of particularly sensitive information *access rights* may only be granted to staff on a strictly 'need-to-know' basis. This restricts access to certain files and facilities. Document files can also be password protected. Screen savers can be useful so that people walking past do not see what is on your screen when you are absent from your desk. These can be password protected too. Passwords should be difficult for anyone else to guess (eg not family names or birthdays) and changed frequently. They should, of course, never be divulged to an unauthorised individual and should not be written down.

Computers should be sited in places that:

- are not easily accessible, so that they cannot be stolen (they should be security marked so that they can be easily traced if necessary)
- have fire and smoke alarms
- are kept clean and dust free
- do not flood.

The popularity of small battery-powered computers has greatly increased the risk of unauthorised access to confidential information. A laptop computer or PDA may easily be stolen from a car or left on a train, and the stored data misused. Even text messages stored on a mobile phone could provide details of your home and the times when it may be empty, and the address book might contain telephone numbers that might be misused (eg nuisance calls and fraud). In addition to the security issues, loss of information (eg customer contact details and business quotations) may cause considerable inconvenience and unnecessary work. Sensitive data can be particularly vulnerable whilst in transit, on removable disk or via telecommunications. Under these circumstances, security can be improved by using *encryption* techniques to encode data before storage or transmission. The data can then only be decoded by users that possess the correct *encryption key* software. Internet banking and many other forms of e-commerce rely heavily on this method of data security. The allocation of encryption keys must, of course, be strictly controlled as part of an organisation's overall information security policy.

4.3 Computer viruses

A *computer virus* is a program written by someone who wants to cause widespread inconvenience to other computer users. A virus is normally buried within another program and automatically loaded into a user's computer without his or her knowledge or consent. Depending on which type of computer virus is involved, when the user runs the infected program, the virus causes problems that may range from merely irritating (unwanted messages or graphics effects) to devastating (major loss or corruption of data). Most have the ability to attach copies of themselves to other programs that in turn infect more programs. When removable disks were the main source of infection the spread of viruses was relatively slow, but with the growth of the Internet it is now possible to have a worldwide computer epidemic within hours. A list of the more common viruses is given below:

- *Trojan Horse*: the actions of this type of virus are disguised to appear benign, whilst actually causing harm (eg altering an existing program to access restricted data).
- *Time bomb*: this type of virus only causes harm on a specific date or when a program has been run a certain number of times.
- *Logic bomb*: this type of virus only causes harm when it detects specific data.
- *Worm*: this type of virus makes copies of itself throughout a computer's hard disk and RAM. This increasingly uses up resources and overloads the computer until it slows or stops.

Antivirus utility programs are available that alert you to an infection and then remove (*disinfect*) it from your computer. Antivirus utility programs perform this service by searching the computer's memory for the *signature code* (unique pattern) of known viruses and deleting any found. You can set the frequency of antivirus runs so that the software runs automatically and to your requirements. Antivirus utility programs are a good 'insurance' investment, but only if updated on a regular basis to cope with the new viruses that are continually being released. If you are unfortunate enough to have a virus on your computer, contact your IT support department straightaway. They will try to minimise the risk of the virus spreading. If you work alone, close down the computer and restart it using a write-protected *boot disk* (a disk that contains the essential elements of the operating system) and then run an antivirus utility. Since prevention is better than cure, try to know the source of your software and always save and perform a virus check before running it (even software distributed on disks with computer magazines has been known to contain viruses).

Be particularly careful to save and virus-check files that are downloaded from the Internet, or e-mails and their attachments. It may often be simpler to delete a suspicious e-mail message rather than risk opening it. For example, in May 2000 an Internet virus infected about ten percent of business computer systems in the UK and many more worldwide. The virus spread rapidly because people rushed to open the enticingly labelled *Iloveyou* e-mail attachment which then accessed their computer address book and e-mailed itself to everyone listed.

4.4 Copyright issues

Copyright is the exclusive right, granted by law for a certain number of years, to copy and distribute creative work (eg literature, music and software). It is therefore illegal for anyone to copy or distribute such work without the permission of the copyright holder. This legal protection may apply whether the copyright material exists in printed or electronic form. However, on CDs, Zip disks and diskettes etc there are certain exceptions. The law can allow *fair use* of properly credited material (ie not claim the work as your own but credited to the original creator) that forms a small part of a much larger undertaking (eg an educational research project). Another exception applies when copyright has lapsed (after the specified protection period expires); the material may then enter the *public domain* and be freely copied. Always check on the current status of copyright material rather than risk using it illegally. It is particularly important to undertake such checks when attempting to use material from the Internet (eg since it is easy to copy photos and text from a website into a new document, this does not mean that it is legal).

When purchasing copyright-protected software you enter into an agreement (an *end-user licence agreement*) with the manufacturer that places severe restrictions on the product's use. The agreement normally allows you to make a personal backup copy but prohibits the use of the product by a non-licence holder under any circumstances. Unfortunately copyright-protected software is often illegally copied (*pirated*) and widely distributed. To reduce the possibility of accidentally obtaining an illegal copy you should always purchase software from a reputable source and check that it is still sealed in its original packaging. This should clearly display the manufacturer's *product ID number*. You will need to enter the *ID* number when installing the software on your computer and also register it with the software manufacturer to obtain an end-user licence. Once software is installed its ID number can normally be checked on screen (eg via the Help menu in the case of Microsoft Office).

Shareware is software that is available free of charge for the purpose of evaluation (normally) over a specified period of time. If you decide to continue using this software its author will require you to register and pay for it, often in return for additional documentation, technical support and upgrades. Shareware is increasingly being distributed on CDs that are bundled with computer magazines and are also made available via the Internet.

Freeware is software that you can use free of charge for an indefinite period of time. The author retains ownership of the software and control over its redistribution, which includes the ability to restrict its commercial use and the option of charging for future versions. However, any such control would cease if the author decided to relinquish ownership and place the software in the public domain.

4.5 Data Protection Act 1998

The UK Data Protection Act was first passed in 1984 and has been updated (1998) to give full effect to the European Directives on Data Protection. It now not only sets rules for processing personal information on computers, but extends to paper-based records. It gives individuals the right to know about the information held on them. Personal data is kept for many reasons, eg by tax offices, personnel departments, banks, hospitals. Everyone who processes and stores information should register as a data controller with the Data Protection Commissioner. If an individual feels that information is not being properly used, he or she can contact the Data Protection Commissioner who will investigate the claim. There are strict penalties (unlimited fines) for anyone who does not comply with the rules. There are eight principles to ensure that information is handled properly. These are that personal data must be:

- fairly and lawfully processed
- obtained only for one or more specified purposes
- adequate, relevant and not excessive
- accurate and where necessary kept up to date
- not kept for longer than necessary
- processed in line with the rights of data subjects
- kept secure
- not transferred to countries outside the European Economic Area without adequate protection.

1 What is a Graphical User Interface (GUI)? Describe some of the features that help make them easy to use.

2 List the three main items of hardware that form a desktop computer system.

3 What is the most appropriate unit of storage (select from kilobyte, megabyte, gigabyte and terabyte) for the following devices?

    a   RAM
    b   floppy disk
    c   hard disk
    d   CD-ROM.

4 Compared with a traditional camera, what advantages and disadvantages might a digital camera have?

5 List three advantages and three disadvantages of working from home.

6 Explain the main reasons for keeping backup copies of your computer files.

7 What is the most appropriate type of application software to use for the following tasks?

    a   producing a letter
    b   editing images from a digital camera
    c   producing an advertising brochure
    d   looking for information on the Internet
    e   filing customer details
    f   calculating company expenditure.

8 How might you participate in e-commerce and what are some of the advantages and disadvantages of electronic transactions?

9 What precautions should you take before purchasing from a website?

10 List the three main factors that determine computer performance.

11 What is the role of a programmer in developing a computer system?

12 What unit of measurement is used to indicate the speed of a CPU?

13 Name three computer input and three output devices.

14 Why do most PDAs use a form of touchscreen as the main input/output device?

15 For mobile use, what are the main advantages of a PDA compared with a laptop computer?

16 Why should you not dispose of computer parts and consumables in the same way as normal domestic refuse?

17 How might stored data be affected by moving a computer when it is still switched on?

18 Name two types of computer virus. List the measures required to reduce the risk of virus infection.

19 Why must antivirus software be regularly updated to remain effective?

20 List the measures required to avoid the risk of repetitive strain injury (RSI) when using a computer.

21 What basic precautions can be taken to restrict unauthorised access to computer data?

22 Describe the purpose of the Data Protection Act and give examples of how personal data could be misused.

23 Name two government organisations that would routinely exchange information.

24 What is the difference between an intranet and an extranet? Explain how these networks might be used by an organisation.

25 What equipment and facilities would you need to send and receive e-mail using your home computer?

26 Explain the term Asymmetric Digital Subscriber Line (ADSL). What is the main benefit of ADSL when accessing the Internet for home use?

27 How can you minimise the risk of purchasing pirated software?

28 Explain the differences between shareware software and freeware software.

29 What legal constraint might prohibit you from downloading and using creative material from the Internet?

30 Name the most popular service available on the Internet.

    Note: These are only practice tasks. Successful completion does not imply certification of the module by the ECDL Foundation.

Using the Computer and Managing Files

Section 1 / Getting started

In this section you will practise and learn how to:

- start the computer
- use the mouse
- recognise parts of the desktop and parts of an application window
- use Help functions
- reduce/enlarge, resize, rescale and close a desktop/application window
- move windows on a desktop
- shut down the computer
- restart the computer
- shut down a non-responding application

1.1 Windows

Windows is an operating system that ensures all parts of the computer system work together. It controls the hardware and starts and operates software. It provides ways to manage files stored on the computer.

1.2 Starting the computer

Method

1 Ensure that the computer is plugged into the electricity socket.
2 Press the button on the computer system box (and on the monitor, if it has a separate button) to switch the power on.

The computer will perform its start-up checks (**P**ower **O**n **S**ystem **T**est (**POST**)) and load Windows and accessories. You will then see the Windows desktop displayed. The items that appear on this screen depend on how your computer is set up. It will look something like Figure 2.1.

Note: The small pictures that Windows uses to represent programs, files etc are called *icons*.

Info

If you are using a network or password protected computer, you will need to find out what the procedure is to log in to Windows.

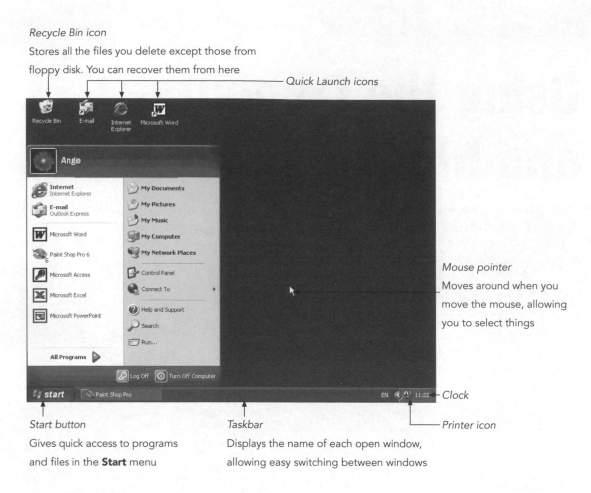

Recycle Bin icon

Stores all the files you delete except those from floppy disk. You can recover them from here

Quick Launch icons

Mouse pointer

Moves around when you move the mouse, allowing you to select things

Clock

Start button

Gives quick access to programs and files in the **Start** menu

Taskbar

Displays the name of each open window, allowing easy switching between windows

Printer icon

Figure 2.1 Windows XP desktop with Start menu displayed

1.3 The mouse

The mouse lets you select and move items on the screen. When you move the mouse on your desk, the mouse pointer moves on the screen in the same direction. You will notice that the mouse pointer changes shape depending on where it is and what it is doing. The mouse has a left and a right button. These can both be used to select and choose options. In Windows, the right mouse button is usually used to access alternative pop-up menus that are relevant to the current task.

Mouse terms

- **Click**: press and release the mouse button.
- **Double-click**: quickly press and release the mouse button twice rapidly. (You may find this quite difficult at first. Ensure that you are not leaving too long a gap between clicks and try to ensure that you do not move the mouse whilst clicking. You will master it!)
- **Drag and drop**: when the mouse pointer is over an object on your screen, press and hold down the left mouse button. Still holding down the button, move to where you want to reposition the object. Release the mouse button.
- **Hover**: place the mouse pointer over an object for a few seconds so that something happens, eg another menu appears or a handy tip (a *ToolTip*).

Practise

An excellent way of practising mouse skills is to play the game of Solitaire that comes with Windows.

Using the Start button

To start Solitaire follow the directions given in Figure 2.2:

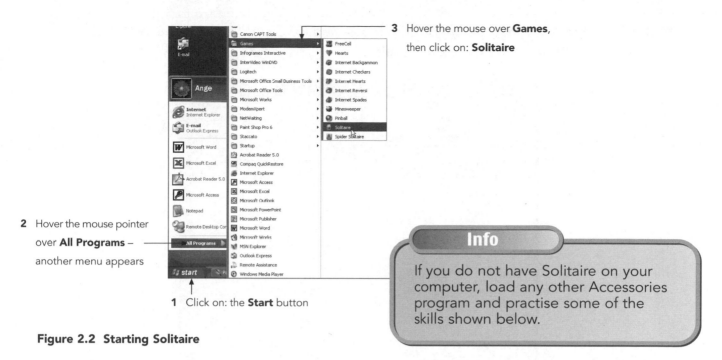

3 Hover the mouse over **Games**, then click on: **Solitaire**

2 Hover the mouse pointer over **All Programs** – another menu appears

1 Click on: the **Start** button

Figure 2.2 Starting Solitaire

The Solitaire window appears (Figure 2.3). Notice that the taskbar, at the bottom of your screen, now displays a button for Solitaire.

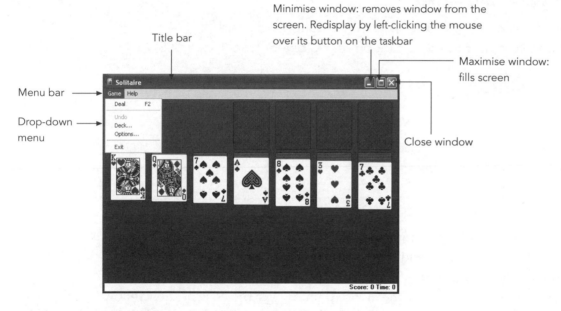

Title bar

Minimise window: removes window from the screen. Redisplay by left-clicking the mouse over its button on the taskbar

Maximise window: fills screen

Menu bar

Drop-down menu

Close window

Figure 2.3 Parts of a window

Play Solitaire

Method

1 On the **Menu** bar, click on: **Help**; a menu appears.
2 Click on: **Contents**; the **Solitaire Help** window appears (Figure 2.4).

3 Click on: the **Contents** tab, if not already selected (on top of **Index** and **Search** tabs).

4 Click on: **Solitaire**, then on: **Play Solitaire**.

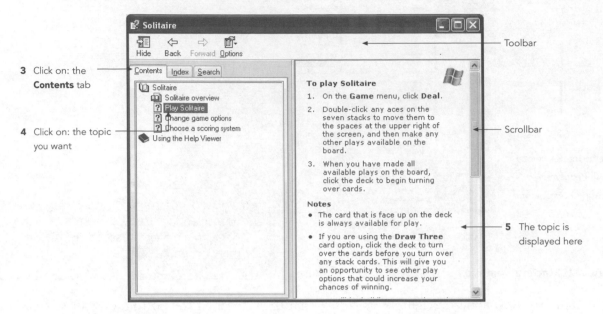

Figure 2.4 Solitaire Help window

5 The rules of the game are displayed in the right-hand pane.

6 When you have read the rules, click on: the **Close** button (Figure 2.5).

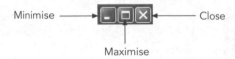

Figure 2.5 The Close button

You are now ready to play Solitaire!

Practise

1 The mouse actions whilst playing the game.

2 Using the menus to get Help and choose other options for the game.

3 Moving the window by pointing to the Title bar and dragging and dropping.

4 Resizing the window by moving the mouse pointer over the edge of the window until a double arrow appears. Press and hold down the left mouse and drag to the required shape. Release the mouse.

Note: To keep the same proportions of the window, drag from a corner.

When you have had enough practising, from the **Game** menu, click on: **Exit**, or click on: the **Close** button.

1.4   Getting Help

You can get Windows XP Help as follows.

Practise

1 Click on: the **Start** button, then on: **Help and Support**. The Help and Support window is displayed.

2 In the **Search** box, key in text for the topic that you want to find out about (Figure 2.6).

Figure 2.6 Help and Support Centre search box

3 Click on: the **Start Searching** button.

4 The search results are displayed (Figure 2.7). A list of date-related topics is given.

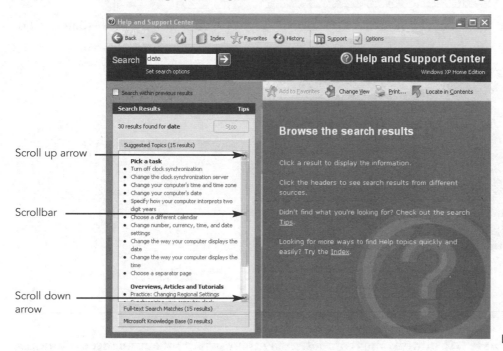

Figure 2.7 Topics Found

5 Choose a topic by double-clicking on it. I have chosen 'Change your computer's date' and the topic appears displaying help in the right-hand pane (Figure 2.8).

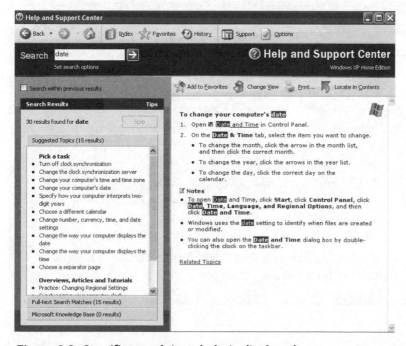

Figure 2.8 Specific search item help is displayed

Scroll bars

When a window is not big enough to display all the information in it, scroll bars appear, vertically and/or horizontally.

Practise

- Clicking on the scroll bar arrows to move through the index entries.
- Dragging the slider along the scroll bar to move more quickly through the entries.
- Searching for other Help topics.

When you have finished searching for Help topics, close the help window by clicking on: the **Close** button.

1.5 Shutting down the computer

1 From the **Start** menu, click on: **Turn Off Computer**. The Turn off computer dialogue box is displayed (Figure 2.9).

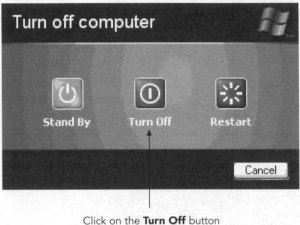

Click on the **Turn Off** button

Figure 2.9 Shutting down Windows

2 Click on: the **Turn Off** button. Your computer may then switch off automatically. If not, when the computer prompts you, you can switch off using the button on the system box.

Info

Do not switch off the computer without closing down Windows correctly when you have finished. Using correct procedures as described above ensures that your work and settings are saved ready for next time. Always save any work that you want to access at a later date and close any applications that you have open. Notice that the **Turn Off Computer** dialogue box (Figure 2.9) also has a **Restart** option. This option closes Windows and then automatically restarts. Sometimes when you are working in an application it will '*crash*', ie you will not be able to interact with the application (eg use the mouse or the keyboard to input data or commands). Depending on the problem, if you can, exit the application and then reload it. When an application has stopped responding and you are unable to close it, you may still be able to access the **Start** menu and **Restart**. If you are unable to access the **Start** menu, pressing the keys: **Ctrl + Alt + Delete** at the same time will display the Windows Task Manager. Select the program that is not responding. Click on: **End Task**. Notice that you can also access the Shut Down menu options, eg **Turn Off** and **Restart**.

Section 1 / Checklist

Are you familiar with the following?

Starting the computer	
Using the mouse	
Recognising parts of the desktop and parts of an application window	
Using Help functions	
Reducing/enlarging a desktop/application window	
Resizing, rescaling and closing a window	
Moving windows on a desktop	
Shutting down the computer	
Shutting down a non-responding application	
Restarting the computer	

Section 2 / Working with icons

In this section you will practise and learn how to:

- recognise icons
- view the computer's basic system information, eg operating system, processor type, installed RAM, version number
- view the computer's desktop configuration: date and time, volume settings, desktop display options, eg background options, screen settings, screen saver etc
- use the Print Screen key
- select and move desktop icons
- create a desktop shortcut icon
- install/uninstall a software application

2.1 / Recognising icons

Method

1 Start the computer as in section 1.2.

2 From the **Start** menu, select: **My Computer**.

3 The My Computer window is displayed (Figure 2.10).

Info

Notice the floppy disk drive icon (drive A:), the hard disk drive icon (drive C:) and the compact disk (CD) drive icon (drive E:). Right-clicking on any of these icons will display a pop-up menu; select: **Properties** for more information, eg free disk space. Try this now by selecting the hard disk drive.

If your list in the right of the window is different, you can change views as follows. From the **View** menu, select: one of the options from the second section. In Figure 2.10 **List** view is selected.

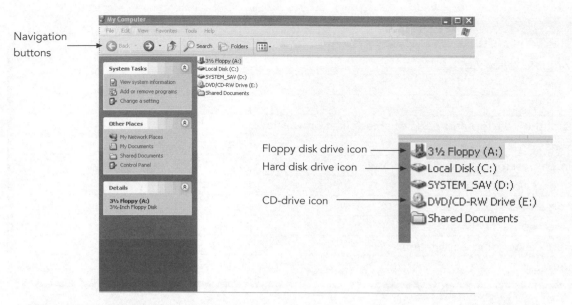

Figure 2.10 My Computer window

Floppy disk drive icon
Hard disk drive icon
CD-drive icon

2.2) Viewing the computer's basic system information

Info

You can use the Control Panel to view and alter numerous settings on your computer. You can also access the Control Panel from the **Start** menu, selecting: **Control Panel**.

Method

1   In the My Computer window, **Other Places** section, click on: **Control Panel**. The Control Panel window and categories are displayed (Figure 2.11).

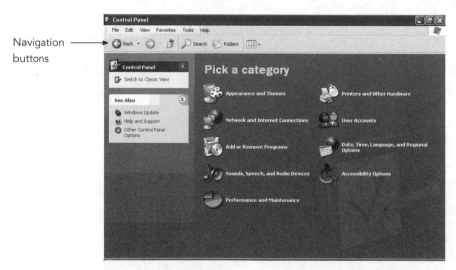

Navigation buttons

Figure 2.11 Control Panel

2   In the **Pick a Category** section, click on: **Performance and Maintenance**.
3   The Performance and Maintenance window is displayed (Figure 2.12).

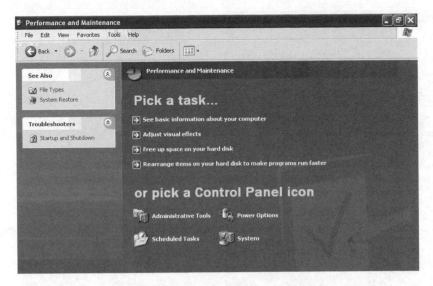

Figure 2.12 Performance and Maintenance window

4   In the **Pick a task** section, select: **See basic information about your computer** (or click on: **System** in the **pick a Control Panel icon** section).

5   The System Properties box is displayed. With the **General** tab selected, you can view the operating system and version number, registration details, processor type and installed RAM (Figure 2.13).

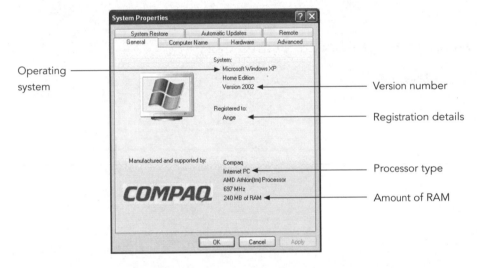

Figure 2.13 System Properties

6   Close the System Properties box by clicking on: **Cancel**.

7   Close the Performance and Maintenance box by clicking on: its **Close** button.

2.3   Viewing and customising the computer's desktop settings

Date and time

Method

1   Access the **Control Panel** (using one of the methods in 2.2).

2   In the **Pick a category** section, select: **Date, Time, Language, and Regional Options**.

3   The Date, Time, Language and Regional Options window is displayed (Figure 2.14).

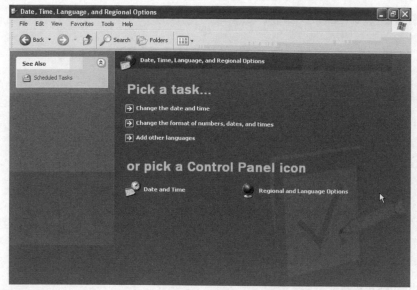

Figure 2.14 Date, Time, Language, and Regional Options window

4   In the **Pick a task** section, select **Change the date and time** (or in the **pick a Control Panel icon** section, select: **Date and Time**).

5   The Date and Time Properties dialogue box is displayed (Figure 2.15).

6   Click in the relevant boxes to change date and time as necessary.

7   Click on: **Apply**.

8   Click on: **OK**.

9   Use the ◀ Back **Back** button to navigate back to **Control Panel**.

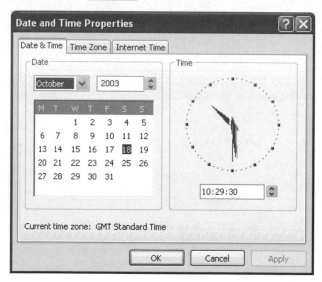

Figure 2.15 Date and Time Properties dialogue box

Note: You can also access the Date and Time Properties dialogue box by double-clicking on: the `10:28` **Date/Time** icon on the taskbar *System Tray*.

Display options

In **Control Panel**, click on: **Appearance and Themes**. In the **pick a Control Panel icon** section, click on: **Display**. The Display Properties dialogue box is displayed.

Figure 2.16 Display Properties dialogue box

Background

> ### Method

1 With the **Desktop** tab selected (Figure 2.16), you can change the desktop background (wallpaper). To do this:
2 Make a selection from the list. A preview will display on the screen graphic above.
3 Click on: **Browse** to select a file that you want to use as a background.
4 (Optional) In the **Position** box, from the list, select the type of display you want.
5 Click on: **Apply**.

Colour settings and resolution

1 Select the **Settings** tab (Figure 2.17).

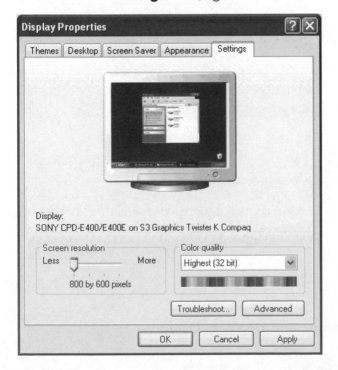

Figure 2.17 Adjusting Settings

2   In the **Color quality** section, click on: the down arrow and click on: a selection.
3   In the **Screen resolution** section, using the mouse, drag the slider for more or less pixel resolution.
4   Click on: **Apply**.

Screen saver

You can set a screen saver that activates when your computer is in use and you have left it idle for a while. Instead of the display showing what you are working on, it shows moving images on the screen. On older monitors, screensavers were originally intended to prolong the life of the screen by preventing 'burn in' of a permanent ghost image (caused by a long time static display). Newer monitors minimise this risk but screensavers are still popular. They can act as a security measure when working in an open office (screen saver passwords can be set) so that your current work is not on view when your computer is unattended. Resume working by pressing a key or moving the mouse.

Method

1   Select: the **Screen Saver** tab to apply/change the screen saver (Figure 2.18). In the **Screen saver** box, click on: the down arrow and then on a screensaver of your choice

Figure 2.18 Setting a screen saver

2   In the **Wait** box, set the time delay before the screen saver is activated.
3   Click on: **Apply**.

By selecting other tabs you can change other desktop settings. Experiment with this now, then close Display Properties (click on: **OK** to save settings) when you have finished.

Note: You can also change desktop settings by right-clicking on the desktop and selecting: **Properties** from the pop-up menu.

Keyboard language

Method

1   In **Control Panel**, select: **Date, Time, Language, and Regional Options**.
2   Click on: **Regional and Language Options**.
3   The Regional and Language Options box is displayed (Figure 2.19).

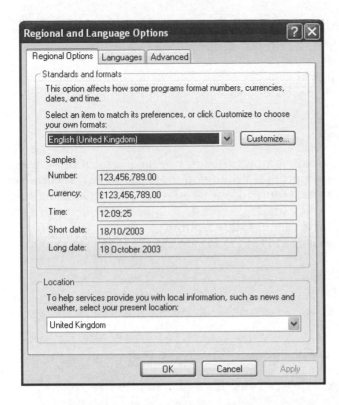

Figure 2.19 Setting Regional and Language Options

4   With the **Regional Options** tab selected, select a language from the drop-down list.
5   Click on: **Apply** and then on: **OK**.

Use the **Back** button to navigate back to **Control Panel**.

Sound settings

1   In **Control Panel**, click on: **Sounds, Speech, and Audio Devices**.
2   Click on: **Sounds and Audio Devices**.
3   The Sounds and Audio Devices Properties box is displayed (Figure 2.20).

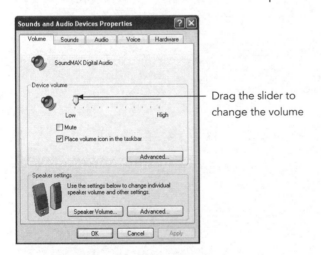

Drag the slider to change the volume

Figure 2.20 Setting sound properties

4   You can adjust your computer's volume by:
5   In the **Device volume** section, drag the slider to the volume you require.
6   Click on: **Apply**.

Note: If you have chosen to display (or already have) a volume icon on the taskbar, double-clicking on it will display the Sounds and Audio Devices Properties box.

7 Click on: **OK**.

8 Click on: the **Close** button to close **Control Panel**.

2.4 Using the Print Screen key

Sometimes you may want to print out information from windows that do not have a print option, eg Windows Explorer. Use the **Print Screen** key for this purpose. When you press the **Print Screen** key, a copy of the screen is saved to the computer's *clipboard*. (You will not be advised that it has done this.) You are then able to open an application that can display images, eg Word and paste the image into a document using the application's **Paste** button or **Edit** menu, **Paste** option.

2.5 Creating a desktop shortcut

Info

It is a good idea to create desktop shortcuts for applications that you use often. You can also create shortcuts for folders and files in the same way. To open an application, file or folder, double-click on its icon. This saves having to go through the **Start** menu. In this example we will create a shortcut for **Notepad**. This is one of the Accessories applications that is part of Windows XP. It is a simple 'no frills' word processor application.

Method

1 Use this method when the application is already accessible through the **Start** menu and sub-menus.

2 From the **Start** menu, select: **All Programs**, **Accessories**, **Notepad**.

3 Hold down the **Ctrl** key and drag **Notepad** onto the desktop.

4 Release the **Ctrl** key.

5 A shortcut icon for Notepad is now displayed on the desktop.

To open an application, file or folder, double-click on its icon.

Info

You can rename a shortcut by right-clicking on it and selecting: **Rename**. Key in a new name and press: **Enter**.

Note: Notepad has not been moved from its original location. You have only created a shortcut to access it in its original location.

2.6 Adding programs to the Start menu

As it is, the *Solitaire* program is rather long-winded to access, tucked away in a sub-sub-menu. If you play Solitaire a lot it is a good idea to add it to the **Start** menu, as in the following example. Other programs can be added in the same way.

Note: You cannot place any new programs below the **Programs** option on the **Start** menu.

Method

1 Open the sub-menus of the **Start** menu until you see **Solitaire**, ie **Start**, **All Programs**, **Games**, **Solitaire**.
2 Right-click on: **Solitaire**.
3 Select: **Pin to Start menu**.
4 The **Start** menu now includes a shortcut to Solitaire.

Info

You can remove programs from the **Start** menu by right-clicking on the program and selecting: **Unpin from Start menu** or **Remove from This List**.

2.7 Recognising more desktop icons

The main types of icons that you see on a normal desktop and that we will be working with are as follows:

- Application/Program shortcut icons such as Notepad, Word, Excel, Access and PowerPoint, shown below:

- File icons, shown below:

A Word file   An Access file   An Excel file   A PowerPoint file

- Folder icons that look like  .

Info

There is more about files and folders in section 3.

2.8 Arranging desktop icons

You can arrange desktop icons by dragging them to the required position on the desktop. If you right-click on the desktop, a pop-up menu appears (Figure 2.21).

Figure 2.21 Arranging desktop icons

Selecting **Arrange icons by**, **Auto Arrange** automatically lines up your icons.
Note: You can delete icons from the desktop by selecting an icon and pressing: **Delete**.

Installing

Installing new software is quite straightforward most of the time. Before you begin ensure that you have the correct system requirements. These are usually listed on the software packaging. You will normally need the registration number or password for your software. This information can also be found on the packaging so ensure that you have any necessary details to hand. During the installation process, you will be given a default location for the software application to reside. If you want to, you can change this default during the installation process.

Method

1   Close any programs that are running.
2   Insert the software CD into the CD drive (if there is more than one CD, they should be labelled so that you know which one to insert first).
3   The CD should start automatically. (If not, follow any instructions included in the package or from the **Start** menu, select: **Run** and key in your CD drive, eg **D:** and click on: **OK**.)
4   Follow the on-screen instructions.

Info

You can also install programs from **Control Panel**. Select: **Add or Remove Programs**. Follow the instructions on screen.

Uninstalling

Method

1   Close any programs that are running.
2   From the **Start** menu, access **Control Panel**.
3   Click on: **Add or Remove Programs**.
4   The Add or Remove Programs dialogue box is displayed (Figure 2.22).

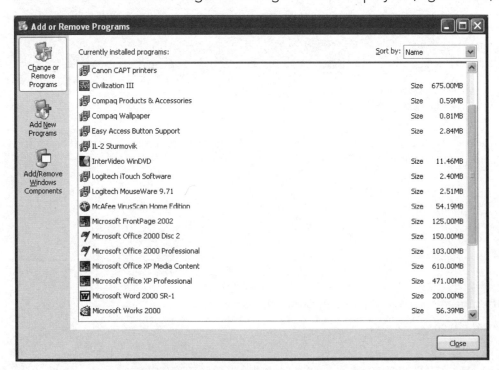

Figure 2.22 Adding or removing programs

Note: Do not follow the next steps unless you are absolutely sure that you want to remove the software application.

5 Click on: the **Change or Remove Programs** button.
6 Scroll and select the software program to uninstall and click on: the **Remove** button.
7 You will be asked to confirm. Click on: **Yes**.
8 When the Application Removal box is displayed, click on: **OK**.

Section 2 / Checklist

Are you familiar with the following?

Restarting the computer	
Recognising icons	
Viewing the computer's basic system information, eg operating system and version, processor type, installed RAM	
Viewing the computer's desktop configuration: date and time, volume settings, desktop display options, eg background options, screen settings, screen saver etc	
Using the Print Screen key	
Selecting and moving desktop icons	
Creating shortcuts on the desktop	
Install/uninstall a software application	

Section 3 / Working with folders and files

In this section you will practise and learn how to:

- use Windows Explorer
- understand basic directory and folder structure
- examine folders/files
- view folder/file attributes
- recognise most widely used file types
- create a folder and subfolders
- rename folders/files
- select an individual file, adjacent files and non-adjacent files

- delete folders/files
- use the Recycle Bin
- copy/move folders/files
- make backups
- format a floppy/Zip disk
- use Find to locate folders/files
- count files
- compress files/folders
- cope with viruses

3.1 / Windows Explorer

Windows Explorer is a program that allows you to view the contents of all the folders and files on your computer. It can be used for disk and file management. Files and folders can be stored on the floppy disk (drive A), the hard disk (usually drive C), the CD drive (usually drive D) and, if you are networked, any network drives that you have access to (see Appendix for details).

Starting Explorer

Method 1

From the **Start** menu, select: **All Programs**, **Accessories**, then **Windows Explorer**.

Method 2

1 Right-click on: **Start**.
2 Select: **Explore All Users** from the pop-up menu.

The Explorer window appears. In this example (Figure 2.23), $3\frac{1}{2}$ Floppy (A:) drive is selected in the left window and the contents of the disk in drive A are displayed in the window on the right.

> **Info**
>
> If your window has a different layout, you may be in a different View. From the **View** menu, select the View you require so that there is a dot next to it.

Toolbar navigation buttons: **Back, Forward** and **Up** one level

Contents of selected object

Status bar gives information about selected object

Figure 2.23 Windows Explorer

The **Desktop** is the top level

My **Computer** is the second level

Disk drives are the next level

This folder has no symbol, indicating that it does not contain any subfolders

This folder has a - symbol indicating that its subfolders are displayed in this pane

This folder has a + symbol indicating that it has subfolders that are not displayed in this pane

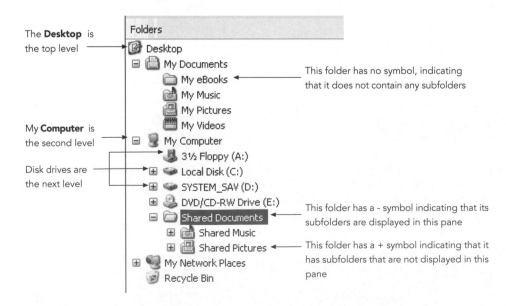

Figure 2.24 Hierarchical structure of computer storage

Figure 2.24 show the hierarchical structure for computer storage. The storage is arranged in a tree-like fashion, branching off to different levels. Disk drives contain folders and subfolders (and subfolders of subfolders), all of which can contain files.

imports

This is an example of a *folder*. Use folders to store related information. Folders can contain files and other folders (that can also contain files). Sometimes folders are referred to as *directories*.

Report.doc

This is an example of a *file*. When you save your work on to a computer disk, it becomes a file. The icon above the filename identifies its type (this is a Word file).

Displaying the contents of a folder

Double-click on the folder.

Info

It is better to double-click the icon rather than the text as sometimes you will not get the action you expect (if you have not double-clicked properly). Instead, a box may appear around the text, waiting for your input. If this happens, press: **Esc** and try again.

Info

Navigating

At some stages you may get lost! Use the navigation buttons shown in Figure 2.23 and the following:

To return to a previously viewed folder, click on: the **Back** button.

3.2 Examining folders and files

You can obtain more information about folders/files.

Method

1 Right-click on the folder/file. A pop-up menu appears (Figure 2.25).

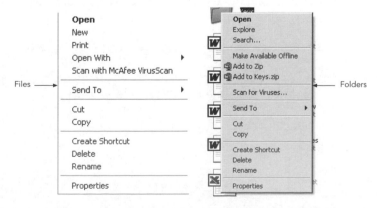

Figure 2.25 Right-click to display pop-up menu

2 Select: **Properties**. The object's properties are displayed (Figure 2.26).

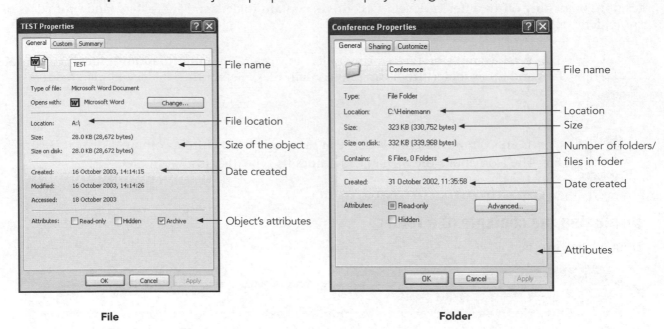

File name — File name

File location — File location

Size of the object — Size of the object

Date created — Date created

Object's attributes — Object's attributes

File name — Location — Size — Number of folders/ files in foder — Date created — Attributes

File   **Folder**

Figure 2.26 Displaying properties

3.3 ▸ Changing file status

When a file is saved, it is normally (by default) given a read-write attribute. This means that it can be opened, read or amended (ie written to). In Figure 2.26, **Attributes** section, the **Read-only** box is empty denoting that this file has a read-write attribute.

Sometimes you may want to make a file *Read-only*. This ensures that you do not accidentally change it.

Method

1 Carry out steps 1 and 2 above.
2 In the **Attributes** section (see Figure 2.26), click in: the **Read-only** box so a tick is displayed.
3 Click on: **Apply** and **OK**.

3.4 ▸ Recognising file types

There are many different types of file and it is useful to be able to recognise those that are most common.

Info

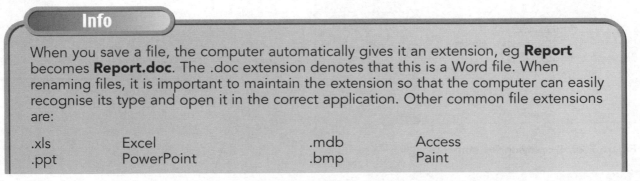

When you save a file, the computer automatically gives it an extension, eg **Report** becomes **Report.doc**. The .doc extension denotes that this is a Word file. When renaming files, it is important to maintain the extension so that the computer can easily recognise its type and open it in the correct application. Other common file extensions are:

| .xls | Excel | .mdb | Access |
| .ppt | PowerPoint | .bmp | Paint |

.rtf	Rich Text Format – this is readable by most of the common word processor applications	.txt	Notepad
		.htm	HTML files used on the World Wide Web
		.tmp	Temporary
.mp3	Music	.gif, .jpg, .tif	Image
.wav, .au	Audio	.exe	Executable program file
.zip	Compressed	.mpeg, .avi	Video
.pdf	Adobe Acrobat		

To view file extensions:

In Windows Explorer, from the **Tools** menu, select: **Folder Options**, **View** tab. In the **Advanced Settings** section, click next to **Hide extensions for known file types** to remove the tick. Click on: **OK**.

The File Properties box now displays the filename plus extension (Figure 2.27) and filenames plus extensions are also displayed in Windows Explorer.

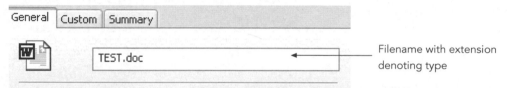

Figure 2.27 File extension

Other information about the file is available by selecting the other tabs. Figure 2.28 shows a summary for the file **TEST**. Access this summary by selecting the **Summary** tab and then clicking on the: **Advanced** button.

Note: This is an example. You will not have this file on your computer.

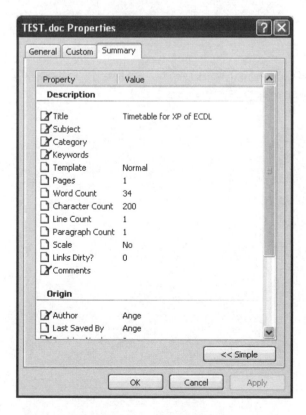

Figure 2.28 Displaying file statistics

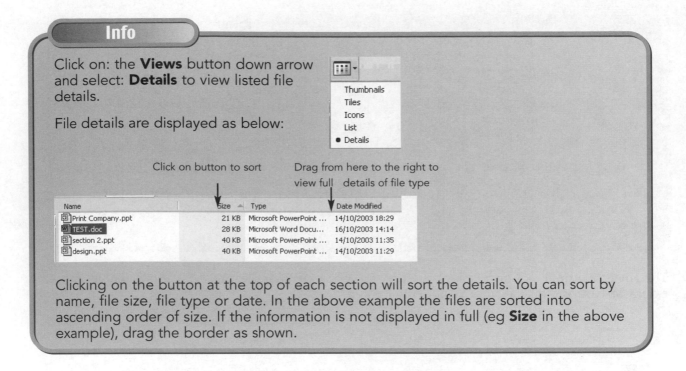

Click on: the **Views** button down arrow and select: **Details** to view listed file details.

File details are displayed as below:

Click on button to sort

Drag from here to the right to view full details of file type

Name	Size	Type	Date Modified
Print Company.ppt	21 KB	Microsoft PowerPoint ...	14/10/2003 18:29
TEST.doc	28 KB	Microsoft Word Docu...	16/10/2003 14:14
section 2.ppt	40 KB	Microsoft PowerPoint ...	14/10/2003 11:35
design.ppt	40 KB	Microsoft PowerPoint ...	14/10/2003 11:29

Clicking on the button at the top of each section will sort the details. You can sort by name, file size, file type or date. In the above example the files are sorted into ascending order of size. If the information is not displayed in full (eg **Size** in the above example), drag the border as shown.

3.5 Creating a new folder and subfolders

You can create new folders in which to store related documents. This is always good practice as it makes for easier location at a later date.

To create a new folder on the disk in drive A:

Method

1 In the left-hand pane, click on: **3½ Floppy (A:)**.
2 The contents of the floppy disk in drive A are displayed in the right-hand pane (Figure 2.23).
3 Right-click in the white space of this section. A menu appears (Figure 2.29)

Figure 2.29 Selecting New

4 Select: **New** and then: **Folder**.
5 The new folder is displayed.

Figure 2.30 Naming a folder

6 Key in the name for the new folder and press: **Enter** (Figure 2.30).

Note: In this example, the new folder name is **Test**.

To create a subfolder within the newly created folder

Method

1 Double-click on: the newly created folder (Figure 2.31).
2 Carry out steps 3–5 above.

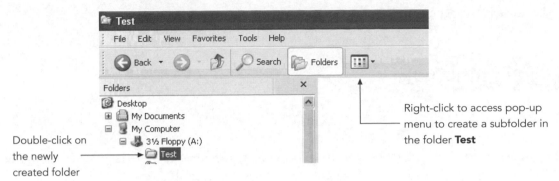

Double-click on the newly created folder

Right-click to access pop-up menu to create a subfolder in the folder **Test**

Figure 2.31 Creating a subfolder

3.6 Renaming a file/folder

Method

1 Right-click on: the file/folder.
2 Select: **Rename** from the pop-up menu.
3 Key in the new name and press: **Enter**.

3.7 Deleting a file/folder

Method

1 Select the file/folder you want to delete by clicking on it.
2 Press: **Delete**.
3 You will be asked to confirm file delete.
4 Click on: **Yes**.

Note: When you delete a folder, its contents are also deleted.

3.8 The Recycle Bin

You can restore a deleted file (*not one deleted from a floppy disk*) from the **Recycle Bin**.

Method

1 In the **Folders** pane, click on: the **Recycle Bin**.
2 Select the file you want to restore.
3 Select: **Restore** from the **File** menu.

Emptying the Recycle Bin

It is a good idea to remove files from the Recycle Bin from time to time. To do this:

1 Click on: the **Recycle Bin** to select it.
2 From the **File** menu, select: **Empty Recycle Bin**.

Note: You can also access the **Recycle Bin** on the desktop by right-clicking on it.

3.9 Copying files/folders

Example

Copy the file **Report** (use any substitute file you have on your computer) so there is a copy in the folder **Word** files.

There are three main ways to copy a file/folder.

Method 1

1 Select the file **Report** by clicking on it, hold down the left mouse button and, at the same time, hold down the **Ctrl** key.
2 Drag the file over the folder **Word files**. Release the **Ctrl** key and the mouse button.

Method 2

1 Select the file **Report**.
2 Hold down the right mouse button and drag the file to the folder **Word files** (it will become highlighted).
3 Release the mouse – a menu appears.
4 Click on: **Copy Here**.

Method 3

1 Right-click on the file Report – a menu appears.
2 Select: **Copy**.
3 Right-click on: the folder **Word files**; select: **Paste**.

Info

The third method is sometimes easier when you have numerous files and folders, as they may scroll out of view when you are trying to drag them. Check the quick reference for keyboard shortcuts and toolbar button methods.

You can check that the file **Report** is in the **Word files** folder by clicking on it to reveal its contents. *Note:* Folders can be copied in the same way. Create a new folder and copy it to the folder **Word files**.

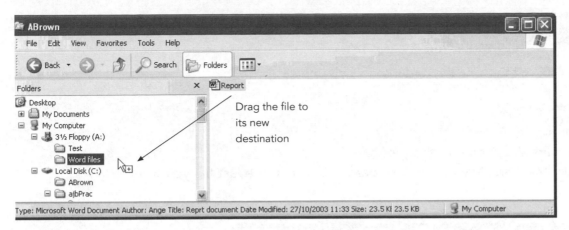

Figure 2.32 Copying/moving a file

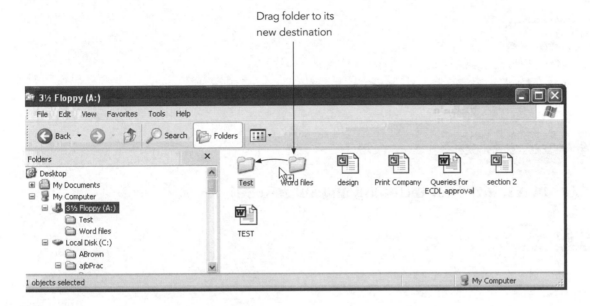

Figure 2.33 Copying/moving a folder

3.10 Moving files/folders

Files/folders can be moved following methods 1, 2 and 3 above, except:

Method 1

Do not hold down the **Ctrl** key when moving files/folders.

Method 2

Select: **Move Here** instead of **Copy Here**.

Method 3

Select: **Cut** instead of **Copy**.

Note: If you drag a file/folder to a new location on the same disk, it will be moved. If you drag it to another disk, it will be copied.

3.11 Selecting adjacent files/folders

You can select more than one file to delete, copy or move.

Method

1 Select: the first file/folder in the group.
2 Hold down the **Shift** key on the keyboard and select: the last file you want.

3.12 Selecting non–adjacent files/folders

Method

1 Select: the first file/folder.
2 Hold down the **Ctrl** key on the keyboard and select: each file in the group.

3.13 Counting files

Counting files in a folder (not including any subfolders)

Method

1 Right-click on: the folder.
2 Select: **Properties**.
3 The Properties box displays the number of files after **Contains**.

Counting files of a specific type in a folder (not including any subfolders)

Method

1 Double-click: on the folder so that the files are displayed in the right-hand pane.
2 Ensure **View** is **Detail**, then click on: the **Type** button (at the top of the list) to sort the files into types so that files of the same type are together.
3 Click on: the first file of the particular type you are counting.
4 Hold down: **Shift** and click on: the last file in the group of the same type.
5 Release: **Shift**.
6 The number of files is displayed on the Status bar.

Counting files of a specific type in a folder (including subfolders)

Method

1 From the **Start** menu, select: **Search**.
2 The Search Results dialogue box is displayed (Figure 2.34).

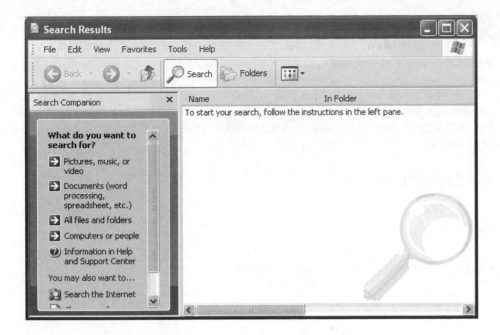

Figure 2.34 Finding files

3   In the **Search Companion**, click on: **All files and folders**.
4   In the **Search Companion**, **All or part of the file name** box, key in the type of files you are counting, eg *.xls (for Excel files), *.doc (for Word files).

Figure 2.35 Entering filename

5   In the **Look in** box, select the location or click on: **Browse** to select the relevant folder.
6   Click on: **More Advanced Options** and ensure that the **Search subfolders** box contains a tick. (*Note*: You can also select the file type here.)
7   Click on: **Search**.
8   When the search is complete, the number of files will be displayed in the **Search Companion**.

> **Info**
>
> You can also find files by date by clicking on the **When was it modified** and by size by clicking on the **What size is it** options.

3.14 Backing up

Backing up means producing exact copies of your files. This is done as a security measure in case anything happens to the originals, eg fire or theft. If you work for a large organisation, backing up is usually carried out for you. However, if you work for a smaller organisation or at home, you will need to create your own backups. Remember to keep the backups somewhere safe and in another location. (See Module 1 for more on backing up.) You need to backup to a removable storage medium, eg a floppy or zip disk, or CD (that you can write to).

Producing a backup of a floppy disk

Method

In Windows Explorer

1 Right-click on: the **3½ Floppy (A:)** drive icon; a menu appears.
2 Click on: **Copy Disk**.
3 Follow the instructions on screen.

3.15 Formatting disks

Most new floppy and Zip disks are already formatted for use on your computer. If not, you will need to format them. Formatting prepares the disk so that it is recognised by your computer, and can quickly and easily store and access information on it. A floppy disk only needs to be formatted once. Formatting a disk will erase any information stored on that disk.

Formatting a floppy disk in Drive A

Method

1 In Windows Explorer, select: **3½ Floppy (A:)**.
2 Right-click: a menu appears (Figure 2.36).

Expand

Explore
Open
Browse with Paint Shop Pro
Search...

Sharing and Security...

Copy Disk...
Scan with McAfee VirusScan

Format...

Cut

Figure 2.36 Formatting a disk

3 Click on: **Format**. The Format dialogue box appears (Figure 2.37).
4 Click on: **Start**.

Figure 2.37 The Format dialogue box

Formatting a Zip disk

Follow the basic procedure above, this time selecting the Zip drive at step 1.

3.16 Finding files

To find a file/folder use the following method.

Method

1 From the **Start** button menu, select: **Search**.
2 The Search Results dialogue box is displayed (Figure 2.38).

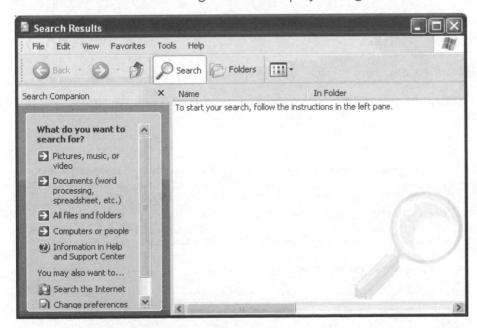

Figure 2.38 Finding files/folders

3 Click on: **All files and folders**.
4 Key in the criteria in the search boxes.

5   Use **When was it modified?** to refine your search to an approximate date (Figure 2.39).

Figure 2.39 Searching by date

6   Use **What size is it?** to refine the search to a specific size (Figure 2.40).

Figure 2.40 Searching by size

7   Use the **Advanced** tab to refine your search to a specific file type and ensure subfolders are included (if appropriate).

8   Click on: **Search**.

Some files can be very large and when e-mailing them or downloading them from the Internet, they can take a very long time. To overcome this problem, files can be compressed (or zipped) so that they are smaller. The files then need to be extracted (unzipped) so that you can open them. Icons for zipped folders look like ▢. The extension for zipped files is .zip.

Special software can be used to compress/extract files, eg WinZip, PKZip. This software can be downloaded from the Internet. However, the following examples use Windows XP software for doing this.

Compressing a file/folder

Method

1   In Windows Explorer, select a location for the compressed folder.
2   In the right-hand pane, right-click in a space, select: **New**, **Compressed (zipped) Folder** (Figure 2.41).

Figure 2.41 Creating a new Compressed (zipped) folder

3   The folder is created (Figure 2.42). Rename it as with any other folder. Remember to keep its extension.

New Compressed (zipped) Folder.zip   **Figure 2.42 New folder**

4   Files or folders can be dragged to the compressed folder and they will automatically be compressed or they can be compressed when moved there by holding down the **Shift** key when moving them.

Info

You can also create a compressed folder and copy a file into it by right-clicking on the file to be compressed and selecting: **Send to, Compressed (zipped) Folder**. The new folder automatically takes the file's name and has the extension .zip.

Extracting a compressed file/folder

Method

1   Select the files/folders to extract.
2   Drag the file/folder out of the compressed folder and it will automatically decompress.

Note: A compressed version will still exist unless you hold down **Shift** at the same time as dragging.

Extracting all files/folders from a compressed folder

Method

1 Right-click on the compressed folder.
2 Select: **Extract All**.
3 Follow the instructions of the Extraction Wizard (see Figures 2.43, 2.44, 2.45).

Figure 2.43 Extraction Wizard (1)

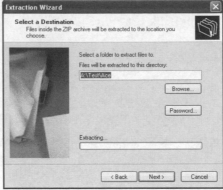

Figure 2.44 Extraction Wizard (2)

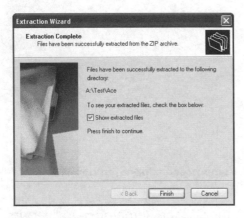

Figure 2.45 Extraction Wizard (3)

3.18 Preventing and coping with viruses

A *computer virus* is a program written by someone who wants to cause widespread inconvenience to other computer users. A virus is normally buried within another program and automatically loaded into a user's computer without their knowledge or consent. Depending on which type of computer virus is involved, when the user runs the infected program, the virus causes problems that may range from merely irritating (unwanted messages or graphics effects) to devastating (major loss or corruption of data). Most have the ability to attach copies of themselves to other programs, that in turn infect more programs. When removable disks were the main source of infection the spread of viruses was relatively slow, but with the growth of the Internet it is now possible to have a worldwide computer epidemic within hours. A list of the more common viruses is given below:

- *Trojan Horse* The actions of this type of virus are disguised to appear benign, whilst actually causing harm (eg altering an existing program to access restricted data).
- *Time Bomb* This type of virus only causes harm on a specific date or when a program has been run a certain number of times.
- *Logic Bomb* This type of virus only causes harm when it detects specific data.
- *Worm* This type of virus makes copies of itself throughout a computer's hard disk and RAM. This increasingly uses up resources and overloads the computer until it slows or stops.

Antivirus utility programs, such as Norton Antivirus and McAfee VirusScan, are available and although the outlay may seem expensive, it will put your mind at rest to know that your valuable data is as protected as possible. Since prevention is better than cure, try to know the source of your software and always save and perform a virus-check before running it (even software distributed on disks with computer magazines has been known to contain viruses).

Be particularly careful to virus-check files that are copied from floppy disks, downloaded from the Internet, or emails and their attachments. It may often be simpler to delete a suspicious email message rather than risk opening it. For example, in May 2000 an Internet virus infected about ten percent of business computer systems in the UK and many more worldwide. The virus spread rapidly because people rushed to open the enticingly labelled *Iloveyou* email attachment which then accessed their computer address book and emailed itself to everyone listed.

Anti-virus software is easy to use. It can be scheduled so that it automatically scans your data at regular intervals, eg every morning when you switch on. You can schedule it so that it scans only certain drives or folders. You are also able to scan individual files or folders when you want to. The software disinfects your computer, ie will alert you to any known viruses found and eliminate them. It may also warn you of any suspicious activity, eg numerous e-mails with the same subject.

Because new computer viruses are becoming apparent all the time, it is important that the software is kept as up-to-date as possible. Most anti-virus software will automatically update when you connect to the Internet.

If you work for an organisation with an IT support team, you should inform them of any viruses that may have spread to/from your computer.

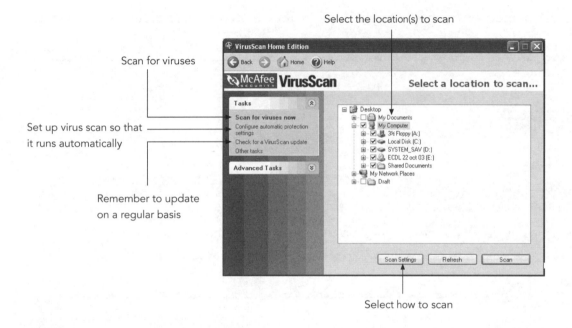

Figure 2.46 Typical virus-scanning selections

Section 3	Checklist	
Are you familiar with the following?		
File handling in Windows Explorer		
Changing file attributes		
Compressing files/folders		
Recognising file types		
Using the Recycle Bin		
Making backups		
Formatting disks		
Coping with viruses		

Section 4 / Using and printing from a text editing application

In this section you will practise and learn how to:

- launch a text editing program and create/open a file
- save the file
- close an application
- print from an installed printer
- change default printer

- install a new printer
- view and manage a print job's progress from a desktop print manager
- move between open windows

4.1 Creating a folder for your file

Exercise 1

Create a folder named **Prac** on a floppy disk (or in your work area) using the methods in section 3.

4.2 Creating a file

Info

For the following exercises we will be using the program **Notepad**.

Note: 'Launching' an application can also be referred to as 'opening' or 'loading' it.

Exercise 2

Launch Notepad and key in the following text:

It was the best of times, it was the worst of times.

Method

1 From the **Start** menu, select: **All Programs**, **Accessories**, **Notepad** *or* double-click on its shortcut icon.
2 The Notepad window appears (Figure 2.47).

Figure 2.47 The Notepad window

3 Key in the text.

4.3 Saving the file

Exercise 3

Save the file.

Method

1 From the **File** menu, select: **Save As** (Figure 2.48).

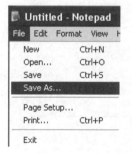

Figure 2.48 File menu, Save As

2 The Save As dialogue box appears (Figure 2.49).

Figure 2.49 Saving the file

3 In the Save in box, select: **Floppy (A:)** (or your preferred location) by clicking on the down arrow and selecting it from the list.

4 Open the **Prac** folder by double-clicking on it.

5 In the **File name** box key in the filename (precede the name with your initials, in my case ajb) **ajb example**.

6 Click on: **Save**.

4.4 Printing the file

Exercise 4

Print the file saved in 4.3.

Method

1 Ensure that the printer is loaded with paper.

2 From the **File** menu, select: **Print**.

4.5 Closing Notepad

Exercise 5

Close the application.

Method

From the **File** menu, select: **Exit**.

4.6 Opening a file

Exercise 6

Launch Notepad and reopen the file you have just saved.

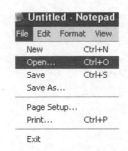

Method

1 Launch Notepad as in 4.2, steps 1 and 2.

2 From the **File** menu, select: **Open** (Figure 2.50).

3 The Open dialogue box is displayed.

4 In the **Look in** box, select: the location of your file.

5 Double-click: on the folder **Prac**.

6 Click on: the file.

7 Click on: **Open**.

Figure 2.50 File menu, Open

4.7　Changing the default printer

Sometimes you may need to change from the default printer, eg to print in better quality. You can usually change from the default printer within the program you are using.

Method 1

In Notepad (or other application):

1　From the **File** menu, select: **Page Setup**.
2　Click on: **Printer**.
3　In the **Name** section, click on: the down arrow and select another printer from the list.
4　Click on: **OK**.

Using Control Panel

Method 2

1　Open Control Panel (**Start** menu, **Control Panel**).
2　Click on: **Printers and Other Hardware**.
3　Click on: **Printers and Faxes**.
4　Right-click on the printer to use as the default.
5　From the pop-up menu, select: **Set as Default Printer**.

A tick is displayed next to the default printer .

Info

You can also change from the default printer and set an alternative printer as the default for your computer using the following methods:

Using the Start menu

1　From the **Start** menu, select: **Settings**, then: **Printers**.
2　The Printers box appears. Right-click on the printer that you want to be the default.
3　Click on: **Set as Default**.

Using My Computer

1　Double-click on: the **Printers** folder.
2　Right-click on: the printer that you want to set as the default.
3　Click on: **Set as Default**.

4.8　Adding a new printer

Method

At step 4 (above) in the **Printer Tasks** section, click on: **Add a Printer**. The Add Printer wizard guides you through the process.

You will need to know:

- if your printer is local (connected directly to your computer) or networked
- the make and model number.

If your printer has an installation disk, you will need to have this ready to insert when requested.

Note: Printers are often 'plug and play', and Windows XP will automatically install the printer when its cable is plugged into your computer.

4.9 Viewing a print job's progress

Method

1 In **Control Panel**, click on: **Printers and Other Hardware**.
2 Click on: **Printers and Faxes**.
3 Double-click on: the default printer icon.
4 The Print Queue is displayed (Figure 2.51).

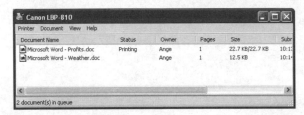

Figure 2.51 Print Queue window

Pausing printing

Method

From the **Printer** menu, select: **Pause Printing** (Figure 2.52).

Figure 2.52 Pausing printing

Restarting printing

Method

From the **Printer** menu, select: **Pause Printing** (notice that a tick appeared next to this option when printing was paused).

Deleting a print job

Method

Select the print job from the list and press: **Delete**.

4.10 Moving between open windows

When you are working you may find that you have more than one window open. The open windows will appear (minimised) on the taskbar (Figure 2.53). In this case the file **ajb example** is visible on screen (the button appears pushed in).

Figure 2.53 Open windows appear on the taskbar

It is easy to switch between windows; just click on the button for the window that you want displayed *or* select it from the **Window** menu.

4.11 Close all open windows

Use one of the methods that you have learnt. You can also close a window by right-clicking on its taskbar button and selecting: **Close**.

Section 4 / Checklist

Are you familiar with the following?

Changing and installing printers	
Viewing a print job's progress	
Moving between open windows	

Module 2) Practice tasks

Note: For these exercises you will need the folder **Module 2**.

1   Copy the folder **Module 2** (including all subfolders) to your work area.

2   Create a folder named **Prac** and two subfolders named **Prac One** and **Prac Two**.

3   Open a text editor program (Notepad). Create an 'Answer' file by keying in your name, the date and the text **ECDL Module 2**. The file will be referred to as **Answer** file.

4   Find all Excel (.xls) files in the **Module 2** folder (include all subfolders) and key in the total number found on the next line of the **Answer** file.

5   How many files are there in the folder (include all subfolders) with '**car**' in the filename? Key in the number found on the next line of the **Answer** file.

6   How many files in total are there in the **Sub3** folder (include subfolders)? Key in the answer on the next line of the **Answer** file.

7   Copy all the Word (.doc) files from **Module 2\Sub1** to **Module 2\Sub5**.

8   Move the three smallest files from **Module 2\Sub2** to **Module 2\Prac\Prac One**.

9   Copy the two oldest files from **Module 2\Sub1** to **Module 2\Prac\Prac Two**.

10   Rename files starting with **Car** so that they start with **aa** eg **carpet** becomes **aapet**.

11   Delete all the PowerPoint (.ppt) files in the **Module 2\Sub8** folder.

12   Set the Access file **Vacations** and the Word file **SAVINGS** to be read-only.

13   Answer the following questions in the **Answer** file:

 a   How do you format a disk?
 b   What is the procedure for shutting down the computer?
 c   What would you do if the computer was not responding to your input?
 d   How do you create a desktop shortcut icon?
 e   How can you view the computer's processor type and installed RAM?
 f   How do you change from the default printer in an application?
 g   When and how would you use the **Print Screen** key?

14   Save and print the **Answer** file.

15   Empty the Recycle Bin.

 Note: These are only practice tasks. Successful completion does not imply certification of the module by the ECDL Foundation.

Using the computer and managing files quick reference

(The following is a list of generally useful tasks associated with this module. For more information on specific items, refer to the chapter content.)

Action	Keyboard	Mouse	Right–mouse menu	Menu
Backup a floppy disk			**Copy disk**	
Copy file/ folder	Select the file/folder			
	Ctrl + C		**Copy**	**Edit**, **Copy**
	Click where you want to copy the file/folder			
	Ctrl + V		**Paste**	**Edit**, **Paste**
Create a new folder	Select where you want the new folder to be			
			New, **Folder**	**File**, **New**, **Folder**
Create a subfolder	Select the folder in which you want the subfolder to be and follow the steps for creating a new folder.			
Delete a file/ folder	Select the file/folder			
	Delete		**Delete**	**File**, **Delete**
Display contents of folder		Double-click: the folder		
Exit Windows Explorer		Click: the ☒ **Close** button		**File**, **Close**
Find files/ folders	**Start**, **Search**			
Format a floppy/Zip disk	Select drive			
			Format	
Load Windows Explorer	In Windows XP desktop			
		Double-click: the **Windows Explorer** shortcut icon	Right-click on: **Start**, **Explore All Users**	**Start**, **All Programs**, **Accessories**, **Windows Explorer**
Move file/ folder	Select the file			
	Ctrl + X		**Cut**	**Edit**, **Cut**
	Click where you want to move the file/folder to			
	Ctrl + V		**Paste**	**Edit**, **Paste**
Notepad, open		Double-click: the **Notepad** shortcut icon		**Start**, **All Programs**, **Accessories**, **Notepad**

Action	Keyboard	Mouse	Right-mouse menu	Menu
Notepad, close		Click: the ☒ **Close** button		**File**, **Exit**
Notepad, saving a document				**File**, **Save** or **Save As**
Notepad, print				**File**, **Print**
Notepad, change default printer				**File**, **Page Setup**, **Printer**
Printer, change default, View print job's progress				**Start**, **Control Panel**, **Printers and Other Hardware**
Recycle Bin, restore files	Double-click on the **Recycle Bin** icon Select the file you want to restore			
			Restore	**File**, **Restore**
Recycle Bin, empty			**Empty Recycle Bin**	
Rename file/ folder			**Rename**	**File**, **Rename**
Select files *adjacent* *non-adjacent*	Click: the first file Holding down: **Shift**, click: the last file Click: the first file Holding down: **Ctrl**, click: each file in turn			
Shortcut, creating	In Windows Explorer			
		Drag object to desktop	**Create Shortcut**	**File**, **Create Shortcut**
Shut down the computer	**Start**, **Turn Off Computer**			
View all file/ folder attributes		Click: the ▦ **Views** button arrow, **Details**		
View individual file/folder attributes	Select file/folder			
			Properties	**File**, **Properties**

Word Processing

Section 1 / Getting started

In this section you will practise and learn how to:

- load Word
- understand the parts of the document window
- understand how to use Help functions
- modify the toolbar display

- create a document: enter text, insert text, delete text
- save a document
- exit Word

1.1 / Loading Word

Exercise 1

Load Word.

Method

1 Switch on your computer and log in until the Windows desktop screen appears.
2 Move the mouse pointer over the **Start** button and click on the left button – a menu appears.
3 Select: **All Programs** by hovering the mouse over it – another menu appears.
   Select: **Microsoft Word** and click the left button (Figure 3.1).

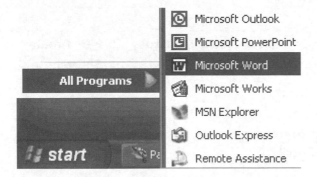

Figure 3.1 Loading Word

If you have a shortcut icon to Word on your desktop, you can load Word by double-clicking on: the **W** **Word** icon.

The Word Document window will be displayed on screen, looking similar to Figure 3.2. This shows a blank document with default values, ie pre-programmed settings such as line spacing, width of margins and font type. These will remain unchanged until you alter them.

If there is no Document window, click on: the □ **New Blank Document** button on the top left of the toolbar *or* select: **New**. **Blank Document** from the Task Pane.

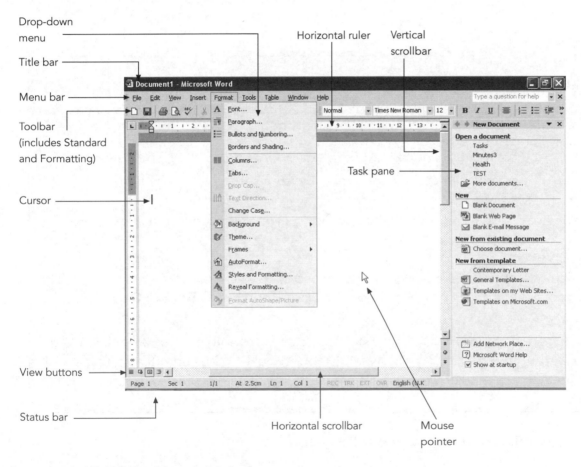

Figure 3.2 The Word Document window

Title bar: This shows the name of the application being used, Microsoft Word, and the current document name, **Document1** (this is the default name).

Menu bar: This has menu names, which can be selected using the mouse/keyboard. A *drop-down menu* then gives you options within that menu. This initially displays options used most recently. After a few seconds, the drop-down menu expands to include all available options. These menus will personalise to display your most recently selected options as you progress through your work.

Toolbar: This contains shortcut buttons for actions that are frequently carried out. For example, to print a document, click on: the **Print** button shown in Figure 3.3.

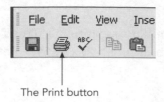

The Print button

Figure 3.3 Standard toolbar buttons

Try to guess what each button on the toolbar does by looking at the icon on the button. To find out what each button does, point the mouse over the button (without clicking) and wait for a few seconds. A *ToolTip* will appear giving a brief explanation of the button. Try this now.

Formatting toolbar: This allows shortcuts to formatting your document, such as underlining text and centring text.

Info

Modifying the toolbar display

By default the Standard and Formatting toolbars are displayed together on the same row. Since these both contain frequently used shortcut buttons, it is useful to display the Standard and Formatting toolbars in full on separate rows (the exercises in this chapter will assume this). To display the Standard and Formatting toolbars in full on separate rows:

1 From the **View** menu, select: **Toolbars**, then **Customize**.
2 Click on: the **Options** tab.
3 Click to place a tick in the **Show Standard and Formatting toolbars on two rows** box.
4 Click on: **Close**.

Note: If you prefer not to alter the default setting and so have more screen area you can still access the remaining options on each toolbar by clicking on: the ⁑ **Toolbar Options** buttons.

You can choose to have more toolbars visible by selecting: **Toolbars** from the **View** menu and then selecting the toolbar to display. Ticks appear next to the currently displayed toolbars. The content of your work will dictate which ones are useful to you.

Cursor: The cursor flashes where your text will appear.

Horizontal ruler: This shows the position of text and can be displayed in centimetres or inches. (See the Appendix to change the default.)

Mouse pointer: This will move when you move the mouse – use to select items in the window. The mouse pointer changes shape depending on where it is on the screen.

Scroll bars: You can quickly scroll through your document using the scroll bars.

Status bar: This provides information about the position of the cursor and the text displayed on your screen.

Task Pane: The Task Pane displays several shortcuts that you may find useful when working. Close it for now by clicking on: its **Close** button.

View buttons: There are different ways of viewing your text. (See section 3 for more information on types of View.)

1.3 Getting help

Note: Throughout this book, the Office Assistant facility has been hidden so as not to distract from the main objectives. More details of the Office Assistant are found in the Appendix.

From the **Help** menu, select: **Microsoft Word Help** *or* click on: the 🔲 **Microsoft Word Help** button *or* press: **F1**. The Microsoft Word Help window is displayed (Figure 3.4).

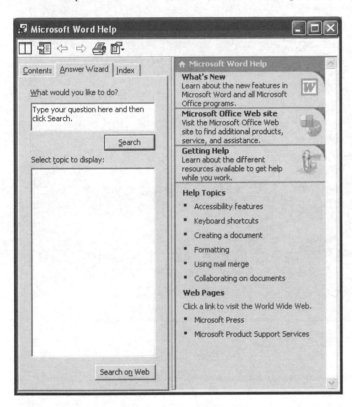

Figure 3.4 Microsoft Word Help

You can select:

- The **Contents** tab for a list of help topics. By double-clicking on a topic, a display of that topic will appear.
- The **Answer Wizard** tab. This allows you to key in a question and then click on: **Search**. The topic will then be highlighted in the contents list and the topic displayed as above.
- The **Index** tab. This allows you to key in key words and click on **Search**. Again, the topic will be highlighted and displayed as above.

To close the Help window, click on: the ❎ **Close** button (at the top right-hand corner).

ScreenTips

From the **Help** menu, select: **What's This?** Then click on the item you want to know about. A short description appears. Press: **Esc** to remove the ScreenTip.

Accessing help in a dialogue box

To access Help in a dialogue box, click on: the ❓ **Help** button in the dialogue box and then click on the item you want help about.

Info

Before you begin entering text you need to be aware of the following:

- You do not need to press the **Enter** key at the end of each line because if the text is too long to fit within the space available it will automatically be carried over to the next line. This is known as *word wrap*.
- You should be consistent with spaces after commas and full stops. One space after a comma and one/two space(s) after a full stop is acceptable, looks neat and is easy to read. You can check that you have been consistent by clicking on: the ¶ **Show/Hide** button. This displays spaces as dots. Therefore each space appears as one dot. Look to see what other hidden characters are displayed as. To turn **Show/Hide** off, click on: the **Show/Hide** button again.
- You should leave a blank line after headings and between paragraphs. To do this press: **Enter** twice.
- To join two paragraphs together, position the cursor before the first word of the second paragraph and press: ← **Del** (**Backspace**) twice.
- To key in capital letters, hold down: **Shift** at the same time as the key for the letter that you want to key in.
- If you are keying in a block of capital letters, press: **Caps Lock** to start keying in capitals and press: **Caps Lock** again to stop. (Also see 'Change case' in the quick reference at the end of the chapter.)
- Don't worry if you make mistakes, you can correct them later.
- You may notice that you have wavy lines under some of your keyed-in text. The reason for this is explained in section 2, so you can ignore it for now.

For more information on layout, see the Appendix.

Exercise 2

With the new Word Document window on your screen, key in the following text:

The wind chill factor should be taken into account when deciding what to wear outdoors in winter.

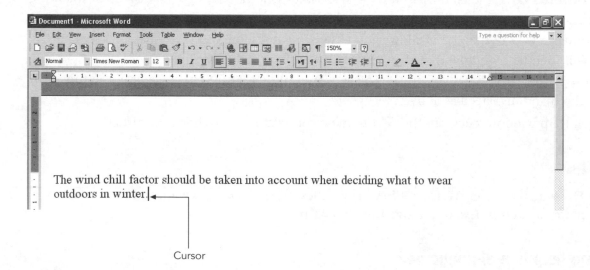

Cursor

Figure 3.5 The keyed-in text will look similar to this

1.5　Moving around your text

Here we will learn three methods to move around the text:

1　Using the arrow keys.

2　Using the mouse.

3　Using two keys together, **Ctrl** + **Home**, and **Ctrl** + **End**.

1　Moving around your text using the arrow keys

The arrow keys ← ↑ → ↓ (located at the bottom right of the main keyboard) allow you to move the cursor (the flashing black vertical line) in the direction of the arrows.

You can move one space forwards or backwards at a time, or you can move up or down one line at a time. If you keep an arrow key pressed down, the cursor will move quickly through the document. Remember to release the arrow key when you reach the required place.

2　Moving around your text using the mouse

As you move the mouse around the screen, you will notice that the I-beam moves with you. Move it until you have reached the required position, click the left mouse button once and the cursor will reposition itself where you clicked.

3　Using Ctrl + Home and Ctrl + End

Hold down: **Ctrl** key at the same time as the **Home** key to move to the top of your text.

Hold down: **Ctrl** key at the same time as the **End** key to move to the bottom of your text.

Info

There are other ways to move around the document and these are included in the quick reference at the end of this chapter.

1.6　Inserting text

Exercise 3

Insert the word **always** between the words **should** and **be**.

Method

Position the cursor at the point where you want to insert text (in this case in the space after the word **should**), and then key in **always** and a space (Figure 3.6).

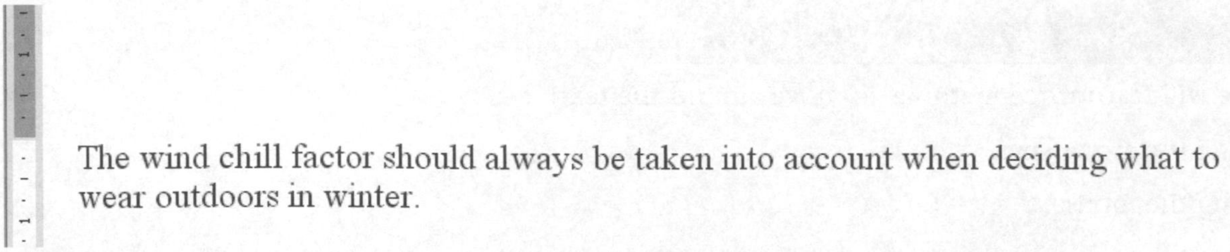

The wind chill factor should always be taken into account when deciding what to wear outdoors in winter.

Figure 3.6 Inserting text

Notice how the text to the right of the cursor moves to make room for the new text.

Info

If your text does not move across but overwrites text already there, check that **OVR** is not displayed on the Status Bar. If it is, press: **Insert** to remove overwrite.

1.7 Deleting text

Exercise 4

Delete the word **outdoors**.

Method

Either:

Position the cursor to the left of the first character that you want to delete, ie the **o** of **outdoors** and press: **Delete** until all the letters of **outdoors** (and the space) have been deleted

or:

Position the cursor to the right of the last character you want to delete and press: ← **Del** (**Backspace**) key (top right of main keyboard) until all the letters of **outdoors** (and the space) have been deleted.

Exercise 5

Now try keying in a longer piece of text.

Method

Click on: the ☐ **New** button.

Key in the following **CAPSULE WITH A VIEW** text (this should not be in bold lettering and the line endings will not necessarily be in the same place):

CAPSULE WITH A VIEW

London Eye

One of the best ways to view London is from the London Eye. It was constructed as a millennium project and is a giant wheel that towers over the River Thames and other world famous landmarks.

How high is it?

The Eye is the sixth tallest structure in London. Only the BT Tower, the Canary Wharf towers and Tower 42 are taller. Other wheels to compare are the giant Prater Wheel in Vienna (half the height) and the previous tallest observation wheel in Yokahama Bay, Japan (thirty metres shorter).

The Capsules

Attached to this giant wheel are passenger capsules, each can accommodate more than twenty people. These capsules are specially designed and positioned on the outside of the wheel to give a spectacular 360 degree panorama from the top. The capsules can be booked for sharing with others or there are also options for private capsule bookings. These include Cupid's Capsule (for couples), capsules for groups and even wedding capsules that can accommodate fourteen guests as well as the bride and groom.

1.8 Saving text

Exercise 6

Save the text.

Method

Info

Note that the text will now be referred to as a file.

1 From the **File** menu, select: **Save As** (Figure 3.7).

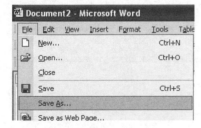

Figure 3.7 Saving a file for the first time using Save As

2 The Save As dialogue box is displayed.

Click on the down arrow to display
locations where you may store your
text. Click on the location, eg **3¹/₂
Floppy (A:)**

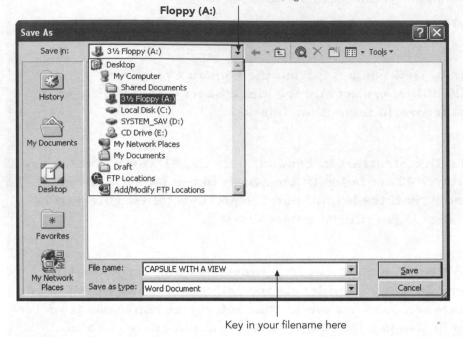

Key in your filename here

Figure 3.8 The Save As dialogue box

3 Click on: the down arrow as shown in Figure 3.8 and click on the location where you want to save your text. (If you are saving to a floppy disk, remember to have your disk inserted in the drive.)

4 Click in: the **File name** box at the beginning of the default name that is already there and delete it by pressing: **Delete**.

5 Key in the filename **Eye** (case does not matter).

6 Click on: **Save**.

Info

Notice that the default filename (**DocumentX**) has been replaced with the new filename (**Eye**) on the Title bar.

1.9 Closing a file

Exercise 7

Close the file **Eye**.

Method

From the **File** menu, select: **Close**.

1.10 Exiting Word

Exercise 8

Exit Word.

Method

Click on: the ⊠ **Close** button in the top right-hand corner.

Info

You will be asked if you want to save the one-sentence practice file. Click on: **Yes** and follow the method above using the filename **Winter**.

Practice 1

1 Load Word, open a new file and enter the following text:

Colours of a rainbow

A rainbow is an arc of colours formed in the sky. They quickly fade and disappear. The perfect arc and the bands of colour make the rainbow a beautiful sight. There is a saying that you may find a pot of gold at the end of a rainbow!

Rainbows appear when the sun comes out whilst it is raining. The light from the sun is known as white light. White light is actually made up of all the possible colours you can think of. Raindrops split the white light into the colours that are seen in the arc of a rainbow. Seven main colours can be identified.

You can demonstrate the formation of white from the seven main colours. Paint the colours, red, orange, yellow, green, blue, indigo and violet, in segments on a cardboard circle. Stick a pin through the centre to make a spinner. When spinning, the colours will recombine and look white.

2 Save the text with the filename: **P1 sec1 rainbow**.

3 Close the file and exit Word.

Practice 2

1 Load Word, open a new file and enter the following text:

Most people live within walking distance of a Post Office. In towns and cities it is somewhere we go to buy stamps, post letters and parcels, collect benefits, pay bills and are able to make use of a whole host of other services. In villages the Post Office is often incorporated in the local village store. In such settings, it can be at the heart of village life where people can chat and catch up with local events.

Post Offices have post boxes or pillar boxes (post boxes shaped like a pillar, often painted red). However, today we take for granted that post/pillar boxes are sited in numerous convenient locations. These were only introduced to mainland Britain in 1879. This was more than two centuries after the introduction of the public use of Royal Mail.

The cost of using the Royal Mail at its time of introduction was 2d (0.8p) for a single sheet travelling up to 80 miles (128.7km). This was paid not by the sender but by the recipient.

2 Save the text with the filename: **P2 sec1 post**.

3 Close the file and exit Word.

In this section you will practise and learn how to:

- open an existing document
- spellcheck and make changes where necessary
- add words to a custom dictionary
- resave a previously saved file
- preview and print a document and print part of the document from an installed printer
- insert/delete text
- overwrite text
- insert a new paragraph
- use the Undo and Redo commands

- select character, word, sentence, paragraph, body text or entire document
- replace words with other words
- use the Find command for a word or phrase within a document
- copy/move text within a document and to another document
- open several documents
- insert special characters/symbols
- modify document setup: page orientation, margins, page size etc
- switch between open documents

2.1) Opening an existing document

Exercise 1

Load Word and open the file **Eye** saved in section 1.

Method

1 Click on: the 📂 **Open** button.
2 In the Open dialogue box (Figure 3.9), in the **Look in** box, click on: the down arrow and then on the location of your file.
3 Click on: the filename, **Eye**.
4 Click on: **Open**.

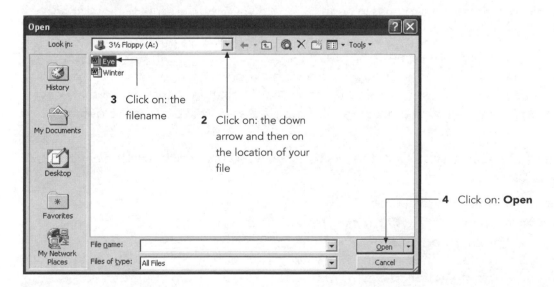

Figure 3.9 Opening a file

Recently opened files appear listed at the bottom of the **File** menu or in the Task Pane. Click on: the filename to open it.

2.2) Proofreading and correcting errors

It is important to proofread your work carefully against the hard copy. This becomes even more important when you are about to print a final finished copy. Then it will be necessary to check that the layout and all other attributes are as expected. At this early stage though, correct any errors in the text using the methods described in section 1.

2.3) Spellchecking

It is always prudent to use the spellchecker before you print a document. The spellchecker compares words in your text with words in its main dictionary and alerts you to any differences. It will pick up most misspelt words and provide you with the chance to correct them. The spellchecker will also alert you to any repeated words, eg 'the the'. Word provides an option to check spelling and grammar together. It also provides the option to check spelling and grammar as it is being keyed in. For a beginner this can be quite distracting since it places wavy red lines under misspelt words and wavy green lines under possible grammatical errors. Throughout this book I have chosen to turn the **Check spelling as you type** off. To do this from the **Tools** menu, select: **Options**. Click on: the **Spelling and Grammar** tab, then in the **Spelling** section, click in the box next to **Check spelling as you type** to remove the tick. Do the same in the **Grammar** section and click on: **OK**.

Note: There are limitations to the spellchecker's abilities and it may not pick up wrong usage of correctly spelt words, eg 'where' and 'were', 'stair' and 'stare'. Although these words are spelt correctly, they may be used in the wrong context. Similarly do not rely unquestionably on the grammar checker. The grammar checker is not always able to work out the correct structure of certain sentences. However it is useful for highlighting obvious errors, eg missing words.

Proper names, such as place names, and very unusual words are not in the spellchecker's main dictionary so these will also be highlighted. If you think that you will use these words often, it is worth adding them to Word's custom dictionary so that they will be ignored when carrying out future spellchecks. To add words to Word's default custom dictionary:

When running the spellchecker, with the word displayed in the **Not in Dictionary** box, click on: **Add to Dictionary**.

To check or edit the custom dictionary:

1 From the **Tools** menu, select: **Options**.
2 Click on: the **Spelling and Grammar** tab.
3 Click on: the **Custom Dictionaries** button.
4 Click on: **Modify**.
5 Words that have been added to the custom dictionary are displayed.
6 Key in or delete words as appropriate.
7 Click on: the ☒ **Close** button.
8 Click on: **OK**.

Run the spellchecker through the document.

Method

1 Position the cursor at the start of the document by pressing: **Ctrl** + **Home**.
2 Click on: the **Spelling and Grammar** button (Figure 3.10).

Spelling and Grammar button

Figure 3.10 The Spelling and Grammar button

3 The Spelling and Grammar dialogue box appears (Figure 3.11).

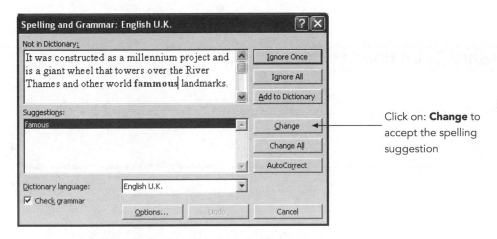

Click on: **Change** to accept the spelling suggestion

Figure 3.11 Spelling and Grammar dialogue box

The spellchecker will go through your text and match it with the words in its dictionary. It will highlight unrecognisable words and offer suggestions. (You may not have made any spelling errors!) In the example above, it has highlighted the word **fammous** and it is offering its preferred replacement, **famous**, also highlighted in the lower box. In this case accept the suggestion by clicking on: **Change**. If you do not want to accept a suggestion that the spellchecker has made, click on: **Ignore**. If you want to accept one of the other suggestions that it may have made, click on it to select it and then click on: **Change**. The spellchecker will repeat this process until it has finished checking all the text. It will then display a message telling you the spellcheck is complete.

2.4   Resaving a previously saved file

Exercise 3

Resave the file **Eye**.

Method

Click on: the **Save** button (Figure 3.12).

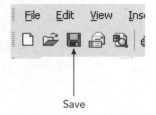

Save

Figure 3.12 The Save button

2.5   Previewing a document

Exercise 4

Print Preview your document.

Method

If you want to see how your document is going to look on the page before printing it, you can use Word's Print Preview facility.

1   Click on: the [🔍] **Print Preview** button. The Print Preview screen appears (Figure 3.13).

Multiple pages

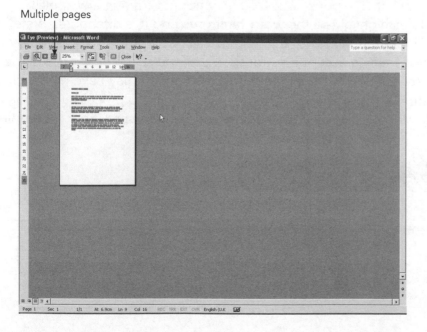

Figure 3.13 The Print Preview screen

The cursor, when placed over the document, appears in the shape of a magnifying glass. You can zoom in to any part of the document by clicking over it with the left mouse button. To zoom out, click again. The **Multiple Pages** button (shown in the figure above) is useful when your document has more than one page.

2   Press: **Esc** or click on: **Close** to return to the document window.

2.6   Printing a document

Exercise 5

Print one copy of the document.

Method

1   From the **File** menu, select: **Print** (Figure 3.14).

Figure 3.14   File menu, Print

2   The Print dialogue box appears (Figure 3.15).

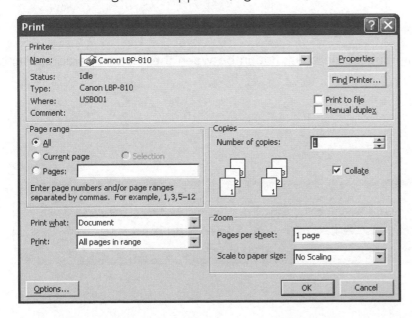

Figure 3.15   The Print dialogue box

3   Check the printer you are using. If it is not the one shown in the **Name** section of the Print dialogue box, click on: the down arrow and select the correct printer so that it appears in the **Name** box. Check that the printer is ready and loaded with paper.

4   There are several other default control options concerning printing (shown in the Print dialogue box – Figure 3.15 and in the Info box below). At this stage, you should not need to change any settings, so just click on **OK**.

Info

Quick method to print

On the toolbar, click on: the 🖨 **Print** button.

Use this if you know that you do not need to alter anything in the Print dialogue box.

Useful printing options

In the **Page range** section, choose which pages to print.

In the **Copies** section, select the number of copies to print.

In the **Print** section, you can select to print only **Odd** or **Even** pages.

2.7   Inserting text

Exercise 6

Using the instructions for inserting text in section 1.6 and below, insert the new paragraph (shown below) after the second paragraph ending… **thirty metres shorter**).

Going round

The London Eye does not stop for you to get on. This may sound alarming! Do not worry. It travels at a very slow speed so that you can hardly notice that it is moving.

Method

1   Position the cursor at the beginning of the blank line in between the second paragraph and the heading **The Capsules**.

2   Press: **Enter**.

3   Key in the text.

4   Press: **Enter**.

Info

Remember when you insert or delete text, check that the spacing between words, sentences and paragraphs is still consistent. Use the ¶ **Show/Hide** button to check this.

In the second sentence of the first paragraph, insert a comma and one space and then the following after **Thames** and before **and**:

Big Ben, the Houses of Parliament

Method

Follow the method given in section 1.6.

2.8 Deleting text

We have already learnt how to delete text using the **Delete** or ← **Del** (**Backspace**) key. However, this is not the quickest method to delete whole sentences or longer portions of text. To do this we need to select the text to be deleted.

Exercise 8

In the second sentence of the final paragraph, delete the words **specially designed and**.

Method

1 Position the cursor at the beginning of the text you want to delete – in this case the **s** of **specially** (Figure 3.16).

> Attached to this giant wheel are passenger capsules, each can accommodate more than twenty people. These capsules are |specially designed and positioned on the outside of the wheel to give a spectacular 360 degree panorama from the top. The capsules can be

Figure 3.16 Positioning the cursor

2 Hold down the left mouse button and drag the I-beam pointer across the words to be deleted (Figure 3.17).

> Attached to this giant wheel are passenger capsules, each can accommodate more than twenty people. These capsules are specially designed and positioned on the outside of the wheel to give a spectacular 360 degree panorama from the top. The capsules can be

Figure 3.17 Selecting text

3 Release the mouse. The highlighting shows the text that is selected. (If you need to cancel the selection, click anywhere on the screen or press any arrow key.)
4 Press: **Delete**.
5 Check for consistency of spacing.

Info

If you want to undo the last action(s), click on: the ↶ **Undo** button on the toolbar. This button is very useful and can be used at any time. When you click on the arrow next to the Undo button, a list of your most recent actions is displayed so you can select exactly which action to undo. You can also use the ↷ **Redo** button if you decide that you did not want to undo an action.

There are many ways to select text. These are given below. There is no right or wrong way and if you experiment you will find your own preferred method.

Selecting what	Action
Whole document	**Ctrl + A**
One word	Double-click on the word
One line	Click once just to the left of the line
One sentence	Hold down **Ctrl**, click anywhere in the sentence
One paragraph	Double-click just to the left of the paragraph
Any block of text	Position cursor at start of text. Hold down: **Shift**, position cursor at end of text and click
Deselect text	Click in any white space

2.9 Finding and replacing text

Info

There is no need for you to scan through text manually to replace text because Word can automatically find and replace text. Since the document you are working on is short, it may not take long to scan through without Word's help. However, it is very useful when working on longer documents.

To find words or phrases quickly:

1 From the **Edit** menu, select: **Find**.
2 Key in the word or phrase that you want to find and click on: **Find Next**.

Exercise 9

The word **giant** appears three times in the text. Replace the word **giant** with the word **gigantic** each time it appears.

Method

1 Move your cursor to the top of the document (**Ctrl + Home**).
2 From the **Edit** menu, select: **Replace** (Figure 3.18).

Figure 3.18 Edit menu, Replace

3 The Find and Replace dialogue box appears (Figure 3.19).

4 Click on: the **Replace** tab (if not already selected).

5 Click in: the **Find what** box, key in the word **giant**.

NB: DO NOT PRESS ENTER YET.

6 Click in: the **Replace with** box, key in the word **gigantic** (lower case).

7 Click on: **Replace All**.

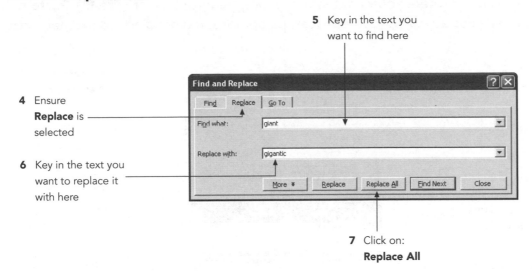

5 Key in the text you want to find here

4 Ensure **Replace** is selected

6 Key in the text you want to replace it with here

7 Click on: **Replace All**

Figure 3.19 The Find and Replace dialogue box

8 A box appears telling you how many replacements have been made (Figure 3.20).

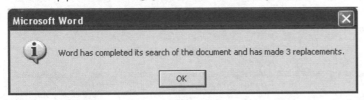

Microsoft Word

Word has completed its search of the document and has made 3 replacements.

OK

Figure 3.20 You are advised how many replacements have been made

9 Click on: **OK**.

10 Click on: **Close**.

Info

There are options available within Find and Replace. The commonly used option is **Match Case**. Use this if you are replacing a word consisting of capital letters. If you do not use it, the replacement word will also have capital letters (it will not have matched the case you have keyed in). To set Match Case, in the Find and Replace dialogue box, click on: **More**, click on: **Match Case** and proceed as before.

2.10 Moving text

Exercise 10

Move the second paragraph and its heading: **How high is it?** so that it becomes the third paragraph.

1 Select the paragraph and its heading using one of the methods in section 2.8.
2 Click on: the ✂ **Cut** button. The text will be saved on to the clipboard (you will not see or be told this).
3 a) Position the cursor where you want the text to reappear; b) click on: the 📋 **Paste** button.
4 You will now need to adjust spacing between paragraphs and headings to maintain spacing consistency.

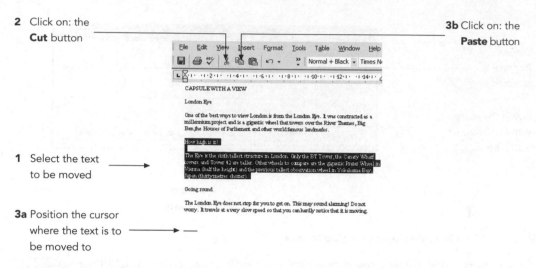

2 Click on: the
   Cut button

3b Click on: the
   Paste button

1 Select the text
   to be moved

3a Position the cursor
   where the text is to
   be moved to

Figure 3.21 Cutting and pasting

Info

The Clipboard

The clipboard is a memory store. Whenever you cut or copy an object, the computer temporarily stores the copy on the clipboard. It can then quickly retrieve it when you want to paste it somewhere else, even into other Office applications such as Excel or PowerPoint. To view what is on the clipboard, from the **Edit** menu, select: **Office Clipboard**. Items on the clipboard are removed when the computer is turned off.

2.11 Copying text

Exercise 11

Copy the heading **CAPSULE WITH A VIEW** so that it is repeated on a new line at the end of the text.

Method

Follow the method shown in section 2.10, except at step 2 click on: the 📋 **Copy** button instead of the **Cut** button.

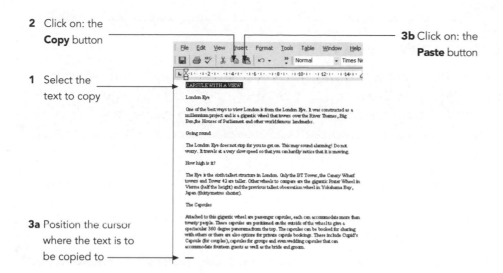

2 Click on: the **Copy** button

1 Select the text to copy

3b Click on: the **Paste** button

3a Position the cursor where the text is to be copied to

Figure 3.22 Copying and pasting

Saving and printing

Exercise 12

Save your file with the filename **Eye1** (as shown in section 1.8) and print one copy.

Info

By saving your file as **Eye1**, you will ensure that the original file is not overwritten. When practising working through assignments you will then be able to go back and correct any errors should this be necessary.

Note: It is good practice to get into the habit of saving your work regularly. If you encounter a problem you can always revert back to the most recently saved version of your work.

2.13 **Copy text to another document**

Exercise 13

Copy the first paragraph beginning **One of the best ways**... of the document currently open, ie **Eye1**, to a new Word document. Do not include the paragraph heading.

Method

1 Select the text to be copied so that it is highlighted.
2 Click on: the ▣ **Copy** button.
3 Open a new Word document by clicking on: the ▯ **New Blank Document** button. A new document appears.
4 Click on: the ▣ **Paste** button.

Exercise 14

Open the file saved as **Winter** in section 1.10 and copy the same piece of text as in Exercise 13 so that it becomes the second paragraph of the document.

Method

1   Open the file **Winter** following the method shown in section 2.1.
2   Position the cursor where you want the copied text to appear.
3   The text should already be on the clipboard so click on: the 📋 **Paste** button.

 Note: You should now have three Word documents open, ie **Eye1**, **Winter** and **Documentx** (which has not yet been given a filename).

Info

You can also move text between documents. To do this use the ✂ **Cut** button (instead of the **Copy** button after selecting the text).

Exercise 15

Save and print the documents **Winter** and **Documentx**, choosing a suitable filename for **Documentx**. Close all three documents.

Method

Use the quick save method for documents **Eye1** and **Winter** as in section 2.4. Save the file **Documentx** using the method in section 1.8 so that you can give the document a filename.

Info

Always give your documents meaningful filenames so that it will be easier to recognise them at a later date.

Exercise 16

Load the file **Eye1** saved in section 2.13 and insert the following text after and on the same line as **CAPSULE WITH A VIEW** at the end of the document:

Things To Do Places To Go Company ©

Method

1 Open the file and position the cursor where you want to key in the text.
2 Key in **Things To Do Places To Go Company**.
3 The © symbol does not appear on the keyboard. To insert this special character, ensure that the cursor is positioned where you want the character to appear.
4 From the **Insert** menu, select: **Symbol** (Figure 3.23).

Figure 3.23 Inserting a special character/symbol

5 The Symbol dialogue box appears (Figure 3.24).

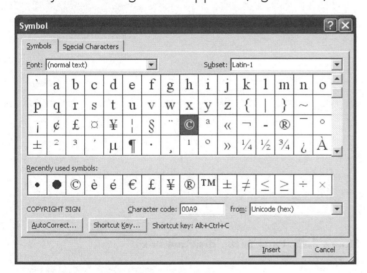

Figure 3.24 The Symbol dialogue box

6 With the **Symbols** tab selected, click on the symbol to insert.
7 Click on: **Insert** and then on: **Close**.

Info

The figure above displays **Font: (normal text)** and **Subset: Latin-1**. There are some other commonly used symbols to choose from, for example, foreign language letters with accents eg é, ä. It is worth taking time to acquaint yourself with some of them. There are other fonts (especially Wingdings and Symbol) that have some useful characters/symbols. Select other fonts from the list in the **Font** box. Click on: the **Special Characters** tab to access special characters such as ™ Trademark, ® Registered. Note © Copyright can also be accessed here.

Exercise 17

Change the document layout to landscape display and to paper size A4.

Info

Portrait and landscape

By default the document will be in Portrait display (the narrow edge at the top of the page).

Portrait

Landscape

Method

1   From the **File** menu, select: **Page Setup**.
2   The Page Setup dialogue box appears (Figure 3.25).

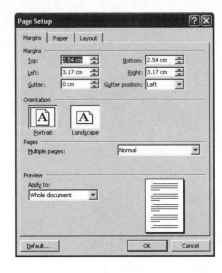

Figure 3.25 Page Setup dialogue box

3   Click on: the **Paper** tab (Figure 3.26).

Paper tab

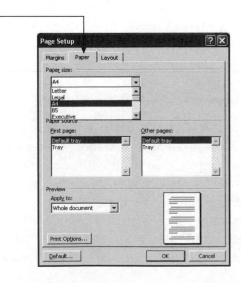

Figure 3.26 Selecting page orientation

4 In the **Paper size** box, click on the down arrow and click on: A4 to select it.

5 Select the **Margins** tab and in the **Orientation** section, click in: **Landscape** to select it.

6 Click on: **OK**.

Note: You can check the new document orientation in Print Preview.

Changing the margins

Exercise 18

Set in both the left and right margins by 2 cm ($\frac{1}{2}$").

Method

1 From the **File** menu, select: **Page Setup**: the Page Setup dialogue box appears (Figure 3.26).

2 Ensure that the **Margins** tab is selected. The default landscape left and right margin width is 2.54 cm. Therefore to set in the margin by 2 cm we will need to add 2 cm to the default width of 2.54 cm. The result is 4.54 cm.

3 Click in: the **Left** margin box and delete 2.54 cm and key in **4.54 cm**. Repeat in the **Right** margin box.

4 Click on: **OK**.

5 Click in a white space to take the highlighting off.

Exercise 19

Change the top and bottom margins to 2 cm. To do this, repeat the steps above, this time altering the figures in the **Top** and **Bottom** boxes.

Info

The default left and right margins in portrait display are 3.17 cm. You will notice that the Page Setup dialogue box allows you to change many of the defaults. Take a look at these now.

2.16 **Printing part of a document**

Exercise 20

Print only the end of the document from and including the heading **The Capsules**.

Method

1 Select the text to be printed so that it is highlighted (Figure 3.27).

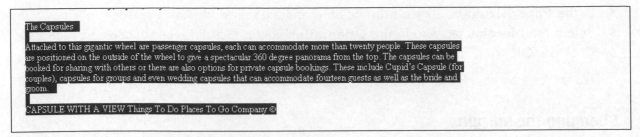

Figure 3.27 Section to be printed is selected

2   Follow the method in section 2.6 but at Step 4 in the **Page range** section of the Print dialogue box, click in: the option button next to **Selection** so that a dot is shown (Figure 3.28).

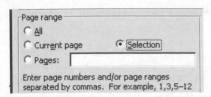

Figure 3.28 Printing part of a document

2.17   Close the file, save changes and exit Word

Info

Section 2.2 mentioned the importance of proofreading and correcting your work. If you are working on your own documents, when preparing final copy always do the following:

1   Spellcheck and correct where necessary.
2   Proofread against original copy (where relevant).
3   Check the layout using Print Preview.
4   Alter settings as necessary, bearing in mind the following:
    * is the document easy to read?
    * would a different page orientation be better?
    * are the fonts acceptable and a good size?
    * do the margins need altering?

These skills are all covered in this module.

Note: For Practice 4 you will need the Word file **Postal**.

Practice 3

1   Load Word and reload the file **P1 sec1 rainbow** saved in section 1.

2   Proofread and spellcheck the document, making corrections where necessary.

3   Quick save the document.

4   Print one copy.

5   Insert a new paragraph after the second paragraph ending …**can be identified**: **Mixing coloured light does not produce the same results as mixing paint. When red and green light are mixed, you get brown, not yellow.**

6   In the second paragraph delete the sentence beginning **Seven main colours**…

7   Replace **arc** with the word **arch** each time it appears.

8   In the first paragraph move the sentence beginning **They quickly fade**… from being the second sentence so that it becomes the last sentence in the paragraph.

9   Change the page orientation to landscape and set the paper to A4.

10 Change the left and right margins so that they are both 5.54 cm.

11 Change the top and bottom margins to 6.25 cm.

12 Save the document with the filename **P3 sec2 rainbow** and print a copy.

13 Print the document.

14 Close the file and exit Word.

Practice 4

1   Load Word and reload the file **P2 sec1 post** saved in section 1.

2   Proofread and spellcheck the document, making corrections where necessary.

3   Quick save the document.

4   Print one copy.

5   In the second paragraph, insert the following text to become the ending of the sentence currently ending in …**mainland Britain in 1879**: …**after roadside boxes had proved successful in Jersey and Guernsey**.

6   In the second sentence of the first paragraph, delete the text **collect benefits**.

7   Move the first paragraph so that it becomes the final paragraph.

8   At the top of the document, insert a heading **Post Services**. Leave one clear line space between the heading and the text below.

9   Copy the heading to a new line at the end of the document.

10 On the line below the copied heading enter the sentence: **Compiled by Chloë Black**.

11 Set in the left and right margins by 2 cm.

12 Save the document with the filename **P4 sec2 post** and print one copy on A4 paper.

13 Copy the text from (and including) the third paragraph to the end of the document to a new Word document.

14 Save the new document with the name **P4 sec2 postnew** and print.

15 Copy the same text to the end of the existing document **Postal** and resave as **Postal2**.

16 Print the file **Postal2** in portrait orientation on A4 paper.

17 Change to landscape orientation and print only the second paragraph.

18 Close all files and exit Word.

Section 3 / Formatting

In this section you will practise and learn how to:

- centre, embolden, italicise and underline text
- format superscript, subscript text
- change case
- apply different colours to text
- change line spacing
- control justification/alignment
- control hyphenation
- change font type and font size
- copy the formatting from a selected piece of text

- indent text
- create a header and a footer, inserting date, author, page numbers, filename and location
- apply headers and footers
- change page display modes
- use the page view magnification tool/zoom tool
- use and change pagination

3.1 Centring text

Exercise 1

Reload the file **Eye1**, saved in section 2 and ensure that it is showing portrait display. Centre the heading **CAPSULE WITH A VIEW**.

Info

When the display is changed back to portrait, the changes that were made to the left and right margins in landscape are now applied instead to the top and bottom margins and those to the top and bottom, to the left and right. We do not need to be concerned with this for the following exercises, but you will need to be aware for future reference.

Method

1 Select the text to be centred or position the cursor on the line where the text appears.
2 Click on: the **Center** button (Figure 3.29).

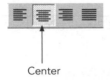

Center

Figure 3.29 The Center button

3 Click in a white space to remove highlighting.

3.2　Emboldening text

Exercise 2

Embolden the heading ...**CAPSULE WITH A VIEW**.

Info

Emboldening, italicising or underlining text is a way of giving emphasis to it.

Method

1 Select the text to be emboldened.
2 Click on: the **B** **Embolden** button.

3.3　Italicising text

Exercise 3

Italicise the text in the second sentence of the second paragraph that reads: **This may sound alarming!**

Method

Follow the method shown in section 3.2 except at step 2 click on: the *I* **Italic** button.

3.4　Underlining text

Exercise 4

At the bottom of the document underline the text **CAPSULE WITH A VIEW**.

Method

Follow the method shown in section 3.2 except at step 2 click on: the **U** **Underline** button.

3.5 Superscript and subscript

Exercise 5

At the end of the document, format the copyright symbol © so that it is superscript.

Method

1 Select the © copyright symbol.
2 From the **Format** menu, select: **Font**.
3 In the Font dialogue box, **Effects** section, click in: the **Superscript** box so that a tick appears.
4 Click on: **OK**.

Info

Select: **Subscript** when appropriate at step 3, eg H_2O.

3.6 Changing case

Exercise 6

Change the case of the text **Things To Do Places To Go Company** so that it is in Uppercase.

Method

1 Select the text to be changed.
2 From the **Format** menu, select: **Change Case**.
3 The Change Case box is displayed (Figure 3.30).
4 Select: **UPPERCASE**.
5 Click on: **OK**.

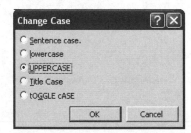

Figure 3.30 Changing case

Note other options that are available in the Change Case box.

3.7 Applying different colours to text

Exercise 7

Change the colour of the text **Cupid's Capsule** in the final sentence of the final paragraph.

1 Select the text to be changed.
2 Click on: the down arrow next to the **A** **Font Color** button to display colour choices (Figure 3.31).

Click on the down arrow to
display text colour choices

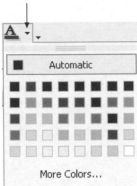

Figure 3.31 Changing text colour

3 Click on your selected colour.

Info

When you print, if you do not have a colour printer, the selected colours will display in grey shades.

3.8   Changing line spacing

Exercise 8

Change the whole document to double line spacing.   1

Info

Word lets you apply a variety of line space settings (the distance between individual lines of text). Examples are:

Single line spacing   this is the default.
Double line spacing   one blank line is left between the lines of text.

This is an example of single line spacing. The default setting is single line spacing where the gap between the lines of text is just over the type size. If the specification for a document is single line spacing, then usually you need do nothing.

This is an example of double line spacing. There is one blank line left automatically

between lines of text without the need to press: **Enter**. It is often used when a section

requires extra emphasis.

Select all the text using the quick method (press: **Ctrl + A**).

2 From the **Format** menu, select: **Paragraph**. The Paragraph dialogue box is displayed (Figure 3.32).

3 Ensure the **Indents and Spacing** tab is selected.

4 In the **Spacing** section, **Line spacing** box, click on: the down arrow and click on: **Double**.

5 Click on: **OK**.

6 Click in a white space to remove highlighting.

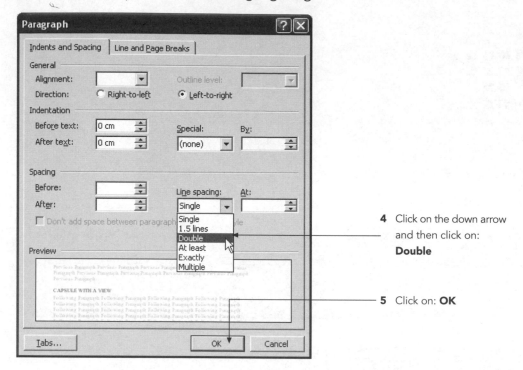

4 Click on the down arrow and then click on: **Double**

5 Click on: **OK**

Figure 3.32 The Paragraph dialogue box – selecting double line spacing

Info

In double line spacing there are usually three lines between paragraphs. If you look on the Status bar in Normal view you will notice that your document now takes up two pages since 2/2 is displayed. When you scroll through your document you will see a line across the page indicating that Word has automatically inserted a page break.

You can apply double line spacing to parts of a document by selecting only the text you require. If you do not want to have the default three lines between paragraphs, select only the individual paragraph and not the line spaces in between.

When working on documents that require specific spacing, it is useful to display paragraph marks and line break marks (without all the other non-printing formatting marks). These display as ¶ . To do this:

1 From the **Tools** menu, select: **Options**.

2 Click on: the **View** tab.

3 In the **Formatting marks** section, click in: the **Paragraph marks** box so that a tick is displayed.

4 Click on: **OK**.

Exercise 9

Justify the text at the right and left-hand margins (full justification).

Method

Info

There are four types of alignment. They can be accessed via the **Formatting** toolbar:

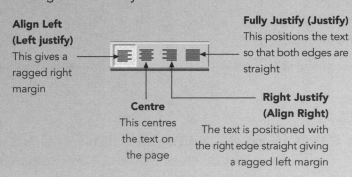

Align Left (Left justify)
This gives a ragged right margin

Fully Justify (Justify)
This positions the text so that both edges are straight

Centre
This centres the text on the page

Right Justify (Align Right)
The text is positioned with the right edge straight giving a ragged left margin

1 Select all of the text (**Ctrl + A**).
2 Click on: the **Justify** button (shown above).
3 Click in a white space to remove the selection.

You will notice that the centred heading **CAPSULE WITH A VIEW** has also justified. Recentre it by following the instructions in section 3.1.

Info

When text is justified, the text is spaced out to sit flush with the margins. In such cases it can look better to hyphenate some words. You can hyphenate automatically or manually. To set hyphenation, from the **Tools** menu, select: **Language** and then: **Hyphenation**. The Hyphenation dialogue box is displayed. Click in: the box to **Automatically hyphenate document**. If you prefer to have more control over which words are hyphenated, deselect: **Automatically hyphenate document**. After keying in the text, select it and from the **Tools** menu, select: **Language**, **Hyphenation** and click on: **Manual**. Word will then ask before it hyphenates a word.

3.10   **Save the file as Eye2**

3.11   **Print one copy on A4 paper**

3.12   **Changing font and font size**

Change the font of the main heading to Arial and the size to 18 pt.

Info

Serif and sans serif fonts

The default font in Word is Times New Roman. This is a serif font. Serifs are small lines that stem from the upper and lower ends of characters. Serif fonts have such lines. Sans serif fonts do not have these lines. As a general rule, larger text in a sans serif font and body text in a serif font usually makes for easier reading. Examples:

Times New Roman is a serif font.

Arial is a sans serif font.

Method

1 Select the heading **CAPSULE WITH A VIEW** so that it is highlighted.
2 Click on: the down arrow in the **Font** box (where **Times New Roman** is displayed, shown in Figure 3.33) to display fonts that are available on your computer.

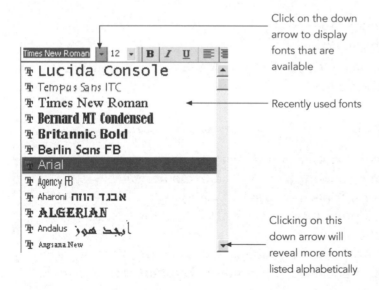

Click on the down arrow to display fonts that are available

Recently used fonts

Clicking on this down arrow will reveal more fonts listed alphabetically

Figure 3.33 Fonts available in Word

3 Click on: Arial to select it.

Changing font size

4 With the text still selected, click on: the down arrow in the **Font Size** box (Figure 3.34).
5 Click on: the size required or key in the new size.

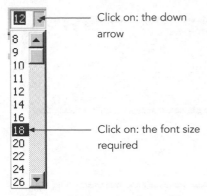

Click on: the down arrow

Click on: the font size required

Figure 3.34 Changing font size

3.13 Copying the formatting from a selected piece of text

Exercise 11

Change all other headings in the document to Arial, size 14 pt.

Method

1 Follow the method shown in section 3.12 to change the first heading, ie **London Eye**.
2 With the changed heading still selected double-click on: the 🖌 **Format Painter** button.
3 Select the other headings in turn. They will automatically reformat.
4 Press: **Esc** to turn the **Format Painter** off.

3.14 Indenting text

Info

Do not confuse indentation with page margins. An indent is the difference between the margin and the text.

Indenting on the left side

Exercise 12

Indent the first paragraph on the left side only. (Do not include the heading.)

Method

1 Select the text to be indented.
2 Click on: the ⬚ **Increase Indent** button.

The **Increase Indent** button moves the text in from the margin by 1.27 cm. Click on it again to increase the indentation further. To remove the indentation, use the ☷ **Decrease Indent** button.

Indenting both the left and right

Exercise 13

Indent the second paragraph on both the left and the right by 2 cm. (Do not include the heading.)

Info

There are two ways to indent on the right-hand side. If you have good control of the mouse, using the ruler is a quick method. It is worth making a note of the measurements already showing on the ruler before altering them. Don't forget, you can use the **Undo** button if you make a mistake.

Indenting using the ruler

Method 1

1 Select the text to be indented.
2 Click and drag the **Left Indent** marker (the square block) on the ruler to the right by 2 cm, as shown in Figure 3.35. The text will indent accordingly.

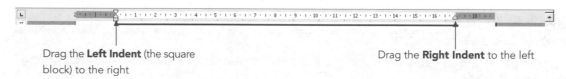

Drag the **Left Indent** (the square block) to the right

Drag the **Right Indent** to the left

Figure 3.35 Indenting using the ruler method

3 Drag the **Right Indent** marker to the left.
4 Click in: a white space to turn the highlighting off.

Indenting using the Format menu

Method 2

1 Select the text to be indented.
2 From the **Format** menu, select: **Paragraph**. The Paragraph dialogue box appears (Figure 3.36).

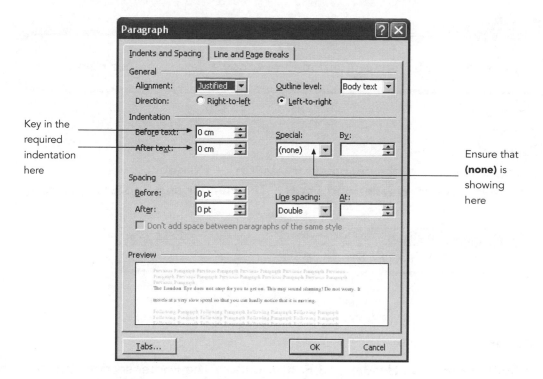

Key in the required indentation here

Ensure that **(none)** is showing here

Figure 3.36 Paragraph dialogue box

3 Ensure the **Indents and Spacing** tab is selected.
4 In the **Indentation** section, click in: the **Before text** (or **Left**:) box and key in the measurement you require.
5 Repeat in the **After text** (or **Right**:) box.
6 In the **Special** box, ensure that **(none)** is displayed.
7 Click on: **OK**.
8 Remove the highlight.

> **Info**
>
> This second method can be used if you need a non-standard-sized indent. It can also be used to create special indents by selecting **First line** or **Hanging** in the **Special** box and keying in the size of the indent in the **By** box.
>
> **First line** indents only the first line of the selection.
>
> **Hanging** does not indent the first line but indents all the following lines.
>
> Note: These special indents can also be achieved using the ruler. See Word Online Help for more detail.

3.15 Creating headers and footers

> **Info**
>
> By default Word leaves a section at the top and bottom of each page so that headers and footers can be printed on documents. Headers and footers can contain information about the document, eg its filename, date and page number. This is a very useful feature, especially when used with multiple page documents. The header and footer need only be set up for one page and will automatically appear on other pages of a long document. Automatic entries can be used, such as date and author's name.

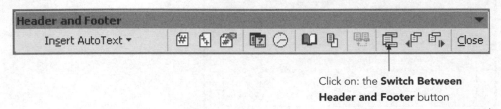

Exercise 14

Create a footer in size 10 pt to display **London Eye**, **today's date** and **your name**.

Method

1 Move the cursor to the start of the document (press: **Ctrl + Home**).
2 From the **View** menu, select: **Header and Footer**. The **Header and Footer** box appears (Figure 3.37).

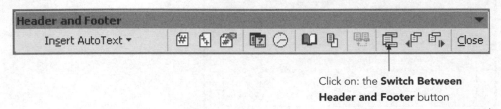

Click on: the **Switch Between Header and Footer** button

Figure 3.37 Header and Footer box

3 Click on: the **Switch Between Header and Footer** button. The Footer section appears (Figure 3.38).

Click on: the down arrow and select options automatically to insert commonly used header and footer information

Switch between header and footer

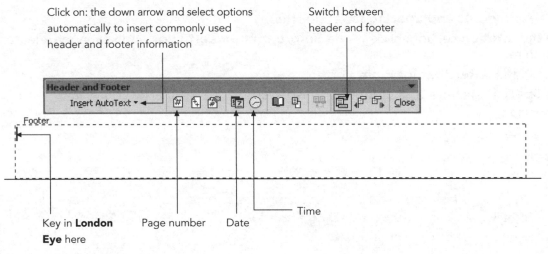

Footer

Key in **London Eye** here   Page number   Date   Time

Figure 3.38 Footer section

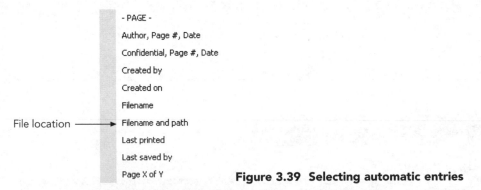

- PAGE -
Author, Page #, Date
Confidential, Page #, Date
Created by
Created on
Filename
File location → Filename and path
Last printed
Last saved by
Page X of Y

Figure 3.39 Selecting automatic entries

4 Key in **London Eye** directly into the **Footer** section.
5 Press: **Tab** (or the spacebar several times) to move the cursor across the page.
6 Click on: the **Insert Date** toolbar button (Figure 3.38) to insert today's date automatically.
7 Press: **Tab** (or the spacebar) again to move the cursor across and then key in your name.
8 It will look something like Figure 3.40.

| London Eye | 21/01/03 | Angela Bessant |

Figure 3.40 Text inserted into footer

Info

Check that the date is correct. The date may not be set up correctly on your computer. If it shows the wrong date, select the date only, then press: **Delete**. Key in the date manually or reset the computer's date (Module 2, section 2.3).

To amend header/footer text, access the header/footer from the **View** menu (as above), select and amend text using the same methods used for the main document.

Note: The **AutoText** fields include filename and file location (for easier location at a later date – see Figure 3.38).

Formatting the footer text

9 Select the footer text and change the size using the formatting toolbar. You may now want to alter the spacing.

10 Click on: **Close**.

Info

You will not be able to see the footer if you are in **Normal View** but it will show up in **Print Layout View** and also in **Print Preview**. (See later in this section for information on different types of view.)

Exercise 15

Add page numbers to the top centre of each page.

There are two ways of adding page numbers.

Method 1

Using the View menu

1 Follow steps 1 and 2 in Exercise 14. The Header and Footer box appears.

2 Click on: the **Center** button on the Formatting toolbar so that the page numbers will appear in the centre.

3 Click on *either* **Insert Autotext**, then **–PAGE–** *or* click on: the **Insert Page Number** button (Figure 3.41).

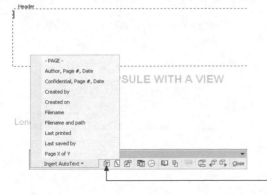

Insert Page Number

Figure 3.41 Inserting page numbers on a header

Using the Insert menu

1 From the **Insert** menu, select: **Page Numbers**.

2 The Page Numbers dialogue box appears (Figure 3.42).

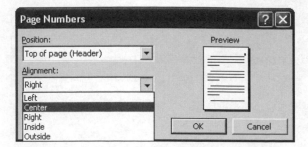

Figure 3.42 Page Numbers box

3 Use the down arrows next to **Position** and **Alignment** to select where you want the numbers to be.

4 Click on: **OK**.

Info

Should you need to adapt page numbers, eg start at a number other than 1, click on: the 🖩 **Format Page Number** button in Method 1. For both methods, click on: **Format** if you need to amend further.

3.16 Changing page display modes

Info

There are four different types of view. The buttons for these are displayed at the bottom left of the Word window.

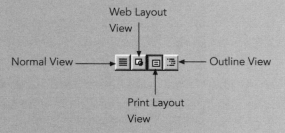

Normal View allows for quick and easy text editing.

Web Layout View displays the document as it would appear on the web.

Print Layout View allows you to see how objects will be positioned on the printed page. It shows margins, headers and footers and graphics.

Outline View allows you to see your document in an outline format. It is also useful when selecting sections of text, eg all the body text (no headings) when styles have been used to format the document. For more on styles, see section 4.

In **Print Layout View**, use the **Zoom** button to magnify the footer text.

Method

1 Click on: the **Print Layout View** button (if not already selected), shown in the Info box above.
2 The header and footer will now be visible. The text, set at size 10 pt, will be small and since header text is greyed out it may be difficult to read. Use the **Zoom** box to enlarge the text on screen as follows:

Using the page view magnification/zoom tool

3 Click on: the down arrow in the **Zoom** toolbar box to reveal default zoom views (Figure 3.43).
4 Select a zoom greater than 100% (or the default) to enlarge text.
5 To revert back, select: zoom 100%.

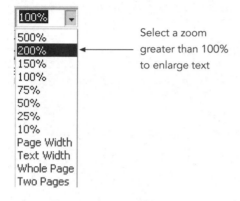

Select a zoom greater than 100% to enlarge text

Figure 3.43 Using Zoom

Insert a page break after the second paragraph ending ...**is moving**.

Method

1 Position the cursor on the line in between the second paragraph and the third paragraph heading.
2 From the **Insert** menu, select: **Break**.
3 The Break dialogue box appears. Ensure that the **Page break** option button is chosen and click on: **OK** (Figure 3.44).

Figure 3.44 The Break dialogue box

It is important to set out the pages so that they are easy to read. Check that the default setting for **Widow/Orphan** control (**Format** menu, **Paragraph**, **Line and Page Breaks**) is ticked. This ensures that paragraphs are not split so that one stray line of text appears at the bottom or top of a page. Always check that headings are not split from the text to which they refer.

Line breaks are used in document layout when you want to start a new line but not a new paragraph.

To insert a line break

Click where you want the break to be. Press: **Shift + Enter**.

To delete a line break

Click on: the **Show/Hide** button.
Select the line break symbol and press: **Delete**.

There are soft and hard page breaks. As your text reaches the bottom margin of a page, a soft page break is automatically inserted by Word. This will reposition itself should you add or delete text from the document. A hard page break is inserted by you. Its position will always remain constant until you decide to alter it.

To delete a hard page break

1 Ensure that you are in **Normal View** by selecting it from the bottom left corner of the document window.

    Normal View ⟶ ▤ ▣ ▤ ▤

2 Position the cursor on the page break (dotted line).

3 Press: **Delete**.

3.18 **Save the document as Eye3**

3.19 **Print one copy on A4 paper**

3.20 **Close the file and exit Word**

Practice 5

1 Load Word and reload the file **P3 sec2 rainbow** saved in section 2.
2 Centre and embolden the heading **Colours of a rainbow**.
3 Change the heading to upper case.
4 Set in the whole document by 2.25 cm at the left margin.
5 Set the document in double line spacing.
6 Change the colour of all the text in the second and fourth paragraph to green.
7 Justify second and third paragraphs only.
8 Change the font in the final paragraph to Arial 14 pt.
9 Add a header containing the text **Colours** and your name.
10 Format the header to 10 pt.
11 Add page numbers at the bottom right, starting at 4.
12 Insert a page break after the first paragraph.
13 Save the document as **P5 sec3 rainbow**.
14 Print one copy on A4 paper in landscape orientation.
15 Close the file and exit Word.

Practice 6

1 Load Word and reload the file **P4 sec2 post** saved in section 2.
2 Change the heading **Post Services** to Arial 16 pt.
3 Centre and underline the heading.
4 Using the **Format Painter**, copy the formatting of the heading to the text at the bottom of the document, **Post Services**, **Compiled by Chloë Black**.
5 Make the second paragraph hanging by 1.5 cm.
6 Increase the font size of the final paragraph by 2 pt.
7 Add a footer with an automatic filename and location.
8 Save the document as **P6 sec3 post**.
9 Print the document on A4 paper and in portrait orientation.
10 Close the file and exit Word.

In this section you will practise and learn how to:

- use lists (bulleted and numbered)
- use and set tabs
- add borders/shading to a document
- save an existing document under another version number, file format
- apply existing styles to a document
- choose an appropriate document template for use in a specified task
- work within a template on a specified task
- modify basic options in Word

4.1 Using lists (bulleted and numbered)

Exercise 1

Open a new Word document and key in the following text, perform a spellcheck and save the document with the filename **bookings**.

ALLSORTS THEATRE

GROUP BOOKING

Benefits of group booking include:

Special discounts
Exclusive events
Exemption from booking fees

Group bookers are very important to us at Allsorts Theatre. We aim to make your visits as simple as possible for you. When booking for a group of 12+ the above benefits are automatically included.

Why not contact us today for an information pack?

We look forward to your call.

Exercise 2

Make the section starting at **Special**... and ending ...**booking fees** into a bulleted list.

Method

1 Select the text to be bulleted.
2 Click on: the ⊟ **Bullets** button.

Bullets/numbering can be selected before keying in the text, if preferred.

Formatting bullets

Bullets can take many forms:

1 From the **Format** menu, select: **Bullets and Numbering**.
2 Select your preferred option and click on: **OK**.
3 Click on: **Customize** if you require a different bullet type.

Numbered lists

Numbering lists is carried out following the same method as for exercise 2 but at step 2 clicking on: the ☰ **Numbering** button. This is useful if lists need to be in a specific order, eg a set of instructions. You can format numbers:

1 Select the list.
2 From the **Format** menu, select: **Bullets and Numbering**.
3 The Bullets and Numbering dialogue box is displayed.
4 Ensure the **Numbered** tab is selcted. Click on: **Customize**.
5 The Customize Numbered List dialogue box is displayed.
6 Select a format from the **Number style** list. Options include Roman numerals and A, B, C etc.

Turning bullets/numbering off

To turn Bullets and Numbering off, select the bulleted/numbered text, and click on: the relevant **Bullets** or **Numbering** button.

4.2 Using and setting tabs

Exercise 3

Using tabs, insert the following paragraph after the line ending …**information pack?**

Please use these numbers: Dylan   **ext 3338**
                                         Carol   **ext 3362**
                                         Nattie   **ext 3363**

Tabs are used to line up columns and Word offers several types of tab:

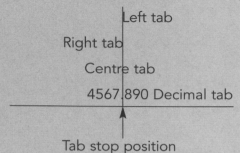

Left tab

Right tab

Centre tab

4567.890 Decimal tab

Tab stop position

By default, tabs are set every 1.27 cm ($\frac{1}{2}$") from the left margin. When a new tab is set, Word clears any default tabs set to the left of the new tab stop. The type of tab stop can be chosen by clicking on the **Tab** button at the left-hand edge of the ruler.

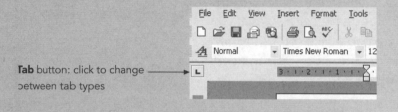

Tab button: click to change between tab types

L – Left tab

⌐ – Right tab

⊥ – Centre tab

⊥ – Decimal tab

Note: The following tabs are also available:

| – Bar tab: This draws a vertical line on a document.

▽ – First Line Indent: This sets the first line of paragraphs.

⊔ – Hanging Indent: This defines the left margin of every line but the first line in a paragraph.

Note: It is useful to have the **Show/Hide** on when setting tabs.

Using pre-set tabs

1   Key in the text **Please use these numbers:** in the correct position in the document.

2   Press: **Tab** once to move to the preset tab stop and key in **Dylan**. *Note*: The **Tab** key is the key (usually to the left of the **Q** key) with a forward arrow and a backward arrow.

3   Press: **Tab** once and key in **ext 3338**. Press: **Enter** (Figure 3.45).

Please·use·these·numbers: → Dylan→ext·3338¶

Figure 3.45 Using tabs

4   Press: **Tab** a number of times until the cursor is lined up under the **D** of **Dylan**.

5   Key in: **Carol**, press: **Tab** once and key in **ext 3362**. Press: **Enter**.

6   Repeat steps 4 and 5 for **Nattie ext 3363** (Figure 3.46).

```
¶
Please·use·these·numbers:  →  Dylan→ext·3338¶
    →       →       →       →   Carol→ext·3362¶
    →       →       →       →   Nattie→ext·3363¶
¶
```

Figure 3.46 Text keyed in displaying hidden characters

Info

In this instance the tab stops are positioned in a convenient place and make the layout clear. Sometimes this is not the case and tab stops need to be positioned manually.

Exercise 4

Underneath the information for Nattie, key in and position the name and extension number **Evangeline ext 3384**.

Method

1 Enter the name and ext number using the above method. You will notice that because the name Evangeline is longer than the other names, the ext number is not lined up (Figure 3.47).

```
Please·use·these·numbers:  →  Dylan→ext·3338¶
    →       →       →       →   Carol→ext·3362¶
    →       →       →       →   Nattie→ext·3363¶
    →       →       →       →   Evangeline →  ext·3384¶
```

Figure 3.47 ext numbers are not aligned

2 To rectify this, add an extra tab space between **Dylan** and **ext**, **Carol** and **ext** and **Nattie** and **ext** (Figure 3.48).

```
Please·use·these·numbers:  →  Dylan→   →    ext·3338¶
    →       →       →       →   Carol→   →    ext·3362¶
    →       →       →       →   Nattie→  →    ext·3363¶
    →       →       →       →   Evangeline →  ext·3384¶
```

Figure 3.48 Extra tab spaces inserted

3 However, now when you take the **Show/Hide** off you will notice that the ext numbers are rather a long way from the names. In order to move them closer to the names we will need to set a left tab stop.

4 Select all the tabulated text.

5 From the **Format** menu, select: **Tabs**. The Tabs dialogue box appears (Figure 3.49).

Figure 3.49 Tabs dialogue box

6   In the **Tab stop position** box, key in the first tab stop position (I am using 4.55 cm). Ensure **Alignment** is set to **Left**. Click on: **Set**.

7   Key in the second tab stop position (I am using 6.55 cm). Click on: **Set**.

8   Click on: **OK**.

9   Your text and ruler will now look similar to that in Figure 3.50. *Note:* You will need to turn **Show/Hide** back on.

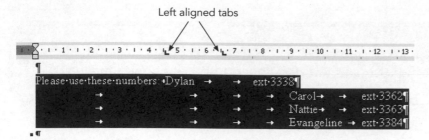

Figure 3.50 Tab set at 4.55 cm and 6.55 cm

10 To realign the text, delete some of the tab spaces, eg position the cursor before the **C** in **Carol** and press: the ← **Del** (Backspace). Repeat for **Nattie** and **Evangeline**. The names will now be aligned. Similarly remove the extra tab spaces between the names, **Dylan**, **Nattie** and **Evangeline** and the ext numbers, ie so that they are aligned with the second tab stop at 6.55 cm (Figure 3.51).

11 Remove the highlighting. Turn **Show/Hide** off.

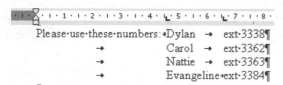

Figure 3.51 Text realigned

Info

Tabs can also be set by:

1   Selecting the tab type by clicking on the **L** **Tab** button until the type you require is showing.

2   Click once on the ruler where you want the tab stop to be.

3   Repeat as necessary.

4   To remove tabs, drag them off the ruler.

Setting leader tabs

Leader tabs have a line for the eye to follow to the tabulated entry, eg:

Dotted line leader . . . . tab
Continuous line leader _____ tab

To set a leader tab:

1   From the **Format** menu, select: **Tabs**.

2   In the **Tabs** dialogue box, set the tab as normal.

3   In the **Leader** section, set the format.

It is well worth practising setting tabs. It is quite difficult to master.

Exercise 5

Add a border to the document.

Method

1　From the **Format** menu, select: **Borders and Shading**. The Borders and Shading dialogue box appears.

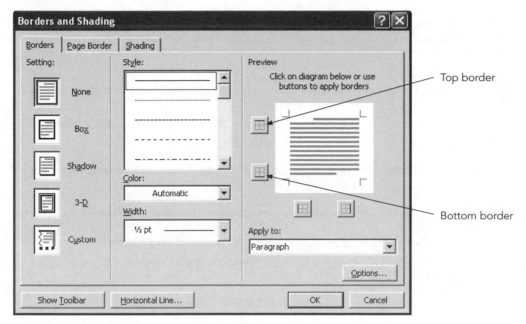

Figure 3.52　Borders and Shading dialogue box

2　Click on: the **Borders** tab and make selections from the various sections, eg **Box**, **Shadow**, **3-D** (Figure 3.52).

　　Note: You do not need to have a border at the top, bottom, left and right. In the **Preview** section, you can select which borders to omit by clicking on the relevant boxes.

3　Click on: **OK**.

Info

You can apply borders to individual paragraphs by first selecting the relevant paragraph. Ensure that the **Borders** tab is selected, format as required, make a selection in the **Apply to** section. Click on: **OK**.

Exercise 6

Add a border and shading to the bulleted list.

1   Select the bulleted list.
2   From the **Format** menu, select: **Borders and Shading**. The Borders and Shading dialogue box appears.
3   Ensure the **Borders** tab is selected. In the **Setting** section, select the border you require. Ensure that **Paragraph** is displayed in the **Apply to** box.
4   Click on: the **Shading** tab.
5   In the **Fill** section, click on a selected shade.
6   Click on: **OK**.
7   Click in a white space to remove highlighting.

4.4   Saving documents under a different file format

Exercise 7

Save the document in the normal way with the filename **theatre groups**. Also save the file with the filename **theatre1** in a format suitable for posting on the web.

Info

By default, Word automatically saves files in the version of Word format that you are using, ie Word XP and adds the extension .doc, eg **theatre groups.doc**. However, it is possible to save documents in other formats.

Method

Save the file with the filename **theatre groups** in the normal way.

Saving a document in web format

1   From the **File** menu, select: **Save As**.
2   The Save As dialogue box appears.
3   In the **Save as type** section, click on: the down arrow to reveal a list. Scroll through to see the formats that the document can be saved as (Figure 3.53). *Note:* You can also save in a different version of the application, eg Word 6.0.
4   Select: **Web Page**.
5   Key in the filename **theatre1**. Click on: **Save**.

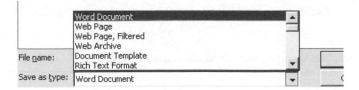

Figure 3.53 File formats available

File type	
Text file (.txt)	Select **Plain text** – all formatting and pictures will be lost.
Rich Text Format (.rtf)	Select **Rich Text Format** – this is readable by most common word processors.
HTML (.htm, .html)	Select **Web Page** – for use on the WWW, LAN or Intranet.
Template (.dot)	Select **Document Template** – use to create a template that can be reused, eg letterhead.
Software-specific file extension	Enter a filename with the file extension, eg [filename].wri (for Microsoft Write).
Version number	Select from one of the versions listed, eg **Word 6/95** – use when you need to share files with users with older versions of Word. Newer versions of Word will be able to read documents saved in previous versions.

Note: You can check the file format by selecting: **Properties** from the **File** menu and then the **General** tab. Figure 3.54 shows the Type as Microsoft HTML Document (this is a web format), the MS-DOS name is **theatre1.htm** instead of **theatre1.doc**.

Figure 3.54 File properties

Exercise 8

Print the saved file **theatre groups** and close both files.

4.5 **Working with templates and applying existing styles to a document**

Info

Word documents are based on a template called **Normal.dot**. Templates act as a document model and store settings. Each template has various set styles associated with it. **Normal** is the default style applied to the default template for Word documents. It has the properties of being left aligned, Times New Roman, 12 pt. Other styles have their own properties which are given next to the example text. Styles are linked to templates so that Heading1 in one template may be Arial, right aligned, 16 pt, and in a different template could be Times New Roman, centred, 20 pt. You will notice that not all styles are suitable as they will upset bulleted lists, tab settings etc. Use the **Undo** button to recover original text style.

More styles are available by selecting: **Styles and Formatting** from the **Format** menu. Also from the **Format** menu, you can experiment with **Autoformat** and **Theme**. As you work through a document, styles that you are using will be added to the Style list.

Open the file **theatre groups** and format it using Word's default template existing styles.

Method

1 With the document open on screen, select the heading **ALLSORTS THEATRE**.
2 Click on: the down arrow in the `Normal ▾` **Style** box.
3 Click on: a suitable style.
4 Format some of the other text within the document in the same way, selecting individual words or paragraphs.
5 Resave and close the document.

Exercise 10

Use a suitable Word template to produce a fax, using your imagination to fill in the details.

Method

1 From the **File** menu, select: **New**.
2 In the Task Pane, **New from template** section, click on: **General Templates**.
3 Click on: the **Letters and Faxes** tab (Figure 3.55).

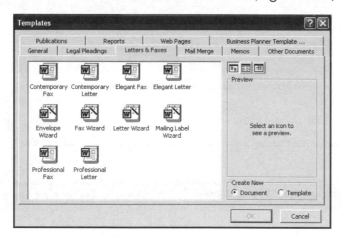

Figure 3.55 Selecting a template

4 Select a suitable template (you will see a **Preview** on the right-hand side) and then click on: **OK**.
5 You may need to use **Zoom** to see all the document details.
6 Overwrite the text with your own.
7 Save the document and print one copy on A4 paper.

Info

Templates have fields that are already set up. These fields are marked in grey. If they are not marked in grey, from the **Tools** menu, select: **Options**. With the **View** tab selected, in the **Show** section, ensure that the **Field shading** box is set to **Always**. You can delete fields by selecting them and pressing: **Delete**. Familiarise yourself with the different templates available in Word.

Creating a new template

1 Create the document that you want to become a template.
2 From the **File** menu, select: **Save As**.
3 Key in the filename and in the **Save as type** box, select: **Document Template**.
4 Choosing **Document Template** automatically takes you to the **Templates** folder where it will be saved.
5 Click on: **Save**.
6 Close the template document.

Opening the new template

1 From the **File** menu, select: **New**.
2 In the Task Pane, **New from Template** section, select: **General Templates**.
3 The **Templates** dialogue box is displayed (Figure 3.55).
4 With the **General** tab selected, you should be able to see your new template.
5 Click on it and then on: **OK**.

4.6   Close the document

4.7   Modify basic options in Word

When you know that you will always be opening/saving files in a particular folder it is worth setting this as the default as follows:

1 From the **Tools** menu, select: **Options**.
2 Select: the **File Locations** tab.
3 In the **File Types** list, click on: **Documents**.
4 Click on: **Modify**.
5 In the **Modify Location** box, select the location and folder where you want the files opened/saved.
6 Click on: **OK**.
7 Click on: **OK** again.
8 The location set will be the default next time you use Word.

You are also able to set a user name that will appear on automatic entries that you insert in your document, eg on headers and footers. The user name set will also display with file properties.

Setting a user name

1 From the **Tools** menu, select: **Options**.
2 Select: the **User Information** tab.
3 In the **Name** box, key in your name.
4 Click on: **OK**.

Note: You can also change a user name for the active document only. To do this:

1 From the **File** menu, select: **Properties**.
2 Select: the **Summary** tab.
3 Key in your name in the **Author** box.
4 Click on: **OK**.

4.8   Exit Word

Practice 7

1 Open a new Word document and key in the following text, formatting as shown. Save the document with the name **Summer breaks**.

SUMMER BREAKS FROM ONLY £69!
MANY DESTINATIONS

Format the 2 headings as follows: sans serif font, 26 pt, bold, font colour red, centre across the page

Try our city breaks, holiday villages and apartments in:

Belgium
France
Holland
Spain
Germany
Italy

Make into bulleted list
Change to upper case

Our prices are keen:
3 night camping Brittany .... **from £99.99**
Eurostar to Brussels .... **from £129.99**
2 night hotel Amsterdam .... **from £130.50**

Tabulate with decimal tab stops and leader dots

Free night deals!
We look forward to your call!

All other formatting is at your discretion using styles. Add a shadow border around the whole document. Add a border of your choice around the bulleted list and shade within this border. Print on A4 paper in portrait display.

2 Save in a format suitable for posting on the web.

Practice 8

1 Load Word and the Professional Memo template. Insert the following text in the appropriate places:

Company name: WINE ROSES
To: Laurent Graham
From: Gita Alahan
Cc: Isobel McGarry
Today's date
Subject: Delivery of Vin de Pays Béthune
Message: Thank you for the delivery that I received this morning. As you know we are opening next Saturday and you would be most welcome to come and join us then. Please let me know if you can make it.
Best Regards

2 Save the document as **Memo wine**.
3 Print one copy on A4 paper.

In this section you will practise and learn how to:

- create standard tables
- insert/delete columns/rows
- add/remove borders on a table
- change cell attributes: formatting, cell size, colour etc

5.1) Creating a standard table

Exercise 1

Open a new Word document and create the following table using the **Table** facility:

Largest Lakes	Longest Rivers	Highest Mountains
Caspian Sea	Nile	Everest
Superior	Amazon	K2
Aral Sea	Mississippi-Missouri	Lhotse

Method

1. With a new document open, position the cursor where you want the top left corner of the table to be.
2. Hold down the left mouse over the ▦ **Insert Table** button: a grid appears.
3. Drag the mouse across and down the grid to result in the number of columns and rows required for the table (3 columns and 5 rows, including a blank row after the headings – Figure 3.56). Release the mouse.

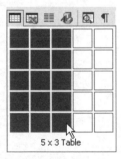

5 x 3 Table

Figure 3.56 Setting cells for a new table

4. The empty table appears in your document.
5. Key in the table's text, pressing: **Tab** to move to the next entry position (or use the arrow keys).

Info

If you press **Enter** by mistake, a line space will appear. Press: ← **Del** (Backspace) key to remove the line space.

Working with borders

6   Remove the borders on the table by positioning the cursor anywhere in the table and from the **Table** menu, select: **Select**, then: **Table**.

7   From the toolbar, click on the down arrow next to the **Border** button. Click on: **No Border** as shown in Figure 3.57.

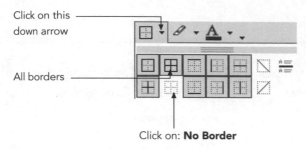

Click on this down arrow

All borders

Click on: **No Border**

Figure 3.57 Deleting borders

8   Reinstate all borders by clicking on: the **All borders** button.

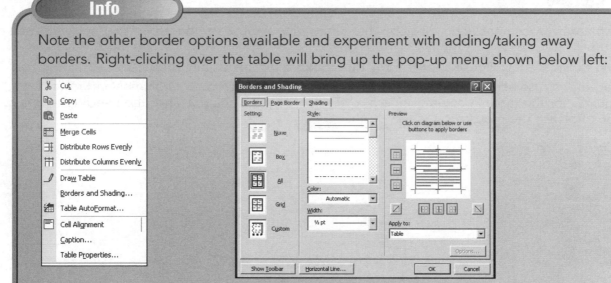
9   Save the document with the filename **Nature**.

Adding rows at the end of a table

Exercise 2

Add a row at the bottom of the table and key in the following in the relevant places:

Huron   **Yenisey-Angara**   **Makulu**

Method

1 Position the cursor after the end of the last table entry, ie the **e** of **Lhotse**.
2 Press: **Tab**. A new row is created.
3 Key in the text and resave the document with its original filename.

Inserting rows within the table

Exercise 3

Insert a row between the one displaying **Superior** and **Aral Sea** and insert the text:

Victoria   **Yangtze-Kiang**   **Kangchenjunga**

Method

1 Select the row below where you want to insert the new row, by dragging the mouse over it.
2 From the **Table** menu, select: **Insert**, then **Rows Above** (Figure 3.58).

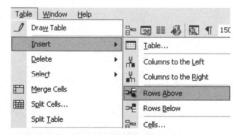

Figure 3.58 Inserting rows

3 Key in the text.

Deleting rows

Exercise 4

Delete the row containing **Caspian Sea**, **Nile**, **Everest**.

Method

1 Select the row to be deleted by dragging the mouse across the row.
2 Right-click over the selection; a pop-up menu appears (Figure 3.59).
3 Select: **Delete Cells**. The Delete Cells box appears (Figure 3.60). Click next to **Delete entire row**, then on: **OK**.

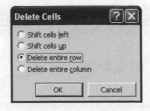

Figure 3.60 Deleting a row

Figure 3.59 Pop-up menu

Deleting columns

Exercise 5

Delete the middle column.

Method

1 Select the column to delete by hovering over the top of the column. When a thick black arrow appears, click the mouse.
2 Right-click over the selection.
3 From the pop-up menu, select: **Delete Columns** (Figure 3.61).

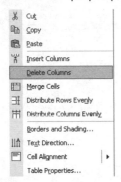

Figure 3.61 Deleting columns

Inserting columns

Exercise 6

Re-insert the deleted column. (For practising purposes, do not use **Undo**.)

Method

1 Select the column to the right of the required position for the new column.
2 Right-click over the selection.
3 From the pop-up menu, select: **Insert Columns**.
4 Key in the text:

Longest Rivers

Amazon

Yangtze–Kiang

Mississippi–Missouri

Yenisey–Angara

Inserting columns to the right of the last column in a table

Exercise 7

Insert a column to become the fourth column of the table and enter the following:

Largest Deserts

Sahara
Arabian
Gobi
Kalahari

Method

1 Click just outside the right-hand column.
2 From the **Table** menu, select: **Select**, then: **Column**.
3 Right-click over selection, select: **Insert Columns**.

Info

Deleting an entire table

Select the table by clicking anywhere in it and from the **Table** menu, select: **Select**, **Table**. Click on: the **Cut** button. Click on: the **Undo** button to reinstate the table!

5.3 Changing cell attributes

Exercise 8

Change the font in the heading row to Arial, 10 pt size, embolden and centre it.

Method

1 Select the heading row.
2 Format it in the usual way using the toolbar buttons.

Exercise 9

Change the background of the heading cells to a colour instead of white.

Method

1 Select the cells and right-click to bring up a pop-up menu.
2 Select: **Borders and Shading**.
3 Ensure the **Shading** tab is selected.
4 Click on: a colour.
5 Click on: **OK**.

Exercise 10

Change the width of the first column so that it is narrower than the other three.

Method

1   Select the first column.
2   Position the cursor on the selected column's side border; the pointer changes to a double-headed arrow pointing to left and right. (*Note*: Ensure the double-headed arrows are not pointing to top and bottom.)
3   Drag the column border to the required position.

Info

Tables are created with standard cell widths and heights. Change them by selecting them and dragging the borders, as in exercise 10. You can use **AutoFit**. With the table or cell(s) selected, from the **Table** menu, select: **AutoFit**, **AutoFit to Contents**.

You can also use, from the **Table** menu, **Table Properties**, **Row** tab, **Specify Height** box and key in a value. Click on: **OK**

or

Column tab, **Preferred Width** box and key in a value. Click on: **OK**.

5.4 **Resave the document and print one copy on A4 paper**

5.5 **Close the document and exit Word**

Practice 9

1 Open a Word file.

2 Key in the following:

More kilocalories are used by males than by females for all activities. This is because men usually are heavier and so have more weight to carry. Also women have more body fat and need less energy to maintain body heat. The table below shows energy requirements by activity.

3 Create the following table:

Activity	Female	Male
Running	420 kcal	600 kcal
Walking uphill	360 kcal	440 kcal
Walking	180 kcal	220 kcal
Sitting	70 kcal	90 kcal
Sleeping	55 kcal	65 kcal

4 Format the headings in bold, centre and make 2 pt larger than the other text.

5 Set the width of the columns so that they are in the same proportions as the columns above.

6 Delete all borders except the outside border and the bottom border of the headings row.

7 Shade the headings row cells in yellow.

8 Insert a row after the one containing **Walking** in the **Activity** column and enter the details:

Standing   100 kcal   120 kcal

9 Save the document with the filename **Calories** and print in landscape display on A4 paper.

10 Print a copy of the table only.

Practice 10

1 Load the file **Calories** saved in Practice 9.

2 Delete the **Male** column from the table (ensure an outside border is maintained).

3 Set in the left and right margins by 2 cm.

4 At the top of the document, add a main heading **Energy Requirements**. Centre the main heading.

5 Change the font throughout the document to Arial 18 pt.

6 Save the file with the filename **Calories female**.

7 Print the document in landscape on A4 paper.

In this section you will practise and learn how to:

- create a data file for use in a mail merge
- merge a data file with a letter document or a label document

What is mail merge?

Mail merge is the name given to the merging of information (usually names and addresses) with a standard document (usually a letter). The names and addresses are keyed in and stored in a database file and can be used with any standard document without having laboriously to key in the information again. Therefore it saves a lot of work. The end result of a mail merge is that the letter (or document) looks personal since it is impossible to tell that a number of other people have received the same letter.

6.1 Creating/opening a merge letter document

Exercise 1

Open a new Word document and key in the following letter. Save the document with the filename **Mail**.

22 September 2003

Autumn and Winter Talks

I am pleased to enclose details of our forthcoming events.

All talks will take place in the main area of the Town Hall. The Montrose multi-storey car park is a short walk away. If you are travelling by public transport, the nearest bus stop is in Ford Road. Please note that we expect these events to be very popular so please book early. We are able to accommodate one guest per member.

I look forward to welcoming you this season.

Yours sincerely

Club Secretary

Enc

Method

Info

In this instance, since we do not already have a letter to merge, we are creating one. If the letter to merge already existed, you would open it in the normal way.

1 Key in the document, proofread, spellcheck and save it.
2 From the **Tools** menu, select: **Letters and Mailings**, **Mail Merge Wizard**.
3 In the **Task Pane**, **Select document type** section, select: **Letters** (Figure 3.62).
4 Click on: **Next: Starting Document**.
5 In the **Select starting document** section, select: **Use the current document** (Figure 3.63).
6 When prompted, select: **Active window** (Figure 3.64).
7 Click on: **Next: Select recipients**.
8 In the **Select recipients** section, select: **Type a new list** (Figure 3.64).
9 Click on: **Create**.

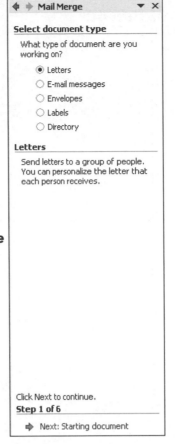

Figure 3.62 Step 1 of 6 Mail Merge

Figure 3.63 Step 2 of 6 Mail Merge

Info

If the data source already existed, you would need to click on: **Use an existing list**. A datafile can be generated from a database application, an Excel file or in Word as follows:

1 Create a table in Word.
2 Position the cursor in the table and from the **Table** menu, select: **Convert Table to Text**.
3 Click in the **Tabs** selection, then on: **OK**.
4 Save as filetype **Plain Text**.

Figure 3.64 Step 3 of 6 Mail Merge

10 The New Address List dialogue box is displayed (Figure 3.65).

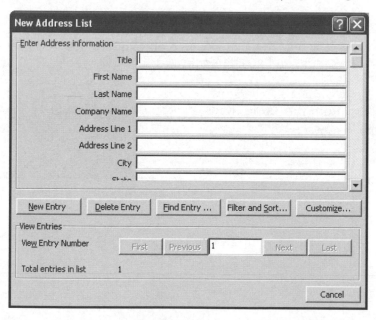

Figure 3.65 New Address List box

6.2 Creating a data source

Use the following information to create the data source:

Miss Alyssa Riley
46 The Briars
Leeds
LS7 6BD

Mr Kevin Anbeh
10 High Street
Harrogate
HG1 9BT

Mrs Colette Fraser
19 George Street
Bradford
BD2 2AH

Mr Jean-Paul Garnier
55 White Quay
Leeds
LS2 4EP

Method

Info

In the data source, each field contains the same type of information, eg in the 'Title' field Mr, Mrs, Miss etc are acceptable. Each addressee's data is called a record. By examining the data source information, you will see that the data has the following six fields: Title, FirstName, LastName, Address Line1, Address Line2 and PostalCode. Word provides commonly used field names, which are displayed in the **Enter Address information** section in Figure 3.65.

1   With the New Address List box displayed, click on: **Customize** (Figure 3.66).

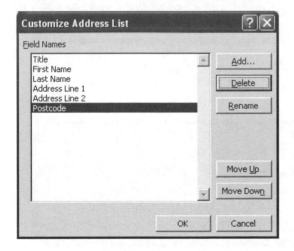

Figure 3.66 Customising the address fields

2   Delete the fields that are not required and rename the **Zip code** field **Postcode**.
3   Click on: **OK**.
4   Enter the first record in the appropriate boxes.
5   Click on: **New Entry**.
6   Repeat for the other records.
7   Click on: **Close**.
8   The Save Address dialogue box is displayed (Figure 3.67).

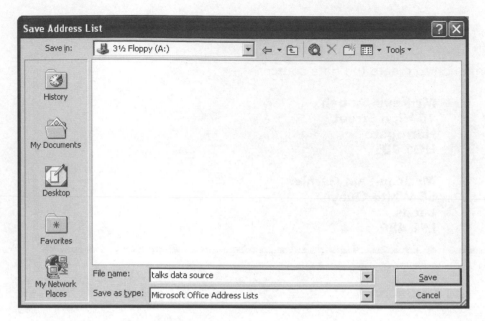

Figure 3.67 Saving the data source

9 Save the data source with the name **Talks data source**.

10 The Mail Merge Recipients dialogue box is displayed. To use all the names and addresses, click on: **OK**.

Exercise 3

Insert merge fields into the document.

Method

Info

In order for Word to know where you want the data in the data source to be merged, it is necessary to insert merge fields. This sounds complicated but is in fact straightforward. When a mail merge is carried out, the actual data (from the data source) will be inserted in the appropriate merge fields. This is demonstrated in the following two exercises.

1 Position the cursor where you want the address to be - in this case under the date of the letter (Figure 3.68).

2 In the Task Pane, **Write your letter** section, click on: **Address block** (Figure 3.69).

22 September 2003

«AddressBlock»

«GreetingLine»
            Autumn and Winter Talks

I am pleased to enclose details of our forthcoming events.

Figure 3.68 Merge fields positioning

Figure 3.69 Step 4 of 6 Mail Merge

3 The Insert Address Block box is displayed providing display options (Figure 3.70).

4 Select any options you require.

5 Click on: **OK**.

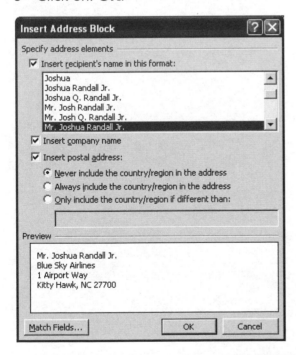

Figure 3.70 Inserting a merge address

6 Position the cursor on the **Greeting line** of the letter.

7 In the Task Pane, select: **Greeting line**.

8 The Greeting Line box is displayed (Figure 3.71).

9 Select the format you require and click on: **OK**.

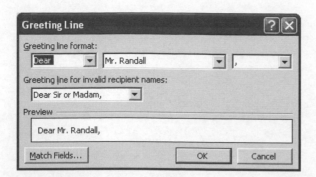

Figure 3.71 Selecting the greeting format

Info

When working on merge documents, you may have other fields to merge. At Step 4 of 6, use the **More items** option to insert individual fields.

6.4 Viewing merged document

Method

1 Click on: **Next: Preview your letters**.
2 The first merged document is displayed.
3 To view the other three, in the Task Pane, use the arrows in the **Preview your letters** section (Figure 3.72).
4 Click on: **Next: Complete the merge**.

Figure 3.72 Step 5 of 6 Mail Merge

6.5 Printing the merged file

1 In the Task Pane, **Merge** section, click on: **Print**. Select **All** and click on: **OK**.

2 Print in the normal way.

6.6 Save all documents with new filenames

6.7 Producing labels

Info

You can also use mail merge to produce address labels. To do this, select: **Labels** at Step 1 Mail Merge. You will need to know what type of labels they are to set up the main merge document. There is a list of standard ones to choose from.

Exercise 4

Use the data file saved as **Talks data source** in section 6.2 to create mailing labels.

Method

1 With a new blank document open, from the **Tools** menu, select: **Letters and mailings**, **Mail Merge Wizard**.

2 In the Task Pane, **Select document type** section, select: **Labels** (Figure 3.73).

3 Click on: **Next: Starting document**.

Figure 3.73 Selecting Labels

4 Select the starting document, in this case **Change document layout** (Figure 3.74). Click on: **Label options**.

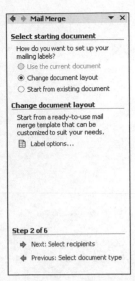

Figure 3.74 Selecting starting document

5 The Label Options dialogue box is displayed (Figure 3.75). Make a selection as appropriate. Click on: **OK**.

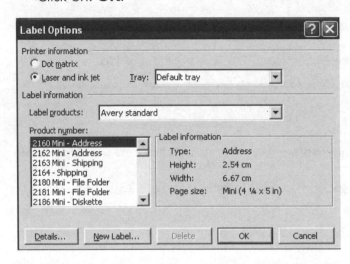

Figure 3.75 Label Options

6 In the Task Pane, click on: **Next: Select recipients**.

7 Select: **Use an existing list** and locate the data file using the **Browse** button (Figure 3.76). Click on: **Next**: **Arrange your labels**.

Note: You could have created a new list at this stage (as in section 6.2).

Figure 3.76 Selecting the data source

8 The Mail Merge Recipients box is displayed (Figure 3.77). *Note:* You can select the recipients for the merge by clicking in their tick boxes. By default they are all selected. Click on: **OK**.

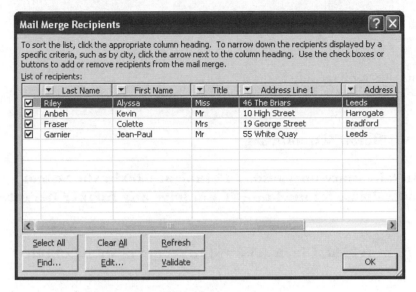

Figure 3.77 Mail Merge Recipients selection

9 Click on: **Next: Arrange your labels**.

10 Select the layout. For this exercise click on: **Address block** (Figure 3.78).

11 Click on: **Update all labels**.

12 Click on: **Next: Preview your labels**.

Figure 3.78 Arranging the labels

13 The labels are previewed. Click on: **Next: Complete the Merge** (Figure 3.79).

14 Click on: **Print** (Figure 3.80).

Figure 3.79 Previewing

Figure 3.80 Printing.

Practice 11

1 Key in the following letter to be used as a merge letter:

Insert date

Bicton School AGM

Please note that the AGM will take place on Tuesday 17 June at 8.00 in the School Hall. I am enclosing the agenda. Please let me know if you have any further items to add.

Coffee and light snacks will be provided. I look forward to seeing as many of our members as possible.

Yours sincerely

Peter Hill

Secretary

Enc

2 Create the data source:

Miss Brown	Dr Doqui	Mrs Allen
8 Winsley Place	91 Hillside Gardens	2 Lavendon Way
Kempston	Silsoe	Harrold
Bedford	Bedford	Bedford
MK67 9NL	BD31 6PT	MK65 2AH

3 Merge the letter with the data source.

4 Save all files.

5 Print the merged letters.

Practice 12

1 Use the data source created in Practice 11 to create mailing labels.

2 Print the labels on to A4 paper.

Pictures, images and other objects

In this section you will practise and learn how to:

- insert a graphic into a document
- resize a graphic
- move/duplicate a graphic within a document and between documents
- delete a graphic

7.1 Adding a graphic to a document

Exercise 1

Open a new Word document and add a piece of ClipArt suitable for a house-warming party.

Method

1 Open a new Word document.
2 Position the cursor, by double-clicking the mouse, where you want the image to appear.
3 From the **Insert** menu, select: **Picture**, then **Clip Art** (Figure 3.81).

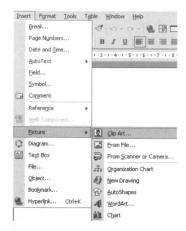

Figure 3.81 Inserting a picture

Info

Notice the other picture options here, notably **From File** (to import an existing picture file) and **Chart**, which are inserted in a similar way. As well as this method, objects including spreadsheets, graphs and graphics can be pasted in from other documents using the **Cut** and **Paste** buttons. When importing using the **Insert File** method, remember to set the file type to that which you are importing. As an example, if the file type is set to the Word document type and you want to insert an Excel file, the Excel file will not be displayed in the files list.

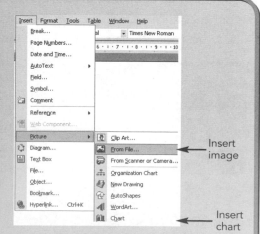

Figure 3.82 Inserting a picture from file or a chart

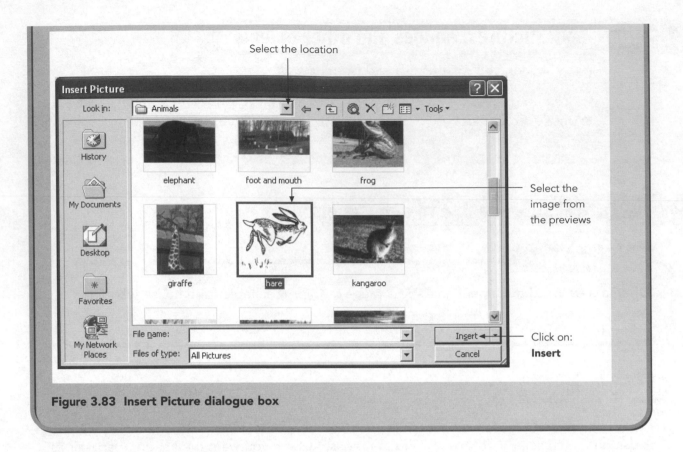

Figure 3.83 Insert Picture dialogue box

4 In the Task Pane, **Search For** section, in the **Search text** box, key in **house** (or a brief description of what you are looking for) (Figure 3.84).

Figure 3.84 Insert ClipArt Task Pane

5 Click on: **Search**.
6 A selection of available ClipArt is displayed (Figure 3.85). Scroll to see more.
7 Select a suitable picture by right-clicking on it.
8 A pop-up menu appears; click on: **Insert**.

Figure 3.85 Results of ClipArt search

9 Close the Task Pane by clicking on its **Close** button.

10 The chosen picture appears in the new document.

Resizing an image

11 Click on the picture to select it. It will have handles on the corners and at the sides (Figure 3.86).

Resize using the corner handles to preserve the aspect ratio ——————

Figure 3.86 A selected picture

12 Hover the mouse over a handle until a double-sided arrow appears. Drag a corner handle inwards to reduce the size of the picture.

13 Centre the picture using the **Center** button.

> ### Info
>
> If you drag from a corner, the picture will keep its aspect ratio (its original proportions). If you try to resize it from the side handles, it will loose its shape. Try it to see what happens. Use the **Undo** button to revert back to the original proportions. A ClipArt picture has been used in Exercise 1. Resize pictures from file (images) and charts in the same way.

> ### Exercise 2
>
> Enter the following text underneath the image. Format the text as you want.
>
> **INVITATION**
> **Jenny and James**
> **invite you to their**
> **NEW FLAT PARTY**
> **Saturday 18 October**
> **9 pm till 2 am**
> **RSVP**

7.2 Moving/duplicating a graphic within a document

> ### Exercise 3
>
> Move the picture so that it appears at the bottom of the text.

Method

1 Select the picture.

2 Click on: the **Cut** button.

3 Position the cursor where you want the picture to appear, then click on: the **Paste** button.

You can also duplicate a picture by clicking on: the **Copy** button at step 2. You can also reposition a picture by selecting it and dragging it to the required position. Use the same method for pictures from file (images) and charts.

7.3 Save the document and print one copy

7.4 Moving/duplicating a graphic between documents

Exercise 4

Open a new Word document. Move the picture used in the document saved in section 7.3 to the new document.

Method

1 Open the document saved in section 7.3 (if not already open).
2 Select the picture by clicking on it.
3 Click on: the **Cut** button.
4 Open a new Word document.
5 Position the cursor where you want the picture to appear. In this case the cursor can be left positioned at the top of the document.
6 Click on: the **Paste** button.

Info

To copy the picture, at step 3, click on: the **Copy** button. Use the same method for pictures from file and charts.

7.5 Deleting a graphic

Exercise 5

Working on the new document and underneath the picture, enter the following text in a sans serif font type, and size 24 pt:

DINNER PARTY INVITATION

Delete the picture that you have just inserted.

Method

1 Enter the text.
2 Click on: the picture to select it.
3 Press: **Delete**.

Complete the invitation with some text of your own and insert a more suitable picture. Format the document as you like, eg add borders, shading, fancy fonts. Use the same method for pictures from file and charts.

Method

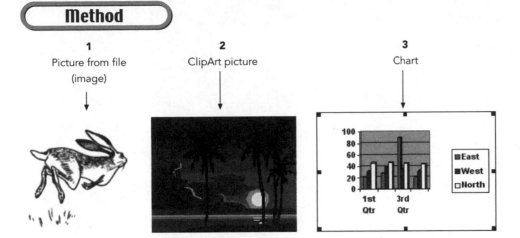

1 Picture from file (image) **2** ClipArt picture **3** Chart

1 Select 1, 2 or 3 by clicking on it.
2 The chart (number 3) has been selected (it has handles).
3 Resize by dragging the handles.
4 Resize and keep proportions by dragging a corner.
5 Delete by selecting and pressing: **Delete** or:
   Move by selecting. Click on: **Cut**, then on: **Paste** or:
   Copy by selecting. Click on: **Copy**, then on: **Paste**.

7.6 Save, print and close the documents and exit Word

Note: No sample answers are given for this exercise since answers will vary.

Note: For this exercise you will need the Word file **visitors**.

Practice 13

1 Open a new Word document.

2 Key in the following text:

Sample Menu

Starter

Tomato Pesto Toasties
Chicken Pittas with Red Coleslaw
Chinese Garlic Mushrooms

Main Course

Tuscan Chicken
Stuffed Plaice Rolls
Cajun Style Cod

Dessert

Fruity Bread Pudding
Apple Foam with Blackberries
Mango and Ginger Clouds

3 Insert a suitable piece of clipart before the **Dessert** heading.

4 Centre the clipart within the left and right margins.

5 Keeping its original aspect ratio, resize the clipart so that it is approximately 4 cm square.

6 Insert a page break after the clipart.

7 At the bottom of the text on the second page, key in the following text:

Visitors by week

The following is a chart displaying the most popular weeks during the summer months.

8 Insert the chart only from the word file **visitors** under the text.

9 Number the pages at the top centre, starting at 5.

10 Copy the items from the second page of the document to a new Word document.

11 Key in your name and the date as the first line of the first page of both documents.

12 Save and print both documents.

Word processing quick reference

(The following is a list of generally useful tasks associated with this module. For more information on specific items, refer to the chapter content.)

Action	Keyboard	Mouse	Right–mouse menu	Menu
Bold text	Select text to embolden			
	Ctrl + B	Click: the **B** **Bold** button	**Font**	**F**o**rmat**, **F**o**nt**
			Select: **Bold** from the **Font style:** menu	
Borders	Select text			
		Click: the **Borders** button		**F**o**rmat**, **B**o**rders and Shading**
	Select the border options you require			
Capitals (blocked)	**Caps Lock** Key in the text **Caps Lock** again to remove			Select text to be changed to capitals: **F**o**rmat**, **Change Cas**e, **UPPERCASE**
Centre text	Select the text			
	Ctrl + E	Click: the **Center** button	**P**a**ragraph**	**F**o**rmat**, **P**a**ragraph**
			Select: **Centered** from the **Alignment:** drop-down menu	
Change case	Select the text to be changed From the **Format** menu, select: **Change Cas**e Select the appropriate case			
Close a file	**Ctrl + W**	Click: the ✕ **Close** button		**F**i**le**, **C**l**ose**
Cut text	Select the text to be cut			
	Ctrl + X	Click: the **Cut** button	**Cu**t	**E**d**it**, **Cu**t
Delete a character	Press **Delete** to delete the character to the right of the cursor Press ← (Backspace) to delete the character to the left of the cursor			
Delete a word	Double-click: the word to select it. Press: **Delete**			
Delete/cut a block of text	Select the text you want to delete			
	Delete *or* **Ctrl + X**	Click: the **Cut** button	**Cu**t	**E**d**it**, **Cu**t

Action	Keyboard	Mouse	Right-mouse menu	Menu
Exit Word		Click: the ❌ **Close** button		**F**ile, E**x**it
Find text	**Ctrl + F**			**E**dit, **F**ind
Font size	Select the text you want to change			
		Click: the ▾ down arrow next to the **Font Size** box Select: the font size you require	**F**ont Select: the required size from the **Size:** menu	F**o**rmat, **F**ont
Font type	Select the text you want to change			
		Click: the ▾ down arrow next to the **Font** box Select: the font you require	**F**ont Select: the required font from the **Font:** menu	F**o**rmat, **F**ont
Formatting, copying	Select text to copy			
	Click: the 🖌 **Format Painter** button Double-click to copy to several pieces of text			
Headers and Footers				**V**iew, **H**eader and Footer
Help	**F1**			**H**elp, Microsoft Word **H**elp
	Shift + F1			**H**elp, What's **T**his?
Hyphenation				**T**ools, **L**anguage, **H**yphenation
Indenting		Click: the 📑 **Increase Indent** button	**P**aragraph, **I**ndents and Spacing	F**o**rmat, **P**aragraph, **I**ndents and Spacing
To remove indent		Click: the 📑 **Decrease Indent** button	In the **Indentation** section, select your options as appropriate	
Insert image, file, chart		Use Cut and Paste method		**I**nsert, *either* **P**icture, **O**bject, Fi**l**e Resize using handles
Insert text	Position the cursor where you want the text to appear Key in the text			

Action	Keyboard	Mouse	Right–mouse menu	Menu
Justified margins	Select the text you want to change			
	Ctrl + J	Click: the ▦ **Justify** button	**P**aragraph	**F**ormat, **P**aragraph
			Select **Justified** from the **Alignment:** drop-down menu		
Line length, changing		Use the ruler (see separate table)		**F**ile, **Page Setup**, **M**argins (see separate table)
Line spacing			**P**aragraph	**F**ormat, **P**aragraph, **I**ndents and **S**pacing
			In the **Spacing** section, select the options you require		
Lists, bulleted and numbered	Click: the ▤ ▤ **Numbering** or **Bullets** button		**B**ullets and **N**umbering	**F**ormat, **B**ullets and **Numbering**
Load Word	In Windows desktop			
		Double-click: the **Word** shortcut icon		**Start**, **All Programs**, **Microsoft Word**
Mail merge				**Tools**, **Letters and Mailings**
Margins				**F**ile, **Page Set**u**p**, **Margins**
Move a block of text	Select: the text to be moved Cut it and paste it where you want it moved to or Select: the text to be moved Click and drag it to the correct position Release the mouse button			
Moving around the document	Use the cursor keys (see separate table for more)	Click: in the required position		
New file, creating	**Ctrl + N**	Click: the ▯ **New** button		**F**ile, **N**ew
Non-printing characters, showing, hiding		Click: the ¶ **Show/Hide** button		

Action	Keyboard	Mouse	Right-mouse menu	Menu
Open an existing file	**Ctrl + O**	Click: the 🖿 **Open** button		**F**ile, **O**pen
	Select the appropriate directory and filename Click: **Open**			
Page break, adding	**Ctrl + Enter**			**I**nsert, **B**reak, OK
Page break, deleting	In Normal View, place the cursor on the page break Press: **Delete**			
Page display	Click: the appropriate ≡ ▫ 目 ☷ **View** button			**V**iew
Page numbering				**I**nsert, **Page** **N**umbers Select the required options
Page Setup				**F**ile, **Page Set**u**p** (Choose from **Margins**, **Paper** **Layout**)
Paper size	(See Page Setup)			
Paragraphs – splitting/joining	*Splitting:* Move the cursor to the first letter of the new paragraph Press: **Enter** twice *Joining:* Move the cursor to the first character of the second paragraph Press ← (Backspace) twice (Press the spacebar to insert a space after a full stop)			
Preferences, set default folder				**T**ools, **O**ptions, **File Locations**
Set user name				**T**ools, **O**ptions, **User Information** or **F**ile, **Proper**t**ies**, **Summary**
Print file	**Ctrl + P** Select the options you need Press: **Enter**	Click: the 🖨 **Print** button		**F**ile, **P**rint Select the options you need and click: **OK**
Print preview		Click: the 🔍 **Print Preview** button		**F**ile, **Print** **Pre**v**iew**

Action	Keyboard	Mouse	Right–mouse menu	Menu
Ragged right margin	**Ctrl + L**	Click: the ☰ **Align Left** button	**Paragraph**	**F**ormat, **Paragraph**
			Select **Left** from the **Alignment:** drop-down menu	
Remove text emphasis	Select text to be changed			
	Ctrl + B (remove bold) **Ctrl + I** (remove italics) **Ctrl + U** (remove underline)	Click: the appropriate button: **B** *I* U	**F**ont	**F**ormat, **F**ont
			Select **Regular** from the **Font Style:** menu	
Replace text	**Ctrl + H**			**E**dit, **R**eplace
Save	**Ctrl + S**	Click: the 💾 **Save** button		**F**ile, **S**ave
	If you have not already saved the file, you will be prompted to specify the directory and to name the file. If you have already done this then Word will automatically save it			
Save using a different name or to a different directory	Select the appropriate drive and change the filename if appropriate Click: **Save**			**F**ile, **Save As**
Save file in a different file format	Save as above, select from **Save as type**			
Special characters/ symbols, inserting				**I**nsert, **Symbol**
Spell check	**F7**	Click: the ✓ **Spelling** button		**T**ools, **Spelling and Grammar**
Adding words to dictionary	When running spellcheck, click on: **Add to Dictionary**			
Styles	Select from the Style box drop-down list Normal			**F**ormat, **S**tyle
Superscript Subscript			**F**ont	**F**ormat, **F**ont
Tables		Click: the ▦ **Insert Table** button		**T**able, **I**nsert, **T**able
	See section 5			
Tabs	See separate information on page 108			

Action	Keyboard	Mouse	Right–mouse menu	Menu
Template, selecting				**File**, **New**, select a template
Text colour	Select the text to colour			
		Click: the **A ▾ Font Color** button	**Font**, **Font color**	**Format**, **Font**, **Font color**
Toolbar, modify				**View**, **Toolbars**, **Customize**
Undo	**Ctrl + Z**	Click: the ↺ **Undo** button		**Edit**, **Undo Typing**
Widows and Orphans				**Format**, **Paragraph, Line and Page Breaks** Select: **Widow/Orphan control**
Zoom	Click: the [100% ▾] **Zoom** button			**View**, **Zoom**

MOVING AROUND THE DOCUMENT	
Move	**Keyboard action**
To top of document	**Ctrl + Home**
To end of document	**Ctrl + End**
Left word by word	**Ctrl + ←**
Right word by word	**Ctrl + →**
To end of line	**End**
To start of line	**Home**

SELECTING TEXT	
Selecting what	**Action**
Whole document	**Ctrl + A**
One word	Double-click on word
One line	Click once in selection border (to left of text)
One sentence	Hold down **Ctrl** and click anywhere in the sentence
One paragraph	Double-click in selection border
Any block of text	Click cursor at start of text, press: **Shift**. Click cursor at end of text and click
Deselect text	Click in any white space

See Appendix for keyboard shortcuts.

Line lengths (portrait orientation A4)

Line length	Margin width
12.7 cm (5")	4.15 cm (1.63")
14 cm (5½")	3.5 cm (1.38")
15.3 cm (6")	2.85 cm (1.13")
16.5 cm (6½")	2.25 cm (0.88")

Hard spaces

It is better not to split some words at line ends, eg Mr Brown – Mr and Brown should be on the same line. A hard space keeps the words on either side of it together. To insert a hard space, instead of just pressing the spacebar between the words, press: **CTRL + SHIFT + Spacebar**.

Note: For these tasks you will need to have the files **water**, **water talks**, **contacts**.

Scenario

You work as a Marketing Officer for the Carlton Spa Centre ®, a company that provides natural healthy lifestyle treatments. You need to prepare some documents relating to a forthcoming promotional tour. The file **Water** is a Word document that is to be used as a handout. It needs to be amended as instructed in Tasks 1 and 2. **Water talks** is a draft letter to be sent to individuals who have shown an interest in the tour. It needs some amendments and additions (Tasks 3 and 4) and then to be merged with the **Contacts** datafile (Task 5). Finally you need to send a reply fax to **Lycée la Vendée** (Task 6).

Task 1

1   Start the word processor and open the file **Water**.

2   Spell check and save the document as **your initials module 3**.

3   Change the font in the document to Arial 12 pt.

4   Italicise the heading **Eight glasses a day**.

5   Centre the heading.

6   Increase the font size of the heading to 18 pt.

7   Embolden the last paragraph beginning **Water is available**... (*Note*: Use Show/Hide to view paragraph marks.)

8   In the third sentence of the second paragraph, delete the text **For Example** so that the sentence starts with **Tomatoes**.

9   In the final paragraph, organise the water types in the sentence beginning **Water comes in many forms:** into bulleted-list format.

10   Insert a blank line between paragraphs.

11   Insert a page break after the third paragraph.

12   Add a header **Water factsheet** and today's date.

13   Format the header to Times New Roman 8 pt.

14   Add page numbers bottom right, starting at 5.

15   Insert your name in the first line of the document (Times New Roman 10 pt, right align).

16   Replace the word **consume** with the word **drink**.

17   Copy the first paragraph so that it appears at the end of the document.

18   Change the line spacing of the first paragraph to 1.5.

19   Fully justify the second paragraph.

20   Insert the following text as a subheading on the line directly under the main heading **Eight glasses a day**:

   Water (H_2O), extract by Carlton Spa Centre ®

21   Save the document with the name **your initials module3 test1**.

22   Print the document on A4 paper in portrait display.

Task 2

1 Create a new document.

2 Copy all the text from the document **your initials module3 test1** to the new document.

3 Change the font in the first paragraph to 10 pt and bold.

4 Use the *Format Painter* to copy the formatting of the first paragraph to the last paragraph.

5 Delete the page break.

6 Set the line spacing to single throughout.

7 Delete the line spaces between the paragraphs.

8 Set the top and bottom margins to 2 cm.

9 Set the left and right margins to 3 cm.

10 Add a border to the bulleted list and shade in grey.

11 Add to the footer an automatic filename.

12 Save the document as **Water info**.

13 Print the document on A4 paper in landscape display.

14 Save the document in a format suitable for posting on the web.

15 Close the documents.

Task 3

1 Open the file **water talks**.

2 Insert the reference **Water03** and your initials in the **Ref** section and add the date.

3 Set a left-aligned tab and align the text on the Ref and Date lines at 11 cm.

4 Spell check the document.

5 Insert a suitable clipart picture at the bottom of the document. Adjust the picture to an appropriate size so that it fits neatly on the page.

6 Save the document as **Task3Merge**.

Task 4

1 Working with the **Task3Merge** document, replace the sender's name with **Hillary Barker**.

2 Insert the following table after the second paragraph ending ...**now been confirmed**.

Bangor	Pier Road	Monday
Llandudno	Great Orme Road	Wednesday
Llandegfan	Cae Gwyn	Tuesday
Menai Bridge	Holyhead Road	Friday

3 Centre the table entries. Format in Times New Roman 14 pt.

4 Insert a heading row at the top of the table as follows:

    Location   **Venue**   **Day**

5 Shade the heading cells and embolden the headings.

6 Use the indent function to indent the first paragraph by approx. 1.5 cm.

7 Enter the following text at beginning of the final paragraph beginning **We look**...

May I take this opportunity to thank you for your interest in our company. We are able to offer a wide range of services that we will be demonstrating.

8   Set the final paragraph with a first line indent of 0.8 cm.

9   Reduce the clipart as necessary to fit the letter on one page.

10 Save the document as **Task4Merge3** and print.

Task 5

Working with the document **Task4Merge3** saved in the last task, merge the letter (ensure it still fits on to one page) with the address list, **contacts**. This has the following fields that will need to be inserted in the merge document:

Title, Last Name, Address1, Town, Postcode

Add the following contacts to the list before merging:

Ms, Jones, Bryn Mawr, Llanfairfechan, LL13 6AW
Dr, Brewster, 1 East Street, Menai Bridge, LL18 4HR

Save, print and close the merged files.

Task 6

1   Open a new document and select the **Contemporary Fax** template.

2   Delete the field above *Facsimile Transmittal*.

3   In the To field key in **Lycée la Vendée.**

4   In the Fax field key in **00 33 23 44 76 98 11**.

5   In the From field key in your name.

6   In the Re field key in **Price details**.

7   In the Pages field key in **1**.

8   Mark the fax **Please Comment**.

9   Enter the message:

    Thank you for your interest. I have posted a brochure to you with the latest price lists.

10 Save the fax as **Prices Vend** and print a copy.

Note: These are only practice tasks. Successful completion does not imply certification of the module by the ECDL Foundation.

Module 4

Spreadsheets

Section 1 / Getting started

In this section you will practise and learn how to:

- load Excel
- understand the parts of the document window
- modify the toolbar display
- use Help functions
- enter spreadsheet contents: insert text, numeric data, simple formulae
- recognise common error messages
- use the Undo/Redo command
- delete cell contents

- save the spreadsheet
- print preview and print the spreadsheet
- use the page view magnification/zoom tool
- fit to specified pages
- modify margins
- close the spreadsheet
- exit Excel

1.1 Loading Excel

Exercise 1

Load Excel.

Method

Load Excel in the same way as other Office XP applications, this time selecting: ![Microsoft Excel] from the **Start**, **All Programs** menu *or* double-click on: the ![Excel] **Excel** shortcut icon (if you have one).

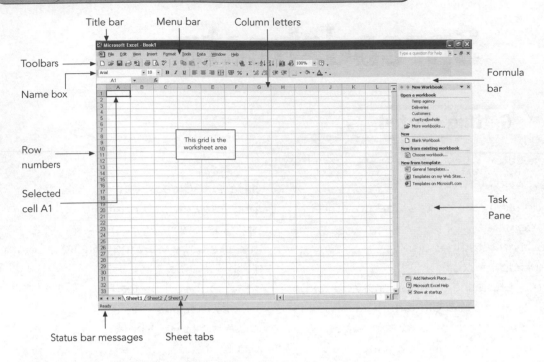

Figure 4.1 The application window

The **Title bar** and **Menu bar** are at the top of the application window.

The **Menu bar** has a set of *drop-down menus* that provide access to all Excel's features.

The **Toolbar** is a row of buttons and selection boxes that, in most cases, provide shortcuts to the menu options or quick ways of entering values. (In Figure 4.1 the **Standard** and **Formatting** toolbars are shown.)

To modify the toolbar display

From the **View** menu, select: **Toolbars**. Click on the toolbar names that you want displayed so that they have a tick next to them. If toolbars that you do not want to display are ticked, click on the toolbar name to remove the tick. Select: **Customize** for further modifications options.

The **Formula bar** displays the data you enter into your worksheet.

The **Name box** displays the active cell reference.

The **Sheet tabs** allow you to move from one spreadsheet to the next.

The **Status bar**, located at the bottom of the window, displays messages about current events.

The **Task Pane** displays several shortcuts that you may find useful when working. For now, close it by clicking on its **Close** button.

The **worksheet area**: this is the area between the **Formula bar** and the **Status bar** where your document (spreadsheet) is displayed. It consists of cells, each with their own cell reference, eg A1, B7, F9. Rows go across horizontally and are labelled 1, 2, 3, 4... Columns go down vertically and are labelled A, B, C, D...

Figure 4.2 shows the position of cell C6.

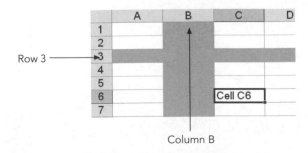

Figure 4.2 Cell references

Note: If you find that the spreadsheet display is too small, use the ⎡100% ▾⎤ **Zoom** box on the Standard toolbar. Click on: the down arrow to select the magnification or key in your own magnification in the **Zoom** box.

Excel refers to a spreadsheet as a *worksheet*. When you open a new Excel document, it automatically consists of three sheets, one is displayed (Sheet1) and there are tabs for Sheet2 and Sheet3 (shown in Figure 4.1). These three sheets together are known, in Excel, as a *workbook*. You can add more sheets to a workbook if required. Throughout this book we will be using the Excel term 'worksheet' and the generic term 'spreadsheet' when referring to a file (when one or more worksheets are saved together in the same file).

Getting Help

From the **Help** menu, select: **Microsoft Excel Help** *or* click on: the ⎡?⎤ **Microsoft Excel Help** button or press: **F1**. Getting help in Excel is the same as with other Office suite applications.

Note: Throughout this book, the Office Assistant facility has been hidden so as not to distract from the main objectives. More details of the Office Assistant are found in the Appendix. You can select:

* The **Contents** tab for a list of help topics. By double-clicking on a topic, a display of that topic will appear.
* The **Answer Wizard** tab. This allows you to key in a question and then click on: **Search**. The topic will then be highlighted in the contents list and the topic displayed as above.
* The **Index** tab. This allows you to key in key words and click on **Search**. Again, the topic will be highlighted and displayed as above.
* To close the Help window, click on: the **Close** button.

ScreenTips

From the **Help** menu, select: **What's This?** Then click on the item you want to know about. A short description appears. Press: **Esc** to remove the ScreenTip.

Accessing Help in a dialogue box

To access Help in a dialogue box, click on: the **Help** button in the dialogue box and then click on the item you want help about.

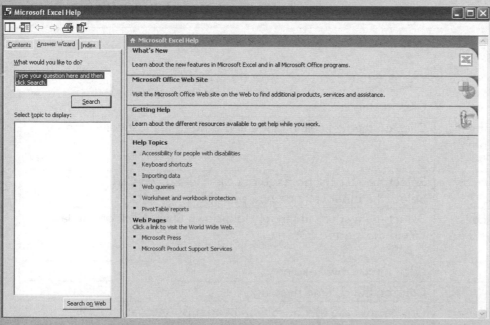

Figure 4.3 The Excel Help screen

Practise

Moving around the spreadsheet:

1 Moving around your document using the scroll bars (Figure 4.4).

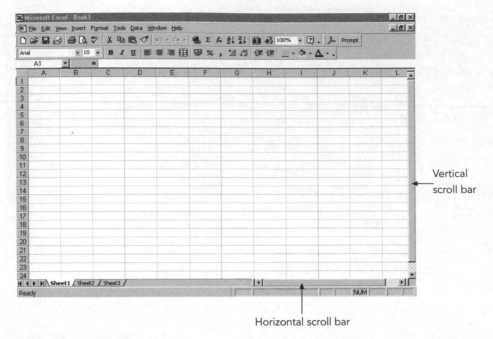

Figure 4.4 Scroll bars

2 Using navigation keys, **Page Up** and **Page Down**, to move up and down a page at a time.

3 Using the arrow keys.

4 Using the **Go To** command in the **Edit** menu. Enter the cell address, eg C5 in the **Reference** text box and click on: **OK**.

5 Click in: the **Name** box and key in the cell address. Press: **Enter**.

6 Point to a cell with the mouse and click.

7 Pressing: **Ctrl + Home** takes you to the top of your spreadsheet. **Ctrl + End** will take you to the last entry on your spreadsheet (only when you have entered data).

Info

Selecting cells

When working on spreadsheets you can makes selections as follows:

Cell	Click on the cell.
Range of adjacent cells (adjacent means next to or adjoining)	Click on the first cell in range and drag to the last cell in range.
Range of non-adjacent cells	Select the first cell or range of cells. Hold down **Ctrl**. Select the other cell or range of cells.
A large range of cells, eg not all displayed on one screen	Select the first cell in range. Hold down **Shift**. Click on the last cell in the range.
An entire row	Click on the row heading.
An entire column	Click on the column heading.
Adjacent rows/columns	Drag across the row or column headings. Alternatively select the first row/column. Hold down **Shift**. Select the last row/column.

Non-adjacent rows/columns	Select the first row/column. Hold down **Ctrl**. Select the other rows/columns.
All cells on worksheet	Click on: the **Select All** button.

Select all ⟶

	A
1	Compu

You can enter:

* text
* numeric data
* formulae

Text entries are used for titles, headings and any notes. They are entries that you do not want to do calculations with. Telephone numbers and stock numbers (although they contain numbers) are text entries.

Numeric data consists of numbers that you want to add, subtract, multiply, divide and use in formulae.

Formulae are used to calculate the value of a cell from the contents of other cells. For instance, formulae may be used to calculate totals or averages. Formulae always start with an = sign. You must enter the formula for it to be activated by pressing: **Enter** or clicking on: the ✓ **Enter** button on the Formula bar. A typical formula could look like:

=A1+A2 *or* **=SUM(A1:A6)**

The following operators (symbols) are used in formulae:

+ ADD   - SUBTRACT * MULTIPLY / DIVIDE

	A	B	C	D
1	**Mileage for essential car users**			
2		**Laurent**	**Martha**	**Erik**
3	**Jan**	267	190	110
4	**Feb**	56	95	34
5	**Totals**	=B3+B4	=C3+C4	=D3+D4

Text entry →
Numeric data →
Formula ↑

Figure 4.5 Types of spreadsheet entry

Info

Excel follows arithmetic protocol when carrying out calculations. It will perform multiplication and division first and then addition and subtraction. (Some people remember this as **M**y **D**ear **A**unt **S**ally.) Sometimes you will need to force Excel to carry out the calculation in a different order. As in arithmetic, this can be achieved by adding brackets around the appropriate part, eg when cells A1, A2 and A3 contain the numbers 4, 3 and 2 respectively.

A1+A2*A3 in numbers is 4 plus 3 times 2, which Excel would calculate to be (carrying out the multiplication first) 10.

Placing brackets around the addition section forces Excel to perform the calculation differently. (A1+A2)*A3 in numbers is (4 plus 3) times 2 and gives the correct result 14.

Inserting text and numeric data

Exercise 2

The spreadsheet below shows the sales figures for three different companies over a four-month period. Enter the data into the spreadsheet.

Method

1 Move to cell A1 and key in **YEAR**.
2 Move to cell B1 and key in **BLUECO**.
3 Move to cell C1 and key in **PINKCO**.
4 Complete the worksheet in this way until it looks like Figure 4.6.

	A	B	C	D
1	YEAR	BLUECO	PINKCO	GREYCO
2	1999	560	700	800
3	2000	120	260	600
4	2001	700	550	540
5	2002	500	1020	330

Figure 4.6 Spreadsheet data

Info

It is especially important to check spreadsheet work very carefully. One simple mistake in a numerical entry will produce inaccurate calculation results in the final spreadsheet. When working with formulae, try to do a mental check to ascertain that the results of calculations are approximately what you expected.

Note: The spellchecker is also available in Excel.

1.5 Entering simple formulae

Exercise 3

Enter simple formulae to add up cell contents.

Method

Remember: Formulae must always begin with the = sign.

1 Move to cell A6 and key in **TOTAL**.
2 We wish to add up the sales figures for **BLUECO**. These are displayed in cells B2, B3, B4 and B5. Move to cell B6 (where you want the answer to appear).

Info

Notice as you key in that the formula appears in full on the Formula bar. It may be too long to fit into the cell but you can ignore this. Cell references can be in upper or lower case. If you make a mistake use the **Undo** button or press: **Esc**. Use the **Redo** button when you want to redo something you have just undone.

Key in:
=B2+B3+B4+B5 and press: **Enter**.
The answer **1880** appears in cell B6.

3 Add up the sales figures for PINKCO in the same way by keying in:
=C2+C3+C4+C5 and press: **Enter**.
The answer **2530** appears in cell C6.

Your spreadsheet will now look like Figure 4.7.

	A	B	C	D
1	YEAR	BLUECO	PINKCO	GREYCO
2	1999	560	700	800
3	2000	120	260	600
4	2001	700	550	540
5	2002	500	1020	330
6	TOTAL	1880	2530	

Figure 4.7 Totalling column B and column C

Using the built-in Sum function

On a large business spreadsheet you might need to add a huge number of cell contents and specifying each cell reference would not be practical. A quicker way to add up figures is by using one of Excel's built-in functions, **SUM**, to work out the formula as follows. To produce a Total for **GREYCO** this time:

1 Move to cell D6 (where you want the answer to appear).

2 Key in =**SUM(D2:D5)** and press: **Enter**.

> **Info**
>
> The colon between the cell references in the formula above means 'to include all the cells in between D2 and D5'.

Your spreadsheet will now look like Figure 4.8.

	A	B	C	D
1	YEAR	BLUECO	PINKCO	GREYCO
2	1999	560	700	800
3	2000	120	260	600
4	2001	700	550	540
5	2002	500	1020	330
6	TOTAL	1880	2530	2270

Figure 4.8 Totalling column D

Practise

Using the **SUM** function:

1 Delete the Totals of **BLUECO** (cell B6) and **PINKCO** (cell C6) by selecting them and pressing: **Delete**.

2 Add the Totals again, this time using the SUM function in cell B6 =**SUM(B2:B5)** and in cell C6 =**SUM(C2:C5)**.

Using the AutoSum button

There is an even quicker way to add cell values using the Σ **AutoSum** button. To practise this, let's add up the totals for the three companies for each year:

1 Move to cell E1 and key in **SALES**.

2 Move to cell E2, the cell where you want the total sales for **1999** to appear.

3 Click on: the Σ **AutoSum** button. You will notice that a dotted line should have appeared around cells B2 through to D2.

Info

In this example Excel should have automatically chosen the correct cells to add. Sometimes it chooses the wrong ones. If this happens, before pressing **Enter**, you will need to select the cells you want by clicking on the cell you want to start with, holding down the left mouse button and dragging the dotted line across the correct cells. Be careful that you don't drag too far by mistake and include the cell where you want the answer to appear. The answer cell cannot be included in the formula. If, in a formula, you try to include the cell reference where you want the answer to appear, an error message will be displayed. Follow the instructions given in the error message.

Common error messages

#####	This indicates that the number in the cell is too long. Increasing the cell width will allow Excel to display the number.
#REF	A deleted cell reference may be present in your formula.
#VALUE	The formula contains text instead of number.
#DIV/0!	You have tried to divide a number by zero.
#NUM	This indicates problems with numbers in the formula.
#NAME	Text in the formula is not recognised.

4 Press: **Enter**.

5 The answer **2060** appears in cell E2.

6 Use this method to calculate the sales total for 2000, 2001 and 2002.

Info

When adding **Sales** for **2001**, you will notice that Excel has mistakenly decided that you now want to add the figures from above the cell and has placed the dotted line around cells E2 and E3. Watch out for this. Remedy by moving the highlight by clicking on the first cell you want to add (B4) and dragging across to D4.

If you have done everything correctly the totals will be as in Figure 4.9.

	A	B	C	D	E
1	YEAR	BLUECO	PINKCO	GREYCO	SALES
2	1999	560	700	800	2060
3	2000	120	260	600	980
4	2001	700	550	540	1790
5	2002	500	1020	330	1850
6	TOTAL	1880	2530	2270	

Figure 4.9 Sales figures for 1999, 2000, 2001, 2002

1.6 Saving the spreadsheet

Exercise 4

Save the spreadsheet with the filename **Income**.

1 Check the spreadsheet and correct any errors.
2 From the **File** menu, select: **Save As**. The Save As dialogue box appears (Figure 4.10).
3 Select the location where you want to save your file and key in: **Income** in the **File name** box.
4 Click on: **Save**.

Click on: this down arrow to display locations where you may
store your file. Click on: the location, eg drive A

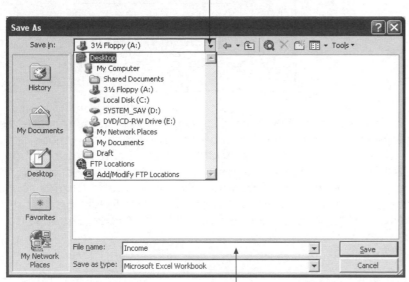

Key in your filename here

Figure 4.10 Save As Dialogue box

1.7) Previewing and printing spreadsheets

Exercise 5

Print a copy of the spreadsheet on to A4 paper.

Method

Previewing a spreadsheet before printing

It is always wise to preview your spreadsheet before printing so that you are sure that the printout
will be exactly what you want. This will save paper as well as effort.

1 Click on: the 🔍 **Print Preview** button.
2 Click on: the **Zoom** option to see your spreadsheet contents. Click on: **Zoom** again to return to
default view.
3 Click on: **Setup**. The Page Setup dialogue box is displayed (Figure 4.11).
4 With the **Page** tab selected, in the **Paper size** box, ensure that A4 is selected. If not, use the
down arrow and click on: the **A4** option.

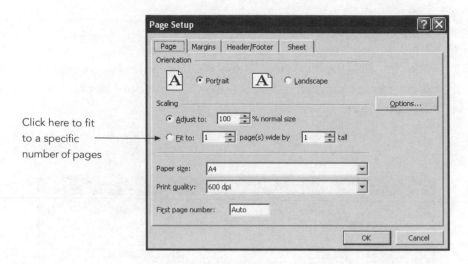

Click here to fit
to a specific
number of pages

Figure 4.11 Page Setup

5   If you are happy with the Print Preview, click **OK**, then click on: **Print**. (You can change default options here if necessary as shown in Figure 4.12. You do not need to change these options for this printout but they will need changing later in this module.) In the **Print range** section, select: **All** by clicking in the **All** button to print all pages or select: **Page(s)** by clicking in the **Page(s)** button and enter the page range in the **From** and **To** boxes. In the **Copies** section, select the number of copies to print. In the **Print what** section, select: **Selection** (to print a current selection), **Entire workbook** (to print all sheets in the file) or **Active Sheet(s)** (to print the current sheet(s).

6   Click on: **OK**.

Info

Should you need to exit Print Preview at step 3, press: **Esc** *or* click on: **Close** to return to the spreadsheet.

Info

Printing on landscape

By default the spreadsheet will print a Portrait display (the narrow edge at the top of the page). If you prefer or if your spreadsheet does not fit across the page, you can change the display to Landscape.

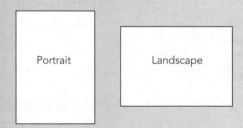

To do this from **Print Preview**, click on: **Setup**:

1   Click on: the **Page** tab, then on the **Landscape** option button.
2   Click on: **OK**.

If not using Print Preview:

1   From the **File** menu, select: **Page Setup**.
2   Click on: the **Page** tab, then on: the **Landscape** option button.
3   Click on: **Print**.

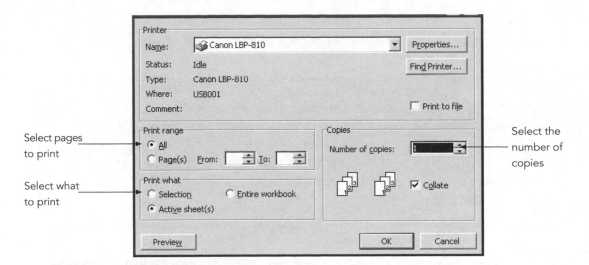

Figure 4.12 Printing options

Select pages to print

Select what to print

Select the number of copies

Exercise 6

Print a copy of the spreadsheet showing the formulae used.

Info

It is useful to display on screen and to have a printout of the formulae used on your spreadsheet so that you can cross-reference for accuracy.

Method

Showing formulae on your spreadsheet

1   With your spreadsheet on screen, from the **Tools** menu, select: **Options**.
2   The Options dialogue box appears. Click on: the **View** tab (if not already selected). Click on: the **Formulas** check box so that a tick appears in this box. Click on: **OK** (Figure 4.13).

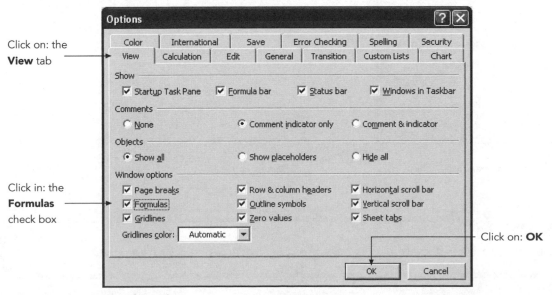

Click on: the **View** tab

Click in: the **Formulas** check box

Click on: **OK**

Figure 4.13 Showing formulae

3 Notice that the columns have widened to accommodate the formulae.

4 If you are unable to see all the spreadsheet at once, use the `100%` ▾ **Zoom** button.

5 Check the spreadsheet using Print Preview (as above).

6 If it fits on one page, print as before.

7 If it does not fit, change it to landscape by following the instructions above.

If you really want to print in portrait display, try the following:

Fitting to one page

From the **File** menu, select: **Page Setup** *or* in **Print Preview**, click on: **Setup**. With the **Page** tab selected, in the **Scaling** section, click in: the option button next to **Fit to 1 page**. (*Note*: You can enter a specified number of pages when appropriate.)

Modifying margins

From the **File** menu, select: **Page Setup** *or* in **Print Preview**, click on: **Setup**. With the **Margins** tab selected, decrease the left, right, top and bottom margin settings (Figure 4.14).

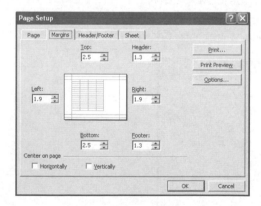

Figure 4.14 Altering margins

Exercise 7

Change the spreadsheet so that numbers are displayed instead of formulae.

Removing showing formulae

1 From the **Tools** menu, select: **Options**.
2 Click on: the **View** tab (if not already selected); click in: the **Formulas** check box so that the tick is removed.
3 Click on: **OK**.

A quicker way to change back to values display is to press: **CTRL+`**.

1.9 Closing a spreadsheet file

Close the spreadsheet file.

From the **File** menu, select: **Close**.

1.10 Exiting Excel

Exit Excel.

From the **File** menu, select: **Exit**.

Practice 1

1 Load Excel.

2 On a new sheet enter the following data:

Note: Leave the cells containing 'formula' blank.

EXPENSES			
	JAN	MAR	APR
FOOD	200	170	190
PETROL	48	50	60
TEL	10	12	20
MOBILE	7	15	18
HOLS	50	50	50
CAR	30	20	100
TOTALS	formula	formula	formula

3 Enter a formula in the TOTALS row to calculate the total expenses for JAN.

4 Save the spreadsheet as **p1 outgoings**.

5 Print a copy of the spreadsheet showing values and another copy showing the formula used.

6 Close the spreadsheet file.

Practice 2

1 On a new sheet enter the following data:

Note: Leave the cells containing 'formula' blank.

COOLKAF						
	Mon	Tue	Wed	Thu	Fri	Total
Bristol	220	660	500	642	1200	formula
Bath	250	121	321	302	321	formula
Wells	380	625	761	700	421	formula
Freshford	210	450	380	439	213	formula
Limpley	88	90	65	203	430	formula
Weston	500	1800	1200	601	500	formula

2 Enter a formula to calculate the Total for the Bristol row.

3 Save the spreadsheet as **p2 branch sales**.

4 Print a copy of the spreadsheet showing values and one showing the formula used.

5 Close the spreadsheet.

In this section you will practise and learn how to:

- open an existing spreadsheet
- make alterations to cell contents
- delete/insert rows/columns
- copy or replicate formulae
- use search, find and replace
- understand relative, absolute and mixed cell references

- save existing spreadsheet
- save the spreadsheet in another file format
- print: part of a spreadsheet; displaying gridlines; displaying row and column headings

2.1) Opening an existing spreadsheet

Exercise 1

Open the spreadsheet **Income** saved in section 1.

Method

1 With Excel loaded, click on: the 📂 **Open** button; the Open dialogue box appears (Figure 4.15).
2 Select the location where your file is stored by clicking on: the down arrow.
3 Click on: the filename **Income**.
4 Click on: **Open**.

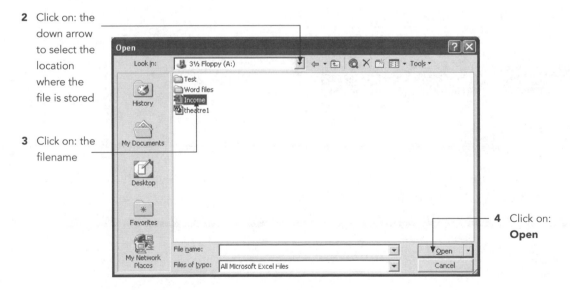

2 Click on: the down arrow to select the location where the file is stored

3 Click on: the filename

4 Click on: **Open**

Figure 4.15 Opening a saved file

2.2 Making alterations to your spreadsheet

Exercise 2

The Sales figures for **BLUECO** should be **405** (not 560) in **1999** and **650** (not 700) in **2001**. We need to change these entries.

Method

1 Move to cell B2 and key in: **405**. Press: **Enter**.
2 Move to cell B4 and key in: **650**. Press: **Enter**.

Info

Notice that the original figures are overwritten. Look what has happened to the **TOTAL** for **BLUECO**. You will see that the formula has been recalculated to give a new **TOTAL**. The **SALES** figures for **1999** and **2001** in column E have also updated to reflect the changes made. This will usually happen; when you change cell contents within a spreadsheet, all the formulae referring to that cell will be automatically recalculated.

Your spreadsheet will now look like Figure 4.16.

	A	B	C	D	E
1	YEAR	BLUECO	PINKCO	GREYCO	SALES
2	1999	405	700	800	1905
3	2000	120	260	600	980
4	2001	650	550	540	1740
5	2002	500	1020	330	1850
6	TOTAL	1675	2530	2270	

Figure 4.16 Updated spreadsheet

2.3 Deleting a row or column

Exercise 3

It has been decided that the figures for **2000** are not required. Delete this row. Close up the space (ie do not leave a blank row).

Method

1 Click in: the box to the left of the row to be deleted, ie row 3. Row 3 is highlighted (Figure 4.17).

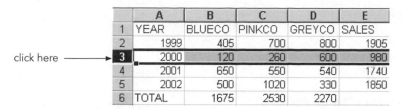

	A	B	C	D	E
1	YEAR	BLUECO	PINKCO	GREYCO	SALES
2	1999	405	700	800	1905
3	2000	120	260	600	980
4	2001	650	550	540	174U
5	2002	500	1020	330	1850
6	TOTAL	1675	2530	2270	

click here ———►

Figure 4.17 Selecting a row

2 Right-click on: the selected row; a pop-up menu appears (Figure 4.18).

Figure 4.18 Right-clicking displays a pop-up menu

3 Click on: **Delete**. The spreadsheet contents move up to occupy the empty space and the figures are recalculated to reflect the change (Figure 4.19).

	A	B	C	D	E
1	YEAR	BLUECO	PINKCO	GREYCO	SALES
2	1999	405	700	800	1905
3	2001	650	550	540	1740
4	2002	500	1020	330	1850
5	TOTAL	1555	2270	1670	

Figure 4.19 Spreadsheet after deletion of the 2000 row

Note: If you want just to delete the cell contents and not the cell, select the cell and press: **Delete**.

Info

When you have a large spreadsheet, it is very difficult to locate cell entries. In such circumstances it is better to use **Search/Find/Replace** from the **Edit** menu to locate/replace entries. Try using this now to locate/replace an entry. When using **Find**, in the **Find what** box, key in the data you want to find. In the **Search** box, select either **By Rows** or **By Columns**. In the **Look In** box, select: **Formulas**, **Values** or **Comments**.

When using **Replace**, in the **Find what** box, key in the entry you want to replace. In the **Replace with** box, key in what you want to replace the entry with. In the **Search** box, select: **By Rows** or **By Columns**. Ensure that the figures are returned to their original values (as in Figure 4.19) before proceeding.

Exercise 4

The figures for **PINKCO** are no longer required; delete this column.

Method

1 Click in: the box at the top of the column to be deleted, ie C; column C is highlighted.
2 Right-click on: the selection; a pop-up menu appears.
3 Click on: **Delete**.

The spreadsheet now looks like Figure 4.20.

	A	B	C	D
1	YEAR	BLUECO	GREYCO	SALES
2	1999	405	800	1205
3	2001	650	540	1190
4	2002	500	330	830
5	TOTAL	1555	1670	

Figure 4.20 Spreadsheet after deletion of PINKCO column

2.4 Copying or replicating formulae

Exercise 5

Replicate the formula used to calculate the **TOTAL** for **GREYCO** so that the **TOTAL** for **SALES** is also calculated.

Method

1 Move to the cell in which the formula that you want to copy is stored. In this case C5.
2 Point the mouse at the bottom right of this cell until a thin black cross + appears, then, holding down the left mouse, drag across cell D5 (where you want the formula copied to). Release the mouse.

The spreadsheet now looks like Figure 4.21.

	A	B	C	D
1	YEAR	BLUECO	GREYCO	SALES
2	1999	405	800	1205
3	2001	650	540	1190
4	2002	500	330	830
5	TOTAL	1555	1670	3225

Figure 4.21 Spreadsheet after replication of formula

Info

If you make an error performing this procedure, click on: the ↶ **Undo** button and try again.

Relative, absolute and mixed cell references

Note: You can now click on cell D5 and examine the formula displayed on the Formula bar. As you can see, when replicating formulae, the cell references change to reflect their new position. A relative cell reference will change relative to its position on the spreadsheet. By contrast, an absolute cell reference will not change even if it is replicated or moved to another part of the spreadsheet. If you need to make a cell reference absolute, add a $ sign in front of the column letter and another $ sign in front of the row number or press: **F4** – eg cell reference C8 becomes $C$8 when it is absolute.

A cell can have a mixed cell reference. In this case the column could be relative and the row absolute, eg C$8, or the row could be relative and the column absolute, eg $C8.

Adding a new column

Exercise 6

Insert a new column, headed **REDCO**, after **BLUECO** and before **GREYCO**. Enter the following information:

1999 600
2001 700
2000 650

Method

1   Click in: the box at the top of the column after where the new column is to appear, ie column C; column C is highlighted (Figure 4.22).

Click here

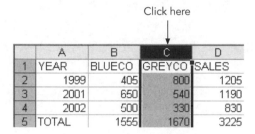

Figure 4.22 Selecting a column

2   Right-click on: the selection; a pop-up menu appears. Click on: **Insert** (Figure 4.23). An empty column appears.

Click on:
Insert

Figure 4.23 Inserting a column

3   Enter the new text and data shown above.

The spreadsheet now looks like Figure 4.24.

	A	B	C	D	E
1	YEAR	BLUECO	REDCO	GREYCO	SALES
2	1999	405	600	800	1805
3	2001	650	700	540	1890
4	2002	500	650	330	1480
5	TOTAL	1555		1670	5175

Figure 4.24 Spreadsheet after addition of REDCO column and data

Calculate the **TOTAL** for **REDCO**, using one of the quicker methods you have learnt. The **TOTAL** is **1950**.

It has been decided to re-insert the figures for **2000**. Insert a new row for **2000** with the following information: **BLUECO 120**, **REDCO 900**, **GREYCO 600**.

Adding a new row

1   Click in: the box to the left of the row below where you want the new row to appear, ie row 3. Row 3 is highlighted (Figure 4.25).

	A	B	C	D	E
1	YEAR	BLUECO	REDCO	GREYCO	SALES
2	1999	405	600	800	1805
3	2001	650	700	540	1890
4	2002	500	650	330	1480
5	TOTAL	1555	1950	1670	5175
6					

Click here →

Figure 4.25 Adding a new row

2   Right-click on: the highlighted row; a pop-up menu appears (Figure 4.26). Click on: **Insert**; an empty row appears.

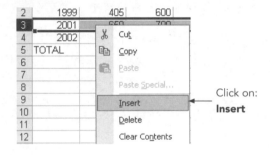

Click on:
Insert

Figure 4.26 Inserting a row

3   Enter the new text and data shown above.

Replicate the formula from cell E2 to produce a **TOTAL** in cell E3 for **2000 SALES**. The **TOTAL** is **1620**.

2.6 Adding a new column or row to create new values

Insert a new column for **ROSECO** after **GREYCO** and before the **SALES** column (see section 2.5 above). Enter the following data:

1999	**621**	**2001**	**700**
2000	**890**	**2002**	**440**

Replicate the formula from D6 to give a Total value in cell E6 for **ROSECO**.

Follow the method in 2.5.

Note: These figures – although at the end of the existing SUM cell range – should be automatically included in the **SALES** column figures. If not, you will need to re-enter the formula in cell F2 and replicate down. This did not happen in earlier versions of Excel. Look out for this as you may not always want Excel to include new data in formulae.

The spreadsheet now looks like Figure 4.27.

	A	B	C	D	E	F
1	YEAR	BLUECO	REDCO	GREYCO	ROSECO	SALES
2	1999	405	600	800	621	2426
3	2000	120	900	600	890	2510
4	2001	650	700	540	700	2590
5	2002	500	650	330	440	1920
6	TOTAL	1675	2850	2270	2651	9446

Figure 4.27 Spreadsheet after adding the ROSECO column

2.7 Save your spreadsheet as Income1 and print one copy on A4 paper

2.8 Saving documents under a different file format

Exercise 9

Save the spreadsheet with the filename **Sales figures** in a format suitable for posting on the web.

Method

1 From the **File** menu, select: **Save As**.
2 Key in the filename.
3 In the **Save as type** section, click on: the down arrow to display type options (Figure 4.28).
4 Select: **Web Page**.
5 Click on: **Save**.

Info

By default Excel automatically saves files in a version of Excel format that you are using, eg Excel 2000, and adds the extension .xls (eg Sales.xls). In Excel the **Save as type** menu includes options specific to spreadsheets (Figure 4.28). Compare this with Word's save options in Module 3, section 4.4.

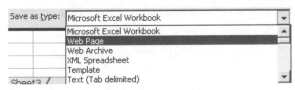

Figure 4.28 Excel's Save as type menu

File type	
Text file (.txt)	Select **Text (Tab delimited)** – all formatting will be lost.
HTML (.htm, .html)	Select **Web Page** – for use on the WWW, LAN or Intranet.
Template (.xlt)	Select **Template** – use to create a template that can be reused when you require the same layout/design.
Software-specific file extension	Enter a filename with the file extension, eg [filename].wks for a Lotus 1-2-3 file.
Version number	Select from one of the versions listed, eg Excel5/95 – use when you need to share files with users of older versions of Excel. Newer versions of Excel will be able to read documents saved in previous versions.

2.9 Printing part of a spreadsheet

Exercise 10

Print only the figures for **BLUECO** (include the year labels).

Method

1 Select columns A and B (by dragging the mouse over the cells) to and including row 6.
2 From the **File** menu, select: **Print**.
3 In the **Print what** section, click in: the option box next to **Selection** (Figure 4.29).
4 Click on: **OK**.

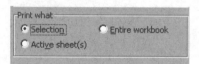

Figure 4.29 Printing a selection

2.10 Other printing options

Info

There are other useful printing options. These include printing gridlines and displaying row and column headings.

Exercise 11

Print the spreadsheet **Income1** with the gridlines and the row and column headings displayed.

Method

1 Display the spreadsheet.
2 From the **File** menu, select: **Page Setup**.

3 With the **Sheet** tab selected (Figure 4.30), in the **Print** section, click in: the **Gridlines** box so that a tick appears. Similarly click in: the **Row and column headings** box so a tick appears.

4 Click on: **Print**.

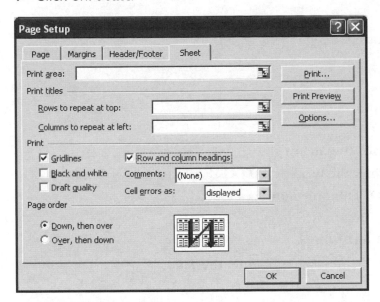

Figure 4.30 Printing options

2.11   Close the files and exit Excel

Practice 3

1 Recall the spreadsheet **p1 outgoings** saved in section 1.

2 Change the following entries:

TEL in **MAR** should be **23** not 12

FOOD in **APR** should be **187** not 190

3 Delete the row containing the CAR data.

4 Replicate the formula for TOTALS for the other months.

5 In the column after the APR column, enter the heading **TOTAL**.

6 Enter a formula to calculate the total FOOD for the months shown.

7 Replicate the formula for the other outgoings.

8 Save the spreadsheet with the name **p3 outgoings**.

9 Insert a new column headed **MAY** after the APR column. Enter the data:

FOOD	**220**
PETROL	**42**
TEL	**17**
MOBILE	**22**
HOLS	**55**

10 Adjust the spreadsheet to show the TOTAL for **MAY**.

11 Calculate an overall total in the TOTALS row/TOTAL column.

12 Save the spreadsheet as **p3 outgoings1** and print one copy.

13 Print only the **TOTAL** column showing the formulae used, including gridlines and column heading.

14 Close the file.

Practice 4

1 Recall the spreadsheet **p2 branch sales** saved in section 1.

2 Change the following entries:

Freshford Tue should be **360** not 450
Bristol Thu should be **541** not 642

3 Delete the **Wells** row.

4 Replicate the formula calculating the Total for Bristol to all other branches.

5 Save the spreadsheet as **p4 branch sales**.

6 Add the heading **Profit** in the column after the Total column.

7 Calculate the profit for the Food department (20% of Total sales).

8 Replicate this formulae for the other branches.

9 Insert a new column headed **Sat** before the Mon column and enter the following data:

Bristol	**1190**
Bath	**1180**
Freshford	**1170**
Limpley	**192**
Weston	**1420**

10 Adjust the spreadsheet formulae as necessary.

11 Save the spreadsheet as **p4 branch sales1** and print one copy.

12 Close the spreadsheet file.

More formulae and functions

In this section you will practise and learn how to generate formulae using the functions: Average, Min, Max, IF and Count

3.1 Using the Average function

Excel has a built-in **AVERAGE** function to work out averages. The syntax is:

=AVERAGE(cell ref:cell ref)

Note: In some spreadsheet applications you can shorten the word **AVERAGE**. Excel does not allow this.

Exercise 1

Open the spreadsheet **Income1** saved at the end of section 2.

Exercise 2

Change the heading **SALES** to **AVERAGE**. Delete all entries in this column.

Exercise 3

Using the **AVERAGE** function, enter a formula to calculate the average sales figures for **1999**. Replicate this formula to cells F3, F4 and F5 to produce averages for the other years.

Method

1   Move to cell F2.
2   Enter the formula **=AVERAGE(B2:E2)**.
3   Press: **Enter**.

    The result of the calculation is **606.5**.

    Note: You can select the cells to average by dragging the mouse over them, as with the **SUM** function.

If you want to find the average of four numbers you need to add up the numbers and divide by 4. For example, to calculate the average of these cells, you could have used the formula **=SUM(B2:E2)/4**. This would have produced the same answer.

However if you were to add another cell to this range, thus making five numbers, then the formula would be incorrect. You would need to divide by 5 not 4. Similarly, if you deleted a cell from the range you would need to divide by 3. Using the **AVERAGE** function incorporates other cell entries, should you insert them at a later date, or eliminates cells that are deleted, without the need to amend the formula.

You can also find averages of numbers that are not in an adjacent cell range using commas to separate the cell references:

=AVERAGE(A1,A6,B7,C4)

4   Replicate the formula in the usual way.

3.2   Using the Min function

Info

The **MAX** and **MIN** functions are used in a similar way to the **AVERAGE** function. For example if you wanted to find the maximum value in a cell range, the formula could be:

=MAX(A1:A5)

or

=MAX(A1,A6,B7,C4)

Use the MIN function in the same way to find the minimum value, eg:

=MIN(A1:A5)

or

=MIN(A1,A6,B7,C4)

Exercise 4

Enter the column heading **MIN** in the cell to the right of the **AVERAGE** cell. Using the **MIN** function, create a formula that generates the minimum sales for **1999**. Replicate this formula for the other years.

Method

1   Move to cell G1 and enter the heading **MIN**.
2   In cell G2 enter the formula **=MIN(B2:E2)**.
3   Press: **Enter**.
4   The result of the calculation is **405**.
5   Replicate down in the usual way.

Enter the column heading **MAX** in the cell to the right of **MIN**. Using the **MAX** function, create a formula that generates the maximum sales for **1999**. Replicate this formula for the other years.

Method

1   Move to cell H1 and enter the heading **MAX**.
2   In cell H2 enter the formula **=MAX(B2:E2)**.
3   Press: **Enter**.
4   The result of the calculation is **800**.
5   Replicate down in the usual way.

3.4 **Using the If function**

Info

The **IF** function is used to test a specified condition and return a verdict. As an example, in this spreadsheet you could determine if the **TOTALS** for each company over the four-year period are good or bad and generate a result of 'Good' or 'Bad' in an appropriate cell. Let's assume a total of over 2000 is good. For **BLUECO** in cell, say B7, the formula could be:

=IF(B6>2000,"Good","Bad")

ie

=IF (test, "value if true", "value if false")

The result would be 'Bad' since the **TOTAL** for **BLUECO** is **1675**.

The > (greater than) symbol is obtained by holding down the **Shift** key and pressing the full stop key.

The < (less than) symbol is obtained by holding down the **Shift** key and pressing the comma key.

Use the following symbols with **IF** functions:

=   is equal to
>   greater than
<   less than
>=   greater than or equal to
<=   less than or equal to
<>   not equal to

Exercise 6

Under the row heading **TOTAL** enter a new row heading **ANALYSIS**. Use this row to generate **PROFIT** or **LOSS** for each company over the four-year period using the **IF** function. Assume that a profit value is over **2300**.

1 Move to cell A7 and enter the heading **ANALYSIS**.
2 Move to cell B7 and enter the formula: **=IF(B6>2300,"PROFIT","LOSS")**.
3 Press: **Enter**.
4 The result is **LOSS**.
5 Replicate this formula for the other companies.

3.5   Using the Count function

Info

COUNT is a useful function. Use it to count the number of cells in a range. Use the **COUNT** function in a formula as follows:

=COUNT(cell ref:cell ref)

Numbers and dates are counted within a specified range. Any cells containing no entries or text entries are not counted.

Exercise 7

Under the row heading **ANALYSIS**, leave one row blank and in the next row enter the heading **NO OF YEARS**. In the cell directly below this heading, using the **COUNT** function, enter a formula to count the number of years covered in the spreadsheet.

Method

1 Move to cell A9 and enter the heading **NO OF YEARS**.
2 Move to cell A10 and enter the formula **=COUNT(A2:A5)**.
3 Press: **Enter**.
4 The result **4** is displayed.

Info

Since this spreadsheet is small, it would be easy to work out some of the results of the formulae above. However, these type of formulae, as well as being more accurate, really save time when working on large spreadsheets.

3.6   Save the spreadsheet as Income2 and print one copy

3.7   Print one copy of the spreadsheet showing the formulae used

Note: Do not resave the spreadsheet.

Info

To show formulae in full, you will need to widen the columns. Do this by double-clicking on the column border: `B  ⊹  C`

3.8   Close the spreadsheet and exit Excel

Practice 5

1 Recall the spreadsheet **p3 outgoings1** saved in section 2.

2 Head the column after the TOTAL column **AVERAGE**.

3 Enter a formula in the AVERAGE column to calculate the average expenditure over the four-monthly period and replicate for each item.

4 In the column next to the AVERAGE heading, enter the heading **MAX**.

5 Enter a formula to display the maximum monthly amount spent on FOOD (use the MAX function). Replicate for each item.

6 In the row below the TOTALS row, enter the heading **MIN**.

7 In the next column, use the MIN function to display the MIN value for the four months in the **TOTALS** row.

8 Save the file as **p5 outgoings2** and print one copy showing values and one showing formulae.

9 Close the file.

Practice 6

1 Recall the spreadsheet **p4 branch sales1** saved in section 2.

2 In the column next to the Profit column, enter the heading **Verdict**.

3 In the Verdict column, use the IF function to display **Good** when the **Profit** is greater then **500** and **Bad** when it is less than **500**. Replicate for all branches.

4 In a row underneath the branch names, enter the heading **No of branches**.

5 In the row directly underneath this heading, use the Count function to display the number of branches in the spreadsheet. (*Note*: You will need to use a column other than the branches column since the entries in this column are text entries and will not be counted.)

6 Save the spreadsheet as **p6 branch sales2**.

7 Print the spreadsheet showing values fitting to one page.

8 Print the spreadsheet showing formulae and fitting to one page.

9 Close both files.

In this section you will practise and learn how to:

- align cell contents
- add borders
- apply colours
- copy formatting
- apply text wrapping
- modify column width and row height
- change text: font, size and colour, italicise, embolden, underline, double underline, orientation

- format number styles: decimal places, integers, with commas
- display numbers as percentages
- format currency symbols
- format different date styles
- add header/footer
- add additional cell content

4.1 / Aligning cell contents

Info

When data is first entered, text is placed on the left of the cell and numbers line up on the right.

Aligning cell content horizontally

Three toolbar buttons can be used to apply a new alignment to a range that is selected.

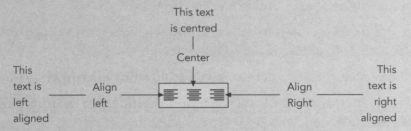

To align cell contents:

1 Select the cells to be realigned.
2 Click on: the appropriate toolbar button.

Aligning cell content vertically

1 From the **Format** menu, select: **Cells**.
2 With the **Alignment** tab selected, in the **Text Alignment** section, **Vertical** box, make a selection.
3 Click on: **OK**.

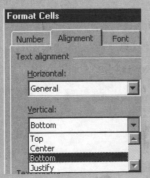

1 Reload the spreadsheet **Income2** saved at the end of section 3.
2 Display the headings so that **YEAR** is left aligned and **BLUECO**, **REDCO**, **GREYCO** and **ROSECO** are right aligned.

Method

The heading **YEAR** is already left aligned. To right align the other headings:

1 Select cells B1 to E1 (Figure 4.31).

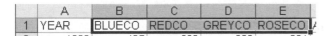

	A	B	C	D	E
1	YEAR	BLUECO	REDCO	GREYCO	ROSECO

Figure 4.31 Cells selected to right align

2 Click on: the **Align Right** toolbar button.

Exercise 2

Enter a main heading **FURNITURE COMPANY SALES** and centre it across the top of the spreadsheet.

Method

1 Insert a row at the top of the spreadsheet.
2 Key in the text in cell A1. Press: **Enter**.
3 Select cells A1 to H1, ie the full extent of spreadsheet columns.
4 Click on: the ▦ **Merge and Center** button.

Info

Although the text in cell A1 has now moved across the spreadsheet, if you need to amend it, it still resides in cell A1.

4.2 Modifying column width/row height, adding additional cell content

Info

By default each column starts with a width of about nine numeric characters. You can adjust the column width so that it accommodates the entry within.

Exercise 3

Change the heading **AVERAGE** so that it becomes **SALES AVERAGE**.

1 Move to cell F2.
2 Click the cursor in front of the **A** of **AVERAGE** (Figure 4.32) on the Formula bar and key in **SALES** and a space.
3 Press: **Enter**.

Click cursor here

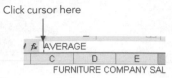

FURNITURE COMPANY SAL

Figure 4.32 Positioning the cursor to alter a heading

4 The entry is now too long to fit the cell. There are several ways to widen the column:

Info

Click on: the **Undo** button after trying each method so that you can practise.

a Position the cursor at the column border; a double arrow appears. Drag the right-hand edge of the column border (next to the column letter) to the right (Figure 4.33).

Position the cursor here
and drag to the right

Figure 4.33 Changing column width

b Position the cursor as above and double-click the mouse (this action widens to fit the longest entry exactly).
c With the cell selected, from the **Format** menu, select: **Column**, **AutoFit Selection** (Figure 4.34).
d Select the column, right-click and from the pop-up menu select: **Column Width**. Key in the new width.
e Click on: **OK**.

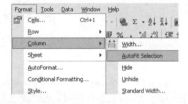

Figure 4.34 Widening a column using the menus

Info

Row height can be changed following these methods substituting Row for Column.

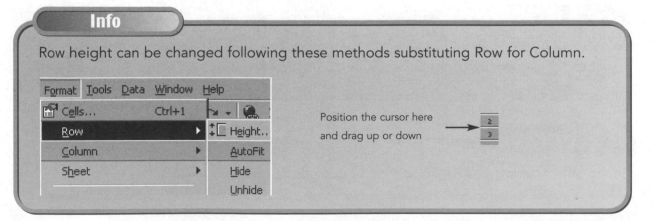

Position the cursor here
and drag up or down

Exercise 4

In the **TOTAL** row, change the numeric entries to font size 16 pt and text colour to blue. Italicise and embolden these entries only.

Method

1   Select the cells to format by dragging the mouse over them.
2   Use the **Font Size** button to change to 16 pt.
3   Use the **A ·** **Font Color** button to change the text to blue. Click on: its down arrow and click on: a colour.
4   Use the **Italic** and **Bold** buttons to italicise and embolden.

Info

The font type can also be altered in this way. Excel's default font is Arial, point size 10.

Exercise 5

Underline the figures in the **MIN** column and double underline the figures in the **MAX** column.

Method

1   Select the cells in the **MIN** column.
2   Click on: the **U** **Underline** button.
3   Select the cells in the **MAX** column.
4   From the **Format** menu, select: **Cells**.
5   The Format Cells dialogue box is displayed.
6   Select: the **Font** tab (Figure 4.35).
7   In the **Underline** section, click on the down arrow and select: **Double**.
8   Click on: **OK**.

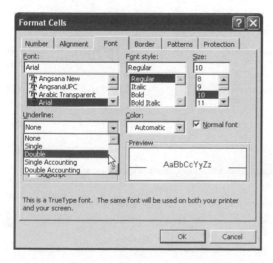

Figure 4.35 Double underlining cell contents

Locate the cell containing the word **ANALYSIS**. Give the text an orientation of **90°**.

Method

1 Select the cell containing the text **ANALYSIS**. (*Note*: If you were working on a larger spreadsheet, you could use **Find** from the **Edit** menu.)
2 From the **Format** menu, select: **Cells**.
3 Select: the **Alignment** tab (Figure 4.36).
4 In the **Orientation** section, enter **90** in the **Degrees** box (or move the Text hand using the mouse).
5 Click on: **OK**.

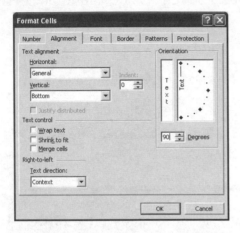

Figure 4.36 Setting text orientation

4.4 Applying text wrapping

Locate the cell containing **NO OF YEARS**. Apply text wrapping so that the text fits within the cell width.

Method

1 Select the cell containing the text **NO OF YEARS**, ie A10.
2 From the **Format** menu, select: **Cells**.
3 The **Format Cells** dialogue box is displayed (Figure 4.36).
4 Select the **Alignment** tab, then in the **Text Control** section, click in: the **Wrap text** box so that a tick appears.
5 Click on: **OK**.

4.5 Adding borders

Add a border around the entire spreadsheet and a double line border under the heading row **FURNITURE COMPANY SALES**.

Method

1 Select the spreadsheet by dragging the mouse over its cells.
2 Click on: the down arrow of the ▦ ▾ **Borders** button.
3 Select: **Outside Borders** as shown in Figure 4.37.

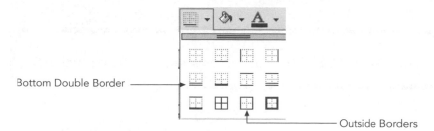

Bottom Double Border ——————————— Outside Borders

Figure 4.37 Setting borders

4 Select the heading row.
5 Using the **Borders** button, select: **Bottom Double Border** (Figure 4.37).

4.6 Shading cells

Exercise 9

In the **ANALYSIS** row, shade the cells showing a profit with a light blue background and the cells showing a loss with a light red background.

Method

1 Select the cell(s) to shade. (Hold down: **Ctrl** when selecting non-adjacent cells.)
2 Click on: the down arrow of the 🪣 ▾ **Fill Color** button.
3 Click on: a colour.

4.7 Copying formatting

Exercise 10

In the cells showing **PROFIT** and **LOSS**, change the font to Times New Roman, pt 12, italic.

Exercise 11

Copy the formatting in the **PROFIT** and **LOSS** cells to the **Company Names** cells, keeping the blue and red shading in the appropriate company name cells.

Method

1 Select the cell to copy from, ie **LOSS**, cell B8.
2 Click twice on: the 🖌 **Format Painter** button.

3 Click on: the cells to copy the formatting to.

4 Press: **Esc** to turn the **Format Painter** off.

5 Repeat for the **PROFIT** cells.

4.8 Using integer and decimal format to display numbers

Exercise 12

Display the numeric data in the **SALES AVERAGE** column as integers (whole numbers).

Method

1 Select the column entries, ie cells F3 to F6.

2 Right-click the highlighted area; a pop-up menu appears (Figure 4.38).

Figure 4.38 Formatting cells

3 From the menu, select: **Format Cells**; the Format Cells dialogue box is displayed.

4 Click on: the **Number** tab (Figure 4.39).

5 In the **Category** box, click on: **Number**.

6 In the **Decimal places** box, use the down arrow to set to zero (0).

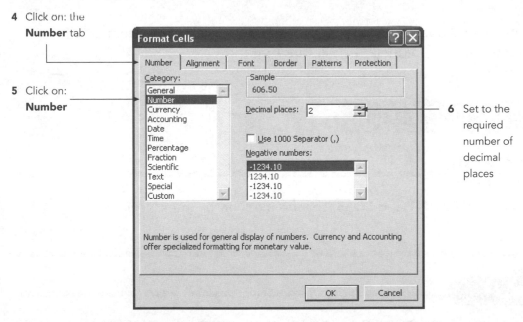

Figure 4.39 Format Cells dialogue box

7 Click on: **OK**.

The **SALES AVERAGE** column will now look like Figure 4.40.

SALES AVERAGE
607
628
648
480

Figure 4.40 Sales Average figures displayed as integers

Exercise 13

Change the display of the numeric data in the **SALES AVERAGE** column to 2 decimal places, ie 2 places after the decimal point.

Info

General is the default number format in Excel and displays numbers with decimal places. If a number has a zero positioned, as in 577.50 (the zero here is said to be 'trailing'), Excel will only display 577.5 in the General format.

You can also use the $\substack{+.0 \\ .00}$ $\substack{.00 \\ +.0}$ **Increase Decimal/Decrease Decimal** buttons to increase and decrease decimal places.

The **SALES AVERAGE** column should now look like Figure 4.41.

SALES AVERAGE
606.50
627.50
647.50
480.00

Figure 4.41 SALES AVERAGE figures displayed with 2 decimal places

4.9 Save the spreadsheet as Furniture and print one copy on A4 paper

4.10 Adding commas and currency symbols

Exercise 14

In the **TOTAL** row, display the numeric entries with the UK currency symbol (£).

Method

1 Select the relevant cells, ie B7 to E7.
2 Click on: the 🖫 **Currency** button.

Info

Excel inserts the £ symbol, a comma to denote thousands and 2 decimal places so that pence can be displayed. Other currency options can be chosen by selecting: **Cells** from the **Format** menu.

With the **Number** tab selected, in the **Category** section, select: **Currency** and then choose from the drop-down list in the **Symbol** section.

Commas to denote thousands (so that 1234 becomes 1,234) can be inserted in numeric data using the **,** **Comma Style** button.

4.11 Displaying numbers as percentages

Exercise 15

Insert a column between **SALES AVERAGE** and **MIN**. Enter the heading **COMMISSION RATES**. Wrap this text. Enter the following commission rates for the years **1999**, **2000**, **2001** and **2002** respectively: **0.05**, **0.08**, **0.1** and **0.025**. Display these commission rates as percentages.

Method

1 Enter the text and data in the usual way.
2 Select the cells containing the commission rates.
3 Click on: the % **Percent Style** button. The commission column now looks like Figure 4.42.

COMMISSION RATES
5%
8%
10%
3%

Figure 4.42 Commission figures changed to percentages

4.12 Save the spreadsheet as Furniture2 and print one copy on A4 paper, landscape display and fit to 1 page

4.13 Changing date format

Exercise 16

A few rows below the existing spreadsheet content, enter the following employee information:

Surname	**First Name**	**Start Date**
Young	**Julian**	**12/03/1997**
Gill	**Sanjit**	**10/11/1999**
Lopez	**Dominic**	**29/09/1998**
Young	**Georgie**	**02/05/2001**

Save the spreadsheet with the name **People**. Change the date format so that the date is displayed in the format 12 March 1997.

Method

1 Enter the data.
2 Check for errors.
3 Save the file with the name **People**.
4 Select the cells to format.
5 From the **Format** menu, select: **Cells**.

6 The Format Cells dialogue box is displayed (Figure 4.43).

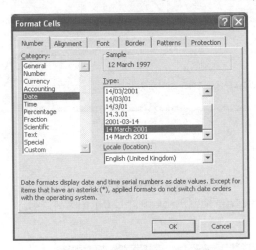

Figure 4.43 Formatting date styles

7 Ensure **Number** tab is selected.

8 In the **Category** section, click on: **Date**.

9 In the **Type** section, select the relevant format and click on: **OK**.

4.14 Formatting numbers as text

Exercise 17

Key in **Tel** in the cell next to **Start Date** and underneath key in the employee telephone numbers as follows:

Sanjit	**01234 752999**
Georgie	**01234 621900**
Julian	**01908 554211**
Dominic	**01908 338554**

Info

Entries such as telephone numbers or stock references, although consisting of numeric data, should be entered as text so that they will be ignored in calculations.

Method

1 Select the cells that are to contain the telephone numbers.

2 From the **Format** menu, select: **Cells**.

3 With the **Number** tab selected, in the **Category** section, select: **Text** from the list.

4 Click on: **OK**.

5 Key in the telephone numbers.

Note: If you are entering the telephone numbers without spaces or brackets, it is essential that you format the cells *before* entering the telephone numbers. If you include spaces or brackets, they automatically format as text.

Add the header **Produced by (your name)** and the **date** to the spreadsheet.

Method

1 With the spreadsheet displayed, from the **File** menu, select: **Page Setup**.
2 The Page Setup dialogue box appears. Click on: the **Header/Footer** tab (Figure 4.44).
3 Click on: **Custom Header**.

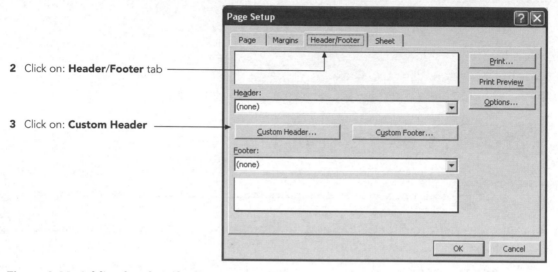

2 Click on: **Header/Footer** tab

3 Click on: **Custom Header**

Figure 4.44 Adding headers/footers

4 The **Header** dialogue box appears. Click in: the **Left section** and key in: **Produced by (your name)**. Click in: the **Center section** and key in the date (or click on: the **Date** button (Figure 4.45) if you are certain that your computer's date is set correctly – the actual date will not be displayed here but you can practise and see what appears on your Print Preview).
5 Click on: **OK** and on: **OK** again.

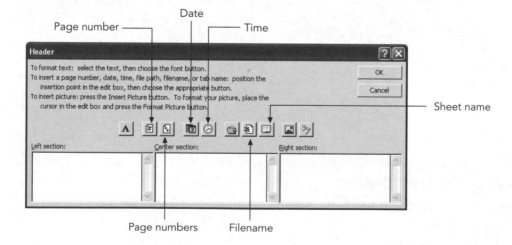

Date

Page number ——   — Time

Sheet name

Page numbers   Filename

Figure 4.45 Inserting an automatic date into a header

Note: In addition to the **Date** button, there are buttons for other automatic fields that can be added to headers/footers (Figure 4.45).

4.16 Modifying headers/footers

Method

1 Access the header/footer as in Exercise 18.
2 Select the entry to modify and amend as necessary.
3 Click on: **OK**.

4.17 Save the spreadsheet with the name People1 and print on A4 paper

4.18 Close the file and exit Excel

Practice 7

1 Recall the spreadsheet **p5 outgoings2** saved in section 3.

2 Right align all the column headings.

3 Change the row headings to Times New Roman, 12 point, red, bold.

4 Widen the column containing the row headings so that the contents are displayed in full.

5 Display all the numeric data in the months columns to 1 decimal place.

6 Display the numeric data in the TOTAL column in UK pounds to 2 decimal places.

7 Change the AVERAGE heading to read **AVERAGE SPENT**.

8 Set the AVERAGE SPENT column width to 20.

9 Display the numeric data in the AVERAGE column in integer format.

10 Centre the heading EXPENSES across the top of the spreadsheet.

11 Embolden the EXPENSES heading and set to 16 pt.

12 Locate the cell containing MIN and set to an orientation of **90 degrees**.

13 Double underline the MIN value in the cell to the right of MIN.

14 Add a border around the entire spreadsheet.

15 Shade the AVERAGE SPENT column.

16 Add a footer containing your name and an automatic filename.

17 Save the spreadsheet as **p7 expenses2**.

18 Print in landscape orientation.

Practice 8

1 Recall the spreadsheet **p6 branch sales2** saved in section 3.

2 Embolden and centre the column headings.

3 Display all the numeric data, except the number of branches, to 2 decimal places.

4 Change the row heading Limpley to **Limpley Stoke**.

5 Insert a column before the Profit column headed **Predicted Increased Sales**. Wrap the text in this cell and change its width to 10 and height to display the entry in full.

6 In the **Predicted Increased Sales** column, enter **0.012** in the **Bristol** row and **0.035** in the **Bath** row.

7 Format the figures in this column as %.

8 Add a border around the spreadsheet and between the cells.

9 Locate the cell containing Sat and replace with the date **21 June 2003**. Format to **21-Jun-03**.

10 Format the heading CoolKaf to bold, Arial 16 pt.

11 Copy this formatting to the cell containing No of Branches.

12 Save the spreadsheet as **p8 branches**.

13 Print the spreadsheet fitting to one page.

14 Close both files.

In this section you will practise and learn how to:

- open several spreadsheet files
- use copy/cut and paste to duplicate/move cell contents in another part of the spreadsheet
- move cell contents between active spreadsheets
- work with worksheets: insert new, delete, rename, duplicate, move

- freeze/unfreeze row/column titles
- sort data into ascending/descending alphabetical/numerical order
- use Autofill to increment entries
- modify basic options

For this section you will need to access the spreadsheet files **Davies profits** and **Office items** on the CD-ROM.

5.1   Opening and saving an existing file

Exercise 1

Open the spreadsheet file **Davies profits**. Change the header so that it displays **Amended by (your name)**. Save the file to your own work area using the name **Davies profits (your initials)**.

5.2   Copying and pasting/moving

Exercise 2

Copy the heading so that it appears in cell A11.

Method 1

Using drag and drop

1 Select the cell where the heading is displayed.
2 Hover the mouse over the selection border; the mouse pointer appears.
3 Hold down the **Ctrl** key; a + appears alongside the arrow.
4 Hold down the left mouse button and drag the selection to its new position, ie cell A11.
5 Release the mouse.

Info

To move instead of copy, do not hold down the **Ctrl** key at step 3.

Copy the row containing the headings **ITEM**, **COST PRICE** etc (ie row 2) together with the **INKJET PRINTER PAPER** row so that they appear adjacent underneath the heading you have just copied.

Method 2

Copying using the Copy and Paste buttons
Moving using the Cut and Paste method
Selecting non–adjacent columns/rows

Info

Adjacent means that the cells are next to one another. Non-adjacent means that they are not. The rows in this exercise are non-adjacent.

1 Select the headings row, hold down the **Ctrl** key and select the **INKJET PRINTER PAPER** row.
2 Click on: the **Copy** button. Flashing dotted lines appear around the selected rows.
3 Select the cells where you want to copy to, eg A12 to D13.
4 Click on: the **Paste** button.
5 Press: **Esc** to remove flashing lines.

Info

Similarly you can cut and paste. At step 2, click on: the **Cut** button.

5.3 Opening several spreadsheets

Exercise 4

Keeping the current spreadsheet open, open a new spreadsheet. Copy the main heading **DAVIES & SON PROFITS** to cell A1 of the new spreadsheet. Save the new spreadsheet with the filename **Employees**.

Method

1 Click on: the ⬚ **New** button.
2 Return to the **Davies profits (your initials)** spreadsheet display (**Window** menu, click on: the filename *or* click on: the filename on the taskbar).
3 Select: the cell to copy, then click on: the **Copy** button.
4 Return to the new spreadsheet, select cell A1 and click on: the **Paste** button.
5 Press: **Esc** to remove the selection from the **Davies profits (your initials)** spreadsheet.
6 Save the new spreadsheet.

5.4 Sorting data into ascending/descending alphabetical/numerical order

> **Exercise 5**
>
> Working on the **Davies profits (your initials)** spreadsheet, display the **ITEM** names in ascending alphabetical order.

Sorting using the toolbar Ascending/Descending buttons

> **Method**

1 Select the cell range containing the item details, ie A3 to D9.

   Note: It is necessary to select the **COST PRICE**, **SHOP PRICE** and **NO SOLD** columns so that they will be kept together when sorted.

2 Click on: the [A↓Z] **Ascending** button.

> **Info**
>
> The Ascending button will sort from A to Z or from the lowest number to the highest number in the selection. There is also a [Z↓A] **Descending** button to use when necessary. This sorts from Z to A and from the highest number to the lowest number in a selection.

5.5 Copying between worksheets

> **Exercise 6**
>
> Copy the whole of the **Davies profits (your initials)** spreadsheet to a second sheet within the same workbook. Name the new sheet **Analysis**.

> **Method**

1 Select the spreadsheet contents.
2 Click on: the **Copy** button.
3 Open a new sheet by clicking on: the **Sheet2** tab (Figure 4.46).

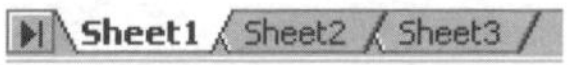

   ▶ \ **Sheet1** / Sheet2 / Sheet3 /

   Figure 4.46 Selecting a new sheet

4 The new sheet appears.
5 Click on: the **Paste** button.
6 Resize the cells as necessary.

Note: To save having to resize column widths, before step 5 clicking on: **Paste**, from the **Edit** menu, select: **Paste Special**, then click in: the **Column widths** option button in the **Paste** section. Click on: **OK**. Move to cell A1, then click on: the **Paste** button.

7   Right-click on: the new sheet tab (Sheet2), from the pop-up menu (Figure 4.47), select: **Rename**. Key in the new sheet name **Analysis** to overwrite the original name.

Figure 4.47 Sheet tab menu

> **Info**
>
> This method can be used to move individual cell contents and cell ranges, except at step 2, select: **Cut**.

Note: You can select other options from the sheet tab menu when appropriate, for example:

Insert a worksheet

Select: **Insert**, **Worksheet**, **OK**.

Delete a worksheet

1   Select: **Delete**.
2   Click on: **OK** to confirm delete.

Move or copy a worksheet

1   Select: **Move or Copy**.
2   The Move or Copy dialogue box is displayed (Figure 4.48).
3   In the **To book** box, click on: the down arrow and select the location to copy/move to.
4   In the **Before sheet** section, click on: a position for the sheet.
5   If you are copying and not moving, click in: the **Create a copy** box so a tick appears.
6   Click on: **OK**.

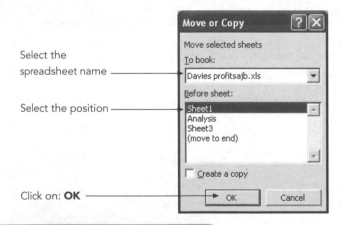

Figure 4.48 Moving or copying a sheet

5.6   Using AutoFill

> **Exercise 7**
>
> On the **Analysis** sheet, add the following row headings in column A, starting at row 15:
>
> **Week1**, **Week2**, **Week3**, **Week4**

Info

If a cell contains a number, date or time period that can extend in a series, by dragging the fill handle of a cell, you can copy that cell to other cells in the same row or column. The values are incremented. For example, if a cell contains **MONDAY**, Excel can quickly fill in other cells in the row or column with **TUESDAY**, **WEDNESDAY** and so on.

To view **AutoFill** options, from the **Tools** menu, select: **Options**, **Custom Lists** tab. Use **AutoFill** to copy entries too, eg key in name in a cell then follow steps 2 to 4.

When a cell does not contain an entry that can be extended in a series, dragging the fill handle of the cell will copy the exact content of the original cell to the cells you want to fill.

1 Enter **Week1** in cell A15, press: **Enter**. Move back to cell A15.
2 Hover the mouse over the **Fill handle** at the bottom right of the cell; a thin black cross appears.
3 Hold down the left mouse and drag across the cells you want to Autofill, ie A16, A17 and A18.
4 Release the mouse.

5.7 **More formulae and printing**

Exercise 8

On the **Analysis** sheet of the **Davies profits (your initials)** spreadsheet, carry out the following tasks:

1 Key in the column heading **TOTAL REVENUE**, adjacent and to the right of the **NO SOLD** heading. Wrap this text in the cell and set the cell width to **14**.
2 Generate a formula for the **TOTAL REVENUE** (**NO SOLD** multiplied by **SHOP PRICE**) for **BALL POINT PENS**.
3 Replicate this formula for the other items.
4 Adjacent to and to the right of the **TOTAL REVENUE** heading, key in the heading **OUTLAY**.
5 Generate a formula to calculate the **OUTLAY** (**COST PRICE** multiplied by **NO SOLD**) for **BALL POINT PENS**.
6 Replicate this formula for the other items.
7 Insert a new column, with the heading **PROFIT**, in between the headings **ITEM** and **COST PRICE**.
8 Generate a formula to calculate the **PROFIT** (**TOTAL REVENUE** minus **OUTLAY**) for **BALL POINT PENS**.
9 Replicate this formula for the other items.
10 Set a footer for this sheet as follows. Insert an automatic date at the left, the text **Analysis of sales** in the centre, and your name on the right.
11 Save the spreadsheet with the name **Profits** and print one copy of the **Analysis** sheet only.
12 Name Sheet1 as **Source**.
13 Save the spreadsheet and print the **Source** sheet.

1 Copy rows 2–9 (incl.) of the **ITEM**, **PROFIT**, **TOTAL REVENUE** and **OUTLAY** columns, including headings from the **Profits** spreadsheet file, **Analysis** sheet, to the **Employees** spreadsheet, created in Exercise 4, starting at cell A2.

2 In column A, a few lines below the entries, enter the heading **COMMISSION RATE**. In the cell below this heading, enter the rate of **0.01**.

3 In column E to the right of the heading OUTLAY, enter the heading **EMPLOYEE COMMISSION**. Widen this column so that the contents are displayed in full.

4 Generate a formula to calculate the **EMPLOYEE COMMISSION** for **BALL POINT PENS** (**PROFIT** multiplied by **COMMISSION RATE**). Make the **COMMISSION RATE** cell reference absolute when creating this formula (see Section 2.4 INFO box).

5 Replicate the formula for the other items.

6 Format the cells to display 2 decimal places.

7 Add a header with your name and an automatic filename insertion.

8 Save the spreadsheet as **employees2**.

9 Print one copy showing the formulae and then close it.

10 Close the **Profits** spreadsheet (if still open).

5.8 Freeze/unfreeze row/column titles

Info

When spreadsheets do not display in their entirety on screen, it is useful to be able to keep rows or columns visible so that when scrolling through you can still see what the cell contents relate to. Excel allows you to freeze row/column headings so that they are visible even when they should have scrolled out of view.

Exercise 10

Open the spreadsheet **Office items**. Freeze row 6, with headings content.

Method

1 Select the row below the one to freeze, eg row 7.

2 From the **Window** menu, select: **Freeze Panes** (Figure 4.49).

Figure 4.49 Freezing panes

3 A solid black line is displayed on the spreadsheet. You can now scroll through with the headings always displayed.

4 To unfreeze, from the **Window** menu, select: **Unfreeze Panes**.

Note: You can freeze columns by selecting the column to the right of where you want the split to appear. You can also freeze rows and columns at the same time by selecting the cell below and to the right of where you want the split to appear.

Exercise 11

Print the spreadsheet **Office items** in landscape display. Do not fit to page. Display the headings row on all pages.

Method

1 From the **File** menu, select: **Page Setup**.
2 Ensure landscape display is selected.
3 Click on: the **Sheet** tab.
4 In the **Print titles** section, click on: the collapse dialogue button in the **Rows to repeat at top** box (Figure 4.50).

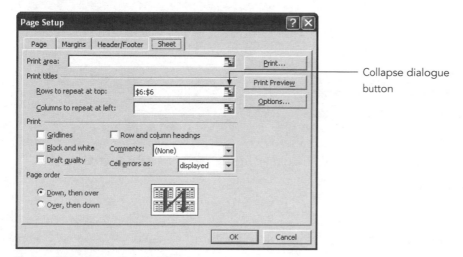

Collapse dialogue button

Figure 4.50 Page Setup, Sheet

5 Select the row to repeat (Figure 4.51).

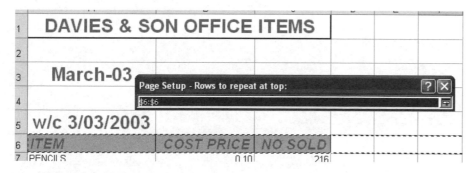

Figure 4.51 Selecting the row to repeat

6 Press: **Enter**.
7 The row reference is now displayed in the **Rows to repeat at top** box (Figure 4.52).

Figure 4.52 Row reference displayed

8 Click on: **OK** and then on: the **Print** button.
   Note: You can also select columns to repeat.

5.11 · Modify basic Excel options

When you know that you will always be opening/saving files in a particular folder it is worth setting this as the default. Set your user name so that it appears on automatic entries, eg in headers and footers.

1   From the **Tools** menu, select: **Options**.

2   Select: the **General** tab (Figure 4.53).

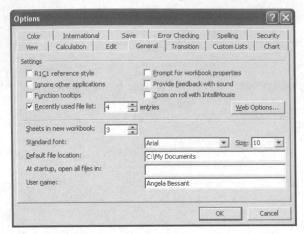

Figure 4.53 Setting user options

3   Key in the location of the folder to save and store files in the **Default file location** box.

4   Key in your name in the **User name** box.

5   Click on: **OK**.

6   The location and name set will be the default next time you use Excel.

Note: You can also change a user name for the active document only. To do this:

1   From the **File** menu, select: **Properties**.

2   Select: the **Summary** tab.

3   Key in your name in the **Author** box.

4   Click on: **OK**.

5.12 · Close the file and exit Excel

Note: For this exercise you will need the file **Cars**.

Practice 9

1   Open the spreadsheet **cars**.

2   Delete the current header and add **Amended by (your name)** in the centre and **ECDL** at the right.

3   Autofill the entries in row 38 to display the months to Aug-03 in this row.

4   Format the month entries in full as in this example: **March 03**.

5   Save the file as **cars (your initials)**.

6   Copy the heading **CAR RENTAL REVENUE** to cell A40.

7   Open a new spreadsheet and copy the column headings and LEISURE section only to the new document. Adjust cell widths, as necessary, to display all entries in full.

8   Save the new spreadsheet as **Leisure**.

9   Sort the data in the **Leisure** spreadsheet into ascending order of REG NO.

10 Resave the Leisure spreadsheet, print one copy and close it.

11 Working on the **cars (your initials)** spreadsheet, copy the REG NO and RENTAL BAND COST columns to a new sheet in this file.

12 Name the new sheet **Predict**.

13 On the new sheet, insert a row at the top.

14 In the first column of this row enter the text **Changing Cost Prediction**. Wrap the text in this cell and give it an orientation of 90 degrees. Change the row height so that each word is not split.

15 In the cell to the right of the new text enter the number 10.

16 Add a new column heading **PREDICT** to the right of RENTAL BAND COST.

17 Copy the formatting from the other column headings to the new heading and widen the column so that the new heading is displayed in full.

18 Enter a formula in the **PREDICT** column to calculate the cost + 10 (**RENTAL BAND COST** + the **Changing Cost Prediction**) for the first REG NO. Make the cell reference of the changing cost prediction absolute.

   Note: When replicating, ensure that entries are deleted for blank rows.

19 Print the **Predict** sheet only.

20 Change the **Changing Cost Prediction** value to **15**.

21 Print the **Predict** sheet only.

22 Return to Sheet1 and name it **rentals**.

23 Freeze the headings in rows 4, 5 and 6, ie **TYPE, REG NO**...

24 Save the spreadsheet file as **cars2**.

25 Move the row containing the dates so that it is below the row CAR RENTAL REVENUE at the bottom.

26 Print the sheet **rentals** only in landscape display applying automatic titles (rows 4, 5 and 6) on each printed page.

27 Close the file.

In this section you will practise and learn how to:

- produce different types of charts/graphs from spreadsheet figures to analyse data: pie charts, column charts, bar charts, line graphs, comparative charts

- edit or modify a chart/graph: add/remove a title or label, change the scale, change the colours
- change the chart/graph type
- copy/move and delete charts/graphs
- resize charts/graphs

6.1 / Different types of display

There are many different ways of graphically displaying data in Excel. The main ones that we will be looking at are pie charts, column/bar charts, line graphs and comparative charts.

Info

Excel uses the word 'chart' and not 'graph' for all its graphical displays. In the UK we tend to differentiate between charts and graphs. For our purposes we can assume that they are the same thing.

6.2 / Pie chart

A pie chart consists of a circle divided into a number of segments. In this example (Figure 4.54), there are three segments representing eye colours: blue, brown and green, in Tutor Group A. The largest segment is brown and it tells us that 44% of Tutor Group A have brown eyes, the next largest is green with 30%, and the smallest blue with 26%. There is a legend (key) to show us which colour or shade represents which eye colour.

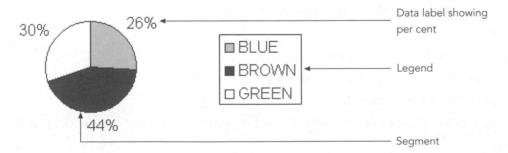

EYE COLOUR TUTOR GROUP A ← Chart Title

26% ← Data label showing per cent

□ BLUE
■ BROWN ← Legend
□ GREEN

Segment

Figure 4.54 Pie chart

Chart components

Chart title: The chart title should be descriptive and clear.

Data labels: On a pie chart you can show percentage values or actual values. You can show the labels next to the segments instead of a legend.

Legend: A legend is a key showing the different colours/shades that correspond to the data represented in the pie chart.

Segment: The pie chart is made up of segments that represent different data types.

6.3 Column and bar charts

A column chart uses bar columns to represent values. The chart has two axes, the *x* (horizontal) axis and the *y* (vertical) axis. The *x* axis usually represents data that does not change, such as days of the week. The *y* axis usually represents values that fluctuate, such as monetary values or temperatures. This type of chart is useful for showing comparisons.

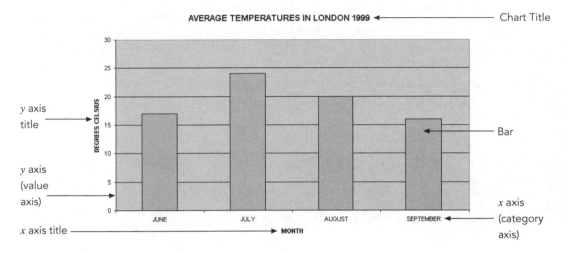

Figure 4.55 Column chart

The column chart (Figure 4.55) shows the comparison of average temperatures in London. The tallest column, July, shows the overall hottest average temperature. The shortest column, September, shows that it was the coolest month of those shown.

Bar charts can also have horizontal bars. These show the categories vertically and the values horizontally.

6.4 Line graph

A line graph shows trends in data at equal intervals. Points on the graph are joined together to form a continuous line. It has properties in common with a column/bar chart, such as *x* and *y* axes and axes titles.

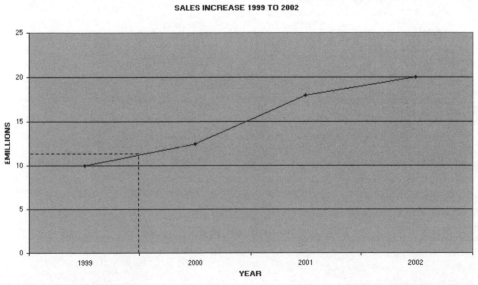

Figure 4.56 Line graph

The line graph (Figure 4.56) shows that the trend is up, as the line is going up and not down. Sales have been increasing steadily since 1999. I have drawn a line from the *x* axis, at the end of 1999, to the plotted line and then drawn a line to the *y* axis. Where this line joins the *y* axis the value can be read, approximately £12 million. This was the value of sales at the end of 1999.

6.5 Comparative charts

A comparative chart is used to compare sets of data. The display shows two or more columns (if a comparative column chart, Figure 4.57) or two or more lines (if a comparative line graph, Figure 4.58) of the same item.

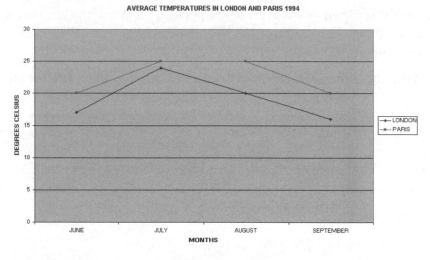

Figure 4.57 Comparative column chart

Figure 4.58 Comparative line graph

6.6 Creating a pie chart

Exercise 1

Produce a pie chart showing the branch sales percentages for Musicmania for the months January to June 2003.

1 Load Excel as shown in section 1.

2 Enter the data so that the spreadsheet looks like Figure 4.59.

	A	B
1	CARDIFF	25
2	LIVERPOOL	14
3	MANCHESTER	20
4	EDINBURGH	41

Figure 4.59 Data entered into spreadsheet

3 Save the spreadsheet as **musicmania**.

Exercise

Now create the pie chart including labels for each of the segments. Enter the following heading **BRANCH SALES PERCENTAGES – JANUARY TO JUNE 2003**.

Method

1 Select all the data entered, ie cells A1 to B4.

2 Click on: the 📊 **Chart Wizard** button.

3 Step 1 of 4 Chart Wizard dialogue box appears: **Chart Type** (Figure 4.60):

   a The **Standard Types** tab is selected. In the **Chart type** box, click on: **Pie**.

   b In the **Chart sub-type** box, click on: the top left pie type, as shown. This is usually already selected as the default setting.

   c Click on: **Next**.

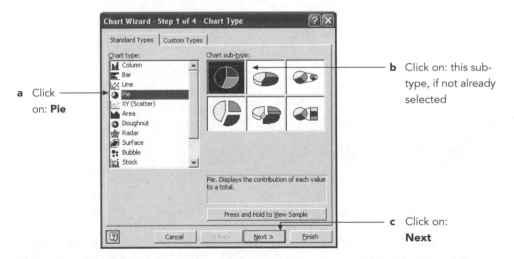

Figure 4.60 Step 1 of Chart Wizard

Info

There are many different types of pie charts that you can choose. To view and learn the names of charts, click and hold the mouse on: **Press and hold to view sample**. Try experimenting with the different types.

4 Step 2 Chart Wizard dialogue box appears: **Chart Source Data** (Figure 4.61). There is a preview of the pie chart together with a legend – a key to the different segments of the pie. With the **Data Range** tab selected, the data range selected is shown as:

=Sheet1$A$1:$B$4

Ignoring the $ signs, this represents Sheet1, cells A1 to B4. Click on: **Next**.

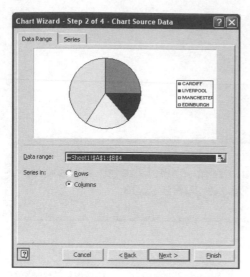

Figure 4.61 Step 2 of Chart Wizard

Info

Data points and data range/series

A data point is the name given to each plotted item and its related value, eg CARDIFF, 25 represents a data point. A data range/series is the name given to all the data points being plotted.

If you have made an error in selecting the data range to chart, at Step 2 of Chart Wizard, either:

a Change the data range by clicking in: the **Data range** box and keying in the correct range *or*

b Click on: the **Collapse Dialog** button, reselect the cell range and click on: the **Collapse Dialog** button again.

In this example we have the data series in columns. You will need to click in the **Rows** option button if the data series is in rows. Should you need to go back a step, after Step 1 of Chart Wizard, click on **Back**.

In some circumstances Excel will automatically make assumptions about what is a data range. It will try to include, for example, years, ie 1993, 1994, 1995 since they are numerical (if they have not been formatted as text). In such cases you will need to carry out steps **a** and **b** (above) to overwrite Excel's assumptions. Then click on: the **Series** tab. In the **Category (X) axis labels**, click on: the **Collapse Dialog** button and select the cell range for year labels. Click on: the **Collapse Dialog** button again.

You can chart non-adjacent rows or columns. Select the first row/column to chart, hold down **Ctrl** when selecting other non-adjacent rows/columns.

---

5 Step 3 Chart Wizard dialogue box appears: **Chart Options** (Figure 4.62):

a With the Titles tab selected, click in the **Chart title** box and key in: **BRANCH SALES PERCENTAGES – JANUARY TO JUNE 2003**.

Click here and key
in chart title

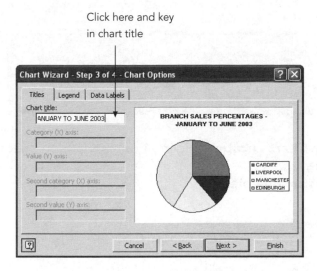

Figure 4.62 Step 3 of Chart Wizard

You will not be able to see all the title as it will scroll out of the visible section. Do not press **Enter** as this will result in moving to the next step of Chart Wizard. If you have pressed **Enter**, click on: **Back**.

b Click on: the **Legend** tab (Figure 4.63).

c Click in: the **Show legend** tick box to remove the tick.

b Click on: the
Legend tab

c Click in: the
Show legend
tick box to
remove tick

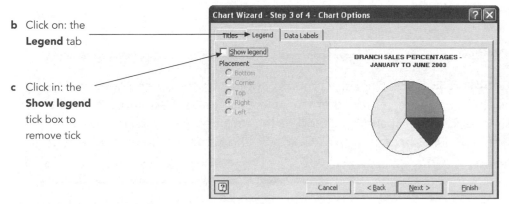

Figure 4.63 Removing a legend

Info

You have been asked to show labels for each of the segments, not a legend. Having segment data labels and a legend duplicates information and will make the chart appear cluttered.

d Click on: the **Data Labels** tab (Figure 4.64).

e Click in: the **Category Name** option button.

f Click on: **Next**.

d Click on: the
Data Labels
tab

e Click in:
Category
name

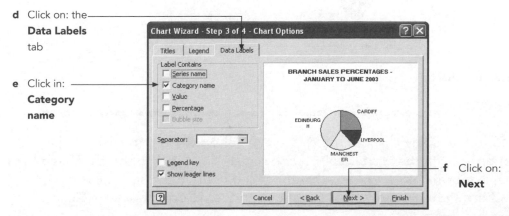

f Click on:
Next

Figure 4.64 Showing labels

6   Step 4 Chart Wizard dialogue box appears: **Chart Location** (Figure 4.65):
    a   Click in: the **As new sheet** option button.
    b   In the box shown, key in the name **Musicmania pie**.
    c   Click on: **Finish**.

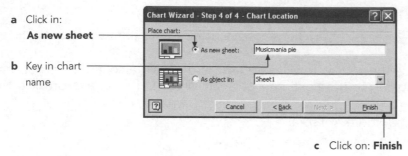

a   Click in:
    As new sheet

b   Key in chart
    name

c   Click on: **Finish**

Figure 4.65 Step 4 of Chart Wizard

The completed pie chart is displayed as shown in Figure 4.66.

Chart Title ⟶ BRANCH SALES PERCENTAGES - JANUARY TO JUNE 2003

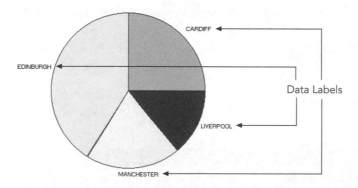

Data Labels

Figure 4.66 Completed pie chart

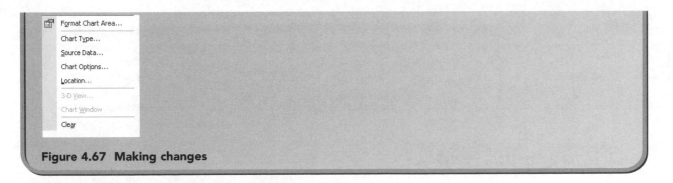

Figure 4.67 Making changes

6.7 Saving the chart

Method

Click on: the **Save** button.

Info

You can use this quick saving method as you have already saved the chart as **Musicmania pie**. The chart and spreadsheet will be saved as one file.

You can swap between chart and spreadsheet display by clicking the relevant tab in the worksheet tab area at the bottom of the currently displayed spreadsheet.

| Musicmania pie | Sheet1 | Sheet2 |

Figure 4.68 Changing sheets

6.8 Printing a chart

Method

1 With the chart displayed on screen, from the **File** menu, select: **Print**. The Print dialogue box appears (Figure 4.69).
2 In the **Print what** section, ensure that the **Active sheet** option button is selected.
3 Click on: **OK**.

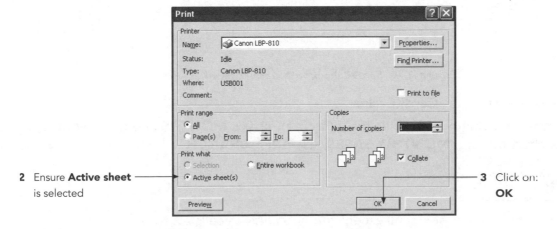

2 Ensure **Active sheet** is selected

3 Click on: **OK**

Figure 4.69 Print dialogue box

Info

By default the chart will print in landscape format. If you have positioned the chart on the same sheet as the data, at step 2, select: **Selected Chart** in the **Print what** section.

6.9 Closing the chart

Method

From the **File** menu, select: **Close**.

Info

You can close with the display on either the chart or the spreadsheet. They will be saved together with the same filename.

6.10 Creating a column chart

Exercise 2

Produce a column chart showing the monthly sales from January to June for the Cardiff branch.

Method

1 Load Excel *or* click on: the **New** button if Excel is already loaded.

2 Enter the data so that your spreadsheet looks like Figure 4.70.

	A	B
1	MONTH	SALES - £
2	Jan	35000
3	Feb	15000
4	Mar	45000
5	Apr	12000
6	May	21000
7	Jun	16000

Figure 4.70 Spreadsheet with data entered

3 Save the spreadsheet as **Cardiff sales**.

Now create the column chart. Title the x (horizontal) axis **MONTHS** and the y (vertical) axis **£**. Give the chart the title **MONTHLY SALES, CARDIFF BRANCH**.

Method

1 From the data entered, select all except the headings, ie cells A2 to B7.

2 Click on: the **Chart Wizard** button.

3 Step 1 (of 4) Chart Wizard dialogue box appears: **Chart Type**:

  a With the **Standard Types** tab selected, click on: **Column**.

  b In the **Chart sub-type** box, click on the top left chart. (This is the default so may already be selected.)

  c Click on: **Next**.

Practise

Clicking on: **Back** to experiment with the different chart types.

4   Step 2 Chart Wizard dialogue box appears: **Chart Source Data**. Click on: **Next**.
5   Step 3 Chart Wizard dialogue box appears: **Chart Options**:
   a   Select the **Titles** tab (if not already selected), click in: the **Chart title** box and key in: **MONTHLY SALES, CARDIFF BRANCH**.
   b   Click in: the **Category** (*x*) axis box and key in: **MONTHS**.
   c   Click in: the **Value** (*y*) axis box and key in: **£**.
   d   Click on: the **Legend** tab.
   e   Click in: the **Show legend** box to remove the tick.
   f   Click on: **Next**.
6   Step 4 Chart Wizard dialogue box appears: **Chart Location**:
   a   Click on: **As new sheet** option button and key in the name **Cardiffbar**.
   b   Click on: **Finish**.

The completed column chart is displayed as shown in Figure 4.71.

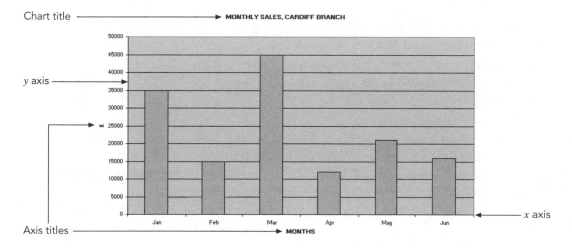

Figure 4.71 Completed column chart

7   Save the chart as in 6.7.
8   Print the chart as in 6.8.
9   Close the chart as in 6.9.

> **Info**
>
> Create a bar chart (with horizontal bars) using this method but selecting **Bar** at step 3(a).

6.11 Creating a line graph

> **Exercise 3**
>
> Produce a line graph showing the monthly sales from January to June for the Liverpool branch.

1 Load Excel or click on: the **New** button.
2 Enter the data so that your spreadsheet looks like Figure 4.72.

	A	B
1	MONTH	SALES - £
2	Jan	15000
3	Feb	25000
4	Mar	41000
5	Apr	46000
6	May	19000
7	Jun	24000

Figure 4.72 Spreadsheet with data entered

3 Save the spreadsheet as **Liverpool sales**.

For the data create a line graph. Enter the x (horizontal) axis title **MONTHS** and the y (vertical) axis **£**. The title for the graph is **MONTHLY SALES – LIVERPOOL BRANCH**.

Method

1 Select the data entered in the cells A2 to B7.
2 Click on: the 📊 **Chart Wizard** button.
3 Step 1 (of 4) Chart Wizard dialogue box appears: **Chart type**:
   a With the **Standard Types** tab selected, click on **Line**.
   b In the **Chart sub-type** box, click on the middle left chart if not already selected.
   c Click on: **Next**.
4 Step 2 Chart Wizard dialogue box appears: **Chart Source Data**. Click on: **Next**.
5 Step 3 Chart Wizard dialogue box appears: **Chart Options**:
   a Select the Titles tab, click in: the **Chart title** box and key in: **MONTHLY SALES – LIVERPOOL BRANCH**.
   b Click in: the **Category** (x) axis box and key in: **MONTHS**. Click in: the **Value** (y) axis box and key in: **£**
   c Click on: the **Legend** tab.
   d Click in: the **Show legend** tick box to remove the tick.
   e Click on: **Next**.
6 Step 4 Chart Wizard dialogue box appears: **Chart Location**:
   a Click on: the **As new sheet** option button and key in the name **Liverpool line**.
   b Click on: **Finish**.

The completed line graph is displayed as shown in Figure 4.73.

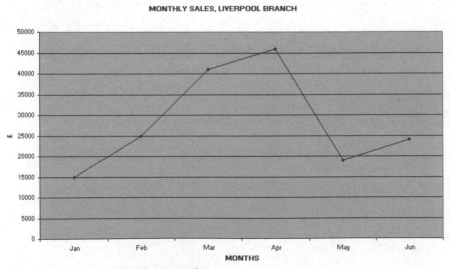

Figure 4.73 Completed line graph

7 Save the graph as in 6.7.

8 Print the graph as in 6.8.

9 Close the graph as in 6.9.

6.12 **Creating a comparative chart**

Exercise 4

Produce a comparative column chart showing Musicmania's daily sales of CDs and DVDs from Sunday to Saturday.

Method

1 Load Excel *or* click on: the **New** toolbar button.

2 Enter the data so that the spreadsheet looks like Figure 4.74.

	A	B	C
1		CD	DVD
2	Sunday	260	180
3	Monday	108	67
4	Tuesday	210	112
5	Wednesday	300	70
6	Thursday	98	102
7	Friday	370	189
8	Saturday	500	210

Figure 4.74 Spreadsheet with data entered

3 Save the spreadsheet as **Daily sales**.

Create a comparative column chart using the data entered. Enter the *y* axis title **DAILY SALES**. Enter the *x* axis title **DAY**. Create a legend to show CD and DVD. The title for the graph is **DAILY CD/DVD SALES**.

Method

1 Select all the data entered, ie cells A1 to C8.

2 Click on: the **Chart Wizard** button.

3 Step 1 Chart Wizard:

    a With the **Standard Types** tab selected, click on: **Column**.

    b In the **Chart sub-type** box, click on the first chart at the top left.

    c Click on: **Next**.

4 Step 2 Chart Wizard. Click on: **Next**.

5 Step 3 Chart Wizard:

    a Select the **Titles** tab, click in: the **Chart title** box and key in: **DAILY CD/DVD SALES**.

    b Click in: the **Category** (*x*) axis box and key in: **DAY**.

    c Click in: the **Value** (*y*) axis box and key in: **NUMBER SOLD**.

    d Click on: **Next**.

6 Step 4 Chart Wizard:

    a Click on: the **As new sheet** option button and key in: **Daily CD DVD**.

    b Click on: **Finish**.

The completed comparative chart is displayed as shown in Figure 4.75.

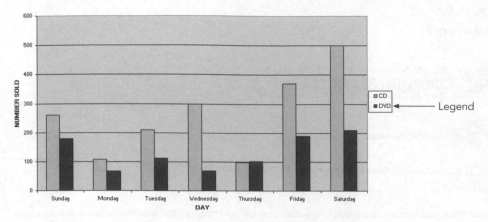

Figure 4.75 Completed comparative graph

> **Info**
>
> In this example, we need to show a legend to indicate which colour bars represent CDs and DVDs. Resize the legend if necessary by clicking on it and dragging its handles.
>
> If you are printing in black and white, the bars and legend will display in differing patterns. If you are printing a comparative line graph to a black and white printer, be careful to choose a chart type that displays different shapes on the lines to distinguish them.

7 Save the chart as in 6.7.

8 Print the chart as in 6.8.

6.13 Changing chart colours

A dialogue box is displayed when you double-click on any part of the completed chart. There are options to change colours, patterns, fonts etc.

Note: When changing pie segment colour, click on: the chart to select it, then click on: the segment to select it. Right-click on: the selection to display a pop-up menu.

Practise this now.

6.14 Changing chart scales

To change the y axis value

1 With the chart displayed on screen, double-click on: the **Value Axis** (Figure 4.76).

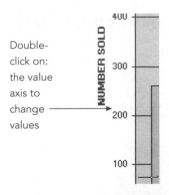

Double-click on: the value axis to change values

Figure 4.76 The Value Axis

2 The **Format Axis** dialogue box appears.

3 With the **Scale** tab selected, change the values in the **Minimum** and **Maximum** boxes.

4 Click on: **OK**.

Practise this now.

6.15 Moving/duplicating a chart

Click on the chart to select it.

Either

Use **Cut/copy** and **Paste** to move it to another sheet or application

or

Drag the chart using the mouse (hover the mouse over the chart) to another location on the same sheet to move it. Hold down **Ctrl** when copying it.

2 Select: **Cut** or **Copy**

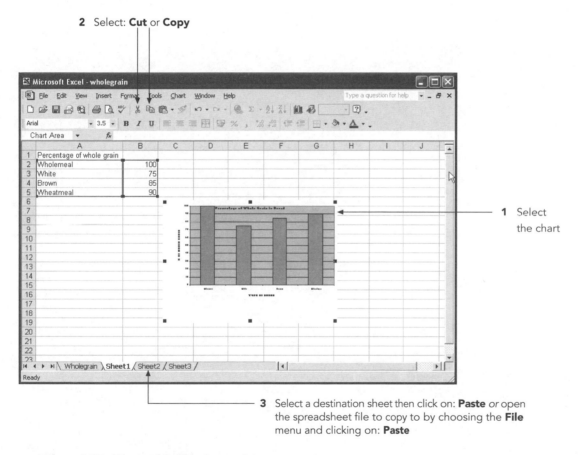

1 Select the chart

3 Select a destination sheet then click on: **Paste** *or* open the spreadsheet file to copy to by choosing the **File** menu and clicking on: **Paste**

Figure 4.77 Moving/duplicating a chart

6.16 Deleting a chart

1 Click on the chart to select it.

2 Press: **Delete**.

6.17 Changing chart type

Method

1 Right-click on the chart.
2 Select: **Chart type** from the pop-up menu.
3 Select a chart type.
4 Click on: **OK**.

6.18 Save and close the spreadsheets and exit Excel

Note: For these exercises you will need the file **weather**.

Practice 10

1   Open Excel and the spreadsheet **weather**.

2   Create a column chart comparing the statistics for Barcelona and Hong Kong.

3   Use the chart title **Weather Comparison (Barcelona, Hong Kong)**.

4   Label the *x* axis **Temperature/Rainfall** and the *y* axis **Degrees C**.

5   Save the chart on a new sheet.

6   Change the scale to display up to 30.

7   Save the file as **weather1**.

8   Print the chart in landscape.

9   Change the chart type to Line with markers displayed at each data value.

10   Save the file as **weather2**.

11   Print the line graph.

Practice 11

1   Using the spreadsheet **weather**, delete the existing chart displayed on the data page.

2   Create an exploded pie chart of the Average daily high temperatures for the cities Istanbul through to Tokyo.

3   Use the chart title **March Highs**.

4   Show value labels and a legend.

5   Save the chart on the same sheet as the spreadsheet data.

6   Change the colour of the segment for Paris to orange.

7   Reposition and resize the chart so that it does not obscure any of the spreadsheet data and shows all the city names.

8   Save the spreadsheet file as **weather highs** and print a copy of the data and chart on one page.

9   Copy the chart to another sheet. Name the sheet **Compare**.

10   Change the chart type to a cluster column with 3-D visual effect.

11   Delete the legend and do not show data label values.

12   Add an *x* axis label **City**.

13   Change the city names on the *x* axis to 14 pt.

14   Amend the chart title to **March Highs Degrees C**.

15   Display the *y* axis from 5 to 35.

16   Ensure that all bars are red.

17   Adjust and use Print Preview to ensure all labels display in full.

18   Print a copy of the chart.

19   Save the file as **weather comp**.

Practice 12

Load any other spreadsheet you have worked on and practise creating different types of chart.

Spreadsheets quick reference

(The following is a list of generally useful tasks associated with this module. For more information on specific items, refer to the module content.)

Action	Keyboard	Mouse	Right–mouse menu	Menu
Absolute cell reference	Add **$** sign in front of the cell reference column letter and in front of the cell reference row number or press: **F4**			
Align cell entries	Select cells to align			
		Click: the relevant button: ▤ ▤ ▤ ▦	**Format Cells**	**Format, Cells**
			Select the **Alignment** tab Select from the **Horizontal:** drop-down menu as appropriate	
Autofill	Select the first cell, drag the **Fill Handle** across the cells			
Bold text	Select cells to embolden			
	Ctrl + **B**	Click: the **B** **Bold** button	**Format Cells**	**Format, Cells**
			Select the **Font** tab Select **Bold** from the **Font style:** menu	
Borders	Select the cells that you want to add a border to			
		Click on the down arrow of the ▦ ▾ **Borders** button. Select the border you require	**Format Cells, Border** tab	**Format, Cells, Border** tab
Capitals (blocked)	**Caps Lock** (Press again to remove)			
Close a file	**Ctrl** + **W**	Click: the ✕ **Close** button		**File, Close**
Colours, apply to cell content		Click: the **A** ▾ **Font Color** button	**Format Cells, Font, Color**	**Format, Cells, Font, Color**
shade cell		Click: the ◆ ▾ **Fill Color** button	**Format Cells, Patterns**	**Format, Cells, Patterns**
Columns, adding	Select the column following the one where you want the new column to appear – by clicking on the column ref box (at top of column)			
			Insert	**Insert, Columns**
Columns, changing width of		Drag the column border `C ╬ D` to fit the widest entry	Select the column(s) by clicking (and dragging) on the column ref box (at top of column)	
			Column Width Key in the width you want	**Format, Column, Width** Key in the width you want or **Format, Column, AutoFit Selection**

Action	Keyboard	Mouse	Right-mouse menu	Menu
Columns, deleting	Select the column you want to delete by clicking on the column ref box (at top of column)			
	Delete		**Delete**	**Edit**, **Delete**
Commas, inserting in numbers		Click: the **›** **Comma Style** button	**Format Cells**, **Number**, **Number**, **Use 1000 Separator**	**Format**, **Cells**, **Number**, **Number**, **Use 1000 Separator**
Copy/cut and paste	Select cell(s) to copy/cut			
	Using drag and drop Copy: Hold down Ctrl and drag to new position Cut: Drag to new position *Using Cut/Copy and Paste* Click: the **Cut/Copy** button. Select where you want to cut/copy to. Click: the 📋 **Paste** button			
Copy (replicate) formulae	Select cell with formula to be copied Drag the mouse from bottom right corner of cell over cells to copy to, release mouse			
Copy formatting	Select cell(s) containing formatting to copy			
		Click: the ⚒ **Format Painter** button		
Currency symbols		Click: the 💲 **Currency** button for UK currency		**Format**, **Cells**, **Number**, **Category**, **Currency**, select: symbol to use
Date, adding	From the **View** menu, select: **Header and Footer** Click: **Custom Header** Click: where you want the date to appear Click: the 📅 **Date** button			
Date, formatting			**Format cells**, **Category**, **Date**, **Type**	**Format**, **Cells**, **Category**, **Date**, **Type**
Decimal places		Click: the **Increase Decimal** button to increase the number of decimal places Click: the **Decrease Decimal** button to decrease the number of decimal places	**Format Cells** Select the **Number** tab Click: **Number** in the **Category:** menu Select the number of decimal places you need	**Format**, **Cells**
Enter text	Click: in the cell where you want text to appear Key in: the text Press: **Enter**			
Enter numeric data	Click: in the cell where you want text to appear Key in: the data Press: **Enter**			

Action	Keyboard	Mouse	Right–mouse menu	Menu
Enter formulae	Click: in the cell where you want text to appear Key in: **=** followed by the formula Press: **Enter**			
Exit the program		Click: the ❎ **Close** button		**F**ile, E**x**it
Find and Replace				**E**dit, **Replace**
Fit to page				**F**ile, **Page Set**u**p**, **F**it to (1) **Page**
Formulae, functions	Click on the cell where the result is required			
	Use: **=SUM(cell ref:cell ref)** for adding a range of cells or Click: Σ **AutoSum** button Click and drag over the cell range Press: **Enter**			
	Use: **=AVERAGE(cell ref:cell ref)** to find the average value in a range of cells			
	Use: **=COUNT(cell ref:cell ref)** to count the number of cells in range			
	Use: **=MIN(cell ref:cell ref)** to find minimum value in range			
	Use: **=MAX(cell ref:cell ref)** to find maximum value in range			
	Use: **=IF(test,"value if true", "value if false")** to return a value for the given test			
Formulae, operators	**+** add **-** subtract ***** multiply **/** divide			
Formulae, showing	**Ctrl + `**			**Tools**, **Options**, **View** Under **Window options**, select **Formulas** so that a tick appears
Formulae, printing	Ensure the formulae are showing			
				File, **Page Set**u**p**, **Page** tab, **Landscape** or **F**ile, **Page Set**u**p**, **Page** tab Under **Scaling**, select **F**it to 1 **page wide** and **1 page tall**
Freeze/Unfreeze				**W**indow, **F**reeze/Unfreeze **Panes**

Action	Keyboard	Mouse	Right-mouse menu	Menu
Gridlines, turn on/off				**File**, **Page Setup**, **Sheet**, **Gridlines**
Headers/Footers				**View**, **Header and Footer**
Help	**F1**			**Help**, **Microsoft Excel Help**
	Shift + F1			**Help**, **What's This?**
Hide columns	**Ctrl + 0**		**Hide**	**Format**, **Column**, **Hide**
Hide rows			**Hide**	**Format**, **Row**, **Hide**
Integers (whole numbers)		Click: the .00 +.0 **Decrease Decimal** button until you have reduced the number of decimal places to zero	**Format Cells** Select the **Number** tab Click: **Number** in the **Category** menu Change the number of decimal places to zero	**Format**, **Cells**
Moving around	Use the cursor keys	Click where you want to move to		
Move to top of document	**Ctrl + Home**			
Move to end of document	**Ctrl + End**			
New file	**Ctrl + N**	Click: the ▢ **New** button		**File**, **New**
Open an existing file	**Ctrl + O**	Click: the 📂 **Open** button		**File**, **Open**
	Select: the drive required Select: the filename Click: **Open**			
Orientation of cell content				**Format**, **Cells**, **Alignment**, **Orientation**
Page number, adding	From the **View** menu, select: **Header and Footer** Click: **Custom Header** Click: where you want the page number to appear Click: the ▢ **Page** button			
Page Setup	From the **File** menu, select: **Page Setup** Choose from **Margins**, **Paper Size**, **Paper Source**, **Layout**			

Action	Keyboard	Mouse	Right–mouse menu	Menu
Percentages, numbers as		Click: the **% Percent Style** button		
Preferences, set default folder				**Tools**, **Options**, **General**
set user name				**As above** _or_ **File**, **Properties**, **Summary**
Print file	**Ctrl + P** Select the options you need Press: **Enter**	Click: the **Print** button		**File**, **Print** Select the options you need and click: **OK**
Print, gridlines				**File**, **Page Setup**, **Sheet**, **Gridlines**
Print, title row on every page				**File**, **Page Setup**, **Sheet**, **Print titles**
Print, orientation	From the **File** menu, select: **Page Setup** Click: the **Page** tab Select: **Landscape** Click: **OK**			
Print, selected cells only	Select the cells to print			
	Ctrl + P			**File**, **Print**
	Select: **Selection** Click: **OK**			
Print Preview		Click: the **Print Preview** button		**File**, **Print Preview**
Remove text emphasis	Select text to be changed			
	Ctrl + B (remove bold) **Ctrl + I** (remove italics) **Ctrl + U** (remove underline)	Click: the appropriate button: **B** _I_ **U**	**Format Cells**	**Format**, **Cells** Select the **Font** tab Click: **Regular** in the **Font Style:** menu
Replicate (copy) formulae	Select: the cell with the formula to be copied Drag the mouse from the bottom right corner of the cell over the cells to copy to Release mouse			
Restore deleted input	**Ctrl + Z**	Click: the **Undo** button		**Edit**, **Undo**
Rows, adding	Select the row by clicking in the row ref box (at side of row) where you want the new row to appear			
			Insert	**Insert**, **Rows**
Rows, deleting	Select the row by clicking in the row ref box (at side of row) that you want to delete			
			Delete	**Edit**, **Delete**

Action	Keyboard	Mouse	Right-mouse menu	Menu
Save	**Ctrl + S**	Click: the 🖫 **Save** button		**File**, **Save**
	If you have not already saved the file you will be prompted to specify the directory and to name the file If you have already done this, then Excel will automatically save it			
Save using a different name or to a different directory				**File**, **Save As**
	Select the appropriate drive and change the filename if relevant Click: **Save**			
Save file in a different file format	Save as above, select from **Save as type**			
Selecting cells Selecting adjacent cells Selecting non-adjacent cells Remove selection	Click and drag across cells Click and drag across cells Select the first cell(s), hold down **Ctrl** and click the others Click in any white space			
Sheets, adding changing				**Insert**, **Worksheet**
	Click on appropriate sheet tab			
copying		Use **Copy** and **Paste** buttons	Right-click on sheet tab. Select: **Move or Copy**. In the **Before sheet** section, select appropriate sheet. Ensure **Create a copy** is ticked. Click: **OK**	
deleting			Right-click on Sheet tab. Select: **Delete**	
renaming			Right-click on sheet tab. Select: **Rename**	
Sorting data	Select cells in the range to sort			
		Click: the ⬇ **Ascending** or the ⬆ **Descending** button		
Spell check	Move cursor to top of document			
	F7	Click: the ✓ **Spelling** button		**Tools**, **Spelling**
Text formatting:	Select cell(s) to format			
font, size, colour, italicise, embolden, orientation	**Ctrl + B** Embolden **Ctrl + I** Italicise **Ctrl + U** Underline	Click: the relevant toolbar button on the formatting toolbar	**Format Cells**, **Font** tab For orientation: **Alignment** tab	**Format**, **Cells**, **Font** tab For orientation: **Alignment** tab
Toolbar, modify				**View**, **Toolbars**, **Customize**
Undo	**Ctrl + Z**	Click: the ↰ **Undo** button		**Edit**, **Undo**

Action	Keyboard	Mouse	Right-mouse menu	Menu
Unhide columns	Select the columns on either side of the hidden ones			
	Ctrl + Shift + 0		**U**nhide	**F**ormat, **C**olumn, **U**nhide
Unhide rows	Select the rows on either side of the hidden ones			
			Unhide	**F**ormat, **R**ow, **U**nhide
Wrap cell content				**F**ormat, C**e**lls, **Alignment**, **Wrap text**
Zoom		Click: the 100% ▼ **Zoom** button		**V**iew, **Z**oom

Charts using Excel quick reference

(The following is a list of generally useful tasks associated with this module. For more information on specific items, refer to the module content.)

Action	Keyboard	Mouse	Right-mouse menu	Menu
Change graphical display	*To change the scale ratios:* With the graph on screen Select: the **Plot Area** Drag the corner handles inwards (to reduce the scale) and outwards (to increase the scale) *To set upper and lower limits for y (vertical) axis:* With the graph on screen Double-click: the **Value Axis** In the **Format Axis** dialogue box: Click: the **Scale** tab Key in: the new values in the **Maximum** and **Minimum** boxes Click: **OK** *To set intermediate values:* With the graph on screen Double-click: the **Value Axis** In the **Format Axis** dialogue box: Click: the **Scale** tab Change the **Major** unit to the required value Click: **Close**			
Create a chart	Select the data to chart			
		Click: the █ **Chart Wizard** button		**Insert**, **Chart**

Action	Keyboard	Mouse	Right–mouse menu	Menu
	STEP 1	Select: the chart type Click: **Next**		
	STEP 2	Check that the source data is correct, if not change it Click: **Next**		
	STEP 3	Select: the **Titles** tab Key in the title Select: the **Legend** tab Click in: the **Category Name** box to add/remove tick as appropriate *(For pie charts only)* Select: the **Data Labels** tab Click: **Show label** if appropriate Click: **Next**		
	STEP 4	Click: **As new sheet** or **As object in** Key in: the chart name Click: **Finish**		
Delete a chart	Select the chart. Press: **Delete**			
Edit a chart			Right-click on the chart. Select from options	
Move a chart	Select the chart. Use **Cut** and **Paste** buttons or drag and drop to new location			
Print a chart	With the chart displayed on screen			
	Ctrl + P Ensure **Active sheet** is selected. Click: **OK**	Click: the 🖨 **Print** button (this will automatically print the sheet)		**File**, **Print** Ensure **Active sheet** is selected. Click: **OK**
Resize a chart		Select the chart and drag its handles		
Save a chart	**Ctrl + S**	Click: the 💾 **Save** button		**File**, **Save**
Sheets, changing	Click on appropriate sheet tab			

Note: For the following tasks you will need the files **Part time** and **Part time pay 2003**.

Scenario

You work as an administrator in the accounting department of a large company. You have been asked to complete and amend a spreadsheet that displays and calculates payments for part-time staff. You also need to create a chart from the data contained in the amended file. The manager has asked you to work on another spreadsheet so that it is ready to insert final monthly totals for part-time employees. She wants to use this data in her calendar-year report.

The company has international customers and you have been advised that it would be a good idea to prepare a currency conversions spreadsheet for future reference. This will be used for working out pricing for goods for the countries that you export to.

Task 1

1   Open the spreadsheet file **Part time**.

2   Save the spreadsheet as **(your initials) pay**.

3   Enter your name in the upper left corner of the spreadsheet.

4   Add a header with the text centred **Updated by (your name)**.

5   Add a footer with a centred automatic date and automatic time at the right.

6   Wrap the headings, ie **Surname**, **First name**....

7   Format all dates in the **Date started** column to DD-MMM-YY, eg 10-Mar-02.

8   Insert a column headed **Weekend rate** in between the columns **Hourly rate** and **Weekend hours**.

9   Sort the data in alphabetical order of **Surname**.

10 Change the hourly rate for Ruby Davis to 8.10.

11 Use search and replace to replace all entries of 6.00 with 6.25.

12 Create a formula to calculate the Weekend rate for each employee:

    Weekend rate is 25% more than hourly rate
    Formula = 125/100*Hourly rate

13 Create a formula to calculate Hourly rate total **Hourly rate * weekly hours**.

14 Create a formula to calculate Weekend total **Weekend rate * Weekend hours**.

15 Create a formula to calculate Total pay due for each employee: **Hourly rate total + Weekend total**.

16 Format all columns with monetary amounts to £ currency, 2 decimal places.

17 Add a title row with the text **Part time staff payments** centred across the columns.

18 Italicise the title and change the font size so that it is 2 pts larger than the rest of the spreadsheet.

19 Add a row at the bottom with the heading **Total p/t pa due**.

20 In the cell below the new heading, enter a formula to calculate the Total p/t pay. Use *SUM*. Add a double underline to this cell.

21 Change the Surname column width to 16.

22 Embolden the column headings.

23 Put a border around the whole table and between each cell.

24 Save the spreadsheet as **(your initials) pay1**.

25 Print with landscape orientation with gridlines and the column and row headings displayed.

Task 2

1 Working with the **(your initials) pay1** file, create a 3-D column chart on the same sheet to show the Total pay due for each part-time employee (display a surname only).

2 Use the title **Part time Pay**.

3 Resize and move the chart so that it does not obscure any spreadsheet data.

4 Reduce the font size of the names on the *x* axis so that all names are displayed.

5 Insert a new sheet in the same workbook with the name **PT Pay Bar**.

6 Copy the chart to the **PT Pay Bar** sheet.

7 Print the **PT Pay Bar** sheet only.

8 Delete the chart from the original sheet and print the original sheet only.

9 Save the spreadsheet as **PTchart**.

Task 3

1 Open the spreadsheet **(your initials)pay1** saved in Task 1.

2 Insert a column before the **Total Pay due** column with the heading **Bonus1 due**.

3 In a cell at the bottom of the spreadsheet enter the text **2003 Bonus Pay**.

4 In the cell directly below the **2003 Bonus Pay** entry, enter **Bonus1**.

5 In the cell to the right of **Bonus1**, enter **Bonus2**.

6 Centre the **2003 Bonus Pay** heading across the **Bonus1** and **Bonus2** cells.

7 In the **Bonus1** column, enter the Bonus figure of 75.

8 In the **Bonus2** column, enter the Bonus figure of 50.

9 In the **Bonus1 due** column, use the *IF* statement to display whether a bonus1 payment is due. A bonus is due if the employee has an hourly rate of less than 6.50. If a bonus is due display **Yes**, otherwise display **No**.

10 Insert a new column to the right of the **Bonus1 due** column headed **Bonus2 due**.

Note: All part-time staff are automatically paid Bonus2.

11 In the **Bonus2 due** column enter a formula to calculate the Total pay due plus the bonus2. Use an absolute cell reference for the bonus2 value cell.

12 Insert two new rows under the title heading **Part time staff payments**.

13 Give the first new row the heading **Max** and the second new row **Min**.

14 Create a formula for each of these rows to display the maximum and minimum in the **Total Pay due** column.

15 Shade the **Max** and **Min** cell headings in light blue and set to Times New Roman, bold, 12 pt.

16 Copy the formatting from the **Max** and **Min** cells to the cell containing the text **2003 Bonus Pay**.

17 Change the spreadsheet margins to: left and right at 1 cm; top and bottom at 4 cm.

18 Print to fit one page in landscape display.

19 Save the spreadsheet file with the name **pay plus**.

20 Print a copy of the spreadsheet (fit to one page) displaying the formulae in full.

21 Close the spreadsheet file.

Task 4

1   Open the spreadsheet **Part time pay 2003**.

2   Autofill the date row so that all months of the year are displayed. (Widen the cells as necessary.)

3   In a cell in column A at the bottom of the spreadsheet, enter the text **No of employees**. Wrap the text and widen so that the word **employees** is not split.

4   In the cell directly below the **No of employees** cell, use the Count function to calculate the number of employees in the spreadsheet.

5   Freeze the row containing the Employee Ref and months headings.

6   Print the spreadsheet in landscape display ensuring that the months row appears on each sheet.

7   Save the spreadsheet file as **(your initials) 2003**.

8   Close the file.

Task 5

Create a spreadsheet to calculate currency exchanges.

1   Set up the following spreadsheet:

Your Pound Sterling Buys

No of pounds for exchange		1,100	
Country	Currency	Exchange rate	Exchange result
France (Euro)	Euro	1.45	formula
Sweden (Kr)	Kr	13.37	formula
US ($)	$	1.67	formula

2   Save the spreadsheet as **(your initials) exchange**.

3   In the **Exchange result** column, enter a formula to convert the currency (use an absolute cell reference for the pounds for conversion).

4   Format all figures in the **Exchange result** column to the appropriate currency format.

5   Centre the title **Your Pound Sterling Buys** across the spreadsheet.

6   Embolden all row headings and increase the font size of these headings by 4 pts.

7   Set the width of the Currency column to 12.

8   Insert a new row below the Sweden row with the following data:

    Belgium (Euro), Euro, 1.45

9   Add a line at the top of the spreadsheet and a line under the bottom cells.

10 Sort in ascending order of Country.

11 Save the spreadsheet as **(your initials) exchange1** and print.

Task 6

1   Create a new spreadsheet file with the filename **Convert**.

2   Copy the spreadsheet saved in Task 5, Step 11, to the new spreadsheet file (workbook).

3   Delete the **France** row.

4   Insert a footer with the text **Converted by (your initials)** on the right.

5   Create an exploded pie chart on a new sheet in the **Convert** workbook showing the Countries and Results of exchange.

6   Include a legend for the countries and include data label values.

7   Title the chart **Exchange results on 1,100 GBP**.

8   Save all documents and print both sheets in the **Convert** file.

    Note: These are only practice tasks. Successful completion does not imply certification of the module by the ECDL Foundation.

Database

In this section you will practise and learn how to:

- open Access
- use Help functions
- modify the toolbar
- change viewing modes
- create a new database
- create a table
- enter data

- define a primary key
- set up an index
- modify table layout attributes
- add records
- modify field attributes
- save a database
- close a database

1.1 Understanding Access basics

A database is a program that allows you to store data in an organised record format. It is sometimes known as an 'electronic filing system'. It is structured to search, retrieve and sort data rapidly and in many different ways. Databases can be saved to disk and printed. They are much faster than a manual paper card-index system and require less office space.

Access is a very powerful database application with numerous features. We will be using only those features necessary to create simple databases and to edit, sort, search and print them. Since Access is quite complicated for the new user, we will start by creating and manipulating a very small database in order to concentrate on understanding the processes involved, without the difficulties of keying in lots of data. Different aspects of Access will be explained as and when we meet them.

Common database terms that are general to all types of database applications include:

Table: A table is a collection of related records.

Record: Each collection of information for each item in a file is called a record.

Field: A record is divided into separate categories, known as fields. There are different types of field. The common ones are:

Alphabetic (in Access called TEXT) fields. These contain text that is manipulated alphabetically.

Numeric (in Access called NUMBER) fields. These recognise numbers and sort in ascending or descending numerical order. In Access CURRENCY and DATE/TIME fields can also be used as number fields where appropriate.

Alphanumeric (in Access called TEXT) fields. These contain numbers and text that do not need to be sorted in number order – telephone numbers for example.

An Access database file contains database objects. We will be using four database objects – Tables, Queries, Reports and Forms. We will meet all the above terms as we progress through this module.

1.2 Creating a new database

Exercise 1

You organise your company's outdoor activities for staff and need to set up a database of activities. Set up a database file using the following field titles:

ACTIVITY	the name of the activity
LOCATION	the location of the activity
DAY	the day the activity takes place
DURATION (WKS)	the number of weeks the activity runs
INSTRUCTOR	the instructor's name

Info

There are five fields in each record of this database file – four text fields, **ACTIVITY**, **LOCATION**, **DAY** and **INSTRUCTOR** and one numeric field **DURATION (WKS)**.

Exercise

Enter the details shown below:

ACTIVITY	LOCATION	DAY	INSTRUCTOR	DURATION (WKS)
HANG GLIDING	FERN DOWNS	SATURDAY	MIKE	12
DIVING	BLUE BEACH	WEDNESDAY	SARA	5
SAILING	BLUE BEACH	THURSDAY	LYNDSEY	20
CANOEING	NORSE BRIDGE	SATURDAY	DYLAN	10
CLIMBING	CHA GORGE	SUNDAY	LEIGH	20
CYCLING	BRIARSWOOD	TUESDAY	LYNDSEY	12

Each row of data (above), excluding field headings, makes up one record. Therefore there will be six records in this database file.

Info

When entering data, you can use codes instead of the full entry. For instance, in the **DAY** field, the codes **M**, **TU**, **W**, **TH** and **F** would be suitable codes for days of the week. This can save time and storage space. Since this database is small we will create it without codes.

Exercise 2

Load Access.

Method

Load Access in the same way as loading other Office applications, this time selecting:

Microsoft Access from the **Start**, **All Programs** menu *or* use the Access shortcut icon if you have one.

The Access window appears.

Info

You will notice that there are many similarities with other Office application windows, for example: Title Bar, Menu Bar and Standard toolbar. Other toolbar buttons will be displayed automatically to reflect the current task as you work through different components of the database. It is worth examining the toolbar buttons as you work through the exercises so that you become acquainted with them. As in other Office applications, you can customise the toolbars to your own preferences by selecting **Toolbars** from the **View** menu. Similarly, help is accessed from the **Help** menu or by pressing **F1**.

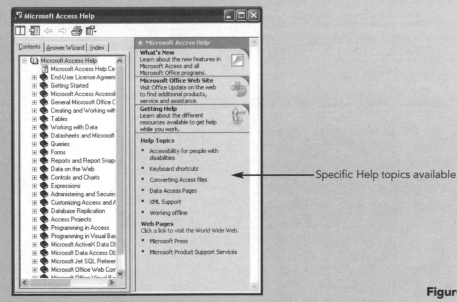

Specific Help topics available

Figure 5.1 Accessing Help

Toolbars

1 From the **View** menu, select: **Toolbars**, then **Customize**.
2 Click on: the **Options** tab.
3 Make selections.
4 Click on: **Close**.

You can choose to have more toolbars visible by selecting: **Toolbars** from the **View** menu and then selecting the toolbar to display. Ticks appear next to the currently displayed toolbars. The content of your work will dictate which ones are useful to you.

Help

Note: Throughout this book, the Office Assistant facility has been hidden so as not to distract from the main objectives. More details of the Office Assistant are found in the Appendix. You can select:

- The **Contents** tab for a list of Help topics. By double-clicking on a topic, a display of that topic will appear.
- The **Answer Wizard** tab. This allows you to key in a question and then click on: **Search**. The topic will then be highlighted in the contents list and the topic displayed as above.
- The **Index** tab. This allows you to key in key words and click on: **Search**. Again, the topic will be highlighted and displayed as above.

To close the Help window, click on: the **Close** button.

ScreenTips

From the **Help** menu, select: **What's This?** Then click on the item you want to know about. A short description appears. Press: **Esc** to remove the ScreenTip.

Accessing Help in a dialogue box

To access Help in a dialogue box, click on: the **Help** button in the dialogue box and then click on the item you want help about.

1.4 Creating a new database

Method

On loading Access, the Task Pane also appears (Figure 5.2).

Note: If the Task Pane does not display, from the **View** menu, select: **Toolbars**, **Task Pane**.

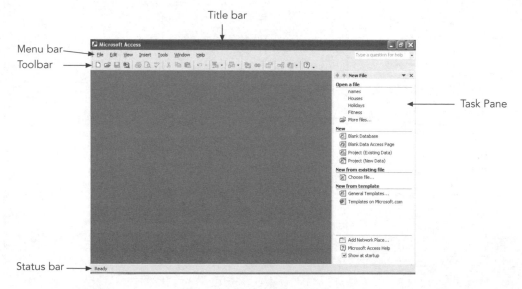

Figure 5.2 The Access window and opening task pane

1 In the Task Pane, **New** section, click on: **Blank Database** in order to create a new one.
2 The File New Database dialogue box is shown (Figure 5.3).

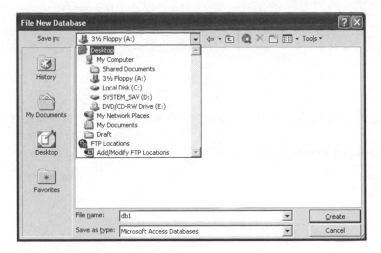

Figure 5.3 The File New Database dialogue box

3 Choose where your file will be located and then key in the filename: **ACTIVITIES**.
4 Click on: **Create**. The **ACTIVITIES: Database** window is shown (Figure 5.4).

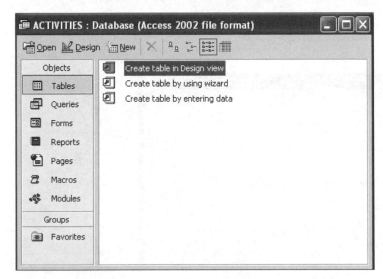

Figure 5.4 ACTIVITIES: database window

> **Info**
>
> Access 2002 may, by default, save files in Access 2000 format (see ACTIVITIES: Database title bar where the version number is displayed). Access 2000 files can be opened in Access 2000 and in Access 2002. Access 2002 files can only be opened in Access 2002. To change the format, from the Tools menu, select: **Options**, **Advanced** tab, **Default File Format**. Click on: **OK**.

> **Info**
>
> The overall database filename is **ACTIVITIES**. There are several different objects that we will be creating and storing within this database file. They are all accessed using the buttons in the **Objects** list. The ones that we will be working with are:
>
> *Tables*: Used to store data in rows and columns.
>
> *Queries*: Used when extracting data from tables.
>
> *Reports*: Used when printouts are required. You can print tables but have limited design options. Reports can be designed for your individual requirements.
>
> *Forms*: Provide a convenient way to view individual records since they can display one record at a time. They do not store data but use the data stored in tables.

Method

1   The **Tables** button is chosen by default (it looks as if it has been pressed in); if not, click it to choose it.
2   Double-click on: **Create table in Design view** (Figure 5.5).

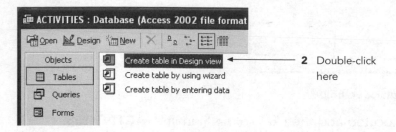

Figure 5.5 Creating a table in Design view

3   The **Table** window in Design view is shown (Figure 5.6).

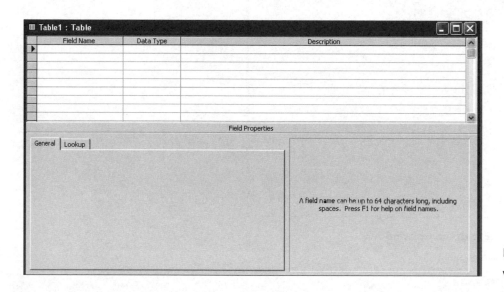

Figure 5.6 The Table window in Design view

Exercise 3

Define the fields in the table.

Method

1   In the **Field Name** column, with the **Caps Lock** on, key in the name of the first field, **ACTIVITY** and press: **Enter** to move to the next column.
2   In the **Data Type** column, keep the default **Text** as this column will contain text entries, ie names of activities. Press: **Enter**.
3   In the **Description** column, you can type a description of the information this field will contain. This is optional, so leave it blank in this case and press: **Enter**.

Repeat steps 1–3 for the other fields except:

Choose Text as the Data Type for **LOCATION**, **DAY** and **INSTRUCTOR**, but **DURATION (WKS)** is a numeric field, ie it contains numbers, therefore choose **Number** as the Data Type. To do this:

In the **Data Type** column, next to the Field Name **DURATION (WKS)**, click in: the **Data Type** box; a down arrow appears. Click on: the down arrow and click on: **Number** (Figure 5.7).

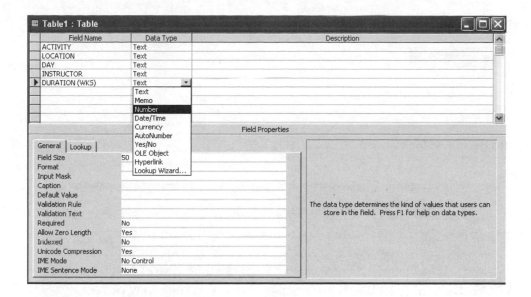

Figure 5.7 Changing the Data Type

Data types

> **Info**
>
> In addition to Text and Number there are other Data Types, as displayed on the drop-down list in Figure 5.7. These are summarised in the table at the end of this exercise.

The Field Properties can then be altered to choose the field size of the number that is required (Figure 5.8).

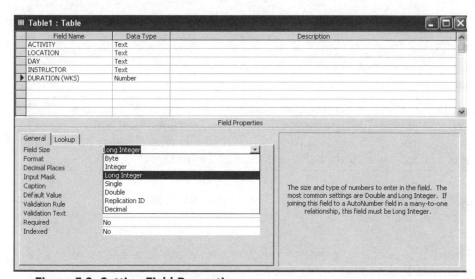

Figure 5.8 Setting Field Properties

1 With the cursor in the **DURATION** field, Data Type Number, in the **Field Properties** section, click in: the box where **Long Integer** (the default) is displayed; a down arrow appears.

2 Click on the down arrow to see the options available.

The options we will use in this module are:

Long integer (integer means a whole number – ie no decimal places).

Double (this allows decimal places).

In this case (as we do not require decimal places) we will leave the Field Size as Long Integer.

3 Click on: **Long Integer**.

The Table design should look like Figure 5.9.

Figure 5.9 The Table design should look like this

Info

In the **Field Properties** section, the field size for text entries is set at 50 characters. This will accommodate most entries and can be left as it is. Should you be very short of storage space (this is unlikely in this instance), then you could save some space by reducing the field sizes as appropriate. It is important that you are careful when altering field sizes in a table. If they are reduced, original entries may not be able to display in full and data may be lost.

If you make a mistake when keying in, you can always go back and make corrections or use the **Undo** button.

Info

If you missed out a field, see section 2 or the quick reference at the end of this chapter for the method to insert it.

Info

Data types

The exercises in this book enable you to practise working with different data types. Note the types and their properties:

Data type	Properties
Text (the default)	The default is 50. There is no need to change this unless requested or short of storage space. *Note*: In the unusual circumstance that your records have more than 50 characters, then this field would need to be changed accordingly so that the entries can be entered in full.
Number	*Field size* Long Integer is the default – this is OK for whole numbers. Double – for numbers with decimal places. *Format* Choose **Fixed** for 2 decimal places to show (even if the last is a zero). Choose **Decimal Places** and enter the number required. (Leave the Format blank for other numbers.)
Date/Time	Choose the most appropriate format for the task. (When entering records in a database, you can key in the date in any format and Access will convert it to the format you have set.)
Currency	Choose **Format Fixed** to display 2 decimal places with no commas or £ symbol.
Yes/No	No need to set.
Memo	No need to set.

Method

1 From **File** menu, select: **Save As** (Figure 5.10).

Figure 5.10 Saving a Table

2 The Save As dialogue box appears (Figure 5.11).
3 Key in: the Table name **OUTDOOR**.
4 Click on: **OK**.

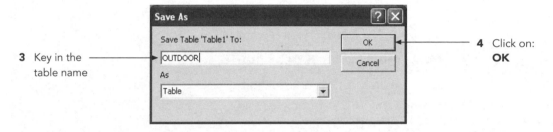

3 Key in the table name

4 Click on: **OK**

Figure 5.11 The Save As dialogue box

A message is displayed as shown in Figure 5.12.

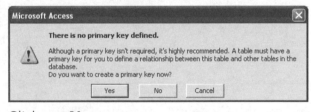

Figure 5.12 Primary Key message

5 Click on: **No**.

Info

Primary keys and indexes

A Primary Key is not essential. It is a field that uniquely identifies each record in a table. Examples of this type of field would be car registration numbers or unique part numbers. In some databases, there is no field that can be guaranteed not to duplicate an entry. In such cases, at the Save stage, Access can create a Primary Key by setting up a field called ID and allocating a number to each record.

Setting a primary key on a specific field

In Table Design view, select the field you want for the primary key and then click on the **Primary Key** button. The 🔑 **primary key** icon appears to the left of the chosen field as shown:

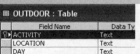

To change the Primary Key

Follow the instructions above again, selecting the new field. Primary Keys speed up data retrieval and are useful when working with large databases or multiple databases. Fields that have a primary key allocated are automatically indexed. With large databases, indexing fields that you often sort and search is another way of speeding up data retrieval. To set up an index:

1   With the table in Design view, position the cursor in the field that you want to index.

2   In the **Field Properties** section, and in the **Indexed** section, select: **Yes(Duplicates OK)** or **Yes(No Duplicates)**, depending on whether the indexed field entries are unique; eg car registration numbers set to **Yes(No Duplicates)**, surnames set to **Yes(Duplicates OK)**. Repeat with any other fields that you want to index.

3   Save the changes to the table design when prompted.

To delete an index

In Table Design view set the Indexed field property to **No**.

To view a list of indexed fields on an existing database:

With the table in Design view, click on: the ⚡ **Indexes** button.

To remove a Primary Key and not set a new one

1   Click on: the ⚡ **Indexes** button. The Indexes dialogue box appears.

2   Select: No from the **Primary** menu.

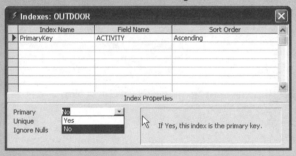

6   Close the database design window by clicking on: the **Close** button (Figure 5.13).

6 Click here to close this design window

Figure 5.13 Closing the Design Window

Info

If you have not remembered to save your design, you cannot exit Design view without being prompted to save.

Should you need to make any changes to the design, click on: the 📐 Design **Design** button, make the changes and resave, this time using the quick method by clicking on: the 💾 **Save** button.

7   You are returned to the **ACTIVITIES: Database** window.

Enter the data.

Method

1 Click on: the **Tables** button, if not already selected

2 Double-click on: **OUTDOOR**

Figure 5.14 Opening a Table

3 The Table window appears (Figure 5.15). The table is now displayed in Datasheet view so that you can enter and manipulate data.

Field names

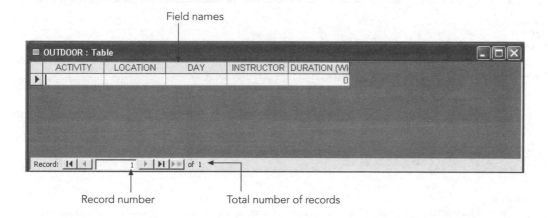

Record number

Total number of records

Figure 5.15 CLASSES table ready for data entry

4 As you can see, the **DURATION (WKS)** field heading does not display in full. Widen this column by dragging the mouse, as shown in Figure 5.16.

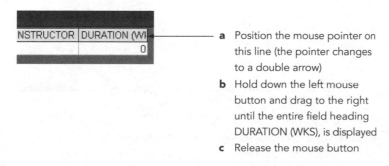

a Position the mouse pointer on this line (the pointer changes to a double arrow)

b Hold down the left mouse button and drag to the right until the entire field heading DURATION (WKS), is displayed

c Release the mouse button

Figure 5.16 Widening columns

Note: To widen the column, you can also double-click where shown in Figure 5.16.

5   Key in the data (section 1.2) in the appropriate fields as shown (Figure 5.17), pressing **Enter**, **Tab** or arrow keys to move from field to field.

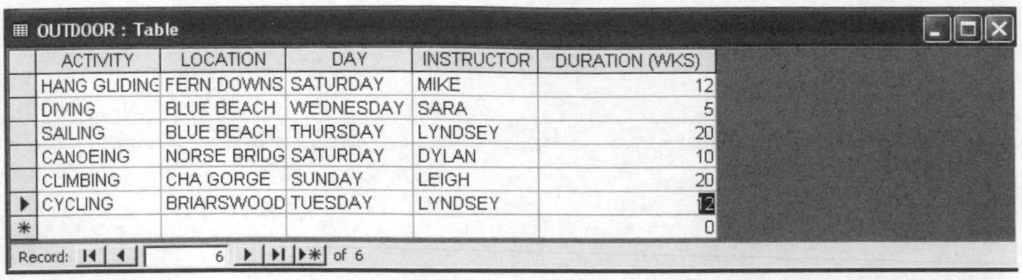

OUTDOOR : Table

ACTIVITY	LOCATION	DAY	INSTRUCTOR	DURATION (WKS)
HANG GLIDING	FERN DOWNS	SATURDAY	MIKE	12
DIVING	BLUE BEACH	WEDNESDAY	SARA	5
SAILING	BLUE BEACH	THURSDAY	LYNDSEY	20
CANOEING	NORSE BRIDG	SATURDAY	DYLAN	10
CLIMBING	CHA GORGE	SUNDAY	LEIGH	20
CYCLING	BRIARSWOOD	TUESDAY	LYNDSEY	12
				0

Record: 6 of 6

Figure 5.17 Data has been keyed in

6   You can see that **HANG GLIDING** and **NORSE BRIDGE** are too long to display in full in the **ACTIVITY** and **LOCATION** field columns; widen these columns as shown in Figure 5.16.
7   Proofread on screen against copy.
8   Correct any errors by clicking to position the cursor on the error, then correct as necessary.

1.8   Saving data and closing the table

Exercise 5

Save the data and close the table.

Method

1   Click on: the **Close** button at the top right of the Table window.
2   The data is saved automatically.
3   If you have made any layout changes, you will be asked if you want to save these; click on: **Yes**.

1.9   Saving the database file

Exercise 6

Save the database file **ACTIVITIES**.

Method

From the **File** menu, select: **Close**.

Info

The database file and its components are automatically saved together. Each individual part, such as the table **OUTDOOR**, has been saved as we have progressed through the exercises. If any parts are not saved, you will be prompted to save before closing.

1.10 Exiting Access

Exercise 7

Exit Access.

Method

From the **File** menu, select: **Exit**.

Practice 1

1 Start up Access.

2 Set up the following database with the filename **salon**.

3 Set the Field **REF NO** to be the primary key.

4 Save the table as **Clients**.

Note: The **TIME** and **PREVIOUS VISITS** should be numeric fields. (Use Date/Time for the **TIME** Field Data Type: Field Properties Format: Short Time.)

Info

To repeat data as in the Stylist field

1 Key in the Stylist's name.
2 Select the name by double-clicking on it.
3 Click on: the **Copy** button.
4 Move to the cell you want to copy to.
5 Click on: the **Paste** button.
6 Move to the next cell to copy to.
7 Click on: the **Paste** button.
8 Repeat as appropriate.

5 Enter the following data:

STYLIST	CLIENT NAME	REF NO	DAY	TIME	PREVIOUS VISITS
BEN	LAURA	J120	WED	09:30	6
BEN	JANE	K345	TUE	12:00	10
BEN	HILARY	J900	SAT	16:00	4
BEN	DON	S559	FRI	13:45	10
CARA	JOHN	L912	SAT	09:00	12
CARA	SUSIE	A519	WED	10:30	0
CARA	DENNIS	J335	SAT	10:00	8
CARA	TONY	B222	FRI	17:45	12
SUSIE	HARRIET	K933	THU	11:00	12
SUSIE	PETER	P210	FRI	18:30	6
SUSIE	CHERIE	L018	SAT	09:30	0
SUSIE	PAUL	H777	SAT	11:00	6
SUSIE	MIKE	J666	WED	15:00	2
BRYONY	ANGIE	L123	WED	10:00	6
BRYONY	JULIE	K572	WED	11:00	6
BRYONY	STEWART	K999	SAT	12:00	10
BRYONY	GEORGE	K909	THU	16:00	10

6 Close the database file and exit Access.

Practice 2

1 Start up Access.

2 Set up the following database file with the filename **Centres**.

4 Save the table as **Details**.

Note: The PRICE and NO OF ROOMS should be numeric fields. Use Currency for the PRICE Field Data Type: Field Properties Format: Fixed.

REGION	TYPE	TOWN	NAME	PRICE	NO OF ROOMS
EAST	COUNTRY HOTEL	NORWICH	MILL MANOR	80.50	15
EAST	BUSINESS CENTRE	CAMBRIDGE	DEAN COURT	98.00	70
EAST	MOTEL	IPSWICH	THE WINDSOR	40.00	55
EAST	COUNTRY HOTEL	PETERBOROUGH	THE BEAUMONT	65.50	25
SOUTH	COUNTRY CLUB	SOUTHAMPTON	RIVERSIDE	120.00	30
SOUTH	BUSINESS CENTRE	LONDON	ECOMMERCE	130.50	106
SOUTH	COUNTRY CLUB	BOURNEMOUTH	SOUTH LAWN	129.99	12
SOUTH	MOTEL	WINCHESTER	THE ALEXANDRA	60.50	44
SOUTH	MOTEL	MAIDSTONE	BON ACCORD	65.99	15
WEST	BUSINESS CENTRE	EXETER	ROOKERY HALL	130.75	75
WEST	COUNTRY CLUB	PLYMOUTH	HEMSLEY HALL	110.50	25
WEST	COUNTRY CLUB	FALMOUTH	THE ACADEMY	65.00	40
NORTH	COUNTRY CLUB	LEEDS	GREEN MAN	75.50	25
NORTH	COUNTRY CLUB	YORK	THE BALMORAL	65.50	26

5 Close the database file.

In this section you will practise and learn how to:

- open an existing database
- print data in table format
- navigate through a table
- modify data
- delete data
- delete/insert records

- add/delete a field
- change field order
- set validation rules and validation text
- set print orientation, page size, print range

2.1 Opening an existing database

Exercise 1

Load Access and the database file **ACTIVITIES** created in the previous section.

Method

Load Access (see section 1). Follow the instructions in Figure 5.18.

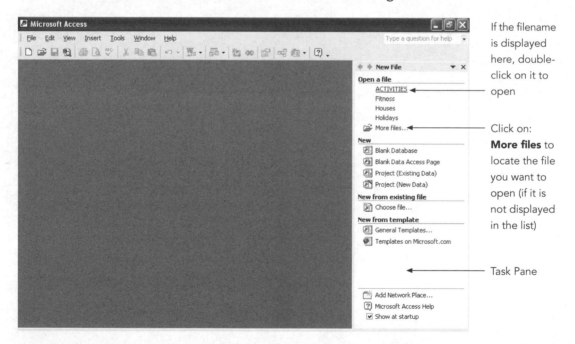

Figure 5.18 Opening an existing database file

Info

The most recently used files will display in the task pane. If you do not see the file ACTIVITIES, click on: **More Files** to locate your file.

2.2 Printing data in table format

Exercise 2

Print the table **OUTDOOR**.

Method

1 Open the table **OUTDOOR**.
2 In the Database window, ensure that the **Tables** tab is selected; if not, select it.
3 Double-click on: **OUTDOOR**.
4 From the **File** menu, select: **Print**.
5 The Print dialogue box appears; we do not need to change any settings.
6 Check that the printer is ready and loaded with paper.
7 Click on: **OK**.

Info

The printout will automatically print the name of the database object (in this case the table name) and the date at the top of the page. In order to ensure that the printout is as expected, use **Print Preview** (from the **File** menu or click on: the **Print Preview** button). The records may appear in a different order from how you keyed them in. You need not be concerned about this at this stage.

2.3 Editing data

Exercise 3

Some errors have been found with the data entered:

- **CYCLING** should be at **NORSE BRIDGE** not **BRIARSWOOD**.
- The **DURATION (WKS)** for **HANG GLIDING** should be **14** not **12**.

Make the necessary changes and reprint the table.

Method

1 Open the table **OUTDOOR** if it is not already open.
2 Alter the data by positioning the cursor in the place where you want to alter data, delete the incorrect data using the **Delete** key or the ←**Del** (Backspace) key and key in the correct data.
3 When all editing is complete close the table by clicking on: the **Close** button.

   The changes will be saved automatically.

Navigating through a table

Move through a table using the Tab or arrow keys. Move quickly to different records as shown below:

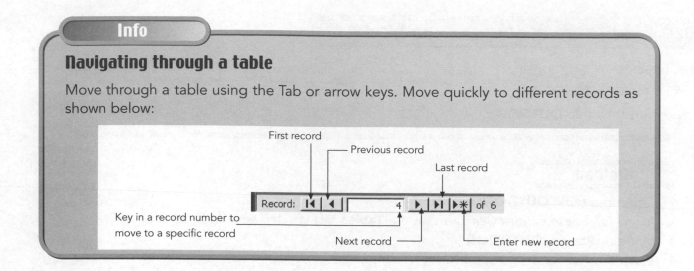

Deleting a record

Exercise 4

CLIMBING at **CHA GORGE** has been postponed. Delete all the details of this activity from the database.

Method

1 Open the table **OUTDOOR** if it is not already open.
2 Click on the row selection box to the far left of the record (Figure 5.19).

Click in this box to select the record CLIMBING

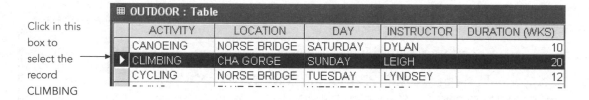

⊞ OUTDOOR : Table				
ACTIVITY	LOCATION	DAY	INSTRUCTOR	DURATION (WKS)
CANOEING	NORSE BRIDGE	SATURDAY	DYLAN	10
CLIMBING	CHA GORGE	SUNDAY	LEIGH	20
CYCLING	NORSE BRIDGE	TUESDAY	LYNDSEY	12

Figure 5.19 Selecting a record

3 An arrow appears in the box; the entire record is highlighted.
4 Right-click anywhere on the selection.
5 A pop-up menu appears (Figure 5.20).

Figure 5.20 Pop-up menu

6 Select: **Delete Record**.
7 You will be asked to confirm that you want to delete this record; click on: **Yes**.

2.5   Adding a record

Exercise 5

A new class is to be started. The class name is **SWIMMING**, it is to be on **FRIDAY** at **BLUE BEACH**, the instructor is **LYNDSEY** and it will run for **15** weeks. Add this record to the file.

Method

1   Open the table if it is not already open.
2   Move the cursor to the last (empty) row (Figure 5.21).

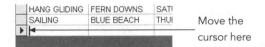

Move the cursor here

Figure 5.21 Adding a record

3   Key in the data in the appropriate fields, pressing **Enter** or **Tab** after each entry.
4   Proofread on screen.
5   Close the table by clicking on: the **Close** button of the Table window. Data is saved automatically.

2.6   Adding a field

Exercise 6

Add the field **STAFF** to the database between the **LOCATION** and **DAY** fields. Use the **Yes/No** data type with Yes = must be a member of staff and No = does not need to be a member, ie can be a guest of a member of staff, as follows:

CANOEING	**No**
CYCLING	**Yes**
DIVING	**No**
HANG GLIDING	**No**
SAILING	**No**
SWIMMING	**Yes**

Method

1   Open the table.
2   Change to Design view by clicking on: the ⊾ **View** button.
3   Position the cursor in the field under where you want to insert the new field, ie in the **DAY** field.
4   Click on: the ╡← **Insert Rows** button.
5   Key in the new field name **STAFF**.
6   Set the Data Type to **Yes/No**.
7   Set the Field Properties format to **Yes/No**.
8   Save changes to the table design.

9 Open the table in Datasheet view and enter the data; clicking in the box for **Yes**, leaving the box empty for **No**.

Info

Deleting a field

1 In Design view, position the cursor in the field to delete.
2 Click on: the ⇛ **Delete Rows** button.
3 You will be asked to confirm the delete.
4 Click on: **Yes**.

2.7 Changing field order

Exercise 7

Rearrange the fields so that the **DAY** field is positioned after the **INSTRUCTOR** field.

Method

1 With the table in Design view, click in the selection box of the title of the field to move, ie **DAY**.
2 Holding down the left mouse button in the selection box again, an arrow and a dotted box appear. Drag the field to the new location.
3 Save the changes to the table.

Info

You can also change field column order in a table in Datasheet view. Select: the column to move. Click and hold down: the mouse on the column heading, and drag to the required position. Release the mouse.

2.8 Adding validation rules to a field

Info

Validation rules

In addition to setting data types and properties, fields can be set up so that only certain entries are allowed. For example, if you are creating a database of items for sale in the price range of £500 or less, you can apply a validation rule to the price field so that an entry of greater than £500 is not allowed.

Exercise 8

Change the day for **DIVING** to **TUESDAY** not **WEDNESDAY**. Add a validation rule to the DAY field so that **WEDNESDAY** cannot be accepted by the database in this field. Add the validation text: **There are no activities on Wednesdays due to staff training.**

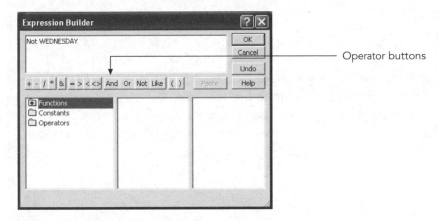

Method

1 Open the table **OUTDOOR** in Datasheet view. Make the amendment to the **DIVING** record.
2 Switch to Dcsign view and click in: the **DAY** field.
3 In the **Field Properties** section, click the cursor in the **Validation Rule** box (Figure 5.22).

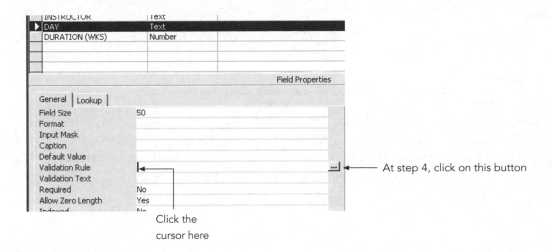

At step 4, click on this button

Click the
cursor here

Figure 5.22 Setting Validation Rules

4 Click on: the button next to the **Validation Rule** box (shown in Figure 5.22).
5 The Expression Builder box is displayed (Figure 5.23).

Operator buttons

Figure 5.23 Expression Builder box

6 Click on: the **Not** button so that **Not** appears in the top box.
7 Key in **WEDNESDAY** after **Not** (Figure 5.24).

Figure 5.24 Expression keyed in

8 Click on: **OK**.
9 The validation rule 'Not WEDNESDAY' is now displayed in the **Validation Rule** box.
10 Click in: the **Validation Text** box.
11 Key in: **There are no activities on Wednesdays due to staff training.**
12 Save the table design.
13 A message is displayed (Figure 5.25).

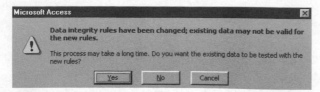

Figure 5.25 Access alert message

14 Click on: **Yes**.

It will now be impossible to enter WEDNESDAY in the DAY field. Have a try! Make up a record and enter it and see what happens.

2.9 Printing the table options

Exercise 9

Print the whole table on A4 size paper and in landscape orientation.

Method

Open the table and use **Page Setup**, **Page** tab to select paper size and orientation. Use **Print Preview** to check that fields display on one page and to determine when landscape orientation is appropriate.

Note the printing range options available in the Print box (Figure 5.26).

Figure 5.26 Print Range options

2.10   Close the database file and exit Access

Practice 3

1 Start up Access and reload the database file **salon**, saved in section 1, Practice 1.

2 Print out the complete file in table format.

3 Change the following records:

The appointment for **Don** to see **Ben** should be on **SAT** not FRI.
The appointment time of **Susie's** client **Mike** should be at **16.00** not 15.00.

4 Cara's client Dennis has cancelled. Delete his details.

5 Add the following new client for **Cara**. Her name is **Dawn Green** and she has booked an appointment for **Saturday** at **10.00**. Her reference number is **S890**. She has **not** visited the salon before.

6 Save the file.

7 Add a new field to the database. Insert **SURNAME** after CLIENT NAME. Enter the clients' surnames as follows:

CLIENT NAME	SURNAME
TONY	BLACK
PETER	DALL
JANE	HATHEY
JOHN	HILFINGER
HARRIET	HILL
GEORGE	HUNTER
ANGIE	KESSIN
PAUL	KILE
JULIE	LINES
MIKE	LOND
HILARY	MALIK
STEWART	McBRIDE
DON	QUORN
CHERIE	UNIHA
LAURA	WATSON
SUSIE	TOLKEIN

8 Change the order of the fields so that the REF NO field is before the CLIENT NAME.

9 Set a validation rule in the DAY field **Not MON**. Set the validation text to **Closed on Mondays**.

10 Save and print the table in landscape orientation.

11 Close the database file.

Practice 4

1 Reload the database file **Centres**, saved in section 1.

2 Print out the complete file in table format.

3 Change the following records:

The **COUNTRY CLUB** in **SOUTHAMPTON**, **SOUTH**, is called **LAKESIDE** not RIVERSIDE.
In **PLYMOUTH**, the **NO OF ROOMS** at **HEMSLEY HALL** is **30** not 25.

4 Delete all entries in the North region.

5 Add two more hotels in the South region as follows:

TYPE	TOWN	NAME	PRICE	NO OF ROOMS
COUNTRY CLUB	DOVER	CHANNEL VIEW	90.50	28
MOTEL	WATFORD	NIGHT STOP	29.99	100

6 Add a new field **RESTAURANT** after the **No of Rooms** field to the database. Set the field as YES/NO. All types have Restaurants (so should be set to **Yes**) except the motels (set these to **No**).

7 Change the field order so that the TOWN field comes before the TYPE field.

8 Save and print the table.

9 Close the file.

Section 3 — Sorting and searching

In this section you will practise and learn how to:

- find a record on given criteria
- add/remove filters
- create a simple query
- create a query with multiple criteria
- save a query

- add/remove/hide/unhide fields in a query
- select and sort records based on given criteria
- select and sort records using logical operators

3.1 — Sorting data

Exercise 1

Sort the database file **ACTIVITIES**, saved in section 2, into alphabetical order of **INSTRUCTOR**.

Info

There are three main methods to sort the database. Use the toolbar button method when you do not need to save the sort. Use the filter or the query method when you want to save the sort and not overwrite any other sort.

What is filtering?

Once you have stored information in your database, you will want to sort and question the database to obtain information in different forms. When you want to see a subset of the records in a table or you want to sort the table and save it (or do all of these) you can use filtering.

What is a query?

A query is a more sophisticated method of sorting and searching a database. It has advantages over a filter as it can:

- enable you to select only certain fields to be displayed
- be used when a table is closed
- calculate sums, averages and other types of totals.

3.2 — Sorting using the Sort buttons

Method

1 Reload the saved file **ACTIVITIES** so that the **ACTIVITIES: Database** window is displayed.
2 Open the table **OUTDOOR** in Datasheet view.

3 Click on: the Field Name **INSTRUCTOR** at the top of the field column so that the column is selected.

4 Click on: the ⬇️ **Sort Ascending** button.

3.3 Sorting using a filter

Exercise 2

Sort the database file into descending numerical order of **DURATION (WKS)** and ascending order of **INSTRUCTOR**.

Info

Using the filtering method allows you to sort more than one field. This is called a multiple criteria sort as opposed to sorting on a single criterion, as in Exercise 1.

Method

1 With the table **OUTDOOR** displayed in Datasheet view, position the cursor in the **DURATION (WKS)** field.

2 From the **Records** menu, select: **Filter, Advanced Filter/Sort** (Figure 5.27).

Figure 5.27 Applying a filter

3 The Filter dialogue box appears. In the first Field column box, click on the down arrow, and click on: **DURATION (WKS)** (Figure 5.28).

4 In the Sort box, click on: the down arrow and click on: **Descending**.

5 In the second field column box, click on: the down arrow and click on: **INSTRUCTOR**.

6 In the **Sort** box, click on: the down arrow and click on: **Ascending**.

7 From the **File** menu, select: **Save As Query** and key in the query name **Duration des and instructor asc**. Click on: **OK**. Close the filter. Return to the **ACTIVITIES: Database** window.

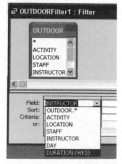

Figure 5.28 The Filter dialogue box

8   To view the result of the filtering, click on: the **Queries** button in the **ACTIVITIES: Database** window.
9   Double-click on: the query name.
10 Close the query by clicking on: its **Close** button.

3.4   Printing a query

Exercise 3

Print the query saved as **Duration des and instructor asc**.

Method

1   In the **ACTIVITIES: Database** window, click on: the **Queries** button.
2   Right-click on: **Duration des and instructor asc**.
3   From the pop-up menu, select: **Print** (or **Print Preview**, then: **Page Setup** from the **File** menu to change to landscape if necessary). Check that the printer is ready and loaded with paper.
4   Click on: **OK**.

3.5   Sorting in a query

Exercise 4

Sort the database file into alphabetical order of **DAY**.

Method

1   In the **ACTIVITIES: Database** window, click on: the **Queries** button (Figure 5.29).
2   Double-click on: **Create query in Design view**.

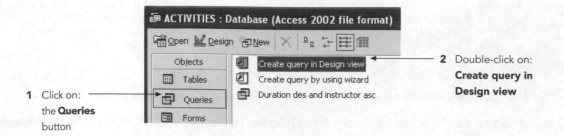

Figure 5.29 Creating a Query

3 The Show Table dialogue box appears (Figure 5.30).

4 The table **OUTDOOR** is selected (there may be more than one table to choose from). Click on: **Add**, then on: **Close**.

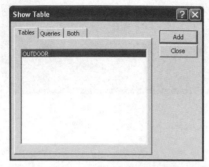

Figure 5.30 Show Table dialogue box

5 The Query – Design view window is displayed (Figure 5.31).

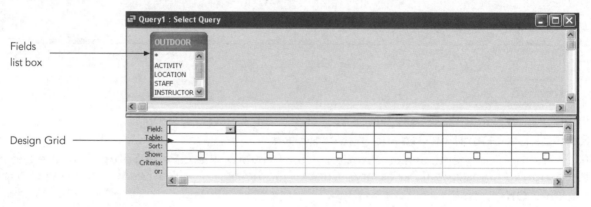

Figure 5.31 Query Design

6 The fields of the **OUTDOOR** table are displayed in a Fields List box. Place the fields in the Design Grid as follows:

a In the Design Grid, click in: the first field column.
b Click on: the down arrow.
c Click on: the name of the field that you want to appear, ie **ACTIVITY**.
d Click in: the next field column, click on: the down arrow.
e Click on: the name of the next field you want to appear, ie **LOCATION**.
f Repeat steps (d)–(e) until all the fields are on the grid.

> **Info**
>
> There are other ways to place the fields in the Design Grid:
>
> • Double-click on: the field name that you want in the Design Grid.
> • Drag the field name on to the Design Grid.

7 In the field **DAY** column, click in: the **Sort** row, then click on the down arrow, then on: **Ascending** (Figure 5.32).

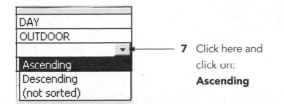

Figure 5.32 **Sorting into Ascending order**

Note: **Descending** option sorts Z–A or in descending numerical order.
Ascending option sorts A–Z, or in ascending numerical order.

7 Click here and click on:
Ascending

8 To save the query, from the **File** menu, select **Save As**. Replace the default name **Query1** by deleting it and keying in the query name **Day asc**. Click on: **OK**.

9 Return to the ACTIVITIES: Database window.

10 View the results of the query as in 3.3.

11 Print the query.

> ### Info
>
> Scan the result of the query. If there is no data or if incorrect data is displayed in Datasheet view, click on: the 📐 **View** button again to return to Design view and check the query design.
>
> You can create queries using the Query Wizard if you prefer. You will need to modify them to suit your needs. Practise this method.

12 Click on: the **Close** button in the top right-hand corner of this window to return to the ACTIVITIES: Database window.

> ### Info
>
> As with advanced filtering, in queries you can also do multiple criteria sorts.

3.6   Finding records specified by a single criterion

> ### Exercise 5
>
> Search the file for all classes taking place at **BLUE BEACH**.

> ### Info
>
> There are several ways to find records. You can search manually, navigating your way through the database using the methods already learnt. This is too time-consuming and not recommended for large databases. Using *Find* is a quicker method. You can also use a filter or create a query.

Method

1 With the table displayed in Datasheet view, position the cursor in the field that you want to search on, ie **LOCATION**.
2 Click on: the 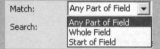 **Find** button. The Find and Replace dialogue box appears (Figure 5.33).
3 In the **Find What** box, key in the data that you want to find, ie **BLUE BEACH**.
4 In the **Look In** box, select: **LOCATION** (**LOCATION** will already be selected if you positioned the cursor in this field at step 1).
5 Click on: **Find Next**.

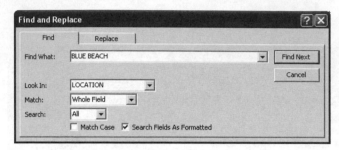

Figure 5.33 Find and Replace dialogue box

6 Access will find each record in turn. *Note*: You may need to reposition the Find box to view the found records.
7 When you have finished searching, close the dialogue box by clicking on: the **Close** button or on: **Cancel**.

Info

Refining finds

As an example, assume that we entered **GYM** in the **Find What** box.

Using Match

Any Part of Field: This finds any data with **GYM** in it, eg **GYM**NASIUM, SPORTS **GYM**.

Whole Field: This finds only GYM not GYMNASIUM or SPORTS GYM.

Start of Field: This finds data at the beginning with GYM, eg GYMNASIUM but not SPORTS GYM.

The **Search** option in the Find and Replace dialogue box allows further refinements as shown:

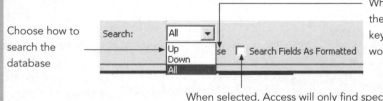

Choose how to search the database

When selected, Access will only find the case that you have used when keying in, eg if you keyed in Gym, it would find GYM but not gym

When selected, Access will only find specific formats of data, eg if your dates are formatted as 10/03/03, Access will only find dates in this format and not 10-October-03

Finding numbers

In the **Find What** box, key in the number.

Finding dates

In the **Find What** box, key in the date (ensure **Search fields as formatted** is not ticked, see above).

Method 1

1   With the table displayed in Datasheet View, position the cursor in a cell containing the data you want to find, ie **BLUE BEACH**.
2   Click on: the 🏳️ **Filter by selection** button.
3   All the records with **BLUE BEACH** are displayed.

Info

You can refine your search further by selecting another data entry, eg all activities at **BLUE BEACH** lasting 15 weeks. With the filtered **BLUE BEACH** records displayed, repeat steps 1 and 2, this time positioning the cursor in a cell containing 15.

You can also select any part of a data entry, eg if you wanted to find all records beginning with the letter B, select only the B and run the filter.

Note: If you are filtering a Yes/No field, you will change the data when you click in the cell containing it. To overcome this, click it twice so that it keeps its original setting before filtering.

4   To remove the filter, click on: the ▽ **Remove Filter** button.
     Note: You cannot save the filter as a query using this method.

Method 2

1   With the table displayed in Datasheet view, from the **Records** menu select: **Filter**, **Advanced Filter/Sort**.
2   The **Filter** box dialogue is displayed.
3   Select the field that contains the data you want to find, ie **LOCATION** by clicking on the arrow in the **Field** row.
4   In the **Criteria** row, key in: **BLUE BEACH**.
5   Click on: the 💾 **Save As Query** button to save the filter as a query, named **Blue Beach**.
6   Close the filter and table.
7   View the results of the filter by clicking on: the **Queries** button and double-clicking on the query name.

Info

Using Method 2, you can search with more than one specified criterion and also sort data.

3.9 Finding data using a query

Method

Follow steps 1–6 in 3.5.

7 In the field **LOCATION** column and the **Criteria** row, key in: **BLUE BEACH** and press: **Enter** (Figure 5.34).

Field:	ACTIVITY	LOCATION	STAFF
Sort:			
Criteria:		"BLUE BEACH"	
or:			

Figure 5.34 Selecting criteria

Info

Quotation marks appear around the keyed text, ie **"BLUE BEACH"**. It does not matter if you key in **Blue Beach** in upper or lower case. Beware: if you spell the entry wrongly, it will not be recognised and Access will be unable to find any records since it only looks for an exact match.

8 View the results of the query by clicking on: the ▦ **View** button. (*Note:* This button changes its icon depending on whether you are in Design view or Datasheet view.)
9 Save the query with the filename **Location Blue Beach**.
10 Print as in 3.4.

3.10 Selecting records specified by more than one criterion

Exercise 6

Using the query method, find all the records for classes taking place at **BLUE BEACH** lasting **less than 16 weeks**. Print details of the selected records and show all fields.

Info

Mathematical operators used in queries

> (greater than) symbol is obtained by holding down the **Shift** key and pressing the **full stop** key.

< (less than) symbol is obtained by holding down the **Shift** key and pressing the **comma** key:

>	greater than (or more recent than in the case of a date)
<	less than (or before in the case of a date)
>=	greater than or equal to
<=	less than or equal to
<>	not equal to
And	Use **and** when you need to restrict results, eg >5 and <10
Or	Use **or** when more than one entry could match, eg red or green

Method

1 From the **ACTIVITIES: Database** window, click on: the **Queries** tab, double-click on the query **Location Blue Beach**, then on: the **View** button to switch from Datasheet view to Design view.

2 In the Design Grid, **DURATION** field column and the **Criteria** row, key in **<16** and press: **Enter** (Figure 5.35).

3 Check that the query design works by switching to Datasheet view by clicking on: the ▦ **View** button. (*Note:* You can also run the query by clicking on: the ❗ **Run** button.)

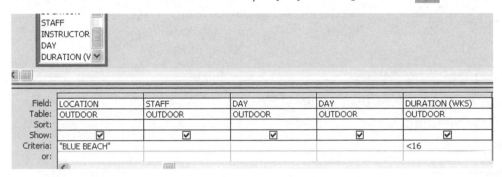

Figure 5.35 Selecting more than one criterion

4 Save the query as **Blue Beach less than 16 wks** and print.

3.11 Printing specified fields from selected sorted records

Exercise 7

Find all the records with the instructor **LYNDSEY lasting more than 15 weeks**. Sort the records into alphabetical order of **ACTIVITY**. Print the details of only these records. Show only the information for **ACTIVITY**, **DAY** and **DURATION (WKS)** fields.

Method

Follow steps 1–6 in section 3.5.

7 In the Design Grid, **INSTRUCTOR** field column and **Criteria** row, key in: **LYNDSEY** and press: **Enter**.

8 In the field **DURATION (WKS)** column and **Criteria** row, key in **>15** and press: **Enter**.

9 In the **ACTIVITY** field, **Sort** row, select: **Ascending** (Figure 5.36).

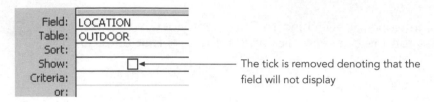

Field:	ACTIVITY	LOCATION	STAFF	INSTRUCTOR	DAY	DURAT
Table:	OUTDOOR	OUTDOOR	OUTDOOR	OUTDOOR	OUTDOOR	OUTD
Sort:	Ascending					
Show:	☑	☑	☑	☑	☑	
Criteria:				"LYNDSEY"		>15
or:						

Figure 5.36 Selecting more than one criterion and sorting in the same query

10 To show only the **ACTIVITY**, **DAY** and **DURATION (WKS)** fields, in the **Show** row and **LOCATION** field column, click the tick in the box. The tick is removed (Figure 5.37). Repeat for the **INSTRUCTOR** and **STAFF** fields. This leaves ticks in the **ACTIVITY**, **DAY** and **DURATION (WKS)** fields only.

Note: If it is decided to show a field that was previously hidden, the tick can be reinstated by clicking on an empty box.

Field:	LOCATION
Table:	OUTDOOR
Sort:	
Show:	☐ ◄——— The tick is removed denoting that the field will not display
Criteria:	
or:	

Figure 5.37 Showing only certain fields

11 Save the query as **Lyndsey more than 15 weeks**.
12 Check the result in Datasheet view.
13 Print the query.

Info

- You will notice that only the fields with ticks will appear on the printout.
- *Remember*: It is always a good idea to check that your query is showing the correct result, so view it in Datasheet view before printing. If it is not showing what you think you have asked for, return to Design view by clicking the **View** toolbar button and checking the details you have entered.
- You can sort and search within the same query.

You can rearrange the field order in a query as follows:
- In the query Design Grid, select the field column to move by clicking on the top of the column.
- Hold down the left mouse button and drag the column to the new position.

You can delete a field from the query Design Grid by selecting the field column, then pressing: **Delete**.

Common errors

- Misspelling the criteria so that the query does not find an exact match (this can also be due to a spelling error in the data in the database).
- Making the criteria plural, eg **BIKES** instead of **BIKE**. The query will not find **BIKES** if the entry was singular, ie **BIKE**. If the entry is not what was entered in the database and therefore not an exact match, the record(s) will not be found.
- Leaving spaces where they should not be.

3.12 Close the database file and exit Access

Practice 5

1   Reload the database file **salon** saved in Practice 3, section 2.
2   Sort the file into alphabetical order of client name and print all the details.
3   Sort the file into ascending numerical order of previous visits and print all details.
4   Search for all the clients whose appointment day is Wednesday. Print details of the selected records showing all fields.
5   Find all the records of clients whose appointments are before 12.30 and after 10.00 and have previously visited fewer than 8 times. Print only the information in the Client Name and Time fields.
6   Save and close the file.

Practice 6

1   Reload the database file **Centres**, saved in Practice 4, section 2.
2   Sort the file into alphabetical order of Town and print.
3   Sort the file into descending numerical order of price and print all details.
4   Search for all the hotels with more than 60 rooms in the EAST or the SOUTH. Print details of these only.
5   Find all records of MOTEL costing more than £50.00. Print only the Region, Town, Name and No of rooms fields.
6   Automatically find and replace all BUSINESS CENTRE types with COMMERCE CENTRE.
7   Save and close the file.

In this section you will practise and learn how to:

- create reports
- present selected data in a particular sequence on screen and in reports
- modify a report

- create and customise headers and footers
- group data in a report – totals, subtotals etc

4.1 Creating a report

Exercise 1

Open the database file **ACTIVITIES**, saved in the last section, and create a report in table format based on the table **OUTDOOR**, displaying all the records.

Note: Reports can also be produced from Queries.

Method 1

Using AutoReport

1 With the **ACTIVITIES: Database** window displayed, click on: the **Reports** button.
2 Click on: the ⬚ New **New** button.
3 The **New Report** dialogue box is displayed (Figure 5.38). Select: **AutoReport: Tabular**.
4 In the **Choose the table...** box, click on: the down arrow and select the table **OUTDOOR** from the drop-down list.
5 Click on: **OK**.

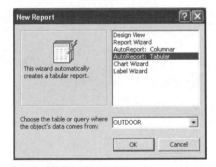

Figure 5.38 Creating an AutoReport

6 The report appears in Print Preview mode.
7 Print the report.
8 Close the report (by clicking on its **Close** button). Do not save.

Info

In this instance the report looks very good – it fits on the page and is clearly laid out. Sometimes this is not the case and you will need to use the Report Wizard to create your report. Creating reports without the aid of the wizard is very advanced and time-consuming.

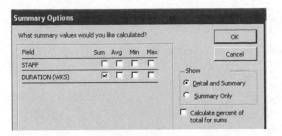

Figure 5.43 Summary Options dialogue box

Note: When required Average, Minimum and Maximum values can be calculated using this box.

12 The next Report Wizard box appears (Figure 5.44). Use your discretion for the best Layout and Orientation. This report, because it is going to show all the fields, will be wide, therefore it is best suited to a landscape display. Click on: the **Landscape** option button. Ensure the **Adjust the Field width** box is ticked.

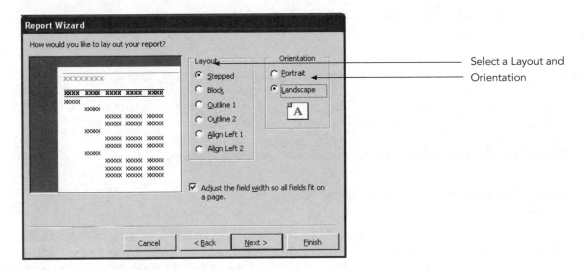

Figure 5.44 Selecting Layout and Orientation

13 Click on: **Next**.

14 The next Report Wizard box appears (Figure 5.45). Experiment with the styles. Each time you choose a style, example reports are displayed in the left box. **Corporate** is a good style because the layout is compact and the data will usually fit on one page.

15 Click on: **Next**.

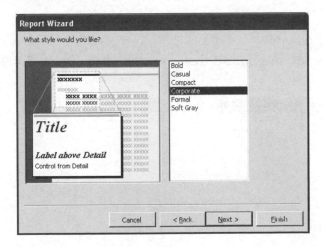

Figure 5.45 Selecting a style

16 The next Report Wizard appears (Figure 5.46). Key in a Report title.

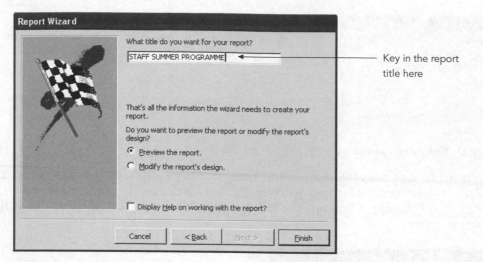

Figure 5.46 Adding a title

Info

This may scroll out of view as you type. Do not worry. Always choose a descriptive title for your report. This will become the report name when it saves automatically.

17 Ensure that the **Preview the report** button is selected.

18 Click on: **Finish**.

19 Check the report (zoom in and out by clicking the mouse over it) to ensure that all details are displayed in full. Access has a habit of cutting off the edges of some of the longer entries! This will not always happen. In this case, using the **Corporate** style, my report has displayed all the entries.

20 You will notice that details of the calculations appear on the report (Figure 5.47). Since these are distracting, we can delete them.

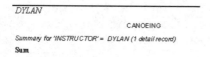

Figure 5.47 Details of calculations can be deleted

21 Click on: the **View** button to switch to Design view.

22 Delete the details of calculations by clicking on the box so that it has handles (Figure 5.48). Press: **Delete**. Similarly delete **Sum**.

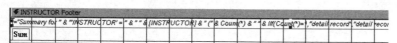

Figure 5.48 Select the detail to delete it

23 Review and save the report.

4.2 Printing a report

Exercise 2

Print the report including the field headings. Close the report.

Add the header: **Report produced by (your name)**.

Add the footer: **Report designed to show weeks for each instructor**.

Method

1 With the report displayed in Design view, display the **Toolbox** (if not already displayed). (Use the **View** menu, **Toolbox** or **View** menu, **Toolbars**, **Toolbox** to display the Toolbox.)

2 Click on: the **Label** button (Figure 5.54).

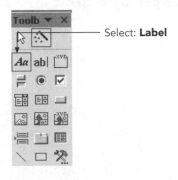 — Select: **Label**

Figure 5.54 The Toolbox

3 In the **Report Header** section, click and drag out a text box.

4 Key in the header text. Press **Enter** and while the text box is selected, select the font, size etc.

5 Repeat for the footer text.

6 Save, preview and print the report.

Info

You can format any of the report text by clicking on it to select it and then formatting. To select more than one text box, hold down the **Shift** key. Resize the boxes as necessary or move them by pointing to a box border until a hand appears and then drag to the new position.

4.5 **Close the database file and exit Access**

Practice 7

1 Reload the database file **salon** saved in Practice 5, section 3.
2 Produce a report as follows:
   a Display all the fields and all the records.
   b Group by Stylist.
   c Sort in descending order of Client Name.
   d Title the report **Clients grouped by stylist**.
   e Add a header with your name and current time of day in Arial, bold, 14 pt.
3 Print the report on one page.
4 Change the report title to **Client appointments this week, grouped by stylist**.
5 Save and print the report.
6 Close the database file.

Practice 8

1 Reload the database file **Centres** saved in Practice 6, section 3.
2 Produce a report as follows:
   a Include all fields except Town.
   b Group the report by Region.
   c Add summary values, Average for the field **Price** and Sum for the **No of Rooms** field.
   d Sort the report into ascending order of Price.
   e Add a title **Venues Available**.
   f Add a footer containing the text: **Report produced by (your name)**.
3 Save and print the report on one page.

Section 5 / Forms

In this section you will practise and learn how to:

- create a simple form
- enter data
- format text

- change background
- change arrangement of objects within a form layout

5.1) What is a form?

Info

Once you have created an Access database table you are able to view the data in Datasheet view. There are limitations to layout design in this view and so Access provides another way to view the same data so that you can see one complete record at a time, arranged to your liking. This is called a *Form*. There are three ways to create a form:

1 Using AutoForm.
2 Using a Form Wizard.
3 Manually.

We will be using the first two methods as we work through this section.

5.2) Creating forms using AutoForm

Exercise 1

Open the **ACTIVITIES** database and create a form from the table **OUTDOOR**.

Method

1 With the **ACTIVITIES: Database** window open, in the **Objects** section, click on: the **Forms** button.
2 Click on: the ⬛New **New** button.
3 The **New Form** dialogue box appears (Figure 5.55). Select: **AutoForm: Columnar** and select the table **OUTDOOR**.
4 Click on: **OK**.

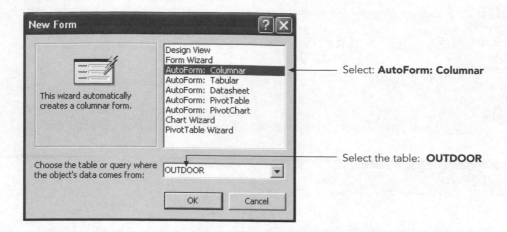

Select: **AutoForm: Columnar**

Select the table: **OUTDOOR**

Figure 5.55 Creating a Form using AutoForm

5 The AutoForm is displayed as shown in Figure 5.56.

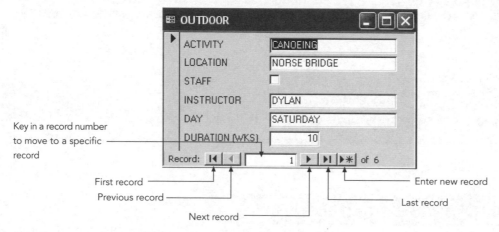

Key in a record number to move to a specific record

First record
Previous record
Next record
Enter new record
Last record

Figure 5.56 A record in the table OUTDOOR in Form layout

Info

The first record of the database is displayed. To see the others, use the arrow buttons at the bottom as described in section 2. You can carry out all the procedures in a form that you can do in a table, ie edit, add, delete records etc. When you make alterations in Form View, the contents of the table **OUTDOOR** are also changed.

6 Close the form. Do not save.

5.3 Creating forms using the Form Wizard

Exercise 2

Create a form based on the table **OUTDOOR** using the Form Wizard. Set out the form so that it is easy to read and attractive to look at.

Method

1 With the ACTIVITIES: Database window open, in the **Objects** section, click on: the **Forms** button.

2 Double-click on: **Create form by using wizard**. A Form Wizard box appears (Figure 5.57). Ensure that the table **OUTDOOR** is selected. Move all the fields across to the **Selected Fields** section using the `>>` double arrow forward button. Click on: **Next**.

Info

You can select to show only some of the fields on a form using the single forward arrow.

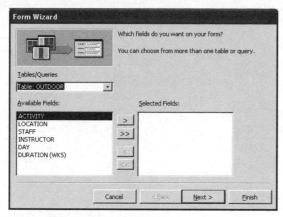

Figure 5.57 Form Wizard

3 The next Form Wizard box appears (Figure 5.58). Select the layout you require (you are given a preview in the box to the left). In this instance select: **Columnar**. Click on: **Next**.

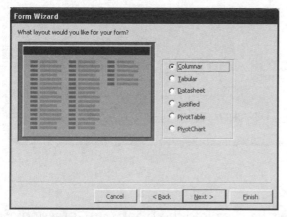

Figure 5.58 Choosing a layout

4 The Next Form Wizard box appears (Figure 5.59). Here you can select a suitable style for your form. Examine the different styles. I will choose **Expedition**. Click on: **Next**.

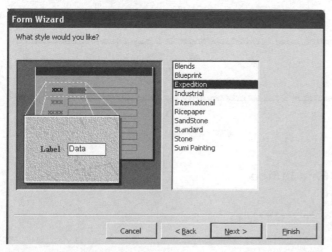

Figure 5.59 Selecting a style

5 The next Form Wizard box appears (Figure 5.60). Give the form a suitable name, eg Staff Events, and click on: **Finish**.

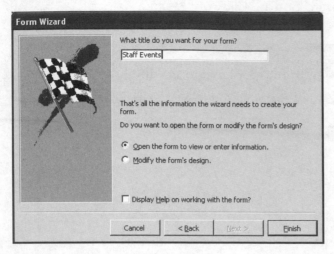

Figure 5.60 Giving the form a title

6 The completed form appears on screen showing the first record.

7 Save the form using **Save As** from the **File** menu.

5.4 Entering and editing data in a form

Exercise 3

Enter the following new record:

ACTIVITY	LOCATION	STAFF	INSTRUCTOR	DAY	DURATION (WKS)
TENNIS	FERN DOWNS	YES	SAMA	TUESDAY	20

Amend the record for HANG GLIDING to display INSTRUCTOR as MICHELLE, not Mike.

Method

1 Click on: the ▶* **New Record** button and enter the data into the blank form, pressing: **Enter** after each field entry.

   Note: In the **STAFF** field, click in the box so that a tick is displayed.

2 Access the HANG GLIDING record. Click in the INSTRUCTOR field entry and amend. Press: **Enter**.

Exercise 4

Delete the record for **DIVING**.

Method

1 Find the **DIVING** record using the 🔍 **Find** button.

2 Click on: the ✖ **Delete Record** button.

3 Click on: **Yes** to confirm the delete.

1   From the **File** menu, select: **Print**, then click on: **OK** *or* click on: the **Print** button.
2   Click on: the **Close** button.

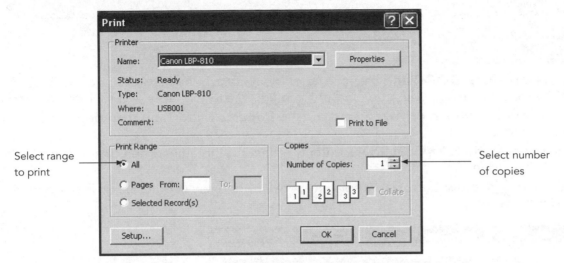

Figure 5.49 Print dialogue box

With **Page** tab selected

Select orientation

Select paper size

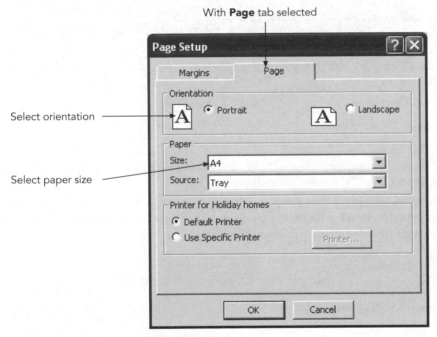

Figure 5.50 Page Setup dialogue box

Note: In the Print box, you can select the print range, ie all the report or selected pages only. Change orientation and margins when appropriate using **Page Setup** from the **File** menu.

4.3   Further adjusting a report design

Exercise 3

In the Table **OUTDOOR**, in the **ACTIVITY** field, change the entry **HANG GLIDING** to **HANG GLIDING (COMPLETE BEGINNERS)**. Review the report created in 4.1 and adjust as necessary.

Method

1 Open the table **OUTDOOR** and change the entry in Datasheet view. Change the width of the **ACTIVITY** field to display the amended entry in full. Close the table and save the amendments.

2 Open the report saved in 4.1 by clicking on: the **Reports** button and then double-clicking on: the report name.

3 You will see that the **HANG GLIDING** entry is reflecting the amendment made but is now no longer displayed in full.

4 Click on: the ![View icon] **View** button to display Report Design view (Figure 5.51). The report is divided into panes.

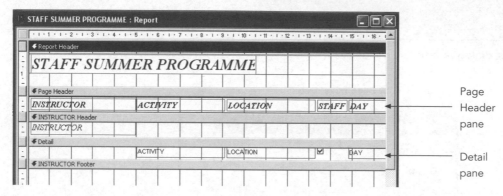

Figure 5.51 Report Design view

5 Using the scroll bars, ensure that the item that you want to alter is in view. In this case the item should already be visible, ie **ACTIVITY** in the **Detail** pane.

6 Click on: the **ACTIVITY** box to select it. Drag the handle to the right to widen the box so that it is wide enough to display all the detail (Figure 5.52). (You will have to make a guess how wide to make the box since the detail does not appear in Report Design view.)

Figure 5.52 Widening the ACTIVITY field detail box

7 Unfortunately the last action has obscured some of the **LOCATION** Detail. Therefore we need to resize both the **LOCATION** Detail and the **LOCATION** Header (so that they line up). To do this, select the **LOCATION** Header by clicking on it; drag the handle to the right (Figure 5.53).

Figure 5.53 Resizing the LOCATION field

8 Similarly resize the **LOCATION** Detail.

9 Click on: the **View** button (its icon has now changed to Print Preview) to return to Report Preview.

10 From the **File** menu, select: **Save**, to save the report design. (This is necessary, even if your report is still not perfect, as failure to save at this point will result in losing the changes that you have already made.)

11 Check the Report Preview and continue to fine tune and save the design as above until you are happy with it.

Sort the database into descending alphabetical order of **ACTIVITY**.

Method

This is done the same way as in Tables (see section 3.2). Remember to position the cursor in the correct field before sorting. Use the ⊞ **Sort descending** button.

Info

You can also perform a multiple criteria sort as in Tables, ie from the **Records** menu, select: **Filter**, **Advanced Filter/Sort** and save it as a query.

Info

You can Filter by selection, as in Table View. The number of records found by the filtering is shown beside the navigation buttons. You can also use **Filter by Form** from the **Records** menu or by clicking on: the ⊞ **Filter by Form** button. In this case a blank form is displayed. Key in what you want to find, then click on: the ▽ **Apply Filter** button. Click on: the button again to remove the filter.

You can also perform an Advanced Filter and save it as a query as for Tables.

5.5) **Modifying a form**

Info

You can change the appearance of a form in a similar way to changing a report's appearance. The exercises below will allow you to practise this.

Exercise 6

Change the text in the form to a different font and reduce the text size.

Method

1 In the **ACTIVITES: Database** window, click on: the **Forms** button.
2 Click on: the form you created above and click on: the ☒ Design **Design** button.
3 The form appears in Design view (Figure 5.61).

Figure 5.61 Form in Design view

4 As with Report designing, select the boxes containing the text to alter. (You need to hold down **Shift** to select more than one box.)

5 Format the text using the toolbar buttons.

Exercise 7

Change the layout of the form so that the data is displayed in full, eg **HANG GLIDING (COMPLETE BEGINNERS)** is cropped. Rearrange the form in any order you like.

Method

Working in Design view, use the methods described for Reports in section 4.

Exercise 8

Change the background colours in the text boxes.

Method

With the form in Design view, select the objects to change. Right-click the mouse to view and select from a pop-up menu.

Practise changing other options. Save the form design when you are happy with it.

5.6 Adding headers and footers

Exercise 9

Add headers and footers to the form design.

Method

Working in Design view, from the **View** menu, select **Page Header/Footer**. Use the same methods as for Reports as follows:

1   With the form displayed in Design view, display the **Toolbox** (if not already displayed). (Use the **View** menu, **Toolbox** or **View** menu, **Toolbars**, **Toolbox** to display the Toolbox.)
2   Click on: the **Label** button (Figure 5.62).

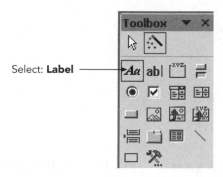

Select: **Label**

Figure 5.62   The Toolbox

3   In the **Form Header** section, click and drag out a text box.
4   Enter the header text. While the text box is selected, select the font, size etc.
5   Repeat for the footer text.

5.7   Print the file in form layout

Method

1   Display the database form that you have just created.
2   Print in the normal way.

    Note: Print Range can be set up in the Print dialogue box, ie All, Selected Pages or Selected Records. Use **Print Preview** before printing.

    To select records in a form, click on: the record selector (Figure 5.63) for each record in the selection.

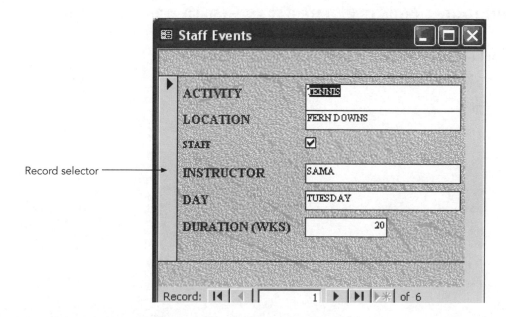

Record selector

Figure 5.63   Record selector

5.8   Close the file and exit Access

Practice 9

1 Reload the database file **salon** saved in Practice 7, section 4.
2 Create a simple form using the table **Clients**.
3 Change the text of the Field headings to Times New Roman, italic.
4 Change the colour of the background in the Field headings boxes to green.
5 Add a header displaying your name.
6 Enter the following new records:

STYLIST	REF NO	CLIENT NAME	DAY	SURNAME	TIME	PREVIOUS VISITS
BEN	Z445	KARL	FRI	HENMAN	16.00	2
BRYONY	Z567	JEANNA	TUE	JONES	10.00	0

7 Delete the record of Cara's client **Susie**.
8 Save the database and print in Form format.
9 Close the database file.

Practice 10

1 Reload the database file **Centres** saved in Practice 8, section 4.
2 Create a simple form using the table **Details**.
3 Change the text of the data to Arial, bold, 10 pt.
4 Change the colour of the background in the data boxes to purple.
5 Enter the following new record:

REGION	TOWN	TYPE	NAME	PRICE	NO OF ROOMS	RESTAURANT
EAST	CAMBRIDGE	COUNTRY CLUB	THE BACKS	150.00	25	Yes

6 Move the **Town** field so that it is displayed above the **Region** field.
7 Save the database and print the new record only in Form format.
8 Close the database file.

Section 6 / Working with more than one table

In this section you will practise and learn how to:

- understand why and how to relate tables in a database
- create/delete relationships between tables
- set relationship rules between tables
- delete database objects

Note: For the exercises in this section, you will need the Access file **MFB Supplies** on the CD-ROM.

6.1 Why relate tables in a database?

So far we have been working with single tables within a database. Often, in such databases, field entries are repeated because the information has to fit into the single table structure. This is not really a very efficient way of storing and manipulating data. Using Access it is possible to create *relational* databases. A relational database contains more than one table with relationships existing between the tables.

Suppose you wanted to create a list of participants for each of the outdoor activities entered in the database in section 1. How would you achieve this? You could design a new database. However, it would be rather time-consuming and tedious to have to enter **HANG GLIDING (COMPLETE BEGINNERS)** for every participant in this activity. A better way is to create a new Table within the existing database and relate the new Table to the existing one. An Activity ID field could be inserted, eg for the **HANG GLIDING (COMPLETE BEGINNERS)** activity say **HG** (much easier and less error-prone to enter!) and a new Table of participants could be created with a relationship between the **ACTIVITY ID** field in the original database table, **OUTDOOR**, and the **Course** field in the **Participants** table. The related fields are shown in Figure 5.64.

OUTDOOR : Table

ACTIVITY ID	ACTIVITY	
CA	CANOEING	NI
CY	CYCLING	NI
HG	HANG GLIDING (COMPLETE BEGINNERS)	FE
S	SAILING	BI
SW	SWIMMING	BI
T	TENNIS	FE

These fields are related

Participants : Table

Course	Surname	First name	Staff nu
HG	WATERS	GRAHAM	609
HG	ANDREOU	CARLOS	500
HG	MOORE	ROBERT	321
HG	OLSEN	ANN	291
SW	SHAREEF	SAMA	700
SW	LeBLANC	NICOLE	781
SW	CEDAR	JANIS	752

Figure 5.64 Related tables

When a relationship has been set up, Access is able to match data in the related fields. In the example above, matches can be made between, eg the entry **HG** in the **Course** field of the **Participants** table and **HG** in the **ACTIVITY ID** field of the **OUTDOOR** table. In this example the relationship is the more common *one-to-many*, ie a record in the **OUTDOOR** table has many matching records in the **Participants** table. Relationships can also be *one-to-one*, ie a record in one table has only one matching record in another table. When creating relationships, it is important to set rules so that, for instance, a related field is not deleted.

There are many advantages in creating relational databases. These include:

- related tables enable entries to be brought together in queries and forms
- errors in data entry are reduced
- time spent entering the same data is saved
- the database file is smaller
- related data need only be updated once since updates in related data will be automatic.

6.2 ▶ Create a one-to-one relationship between tables

Exercise 1

Open the database **MFB Supplies** and create a one-to-one relationship between the **Customer ID** field of the **Customer details** table and the **Customer ID** field of the **Payment** table.

Method

1 Open the database **MFB Supplies** so that the MFB Supplies: Database window is displayed with the **Tables** button selected in the **Objects** section (Figure 5.65). Note that this database has three tables.

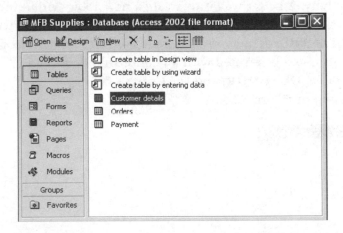

Figure 5.65 Tables in the MFB Supplies database

2 Open the table **Customer details** in Datasheet view and examine the records in it (Figure 5.66).

Figure 5.66 Customer details table in Datasheet view

3 Switch to Table Design view and examine the design of the table. Note that the **Customer ID** field has **primary key** status (it has a key symbol next to it) and no duplicates are allowed (Figure 5.67). When creating one-to-one relationships it is essential that both related fields from each table have primary key status or are uniquely indexed. In a one-to-many relationship, the related field in one of the tables must be primary key or uniquely indexed.

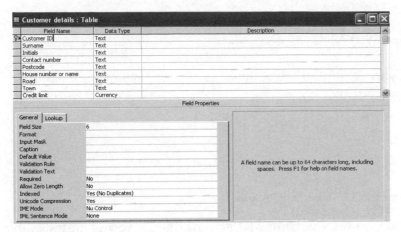

Figure 5.67 Properties of the Customer ID field

4 Close the Table window.

5 Examine the **Payment** table (Figure 5.68).

Figure 5.68 Payment table to Datasheet view

6 With the table displayed in Design view, notice that there is no primary key set.

7 Set the **Customer ID** field to be the primary key by positioning the cursor in the **Customer ID** field and clicking on: the 🔑 **Primary Key** button (Figure 5.69).

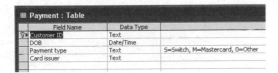

Figure 5.69 Primary key is Customer ID field

8 Close and save the table.

9 From the **Tools** menu, select: **Relationships** (Figure 5.70) *or* click on: the ⊡ **Relationships** button.

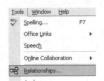

Figure 5.70 Tools menu, Relationships

10 The Show Table dialogue box is displayed (Figure 5.71).

Note: If the Relationships box is displayed at this point, go to step 13.

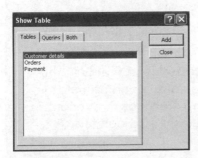

Figure 5.71 Show Table dialogue box

11 With the **Tables** tab selected, click on: the table **Customer details** and click on: **Add**, then click on the table **Payment** and click on: **Add**.

12 Click on: **Close**.

13 The Relationships box is displayed listing the tables and their fields side by side (Figure 5.72).

   Note: The primary key fields are emboldened.

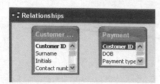

Figure 5.72 Relationships box

14 Hold down the left mouse button on the **Customer ID** field of the **Customer details** table and drag it over the **Customer ID** field of the **Payment** table.

15 The Edit Relationships box is displayed (Figure 5.73). Note that the **Relationship Type** is **One-To-One**.

16 Click in: the **Enforce Referential Integrity** box so that a tick is displayed (see the Info box below for an explanation of this).

17 Click on: **Create**.

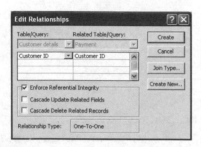

Figure 5.73 Edit Relationships dialogue box

18 The Relationships box now displays the one-to-one relationship between the **Customer ID** fields from each table (Figure 5.74).

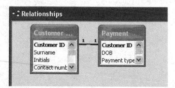

Figure 5.74 Relationship has been created

19 Close the Relationships box by clicking on: its **Close** button and saving changes.

   Note: When the related tables are opened in Datasheet view, you will notice that there is a plus symbol, denoting a relationship, next to the records (Figure 5.75).

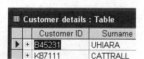

Figure 5.75 Plus symbol denoting relationship

Info

Setting rules/referential integrity

Rules should be applied to relationships so that it is impossible to delete a field in a related table when data still exists in the table it relates to. In Access this is known as *referential integrity*. When rules are set in Access this is known as *enforcing referential integrity*.

Referring to Figure 5.73, note when to select **Cascade Update Related Fields** (if the primary key in a primary table is changed, Access updates the corresponding fields in all related records automatically), and **Cascade Delete Related Records** (if a record in a primary table is deleted, any related records in related tables are also deleted automatically).

Working with the database **MFB Supplies**, create a one-to-many relationship between the **Customer ID** field of the **Customer details** table and the **Customer** field of the **Orders** table.

Method

1 Open the database **MFB Supplies** saved in the last exercise so that the **MFB: Supplies: Database** window is displayed, with the **Tables** button selected in the **Objects** section.

2 You have already examined and amended the table **Customer details** in Exercise 1 and the **Customer ID** field has primary key status in this table. (*Note*: In a one-to-many relationship, the related field in one of the tables must have primary key status or be uniquely referenced. In this instance this is the **Customer ID** field in the **Customer details** table, ie entries in this field have been set so that they cannot be duplicated.) Before creating the relationship, have a look at the **Orders** table. You will notice that in this table, entries in the **Customer** field are duplicated, ie there can be more than one order per customer. When you have finished examining the table, close it.

3 From the **Tools** menu, select: **Relationships** or click on: the **Relationships** button.

4 The Relationships box is displayed. This displays the relationships that already exist for this database. (If there had been no relationships set, the Show Table dialogue box would have been displayed.)

5 Right-click on the Relationships box; a pop-up menu is displayed (Figure 5.76).

6 Click on: **Show Table**.

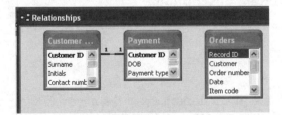

Figure 5.76 Adding a table to the Relationships box

7 Click on: the table **Orders** and click on: **Add**.

8 Click on: **Close**.

9 The Relationships box is displayed with the **Orders** table now present (Figure 5.77).

Figure 5.77 Orders table displayed in Relationships box

10 In the **Customer details** table box, hold down the left mouse button on the **Customer ID** field and drag it over the **Customer** field of the **Orders** table.

11 The Edit Relationships box is displayed (Figure 5.78). Note that the **Relationship Type** is **One-To-Many**.

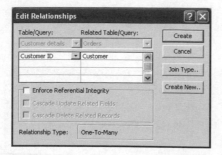

Figure 5.78 Edit Relationships box

12 Click on: **Create**.

13 Close the Relationships box and save changes.

6.4 ▶ Deleting a relationship

Method

1 Close any tables that are open.

2 Click on: the ⊞ **Relationships** button.

3 The Relationships box is displayed.

4 Click on: the line for the relationship to be deleted.

5 Press: **Delete**.

6.5 ▶ Creating queries or forms using more than one table

Exercise 3

Using the database **MFB Supplies** saved (with relationships created) in exercise 2, create a query to find out what orders have been placed by the customer **McFADDEN**. Save the query with the name **McFadden** and print it displaying the fields:

From the **Customer details** table: **Surname**, **Contact number**.

From the **Orders** table: **Order number**, **Date** and **Item description**.

Method

1 Create the query in the normal way except when the Show Table box is displayed (Figure 5.79) select: the **Customer details** table, click on: **Add**, then select: the **Orders** table and click on: **Add**. Click on: **Close**.

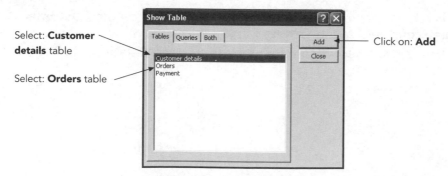

Figure 5.79 Selecting more than one table for a query

2 Both tables are displayed in **Query Design** view.

3 Select the relevant fields from the relevant table so that they are displayed in the **Design Grid**. Enter the search criteria (Figure 5.80).

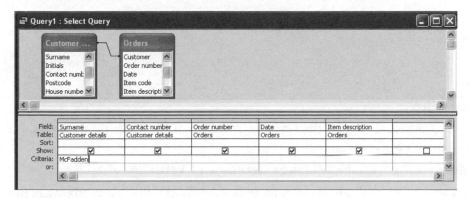

Figure 5.80 Design of query using two tables

4 View, save, print and close the query in the normal way.

6.6 Deleting objects in a database

Exercise 4

In the **MFB Supplies** database, delete the query **Telesales and promotions**.

Method

1 Display the **MFB Supplies: Database** window.
2 In the **Objects** section, click on: the **Queries** button.
3 Click on: the query to select it.
4 Press: **Delete**.

Note: Other objects, eg Tables, Reports, can be deleted using the same method.

6.7 Close the database and close Access

Note: For this exercise you will need the Access file **Garage**.

Practice 11

1   Open the file **Garage**.

2   Delete the query **david pike**.

3   Create a one-to-many relationship between the **Garage ref** field of the **Garage details** table and the **Garage ref** field of the **Vehicles** table.

4   Create the following query using the tables **Garage details** and **Vehicles**:

Find the details of vehicles make FD (Ford), with a price below £5,000. Print the following fields in ascending order of Price:

Garage, Address2, Make, Model, Price

5   Close the database and exit Access.

Database quick reference

(The following is a list of generally useful tasks associated with this module. For more information on specific items, refer to the chapter content.)

Action	Keyboard	Mouse	Right-mouse menu	Menu
Close a database	**Ctrl + W**	Click: the ☒ **Close** button on the database window		**File**, **Close**
Close the Table window		Click: the ☒ **Close** button of the Table window		**File**, **Save As**
Create a database	Load Access In the Task Pane, click: **Blank Database** Select: the location Enter: the filename Click: **Create** Click: **Tables** button Double-click: **Create table in Design view** Enter the field names. These will all appear (by default) as text entries under **Data Type**			
Data Type, changing	(See separate table in section 1 for a guide to Data Types and Field Properties) Click: in the **Data Type** box next to the field name you wish to change Click: the arrow Click: the Data Type you require, eg Number Select the Field properties			
Date format, overall	**Start** menu, **Control Panel**, **Date**, **Time**, **Language and Regional options** (Use **Date** tab to set specific date format for automatic insertions on Headers and Footers)			
Primary key	Select the field for the primary key and click: the 🔑 **Primary Key** button			
	Close the Table window by clicking: its ☒ **Close** button Save the Table design			
Edit data	Open the table (if it is not already open)			
	Click: on the entry you want to edit Delete/overwrite the old data Key in the new data			
Enter data	In the Database window, double-click: the table name Enter the data required in the correct fields. Widen the field columns as necessary. Close the Table window as before. The data is saved automatically			
Field, adding	In Table Design view: Click in the field below where you want to insert a new field			
		Click: the ᴣᴇ **Insert Rows** button	**Insert Rows**	**Insert**, **Rows**
	Add the field details. Resave the table design			
Field, delete	In Table Design view: Select the field to be deleted by clicking to the left of it			
	Delete	Click: the ᴣᴇ **Delete Rows** button	**Delete Rows**	**Edit**, **Delete Rows**

Action	Keyboard	Mouse	Right-mouse menu	Menu
Field order, changing	With the Table in Design view, click: the selection box of the field to move Click: the selection box again (an arrow and dotted box appear) Drag field to new location			
Filters, adding removing	With the object displayed in Datasheet view			
	Select what you want to filter Click: the ⛛ **Filter** button *To remove filter* Click: the **Filter** button again		**Records**, **Filter**, **Advanced** **Filter/Sort**	
Find a record	With the Table displayed, position the cursor in the field you want to search			
	Ctrl + F	Click: the 🔍 **Find** button		**Edit**, **Find**
	In the **Find What** box, key in what you want to find Click: **Find Next** Continue until all records have been found *Note:* You may need to choose a field that has a unique entry to ensure you find the correct record			
Forms, creating	With the database window open, click: the **Forms** button			
	Using Autoform Click: the **New** button Select: **AutoForm: Columnar** Select object(s) that the form is based on, click: **OK** *Using the Wizard* Double-click: **Create form by using wizard** Follow the Wizard's instructions			
Headers and footers in reports, forms	From the **Toolbox**, select: **Label** In the Report header/footer section, click and drag out a box Key in your text			
				(In Design view) **View**, **Page** **Header/Footer**
Help	**F1**			**Help**, **Microsoft** **Access Help**
	Shift + F1			**Help**, **What's** **This?**
Import generic file (CSV)	Load Access In the Task Pane, select: **Blank database** Select: a location and key in filename Click on: **Create** In the database window within Access, click on: the **New** button Click on: **Import Table**, then on: **OK** Select: location of the file (change **Files of type** to **Text Files**) Click on: **Import** **Import Text Wizard** guides you through			
Index, setting up, deleting	With the Table in Design view, position the cursor in the field you want to index In the **Field Properties**, **Indexed** section, make selection			
	Set the **Indexed** field property to **No**			

Action	Keyboard	Mouse	Right-mouse menu	Menu
Load Access	In the Windows desktop			
		Double-click: the **Microsoft Access** shortcut icon		**Start**, **All Programs**, **Microsoft Access**
Margins, altering				**File**, **Page Setup**, **Margins** tab
Open a table In Datasheet view	In the Database window, make sure the **Tables** button is selected			
		Double-click: the table name (Change to Design view by clicking: the **View** button)		
In Design view		Click: the table name (Click: the **Design** Design button)		
Print	Select the object you want to print			
	Ctrl + P			**File**, **Print**
	Make the necessary selections Choose **Setup** if you want to print Landscape Make the necessary selections from the **Setup** dialogue box Click: **OK**, **OK**			
Print, quick		Click: the **Print** button Access will automatically print the whole object		
Query, create in Design view	In the Database window ensure the **Queries** button is selected Double-click: **Create query in Design view** Select object(s) query is based on Click: **Add**, **Close** The fields of the table are now displayed in a list box in the Query window Place the fields that you want to see in your query in the field row of the query grid by double-clicking or dragging them *Note:* Place the fields in the order that you want them to appear Then see *Specify criteria*			
Query, calculations in fields	*Create a new field that calculates using other fields* With the query in Design view, key in a new field name in the field row Key in a colon then the calculation from other fields, eg NO IN STOCK: [NUMBER]-[NO SOLD]			

Action	Keyboard	Mouse	Right–mouse menu	Menu
	Calculations within a field In the query Design Grid, right-click on: the field name Select: **Totals** The **Totals** row is displayed Click on: **Group By** down arrow Select calculation type required			
Query, create a simple query using the Wizard	In the database window, ensure the **Queries** button is selected Click: **Create query by using Wizard** Follow the Wizard's instructions			
Query, sorting	Click: in the **Sort** box of the appropriate field Click: the ▼ arrow Select: **Ascending** or **Descending**.			
Query, specify criteria	Use the **Criteria** row in the grid to specify the conditions in a specific field – e.g. **RED** in the **Color** field			
Query, print specific fields	Use the **Show** row in the grid to choose whether or not to display a particular field in the query. A tick in the **Show** box means that the field will show, no tick means that it will not show. Click to toggle between them.			
Record, adding		Click: the ▶∗ **New Record** button *or* Click: in the blank cell immediately after the last record	(Right-click to the left of any record) **New Record**	**Insert**, **New Record**
Record, deleting	Select the record by clicking to the left of the first field of that record	Click: the ⊠ **Delete Record** button	**Delete Record**	**Edit**, **Delete Record**
	Click: **Yes** to save the change			
Relationships, creating				**Tools**, **Relationships**
Replace field entries	**Ctrl + H**			**Edit**, **Replace**
Report, creating	Ensure the Database window is displayed and that the **Reports** button is selected Double-click: **Create report by using wizard** In the Tables/Queries box, select: the name of the object – eg query, table – that the report is to be generated from Click: **Next** Select the fields to include in the report using the ⏵⏵ or ⏵ buttons Click: **Next** (*If you want to group the report – select the field(s) you want to group by here*) Click: **Next** Sorting (preferably ensure that the original object is sorted. However, if you want to change the sort order here select the field you want to sort by. *Note:* this could rearrange field positions in the final report) Click: **Summary Options** to include calculation results on the report Click: **Next**			

Action	Keyboard	Mouse	Right–mouse menu	Menu
	Select Layout Select the orientation you want – **Landscape** or **Portrait** Click: **Next** Select a style Click: **Next** Key in: the report title Click: **Finish**			
Save a query	**Ctrl + S**	Click: the 🖫 **Save** button		**File**, **Save As**
	To see the results of your query			
		Change to Datasheet view or Click: the **!** **Run** button		**Query**, **Run**
Sort records (quick sort)	Open the Table if it is not already open Select the field that you want to sort by clicking on the Field Name at the top of the field column			
ascending order		Click: the ⬆ **Sort Ascending** button	**Sort Ascending**	
descending order		Click the ⬇ **Sort Descending** button	**Sort Descending**	
Toolbars, customising				**View**, **Toolbars**
Undo		Click: the ↶ **Undo** button		

Important: Always close the database file properly.

Making a copy of a table

Sometimes it is useful to save your original table intact. Follow the steps below:

1 With the table name selected in the Database window, click on: the **Copy** button.
2 Click on: the **Paste** button.
3 In the **Paste Table As** dialogue box, key in the new table name, ensuring **Structure and Data** is selected.
4 Click on: **OK**.

You will now have two exact copies of the same table. Make amendments to one of them, leaving the other one intact.

Note: For this practice you will need to open the Access file **Estate Agents**.

Scenario

You work as an administrator at one of the branch offices of an estate agent. Following up customer enquiries, you have been asked to extract some records from a database of properties for sale at your office. You also need to make some alterations to the database. You have been asked to design and create a new table in the same database and link it to the existing table.

Finally there is a fund-raising event for a local charity coming up. Your company has agreed to accept donations of CDs and sell them. You need to create a database of the CDs so that as they come into the office they can be recorded and added to the circulation list.

Task 1

Using the **Estate Agents** database:

1   Delete the form **today**.

Working with the **Properties** table:

2   Extract all records that have 3 bedrooms. Sort in ascending price order. Save the query as **3 bedrooms** and print, ensuring all data is displayed in full.

3   Extract all records that have a location ending with **ON**. Sort in descending order of location. Save the query as **Location** (ending ON) and print.

4   Extract all records of properties with a single or double garage. Sort in ascending order of **Property ref**. Save the query as **parking** and print only the **Property ref**, **Price** and **Location** fields.

5   Reduce the price of **Property ref 2670** at Combe Down to 115000.

6   Add an additional record to the database as follows:

Property ref	Type	Type2	Beds	Garden	Garage	Price	Location
2999	F	T	1	No	No	68500	FROME

7   Change the **Property ref** 4503 to read **2503**.

8   Set the **Property ref** field to primary key status.

9   In design view, change the **Price** field to currency with a £ sign and 2 decimal places.

10   Change the data type of the **Property ref** field to **Number**.

11   In the **Property ref** field, set a validation rule so that only entries less than 5000 are acceptable. Set the validation text to: **All refs at this office less than 5000**.

12   Sort the database into ascending order of **price** and **location**. (*Note*: Select the adjacent columns together, then sort.)

13   Save and print the table.

14   Create a report titled **Properties for Sale** showing the fields **Type**, **Price** and **Location**. Sort in descending price order. Group by **Type** and include average summary details in the price field.

15   Add a header to the report with **Your name**.

16   Save and print the report in landscape.

Task 2

1   Within the database **Estate Agents**, open the table **Properties** and delete the following properties that have been withdrawn or sold:

Refs: 2755 in High Littleton, 2503, 2090, 2490 and 2300 in Keynsham, 2200 in Monkton Farleigh, 2344 in Paulton, 2500 in Peasedown St John, 2399 in Saltford.

2   Within the database **Estate Agents**, create a new table, **Vendors** with the field names and data as in the table below.

3   Set the date field to **Long Date** format.

4   Set the **Property Ref** field with primary key status.

5   Print the table **Vendors**.

Property ref	Title	Initial	Surname	Date registered	No of viewings
2100	Ms	A	Bloggs	10 Sept 03	1
2400	Mr	C	Higgins	6 June 03	10
2546	Mrs	D	Wells	9 Aug 03	3
2899	Ms	L	Williams	5 July 03	4
2670	Dr	R	Harris	29 Sept 03	6
2139	Miss	H	Kilpink	4 May 03	10
2890	Mr	P	Archer	19 Aug 03	11

6   Create a one-to-one relationship between the table **Property ref** field in the **Properties** table and the **Property ref** field in the **Vendors** table.

7   Using both tables, create a query to display all properties registered after 1/8/03. Sort in descending order of price. Display the fields:

Surname, No of viewings, Price and Location.

8   Save and print the query.

9   Close the database.

Task 3

The task is to create a database of CDs.

1   Create a database table in Design view with 6 fields. Use appropriate data types, distinguishing between text, date etc with the field sizes shown:

Title (40), **Artist** (25), **Release date, Category** (15), **Cost, Top 40** (Y/N)

2   Set the **Release date** field to Long date format.

3   Set the **Artist** field as indexed, duplicates allowed.

4   Set the **Cost** field to display to 2 decimal places.

5   Save the database as **Compact Disks** and the table as **CD**.

6   Create a form from the table.

7   Working with forms, create six records for any CDs (real or not) of your choice.

8   Sort the database in descending order of **Artist**.

9   Save and print the forms.

10 Working with the table, add a field **Label** (20) in between **Release date** and **Category**. Enter suitable label data.

11 Sort in alphabetical order of **Title**.

12 Save and print.

Note: These are only practice tasks. Successful completion does not imply certification of the module by the ECDL Foundation.

Presentation

Section 1 / Getting started

In this section you will practise and learn how to:

- open PowerPoint
- use application help functions
- close PowerPoint
- create a new presentation
- choose an appropriate automatic slide layout
- modify slide layout
- add text
- close a document
- save a presentation
- modify toolbar display
- use page view/zoom

- change view modes
- add an image, resize and move
- format font: italics, bold, underline, case, apply shadow, apply colours
- align text: centre, left, right, top, bottom
- adjust line spacing
- change type of bullets
- resize and move text within a slide
- use spellcheck
- print slides in various views
- select appropriate output

1.1 PowerPoint basics

PowerPoint enables you to create, organise and design effective presentations. These can be used as handouts, overhead transparencies, 35 mm slides and automated presentations on a computer.

1.2 Loading PowerPoint

Exercise 1

Load PowerPoint.

Method

From the **Start** menu, select: **All Programs**, **Microsoft PowerPoint** *or* double-click on: the 🔲 **PowerPoint** shortcut icon if you have one. Either method results in the PowerPoint window being displayed on screen (Figure 6.1).

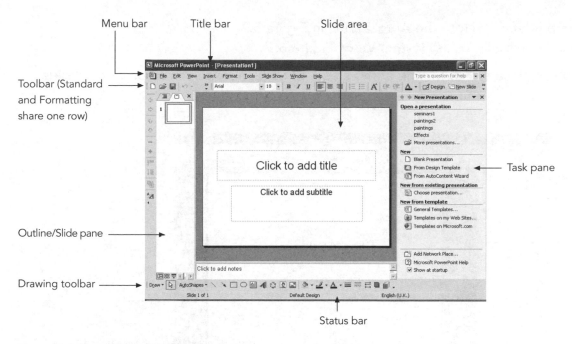

Menu bar   Title bar   Slide area

Toolbar (Standard
and Formatting
share one row)

Task pane

Outline/Slide pane

Drawing toolbar

Status bar

Figure 6.1 PowerPoint's opening window

1.3) Creating a new presentation

Exercise 2

Create slide 1.

Note: PowerPoint uses the word *slide* for each page created, even for the production of paper printouts or overhead transparencies.

Method

1 In the Task Pane, **New** section, click on: **Blank Presentation**. The **New Slide** dialogue box appears (Figure 6.2).

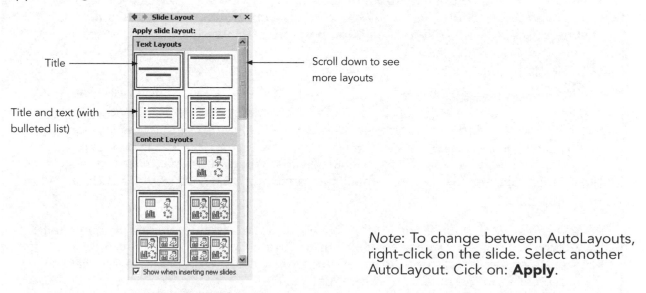

Title

Title and text (with bulleted list)

Scroll down to see more layouts

Note: To change between AutoLayouts, right-click on the slide. Select another AutoLayout. Cick on: **Apply**.

Figure 6.2 New Slide dialogue box

2 Slide layouts are displayed in the Task Pane (Figure 6.2). There are many different AutoLayouts to choose from. Hovering over a slide layout displays the name of the layout. Scroll down to view and familiarise yourself with possible layouts. Click the top left – **Title Slide** (it may already

be chosen by default). Note the AutoLayouts in Figure 6.2.

3   This first slide is displayed in **Normal View** (Figure 6.3).

Note: You can close the Task Pane at this stage, to have more screen display of the slide.

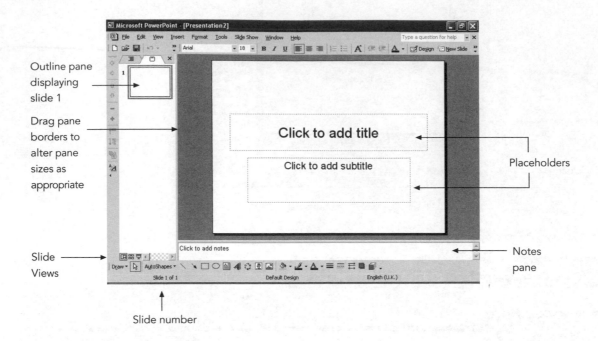

Figure 6.3 Slide in Normal View

Info

It is worth examining the PowerPoint window at this stage, noting Figures 6.1 and 6.3 and the following:

Modifying toolbars

The Standard and Formatting toolbars display (by default) on one row. It is quite useful to leave them like this so that you have more room to work on your slides. If you want to modify the toolbar display, use the **View** menu, select: **Toolbars**, then: **Customize**. Click on: the **Options** tab. Use the **View** menu, **Toolbars**, to select which toolbars to display or hide.

Slide views

The slide is displayed in **Normal View**. It contains three panes: outline, slide and notes. The pane sizes can be adjusted by dragging the pane borders. Normal View displays slides individually and can be used to work on/view all parts of your presentation. The outline pane gives an overview of your presentation (currently there is only one slide). The notes pane allows you to input any notes that you want to make about the slide. These notes aid the speaker when making a presentation. Other views include:

Slide Sorter:

*   You can view all your slides in this view as miniatures (small versions or thumbnails).
*   Zoom in and out for more/less detail using **Zoom** Control.
*   Sort slides into a different presentation order by clicking on the slide you want to move and dragging it to a new location.
*   Add a new slide by placing the pointer between the slides where you want the new slide to appear and clicking on the **New Slide** toolbar button.
*   Delete a slide by selecting it and pressing the **Delete** key. Use the **Undo** toolbar button to reinstate the deleted slide. Use the **Redo** button to redo.

Slide Show: Shows your slides on a full screen, as they will appear when you set a slide show in motion. Select the first slide. Click on: the **Slide Show** button. To view the next slide, press: **Page Down**. When all the slides have been viewed you will be returned to the previous view (this will be covered in more detail later) or pressing: **Esc** will return you to the previous view.

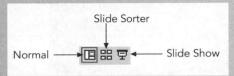

Getting help

Help is obtained, as in other Office applications, ie using the **Help** menu, pressing: **F1** or **Shift** and **F1**.

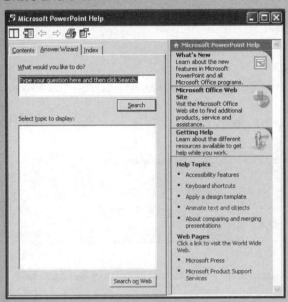

Figure 6.4 PowerPoint Help

Help

Note: Throughout this book, the Office Assistant facility has been hidden so as not to distract from the main objectives. More details of the Office Assistant are found in the Appendix.

You can select:

- The **Contents** tab for a list of help topics. By double-clicking on a topic, a display of that topic will appear.
- The **Answer Wizard** tab. This allows you to key in a question and then click on: **Search**. The topic will then be highlighted in the contents list and the topic displayed as above.
- The **Index** tab. This allows you to key in key words and click on **Search**. Again, the topic will be highlighted and displayed as above.

To close the Help window, click on: the **Close** button.

ScreenTips

From the **Help** menu, select: **What's This?** Then click on the item you want to know about. A short description appears. Press: **Esc** to remove the ScreenTip.

Accessing Help in a dialogue box

To access Help in a dialogue box, click on: the **Help** button in the dialogue box and then click on the item you want help about.

4 The slide is shown as in Figure 6.5. It has pre-set placeholders (boxes with dotted-line borders to hold text, bulleted lists etc).

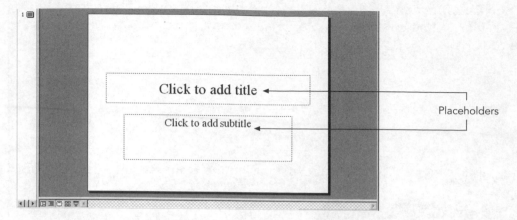

Figure 6.5 Slide View

5 In the slide window, click in: the top placeholder (**Click to add title**) and key in **Presenting with PowerPoint**.

6 Click in: the bottom placeholder (**Click to add subtitle**) and key in your name.

> ### Info
> Title and subtitle can also be referred to as heading and subheading. Body text is usually the text that follows the subheading.

> ### Exercise 3
> Format the text on slide 1.

> ### Info
> PowerPoint bases its default text formats on its default master slide. You will learn more about master slides in section 2.

> ### Method

As in Word, select the text you want to format and then use the **Formatting** toolbar buttons (Figure 6.6) and/or the **Format** menu, selecting **Font** to change the font type, point size, embolden, italicise or underline, apply text shadow.

Change case by selecting: **Change Case** from the **Format** menu.

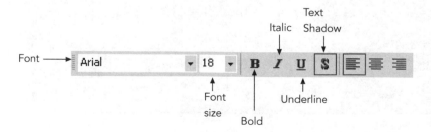

Figure 6.6 Formatting toolbar buttons

Serif and sans serif fonts

Serifs are small lines that stem from the upper and lower ends of characters. Serif fonts have such lines. Sans serif fonts do not have these lines. As a general rule, larger text in a sans serif font and body text in a serif font usually makes for easier reading. For example:

Times New Roman is a serif font.

Arial is a sans serif font.

1   Align the text within the placeholders using the toolbar alignment buttons, ie **Align Left**, **Align Right** and **Center**.

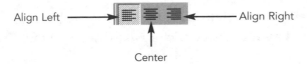

Align Left ⟶   ⟵ Align Right

↑
Center

2   Align the placeholders in relation to the slide:
   a   Select the placeholder.
   b   On the **Drawing** toolbar, click on: **Draw** and then select: **Align or Distribute**.
   c   Click on: **Relative to Slide** so that a tick appears.
   d   Click on: **Draw** again, select: **Align or Distribute** and click on the option you want, ie **Align Top**, **Bottom**, **Left**, **Right** (Figure 6.7).

Figure 6.7 Aligning objects

3   Change the font colour by selecting text, then clicking the down arrow on: the **A ·** **Font Color** button on the **Drawing** toolbar. (By default this toolbar is at the bottom of the working area. If this is not visible, from the **View** menu, select: **Toolbars** and click on: **Drawing**.)

Use the **Undo/Redo** buttons when appropriate or when practising.

1.4   Saving the presentation

Exercise 4

Save the presentation with the name **section1**.

Method

1   From the **File** menu, select: **Save As**.
2   The Save As dialogue box is displayed.

3 In the **Save in** box, select where you want to save the file.

4 In the **File name** box, key in a filename.

5 Click on: **Save**.

Exercise 5

Create a second slide in the presentation.

Method

1 Click on: the 🔲 New Slide **New Slide** button.

2 In the Task Pane, **Other Layouts** section, choose the AutoLayout **Title**, **Text and Clip Art** as shown in Figure 6.8.

Note: You now have two slides in the left-hand pane.

Title, Text and
Clip Art layout

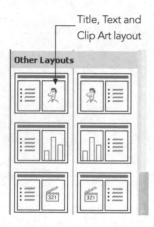

Figure 6.8 Creating slide 2

3 In the **Click to add title** placeholder, key in: **Lists and Pictures**.

4 In the left-hand placeholder, key in the numbers 1 to 4, pressing **Enter** after each number except 4 (the last one). Notice that a bulleted list has been created.

Changing bullet type

5 Select the bulleted text. From the **Format** menu, select: **Bullets and Numbering**.

6 Make your choices from the Bullets and Numbering dialogue box. Click on: **OK**.

Info

Numbered lists

At step 6, you can select a numbered list by clicking on: the **Numbered** tab. You can also add bullets and numbered lists to slides using the appropriate toolbar buttons, ie ⊞ **Bullets** or ⊟ **Numbering**. Click on the relevant toolbar button before keying in text or select the text to be bulleted or numbered and then click on the relevant toolbar button.

Deleting bullets/numbers

Select the list or the line with the bullet/number to delete. Click on: the relevant **Bullets/ Numbering** button.

Changing line spacing

7 Select the list. From the **Format** menu, select: **Line Spacing**.

8 The Line Spacing box is displayed (Figure 6.9).

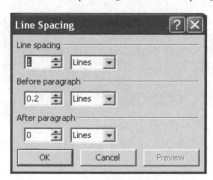

Figure 6.9 Line spacing

9 Select the line spacing required and click on: **OK**.

Adding a picture

10 To insert a picture in the right-hand placeholder, double-click in: the placeholder.

11 The Select Picture dialogue box is displayed (Figure 6.10).

12 Scroll through the Clip Art or key in search text in the **Search Text** box and click on: **Search**. Click on: the **Back** button to return to the categories.

13 When you have decided which to use, click on your chosen one and then on: **OK**.

Note: To return to general Clip Art, delete the entry in the **Search** box, click on: **Search**.

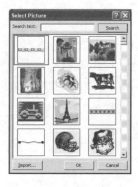

Figure 6.10 Select Picture dialogue box

Slide 2 will now look something like Figure 6.11.

Lists and Pictures

> 1
> 2
> 3
> 4

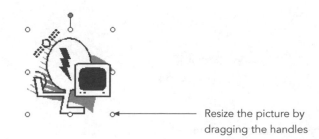

Resize the picture by dragging the handles

Figure 6.11 Slide 2

14 Resize the picture by dragging the handles.

1.6 Moving the elements of the slide

Exercise 6

Reduce the size of the image and reposition it at the bottom right-hand corner of the slide.

Method

1 Click on: the image to select it.
2 Reduce the size as in step 14 above.
3 With the graphic still selected, hover the mouse over it; an arrowhead cross appears.
4 Holding down the left mouse button, drag the graphic to the required position.

Your slide will now look something like Figure 6.12.

Lists and Pictures

➤ 1
➤ 2
➤ 3
➤ 4

Figure 6.12 Graphic resized and repositioned

5 Save your work using the **Save** button method.

1.7 Adding text and pictures to a blank layout

Exercise 7

Create slide 3 using the blank AutoLayout. Decide on your own text for this slide.

Method

1 Click on: the **New Slide** button.
2 In the Task Pane, **Content Layout** section, select: **Blank** AutoLayout.
3 Experiment with adding your own text and graphics.

Adding text

1 Click on: the  **Text Box** button on the **Drawing** toolbar.
2 Click where you want the text to start. *Note*: You need not drag out a box, as the text will expand the box to fit.
3 Key in the text and format it as required.
4 Click in any white space on the slide when finished.
5 Adjust the text box size so that the text fits neatly on the slide.

Adjusting line spacing

When you have more than one line of text, you can adjust the line spacing.

Method

1 With the cursor positioned in the text box, from the **Format** menu, select: **Line Spacing**.
2 Make your choices from the Line Spacing dialogue box.

To add a picture

1 From the **Insert** menu, select: **Picture** and then **Clip Art** (Figure 6.13).
2 In the Task Pane, search and select the Clip Art you want to insert.

Figure 6.13 Adding a picture

Note: The picture is placed in the centre of the slide. Resize and reposition it as necessary following the method given above.

Use your imagination and practise adding and changing elements on this slide. When you are happy with the result, save your work.

You now have three slides in the presentation.

1.8 Viewing the slides

There are several ways to view your slides (see section 1.3). Practise using these views now.

1.9 Implementing a colour scheme

Exercise 8

For all three slides, change the background colour to light green and the title text to red.

Method

1 From the **Format** menu, select: **Slide Design**.
2 You can experiment with the colour schemes provided. However to create your own scheme, click on: **Color Schemes**. Then click on: **Edit Color Scheme**.
3 The Edit Color Scheme dialogue box is displayed.
4 With the **Custom** tab selected, in the **Scheme Colors** section, click on: **Background**, then on: the **Change Color** button (Figure 6.14).

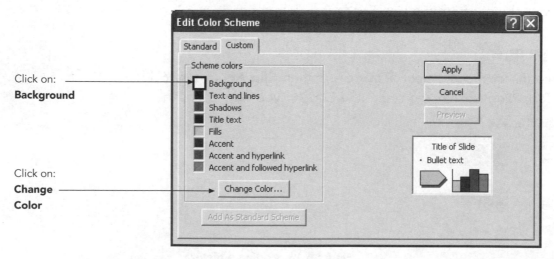

Figure 6.14 **Edit Color Scheme dialogue box**

5 The Background Color dialogue box appears. With **Standard** selected, click on: a shade of light green, then on: **OK** (Figure 6.15).

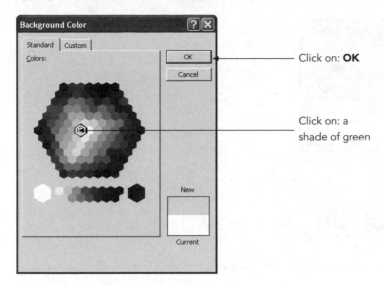

Click on: **OK**

Click on: a shade of green

Figure 6.15 Adding a background colour

6 You are returned to the Edit Color Scheme dialogue box. This time select: **Text and lines** and follow the instructions above, choosing the colour red for the Title text.

7 When you are returned to the Edit Color Scheme dialogue box, click on: **Apply**. You are automatically returned to your slide.

Note: You can apply colours to selected slides by selecting them in the slide pane at step 1.

8 Change to **Slide Sorter View** and see how your slides look with this colour scheme.

Note: The text colour has not been applied to the Title text. **Title Text** is not included in **Text and Lines** and must be chosen separately at step 1.

9 Save your presentation with the name **section2**. (You will use this file for section 2.)

1.10 Spellcheck the presentation

Exercise 9

Spellcheck and resave the presentation.

Method

1 Press: **CTRL + Home** to move to Slide 1.
2 Click on: the **Spelling** toolbar button.
3 The Spelling dialogue box is displayed (Figure 6.16).

Select correct word from list or key in the word in the **Change to** box

Click on: **Ignore** to leave text unchanged

Click on: **Change** to correct

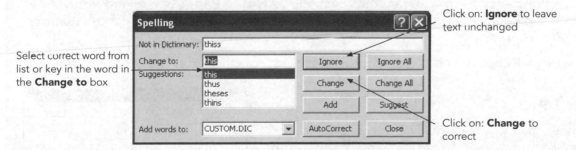

Figure 6.16 Checking spelling

4 Make changes as appropriate.

5 Always resave your work after spellchecking to save any corrections.

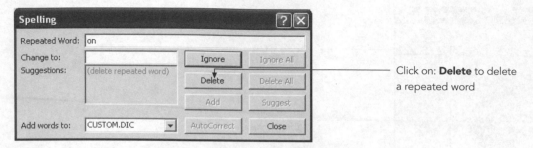

Click on: **Delete** to delete a repeated word

Figure 6.17 Deleting repeated words

1.11   Printing your presentation

Exercise 10

Print the presentation of three slides, one slide per page.

Method

From the **File** menu, select: **Print**. The Print dialogue box appears (Figure 6.18).

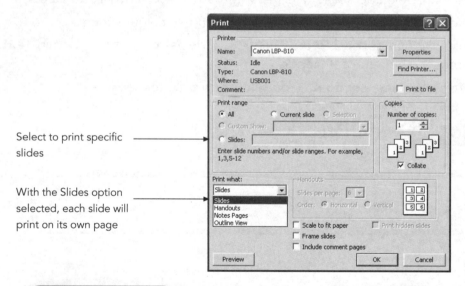

Select to print specific slides

With the Slides option selected, each slide will print on its own page

Figure 6.18 Print dialogue box

Info

In the **Print what** section, you can choose to print slides in various views including as individual slides (one per page), as **Handouts** (several slides on one page, you can select the number per page in the Handouts section), as **Notes Pages** (slides and notes) or **Outline View**. In the **Copies** section, in the **Number of copies** box, select the number of copies to print.

In the **Page Range** section, you can select to print specific slides.

Page setup

You can size the slides for different outputs in the Page Setup dialogue box (**File** menu, **Page Setup**), **Slides sized for** section. In the **Orientation** box, you can select: **Portrait** or **Landscape**.

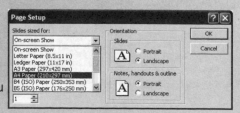

PowerPoint can do design work for you by applying design templates.

Method

1   From the **Format** menu, select: **Slide Design**.
2   In the Task Pane, click on: **Design Templates** (Figure 6.19).
3   Scroll through and click on: a design name, then on its down arrow.
4   From the menu, click on: **Apply to All Sides**.

Figure 6.19 Applying a design template

5   Save your presentation with the name **design** and print as handouts, three per page.

Changing design template

1   From the **Format** menu, select: **Slide Design**.
2   Follow the method above.

1.13   Closing and exiting PowerPoint

Method

1   From the **File** menu, select: **Close**.
2   From the **File** menu, select: **Exit**.

1   Create a three-slide presentation as follows and format it to good effect using the layout given as a guide.

Slide 1

Using Title slide AutoLayout, enter the text shown:

Web Mania Designs
Training Seminar

The Royal York Hotel

Bristol BS8 2TS

Tel 0117 220220

E-mail: jodi@wmdesigns.com

Slide 2

Using the Bulleted list AutoLayout, enter the following. Format the bullets as squares. Add a suitable piece of Clip Art in the bottom right corner.

Basics of Design

✓   Designing for the screen

✓   Controlling layout

✓   Using colour and graphics

✓   Deciding typography

Slide 3

Using the 2 Column Text AutoLayout, enter the following text. Adjust the line spacing in the body text to 1.25 lines. *Note*: Delete the bullets by positioning the cursor in the bulleted line and pressing: the backspace key.

Fonts and Balance

Fonts

Fonts are often grouped in families with plain, italic, bold and bold italic forms. Some families, such as Helvetica, have a much greater range of more than thirty forms, including demi bold, extra bold and compressed.

Balance

Although many designs can work and be acceptable, there are a few basic rules to consider. Positioning text or an object too high or too low can look imbalanced. The eye plays tricks and the visual weight should balance.

---

2   Apply a light yellow background to all the slides.

3   Automatically change the title text on slide 3 to upper case.

4   Set all title text to dark blue.

5   Save the presentation.

6   Print the slides as handouts (three per page).

7   Close the file and exit PowerPoint.

In this section you will practise and learn how to:

- open an existing presentation
- create and use a master slide
- number slides
- add different types of line, move lines, change line colour/modify line width
- add shapes and free-drawn lines
- rotate or flip an object
- change attributes: colour, line type, apply shadow
- set line weights, style and colours in a text box
- use copy/cut and paste to duplicate slides/text/images within presentation(s)

- use cut and paste as above
- reorder slides
- open several presentations
- delete an image/selected text/slides
- use Outline View
- add notes to slides
- save an existing presentation
- save under different file types and version number
- modifying basic options/preferences within PowerPoint

Note: Since answers to the exercises in this section will vary considerably, no sample answers are given.

2.1) **Opening an existing presentation**

Exercise 1

Load PowerPoint and open the presentation with the name **section2** created in section 1.

Method

1 Open PowerPoint as in section 1.
2 In the Task Pane, **Open a presentation** section (Figure 6.20), click on: the filename.
3 If the filename is not visible, to locate it click on: **More presentations**.

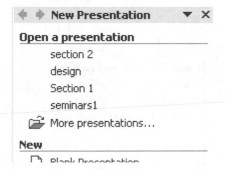

Figure 6.20 Opening an existing presentation

Exercise 2

Create a master slide for the presentation, containing a fixed date of **19 September 2003**, slide number and the footer **PowerPoint Basics**.

Info

The default master slide is always present and your presentation will be based on the default settings if you do not change them. In order that your slides have a common look and feel, it is a good idea to set up a master slide containing common objects that you want to appear on all the slides. These objects cannot then be deleted, except from the master slide.

Method

1 From the **View** menu, select: **Master**, **Slide Master**. The master slide appears (Figure 6.21).

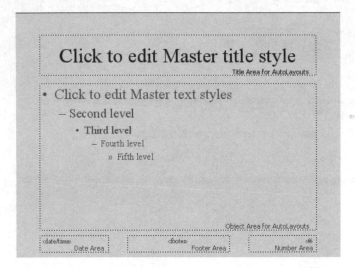

Figure 6.21 The master slide

2 From the **View** menu, select: **Header and Footer**.
3 The Header and Footer dialogue box is displayed (Figure 6.22).

Select: the **Slide** tab to display on slides

Selecting the **Notes and Handouts** tab allows you to display different items on Notes and Handouts

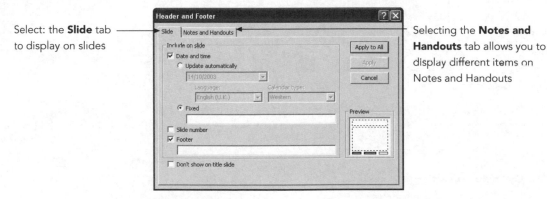

Figure 6.22 Header and Footer dialogue box

4   With the **Slide** tab selected, in the **Include on slide** section, click in: the option box for **Date and time** so that a tick is displayed. Notice the options: **Update automatically** (this option will always display the current date whenever the presentation is opened) or **Fixed** (this will display a static date that you enter in the box below Fixed). In this exercise, click in: the **Fixed** option button and in the box below key in the date **19 September 2003**.

5   Click in: the **Slide number** box.

6   Ensure there is a tick in the **Footer** box. Key in the footer text **PowerPoint Basics** in the footer box. (*Note*: When a footer is not required, you can deselect this box.)

7   Click on: **Apply to All**.

    Note: You can select not to show the footer on the Title slide.

8   Change to **Slide Sorter View** to view the effects of creating a master slide. You may want to increase the Zoom to be able to read the footer text. Change back to the default when you have finished.

Info

You can view and edit the master slide, at any time, by selecting: **Master** from the **View** menu. You can delete objects from a master slide by selecting them and then pressing: **Delete**. You can add pictures, images and drawn objects to the master slide using the methods given in this module for general slides.

You are able to overwrite the footer details on individual slides by selecting the slide and formatting its footer details. Click on: **Apply**.

2.3 Adding lines and shapes

Exercise 3

Create a new slide and practise adding lines and shapes.

Method

1   In **Normal View**, click on: the last slide in the presentation in the Outline pane. (This will ensure that the new slide is correctly positioned as slide 4 of the presentation.)

2   Click on: the **New Slide** button.

3   Select: **Blank** AutoLayout.

4   Ensure that you are in **Slide View** with the Drawing toolbar visible. If not, from the **View** menu, select: **Toolbars**, **Drawing** so that a tick appears next to it. The Drawing toolbar is shown in Figure 6.23.

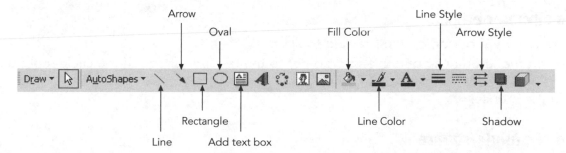

Figure 6.23 Drawing toolbar

Adding a line

1 Click on: the **Line** button.
2 Position the crosshair where you want the line to start.
3 Hold down the left mouse button and drag the mouse to where you want the line to end. Release the mouse.

Formatting the line

1 Select the line by clicking on it. When it is selected, handles appear at each end.
2 Click on: the **Line Style** button.
3 Click on the line style that you want.
4 Click on: the down arrow of the **Line Color** button to choose the line colour.

Note: You can set more precise attributes by selecting: **Autoshape** from the **Format** menu. Make selections in the Format AutoShape dialogue box (Figure 6.24).

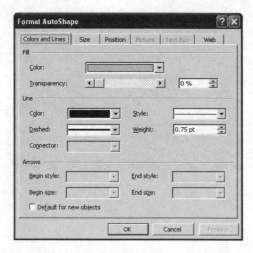

Figure 6.24 Setting precise attributes to lines and shapes

Changing line length and moving a line

1 Click on the line to select it.
2 Change the length by dragging the handles to the required length.
3 Move the line by holding down the mouse anywhere along its length until the arrowhead cross appears and then drag it to the new position.

Adding arrows to lines

1 With the line selected, click on: the **Arrow Style** button.
2 Select: a style or click on: **More Arrows** to display the Format AutoShape dialogue box. Select **Begin** and **End** styles in the **Arrows** section.

Note: You can also add an arrowed line by clicking on: the **Arrow** button.

Adding a circle or ellipse

1 Click on: the **Oval** button on the Drawing toolbar.
2 Hold down the left mouse button and drag out to the required shape. For a circle, hold down **Shift** at the same time as dragging.
3 Release the mouse.

Adding a rectangle/square

Follow the method for a circle/ellipse, shown above, but clicking on: the **Rectangle** button. For a square, hold down **Shift** at the same time as dragging.

Filling a shape with colour

1 Select the shape to fill.
2 Click on: the **Fill Color** button.
3 Click on the chosen colour.

Filling a shape with a pattern

Follow steps 1 and 2 in 'filling a shape with colour' above.

3 Click on: **Fill Effects**. The Fill Effects dialogue box appears.
4 Click on: the **Pattern** tab.
5 Click on: the chosen pattern. Click on: **OK**.

Applying a shadow

1 Select the required object.
2 Click on: the **Shadow** button.

Adding free-drawn lines

1 Click on: the **AutoShapes** arrow button. Select: **Lines**, **Freeform** or **Scribble** (Figure 6.25).

Figure 6.25 Free-drawn lines

2 Hold down the left mouse and draw with the 'pencil'.

Note: Check the other options on this menu – they are very useful.

Resizing objects

Resize objects by selecting them and dragging their handles.

Aligning objects

1 Select the object.
2 Click on: the **Draw** button arrow, select: **Align or Distribute**, **Relative to Slide**.
3 Click on: the **Draw** button arrow again, select: **Align or Distribute**.
4 Click on: the required position.

Rotating or flipping an object

1 Select the object.
2 Click on: the **Draw** button arrow, select: **Rotate or Flip** and then select from the next menu (Figure 6.26).

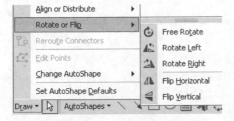

Figure 6.26 Rotating and flipping objects

When there is more than one object and they overlap, you can select the display order as follows:

1 Right-click on the object.
2 On the Drawing toolbar, click on: **Draw**.
3 Click on: **Order** and make a selection (shown below).

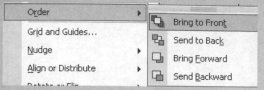

Objects can be grouped so that they stay together. To do this:

1 Hold down **Shift** whilst clicking in turn on the objects to group.
2 Right-click over the selected objects.
3 Select: **Grouping**, **Group**.

Note: You can ungroup using this menu.

Experiment with the other Drawing toolbar buttons to create some stunning effects.

2.4 Setting line weights, styles and colours in text boxes

Exercise 4

Create a text box at the top of the slide. Insert the text **Adding shapes and lines**. Format the text box.

Method

1 Add a text box in the normal way and key in the text.
2 With the text box selected, format it using the Drawing toolbar buttons.

2.5 Copying/cutting and pasting within a presentation

Exercise 5

Copy the text box created in Exercise 4 so that it appears centred on slide 2 under **Lists and Pictures**.

Method

1 In **Normal View**, select the text box.
2 Click on: the **Copy** button.

3 Select slide 2 from the left pane.

4 Click on: the **Paste** button.

5 Position the object as appropriate.

The methods in exercises 6 and 7 apply for Clip Art, text and images.

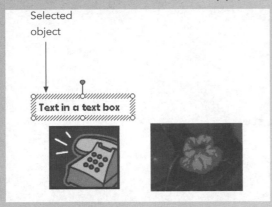

Figure 6.27 Examples of objects

Duplicating

1 Select the object by clicking on it (it displays handles when selected).

2 Click on: the **Copy** button.

3 Go to the location to copy to, ie another slide in the presentation (select from the left pane or use the navigation arrow buttons or switch to another presentation, use the **File** menu, **Open** or **New**, or, if the destination presentation is already open, click on: its button on the taskbar).

4 Click on: **Paste**.

Moving

Follow the instructions above except at step 2, click on: the **Cut** button.

Resizing

With the object selected, drag its handles (drag from the corners to keep proportions).

Deleting

With the object selected, press: **Delete**.

Exercise 6

Move the picture on slide 2 to a new blank slide.

Method

1 Create a new slide using the **Blank** AutoLayout.

2 Select slide 2 from the left pane, and then select the picture.

3 Click on: the **Cut** button.

4 Select the new slide from the left pane.

5 Click on: the **Paste** button.

Copy the picture from slide 3 so that it appears in the box on slide 2 (in place of the moved picture).

Method

1 In **Normal View**, select the picture on slide 3.
2 Click on: the **Copy** button.
3 Select slide 2 from the left pane.
4 Select the picture placeholder and click on: **Paste**.

2.6 Duplicating whole slides

Exercise 8

Duplicate slide 1.

Method

1 In **Slide Sorter View**, select slide 1.
2 From the **Insert** menu, select: **Duplicate Slide**.
3 The duplicate of the slide appears next to slide 1.

Note: You can also duplicate slides by selecting the slide to copy and clicking on: the **Copy** button. Click where you want the slide to appear and click on: the **Paste** button. You can cut and paste whole slides using the **Cut** instead of the **Copy** button.

2.7 Reordering slides

Exercise 9

Reorder the slides so that the duplicate slide becomes the last slide.

Method

In **Slide Sorter View**, hold down the left mouse on slide 2 and drag the slide to the required position.

2.8 Opening more than one presentation

Exercise 10

Open a new presentation and copy slide 2 of the PowerPoint presentation **section1** to the new presentation.

Method

1 Click on: the  **New** button.
2 Select **Blank** AutoLayout.
3 On the **taskbar**, click on: the **section2** button (Figure 6.28).

Figure 6.28 Switching presentations

4 In **Slide Sorter View** select slide 2.
5 Click on: the **Copy** button.
6 On the **taskbar**, switch to the new presentation by clicking on the button **section2**.
7 In **Slide** View, click on: the **Paste** button.
8 Resize to fit the slide if necessary.

Note: Although you have copied this slide, it will not implement the master slide for slides in this new presentation. You can use the methods in section 2.5 for copying/pasting text, pictures and images between applications, switching presentations using the taskbar buttons.

2.9 Deleting pictures/images/text

To delete pictures, images or text from slides, select the picture/image/text and press: **Delete**. Practise this now.

2.10 Deleting slides

Exercise 11

Delete slide 3 from the presentation **section2**.

Method

1 In **Slide Sorter View**, select slide 3.
2 Press: **Delete**.

2.11 Working in Outline View

When editing or reviewing slides it is often quicker to work in Outline View. In **Normal** view, click on: the **Outline** tab in the **Outline** (**Slides**) pane.

Outline tab

Edit text in this pane

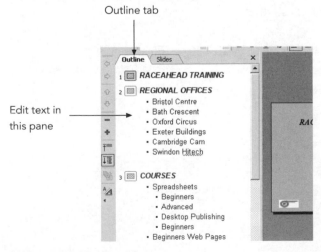

Figure 6.29 Outline View

Click on: the **Outline View** button now and practise editing text in your presentation.

2.12 Adding notes to slides

Info

You can add notes to your slides. These are useful 'prompts' for key points when you are delivering a presentation. You can print notes for each slide together with a small version of each slide as handouts.

Exercise 12

Add a note to slide 1 of the new presentation **'This slide has been copied from another presentation'**. Print the slide together with the notes.

Method

1 Ensure that the correct presentation and slide are displayed.
2 Key in the text in the **Notes** pane.
3 From the **File** menu, select: **Print**.
4 In the **Print what** section, select: **Notes Pages**.
5 Click on: **OK**.

2.13 Saving an existing presentation and in different format or version

Exercise 13

Save both presentations. Save the new presentation in a form suitable for the web.

Method

1 Save the existing presentation by clicking on: the **Save** button.
2 Save the new presentation by clicking on: the **Save** button. The Save As dialogue box is displayed. Select the location where you want to save it.
3 Key in a suitable filename.
4 Click on: the arrow in the **Save as type** box and select: **Web Page** (Figure 6.30).
5 Click on: **Save**.

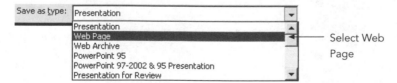

Figure 6.30 Saving as Web page

File formats

Being able to save files in different formats is extremely useful. It means that you can share files with others who do not have the same software or version, eg PowerPoint 95, of software that you are using. Saving in web format will usually reproduce reliably. You can save in a previous version of PowerPoint but beware since some functions may not have been available in earlier versions so some elements may be lost or changed. PowerPoint files have the extension .ppt. Other useful formats include:

Outline/RTF (Rich Text Format) .rtf – this saves the text of the presentation so that it can be opened in Word, for example.

Design Template .pot – this saves the layout so that you can reuse it thus saving time. You need only add content to the slides.

Image formats – use JPEG (.jpg) or GIF (.gif) formats when you want to insert slides on web pages or use them in other graphics programs.

Web page .htm or .html.

2.14 Modifying basic options/preferences within PowerPoint

When you know that you will always be opening/saving files in a particular folder it is worth setting this as the default. Set your user name so that it appears on automatic entries, eg in headers and footers.

1   From the **Tools** menu, select: **Options**.

2   Select: the **General** tab (Figure 6.31).

3   In the **User information** section, key in your name.

4   Select: the **Save** tab. In the **Default file location** box, key in the location (Figure 6.32).

5   Click on: **OK**.

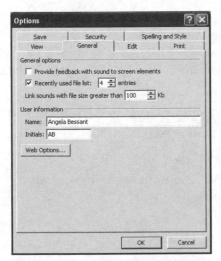

Figure 6.31 Setting user name

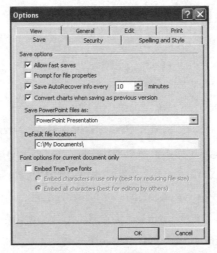

Figure 6.32 Setting default location

2.15 Close both presentations and exit PowerPoint

1   Reload the presentation saved in Presentations Practice section 1.

2   Set the master slide to contain a footer with the date (that updates automatically) and the text **Created by** (**your name**). Do not display the footer on slide 1.

3   Add a suitable graphic to this master slide at the top right. Resize it to approximately 2 cm square (keep the original aspect ratio).

4   Delete the graphic on slide 2.

5   On slide 2 add a line across the page between the text **Basics of Design** and the bulleted list. Give the line a weighting of 6 pt.

6   On slide 2 change the bulleted list to a numbered list.

7   Add a new blank slide at the end of the presentation.

8   Using the Drawing toolbar buttons, create the following diagram in the centre of the newly created slide:

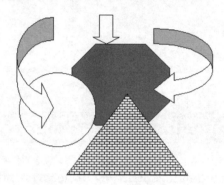

9   Add a text box below the diagram with the text **Using shapes**.

10   Format the text box with a background colour light pink and text colour dark green.

11   Add another new blank slide at the end of the presentation.

12   Copy the text box just created on the previous slide to the new slide.

13   Open a new PowerPoint presentation and use Title slide AutoLayout for the first slide as follows:

   PowerPoint Designs
   (Your name)

14   Add a new blank slide 2.

15   Copy the text box (**Using shapes**) from the original presentation (final slide) to the second slide of the new presentation. Position at the top of the slide.

16   Add a text box in the centre of the slide in step 15 with the text **Using the Drawing toolbar**.

17   Add a note to this slide: **Practising drawing skills in PowerPoint**.

18   Return to the original presentation. Reorder the slides so that slide 1 becomes the last slide.

19   Save the original presentation and print as Handouts (all slides on one page) in portrait display.

20   Print the new presentation as Notes Pages.

21   Save the new presentation in a format suitable for the web.

22   Close both files and exit PowerPoint.

In this section you will practise and learn how to:

- create an organisational chart
- modify the structure of an organisational chart
- create different kinds of chart/graph

3.1 Creating an organisational chart

Exercise 1

Load PowerPoint and a new presentation. On slide 1 enter the text **Types of Chart** and add a bulleted list containing:

- organisational
- bar
- pie

On the master slide for this presentation, insert a footer containing your name and slide number. Save the presentation with the filename **Print Company**. On slide 2 create an organisational chart.

Method

1 Create slide 1 and edit the master slide.
2 Create slide 2 by clicking on: the **New Slide** button and selecting: **Title and Diagram** or **Organization Chart** AutoLayout (Figure 6.33).

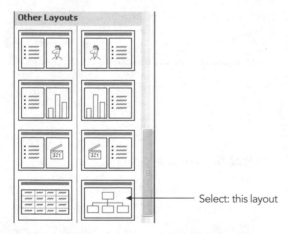

Select: this layout

Figure 6.33 Creating an organisational chart

Figure 6.34 Diagram Gallery

3 Key in: the title **Personnel** in the **Title** placeholder. You can also add a company name here.
4 Double-click in: the chart box to add the organisational chart. The Diagram Gallery window appears (Figure 6.34). Click on: the **Organization Chart** and then on: **OK**.
5 Key in the following details by clicking in: the first relevant box and overwriting the original text. Click on: the second relevant box and so on.

Note: You may find it easier if you enlarge the display. (Use Zoom from the **View** menu.)

Personnel

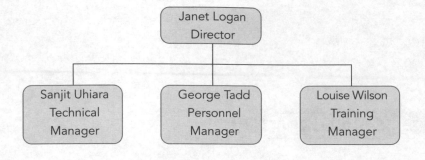

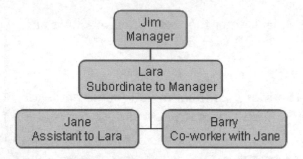

Figure 6.35 Example of a hierarchial layout

Adding chart boxes

Exercise 2

Simeon Harris works alongside Sanjit Uhiara and is also a Technical Manager. Add a Co-worker box and enter his name and his position.

Method

1   Click on: the Sanjit Uhiara box.
2   Click on: the down arrow of the [Insert Shape ▾] **Insert Shape** button.
3   Select: **Coworker**.
4   Key in: Simeon Harris's details.

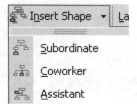

Figure 6.36 Selecting Coworker

Paula Hudson's line manager is George Tadd. Her title is Administrator. Enter a chart box for Paula.

Method

1 Select: George Tadd's box.
2 Select: the **Subordinate** button from the **Insert Shape** menu.
3 Key in: Paula Hudson's details.

Info

You can continue adding as many boxes as necessary to complete an organisational chart. Select the button as appropriate, eg **Manager**, **Subordinate** etc. (Figure 6.35).

3.2 Editing a chart

Exercise 4

George Tadd's name does not have the correct spelling. Change his surname to Tadde.

Method

Click on: the relevant box and amend as necessary.

Exercise 5

Sanjit Uhiara has been promoted to Senior Technical Manager and is now Simeon Harris's line manager. Change the chart hierarchical structure as appropriate.

Method

1 Select Simeon Harris's box.
2 Using the mouse, drag this box over Sanjit Uhiara's box.
3 Release the mouse.
4 Change Sanjit Uhiara's title.

Deleting boxes

In the chart window, right-click on the box to delete. Press: **Delete**. (Make sure you select the *box* and not the *text*. See Figure 6.37).

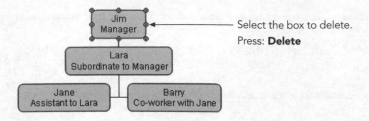

Figure 6.37 Deleting chart boxes

Delete an entire chart by right-clicking on its slide and pressing: **Cut**.

This also applies to data charts (as in Section 3.3).

3.3 Creating a column/bar/line/pie chart

Exercise 6

Create slide 3 containing the title **Weekly Visits – Jun to Aug 2003**. Include a chart showing the sales set out below:

	Week1	Week2	Week3	Week4
Jun	110	95	168	202
Jul	67	89	101	79
Aug	210	250	178	122

Method

1 Click on: the **New Slide** button.
2 In the Task Pane, **Other Layouts** section, select: **Title and Chart** AutoLayout (Figure 6.38).
3 Click on: **OK**.

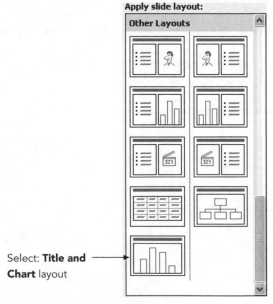

Select: **Title and Chart** layout

Figure 6.38 Chart layout

4 Key in the title in the **Title** placeholder.
5 Double-click to add the chart. A datasheet (Figure 6.39) and a bar chart are displayed (Figure 6.40).

6 Key in the data above in the appropriate cells overwriting the sample data (Figure 6.40).

Print Company - Datasheet						
		A	B	C	D	E
		1st Qtr	2nd Qtr	3rd Qtr	4th Qtr	
1	East	20.4	27.4	90	20.4	
2	West	30.6	38.6	34.6	31.6	
3	North	45.9	46.9	45	43.9	

Figure 6.39 Original datasheet

Print Company - Datasheet						
		A	B	C	D	E
		Week1	Week2	Week3	Week4	
1	Jun	110	95	168	202	
2	Jul	67	89	101	79	
3	Aug	210	250	178	122	

Figure 6.40 Content entered

7 Close the Datasheet window by clicking on: its **Close** button.

Exercise 7

Change the column chart to a bar chart.

Method

1 Double-click on: the chart to select it. Right-click on: the selection and select: **Chart Type** from the pop-up menu.

2 The Chart Type dialogue box is displayed. Select the bar chart you require. Click on: **OK**.

Note: You can change to other chart types, for example, line and pie. Remember that pie charts use only one data series so you may need to hide data on the datasheet to get an accurate result.

Display the datasheet by clicking on: the ▦ **View Datasheet** button.

To Hide data: Select the column(s)/row(s) to hide. Right-click on the selection and select: **Hide**.

To Unhide data: Select the column(s)/row(s) to unhide. Right-click on the selection and select: **Unhide**.

Depending on how you lay out data you can use the buttons to plot by row or by column. Add/delete rows or columns and format as in Excel.

Resizing a chart

1 Click on: the chart to select it.
2 Drag its handles.

Changing chart colours – bars, lines, pie slices

1 Double-click on: the chart.
2 Click on: the section of the chart to change, ie column, bar, line or pie segment so it is selected.

Note: To select individual pie segments, click on: the pie chart and then click on: the individual segment.

3 Right-click: on selection.

4 Select: **Format Data Series**. (For pie charts, select: **Format Data Point**.)

5 The Format Data Series box is displayed (Figure 6.41). (For pie charts, the Format Data Point box is displayed.)

6 In the **Area** section, click on: a colour and then on: **OK**.

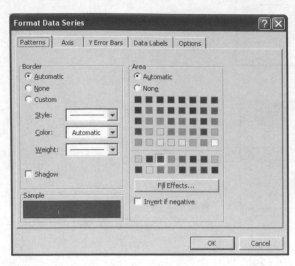

Figure 6.41 Changing chart colours

Changing chart background colour

1 Double-click on: the chart.

2 Right-click on: the centre of the chart.

3 Select: **Format Plot Area**.

4 The Format Plot Area dialogue box is displayed (Figure 6.42).

5 In the **Area** section, click on: a colour and then on: **OK**.

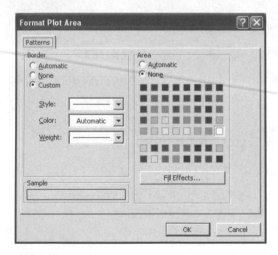

Figure 6.42 Changing background colour

Deleting a chart

1 Select the chart.

2 Press: **Delete**.

Copying/moving a chart

1 Select the chart.

2 Use the Copy/Move and Paste method.

Paula Hudson's line manager is George Tadd. Her title is Administrator. Enter a chart box for Paula.

Method

1 Select: George Tadd's box.
2 Select: the **Subordinate** button from the **Insert Shape** menu.
3 Key in: Paula Hudson's details.

Info

You can continue adding as many boxes as necessary to complete an organisational chart. Select the button as appropriate, eg **Manager**, **Subordinate** etc. (Figure 6.35).

3.2 Editing a chart

Exercise 4

George Tadd's name does not have the correct spelling. Change his surname to Tadde.

Method

Click on: the relevant box and amend as necessary.

Exercise 5

Sanjit Uhiara has been promoted to Senior Technical Manager and is now Simeon Harris's line manager. Change the chart hierarchical structure as appropriate.

Method

1 Select Simeon Harris's box.
2 Using the mouse, drag this box over Sanjit Uhiara's box.
3 Release the mouse.
4 Change Sanjit Uhiara's title.

Deleting boxes

In the chart window, right-click on the box to delete. Press: **Delete**. (Make sure you select the *box* and not the *text*. See Figure 6.37).

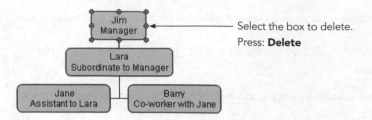

Select the box to delete.
Press: **Delete**

Figure 6.37 Deleting chart boxes

Delete an entire chart by right-clicking on its slide and pressing: **Cut**.

This also applies to data charts (as in Section 3.3).

3.3 Creating a column/bar/line/pie chart

Exercise 6

Create slide 3 containing the title **Weekly Visits – Jun to Aug 2003**. Include a chart showing the sales set out below:

	Week1	Week2	Week3	Week4
Jun	110	95	168	202
Jul	67	89	101	79
Aug	210	250	178	122

Method

1 Click on: the **New Slide** button.
2 In the Task Pane, **Other Layouts** section, select: **Title and Chart** AutoLayout (Figure 6.38).
3 Click on: **OK**.

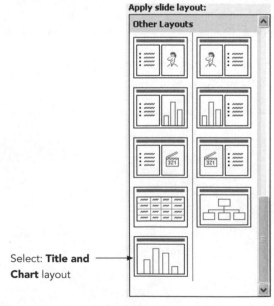

Select: **Title and
Chart** layout

Figure 6.38 Chart layout

4 Key in the title in the **Title** placeholder.
5 Double-click to add the chart. A datasheet (Figure 6.39) and a bar chart are displayed (Figure 6.40).

Working with charts

Duplicating

1 Select the chart by clicking on it (it displays handles when selected).
2 Click on: the **Copy** button.
3 Go to the location to copy to, ie another slide in the presentation (select from the left pane or use the navigation arrow buttons or switch to another presentation (use the **File** menu, **Open** or **New**, or (if the destination presentation is already open) click on: its button on the taskbar).
4 Click on: **Paste**.

Moving

Follow the instructions above except at step 2, click on: the **Cut** button.

Resizing

With the chart selected, drag its handles (drag from the corners to keep proportions).

Deleting

With the chart selected, press: **Delete**.
Note: You can also right-click on the chart and select from the pop-up menu.

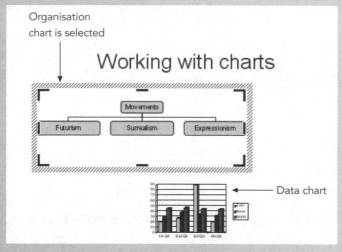

Figure 6.43 Working with charts

3.4 Save and print the presentation (as slides)

3.5 Close the presentation and exit PowerPoint

1   Open a new PowerPoint presentation, choose a design template to be used throughout and create
    the following three slides:

Slide 1

Using the Title slide layout enter the title **Science Faculty, South Downs College** and the
subtitle **Bourton House, Windmill Road, Bristol BS6 8HT e-mail
science@soudowns.ac.uk**

Slide 2

Using the Organization Chart layout, enter the title **Science Faculty Staff**. Enter the
organisational chart as shown:

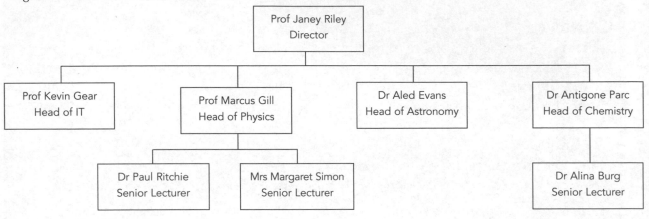

Slide 3

Using the Chart slide layout, add the title **Student Stats**. Use the following chart data to produce a
3-D Bar chart:

	IT	Phys	Astro	Chem
TERM 1	32	21	12	19
TERM 2	65	26	15	47
TERM 3	28	25	19	37

2   Change the text in the title of slide 2 to **September 2003 – Teaching Staff**.

3   Save the presentation and print the slides on separate pages.

4   Close the presentation.

In this section you will practise and learn how to:

- add slide transitions
- start a slide show
- add preset animation effects
- change preset animation effects

4.1 Creating transitional timings

Info

In **Slide Show View** you can see how the slides look on a full screen moving to the next/previous slide using the **Page Up/Page Down** keys (other keys will also perform the same task. Pressing the **Home** key will take you to slide 1 and pressing the **End** key will take you to the last slide). The slides do not run automatically. In order for them to do this you need to set up transitional timings (slide durations) that automatically show the next slide after a set number of seconds.

Exercise 1

Load PowerPoint and load one of the presentations you have created in the last sections. Create an automated presentation with slide durations shown below:

Slide no	Slide duration
Slide 1	5 secs
Slide 2	7 secs
Slide 3	15 sec
Slide 4	10 secs

Method

1 In **Slide Sorter View**, click on: slide 1 to select it.
2 Click on: the ⊞ Transition **Transition** button. *Note:* You may need to click on: the ⁑ **Toolbar Options** button to locate the **Transition** button on the Slide Sorter toolbar.
3 The Task Pane is displayed (Figure 6.44).

Figure 6.44 Slide Transition Task Pane

4 In the **Advance Slide** section, click in: the box **On mouse click** so that there is no tick in the box. Click in: the box **Automatically after** so that a tick is shown, and in the box beneath, key in the slide duration for slide 1, ie 5 (Figure 6.45).

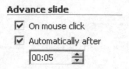

Figure 6.45 Setting timing

5 Click on: **Apply**. Slide 1 now has the duration (00:05) shown underneath at the left-hand side (Figure 6.46).

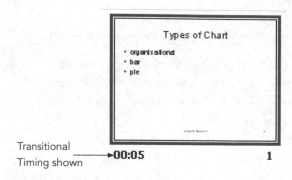

Figure 6.46 Transitional timing

6 Click on: the next slide and repeat steps 4 and 5 for each of the other slides ensuring that you have selected the timing requested.

7 Save the presentation.

Info

You can also add transitional timings by clicking on: the ⬚ **Rehearse Timings** button. Slide 1 is shown with a **Rehearsal** box counting the time in the top left of the screen. Move to the next slide by clicking on the ⬚ arrow at the bottom left of the screen. Select: **Next** from the menu. When all the slides have been shown, you are asked if you want to accept the timings. Click on: **Yes**.

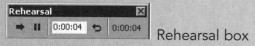 Rehearsal box

---

4.2   Starting a slide show

Exercise 2

Start the slide show created in 4.1.

Method

1 From the **Slide Show** menu, select: **View Show**.

2 The presentation will run automatically with the timings that have been set.

To start the slide show at a slide other than the first slide, select: **Set Up Show** from the **Slide Show** menu. The Set Up Show dialogue box is displayed. In the **Slides** section, key in the slides to view. Note the other options available in this dialogue box.

4.3 Hiding slides in a show

Exercise 3

Hide one of the slides in your show.

Method

1 In **Slide Sorter View**, select the slide to hide.
2 Click on: the ▧ **Hide Slide** button.
   Hidden slides have a cross through their number, eg ▧ .

   Note: Unhide a slide by selecting it in **Slide Sorter View**, click on: the **Hide Slide** button.

4.4 Changing transitional timings

Info

If you are not happy with the timings set, change them by selecting a slide with the time you want to change. Click on: the **Slide Transition** button and edit the time next to the **Automatically after** box. Click on: **Apply**. Repeat for all slides you want to change.

4.5 Creating transitional effects

Info

Transitional effects control how slides appear on the screen during a presentation. They are used to enhance the display and to ensure that the audience of the presentation stays interested in it.

Exercise 4

Create different transition effects for each of the slides.

1 In **Slide Sorter View**, click on: slide 1 to select it.
2 Click on: the **Transition** button.
3 The **Slide Transition** Task Pane is displayed (Figure 6.47).

Figure 6.47 Creating slide transition effects

4 In the **Apply to selected slides** section, click on a transition effect. There are many transition effects to choose from – you can scroll down for more. You will see a preview of the effect on slide 1. Experiment with the different effects. When you find one you like, click on it.
5 An icon appears beneath the slide to show that it has a transition effect applied to it (Figure 6.48).

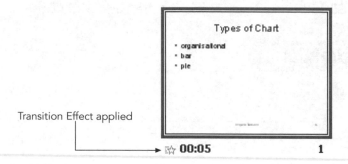

Transition Effect applied

Figure 6.48 Transition Effect applied

6 Repeat for the other slides, choosing a different transitional effect for each one.
7 Save the presentation.
8 You can now run the presentation so that you can view how the transitional effects look.

Info

If you want to apply the same transition effect to more than one slide in the presentation, select more than one slide by holding down the **Shift** key whilst selecting them. It is best not to apply too many transition effects to an automated presentation. Stick to the ones that you think work best. You can define the transition effect further in the **Modify Transition** selection. Here you can choose the speed of the effect and add sound!

If you need to change transition effects, select the slide with the effect you want to change. Click on: the **Transition** button. Select an alternative effect from the Task Pane.

4.7 Creating preset animation effects

Info

Preset animation effects determine the way that text or objects are revealed on a slide. They are usually very effective when applied to bulleted lists but can be applied to any slide.

Exercise 5

Add different preset animation effects to all the slides except slide 4.

Method

1 In **Slide Sorter View**, click on: slide 1 to select it.
2 From the **Slide Show** menu, select: **Animation Schemes**.
3 In the Task Pane, click on: an animation scheme (Figure 6.49).

Figure 6.49 Selecting animation effects

4 To view the animation effect, change to **Slide Show View**. The presentation will begin. To exit the slide show, press: **Esc**.
5 Add preset animation effects to the other slides as appropriate.
6 Save the presentation.
7 View the automated presentation.

Info

If you need to change preset animation effects, select the slide with the effect you want to change. Select an alternative effect. If the preset animation effect is attached/to be attached to one item only, eg text in a placeholder:

1   In **Normal** view, select the item.
2   From the **Slide Show** menu, select: **Animation Schemes**.
3   Click on: an effect.
4   From the **Slide Show** menu, select: **Animation Schemes**.

Info

Effects and timings can be applied to individual objects on a slide, eg images as follows:

1   Right-click on an object.
2   Select: **Custom Animation**.
3   The Custom Animation Task Pane is displayed (Figure 6.50).

Figure 6.50 Custom Animation Task Pane

4   Click on the down arrow of the **Add Effect** button.
5   Select an effect (Figure 6.51).

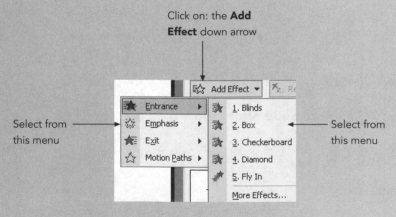

Figure 6.51 Selecting an effect

6 The object with the effect added is now displayed (Figure 6.52).

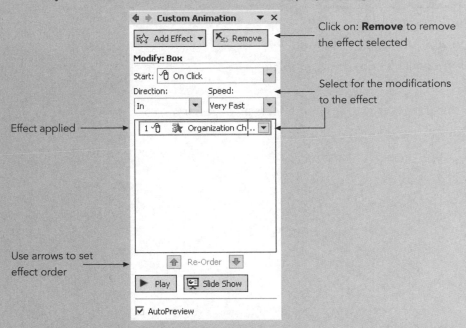

Click on: **Remove** to remove the effect selected

Select for the modifications to the effect

Effect applied

Use arrows to set effect order

Figure 6.52 Modifying effects

7 In the **Modify: Box** you can make further selections. Use the down arrow next to the object to access more choices.

To remove an effect

1 Select the object.
2 Click on: **Remove**.

To add another effect to the same object

1 Select the object.
2 Click on: **Add Effect** or **Change Effect**.

Ordering effects

Use the **Re-Order** arrows to set the order of effects in the slide show.

4.9 **Save and close the presentation and exit PowerPoint**

Section 4 — Presentations practice

1 Reload the presentation saved in Presentation practice section 3.

2 Add transitional timings to the presentation.

3 Add preset animation effects to the presentation.

4 Hide slide 3.

5 Review the slide show and reset timings and effects as necessary.

6 Save the presentation.

Presentation quick reference

(The following is a list of generally useful tasks associated with this module. For more information on specific items, refer to the module content.)

Action	Keyboard	Mouse	Right–mouse menu	Menu
Alignment, in relation to slide		Select object **Drawing** toolbar, **Draw**, **Align or Distribute**, **Relative to Slide** then **Draw**, **Align or Distribute**, select option you want		
Bold text	**Ctrl + B**	Click: the **B** **Bold** button	**Font**	**Format**, **Font**
				Select: **Bold** from the **Font style:** menu
Borders		Select object Drawing toolbar Click: ✏️ **Line Color** button Click: ☰ **Line Style** button		
Bullets, changing type			**Bullets and Numbering**	**Format**, **Bullets and Numbering**
Capitals (blocked)	**Caps Lock** Key in the text **Caps Lock** again to remove			Select text to be changed to capitals: **Format**, **Change Case**, **UPPERCASE**
Centre text	Select the text			
	Ctrl + E	Click: the ☰ **Center** button		**Format**, **Alignment**, **Center**
Change case	Select the text to be changed From the **Format** menu, select: **Change Case** Select the appropriate case			
Chart, inserting data organisation	Select appropriate slide AutoLayout, ie chart or organisation chart: **Insert**, **Chart** Data chart – overwrite sample data, click: ▦ **View Datasheet** button Organisation – select: Organization Chart from Diagram Gallery *or* click on: ✪ **Diagram** on the Drawing toolbar. Key in text			
Close a file	**Ctrl + W**	Click: the ✖ **Close** button		**File**, **Close**
Colours, slide				**Format**, **Slide Design**, **Color Schemes**

Action	Keyboard	Mouse	Right–mouse menu	Menu
Copy/cut text or object	Select the text or object to be cut/copied			
	Ctrl + X	Click: the ✂ **Cut** button or the ▤ **Copy** button	**Cut/Copy**	<u>E</u>dit, Cut/<u>C</u>opy
Delete a character	Press: **Delete** to delete the character to the right of the cursor Press: ← (Backspace) to delete the character to the left of the cursor			
Delete an image	Select the image, press: **Delete**			
Delete a word	Double-click: the word to select it Press: **Delete**			
Delete an slide	Select the slide in Slide Sorter View. Press: **Delete**			
Delete/cut a block of text	Select the text you want to delete			
	Delete or **Ctrl + X**	Click: the ✂ **Cut** button	**Cut**	<u>E</u>dit, Cu<u>t</u>
Duplicate slide				<u>I</u>nsert, <u>D</u>uplicate Slide
Effects, transitional timings	In **Slide Sorter** view			
		Click: the ▣ Transition **Slide Transition** button	**Slide Transition**	Sli<u>d</u>e Show, Slide **Transition**
	In the **Advance Slide** section Select: the timing you require			
Effects, transitional effects	In **Slide Sorter** view			
		Click: the ▾ down arrow next to the **Slide Transition** button	**Slide Transition**	Sli<u>d</u>e Show, Slide **Transition**
	Select: the effect you want from the drop-down menu			
Effects, preset animation	In **Slide Sorter** view			
			Slide Transition	Sli<u>d</u>e Show, Animation Schemes
	Select: the effect you want from the drop-down menu			
Exit PowerPoint		Click: the ✕ **Close** button		<u>F</u>ile, E<u>x</u>it
Font	Select the text you want to change			
		Click: the ▾ down arrow next to the **Font** box Select: the font you require	**Font** Select the required font from the **Font:** menu	F<u>o</u>rmat, <u>F</u>ont
Serif	Serif fonts have small lines at upper and lower ends of characters – eg Times New Roman			
Sans serif	Sans serif fonts do not have lines – eg Arial			
Font colour	Select the text you want to colour			
			Font	F<u>o</u>rmat, <u>F</u>ont

Action	Keyboard	Mouse	Right–mouse menu	Menu
Font emphasis	Select the text you want to emphasise			
		Click on: the appropriate **Bold**, **Italic**, **Underline** button **B** *I* <u>U</u> or **Shadow** S	**Font**	**Format**, **Font**
Font size	Select the text you want to change			
		Click: the ▾ down arrow next to the **Font Size** box	**Font**	**Format**, **Font**
		Select: the font size you require	Select the required size from the **Size:** menu	
Headers and footers				**View**, **Header and Footer**
Help	**F1**			**Help**, **Microsoft PowerPoint Help**
	Shift + **F1**			**What's This?**
Hide a slide		Click: the 🔲 **Hide Slide** button		**Slide Show**, **Hide Slide**
Import graphic, text or other object	From the **Insert** menu, select: **Picture** or **Object** or use copy (in the source application) and paste into PowerPoint			
Insert text	Position the cursor where you want the text to appear Key in the text			
Line spacing	Select text or text box			
				Format, **Line Spacing**
Lines, adding formatting	Use the relevant Drawing toolbar buttons			
Load PowerPoint	In Windows desktop	Double-click: the **PowerPoint** shortcut icon		**Start**, **All Programs**, **Microsoft PowerPoint**
Master Slide setup				**View**, **Master**, **Slide Master**
Move objects within a slide	Select the object and drag to the new location			
New presentation, creating	**Ctrl** + **N**	Click: the ▯ **New** button		**File**, **New**
New Slide	**Ctrl** + **M**	Click: the 🔲New Slide **New Slide** button		**Insert**, **New Slide**
Notes, adding	In **Normal View**, add to the **Notes** pane			

Action	Keyboard	Mouse	Right-mouse menu	Menu
Numbering slides				**Insert**, **Slide Number**
Open an existing file	**Ctrl + O**	Click: the 📂 **Open** button		**File**, **Open**
	Select the appropriate directory and filename Click: **Open**			
Orientation of slides				**File**, **Page Setup**
Print – Slides, Handouts, Notes Pages, Outline View	**Ctrl + P**			**File**, **Print**
	Select from the **Print what:** drop-down menu			
Remove text emphasis	Select text to be changed			
	Ctrl + B (remove bold) **Ctrl + I** (remove italics) **Ctrl + U** (remove underline)	Click: the appropriate button: **B** **I** **U**	**Font** Select: **Regular** from the **Font Style:** menu	**Format**, **Font**
Resize objects	Select the object. Resize using the handles. To preserve aspect ratio, resize from a corner			
Rotate object	Select the object. **Draw** button, **Rotate or Flip**			
Run automated presentation		Click: the 🖵 **Slide Show** button at the bottom left of the screen		**View**, **Slide Show**
Save	**Ctrl + S**	Click: the 💾 **Save** button		**File**, **Save**
	If you have not already saved the file you will be prompted to specify the directory and to name the file			
Save using a different name or to a different directory or in a different format				**File**, **Save As**
	Select the appropriate drive and change the filename and file type if relevant Click: **Save**			
Shadow, adding	On the Drawing toolbar, click: the ⬛ **Shadow** button			
Slide order	In **Slide Sorter** View Click and drag the slide to required position			
Spell check	**F7**	Click: the ✓ **Spelling** button		**Tools**, **Spelling**

Action	Keyboard	Mouse	Right-mouse menu	Menu
Superscript and subscript text			**F**ont, **Effects**	**F**ormat, **F**ont, **Effects**
Templates, using		Formatting toolbar, ☑ Design **Slide Design** button		**F**ormat, **Apply Design Template**
Toolbars, modifying	**V**iew, **T**oolbars, **C**ustomize			
Undo	**Ctrl + Z**	Click: the ↶ **Undo** button		**E**dit, **U**ndo
View		Click: a **View** button ⊞▦☲		**V**iew, **make selection**
Zoom		Click: the 100% ▾ **Zoom** button		**V**iew, **Z**oom

Note: For these exercises you will need the files **colour** and **Art debate**.

You work as a Media Assistant in The Reading Rooms and Events Centre, a cultural centre, open to the public. The centre houses a well-stocked library and organises cultural events. You have been asked to create three slides that will form the basis for future presentations at the centre. You have also been asked to amend a couple of presentations that will be used at a forthcoming event.

Task 1

1   Make a three-page presentation for The Reading Rooms and Events Centre.

2   The first slide is the Title slide. Key in the text: **Reading Rooms and Events Centre** as the title and **Open to All** as the subtitle.

3   On the master slide, add a footer with your name and date, set at 10 October 2003. Insert a suitable piece of ClipArt on the master slide. Resize and position it at the bottom right so it looks effective.

4   On slide 2 key in the text: **Reading Rooms**.

5   Underneath key in the bulleted list:

- **Open every day except Sunday**
- **Opening hours 8.00 to 18.00**
- **Registration card required, cost £5.50**
- **Student registration is free**
- **Minimum age 16 (unless accompanied)**

6   Format the bullets as ticks.

7   Insert a Dash line, 3 pt, across the slide below the list.

8   On slide 3 create an organisational chart entitled **The Team** as follows:

Greg Howe – Rooms Co-ordinator, Paula Brill and Jill Bailey are Managers immediately subordinate to Greg Howe. Matt Quincy and Kiki Grekko are co-workers (Researchers) subordinate to Jill Bailey.

9   Apply a template design that you think will look appropriate.

10   Save the presentation as **reading rooms** and print slides as Handouts (all three on one page).

Task 2

1   Open the presentation **colour**.

2   Replace the word **slide** with **background** throughout.

3   Change the text on the final slide to upper case.

4   Spellcheck and resave as **colour (your initials)**.

5   On slide 1, embolden the text: **Some ideas to think about**.

6   Add the following text to the note on slide 3:

Suggest some other colour combinations that do not work very well.

7   On the master slide change the footer to display the fixed date of 29 October 2003. Replace the name with your name. Do not display the footer on the Title slide.

8   Enter the following text on slide 7:

Colour is the key to good design. Remember that colour is a personal preference and so you will not be able to please everyone.

Add shadow effect to the new text. Align the text in this placeholder to the right and set the background colour to light grey.

9   Move slide 2 so that it becomes slide 3.

10   Delete slide 5.

11   Add a Cover Down transition effect to slide 1.

12   Change the timing of slide 3 to 10.

13   Hide slide 4.

14   Duplicate slide 1 to the end of the presentation.

15   Save the presentation as **colour2**.

16   Print as handouts, four slides per page.

17   Print slide 2 only (with the text **Red text with an orange**…) as a Notes page.

18   Close the presentation.

Task 3

1   Open the presentation **Art debate**.

2   On slide 2, delete the box for the artist **Picasso**.

3   On slide 3, change the colour of the red circle to blue. Display this circle in front of the smiley face. Flip horizontally the yellow, patterned triangle.

4   Create a new slide 4 with the title **Artist Preference**. Add a column bar chart using the data below:

	Group1	Group 2	Group 3	Group 4
Picasso	10	6	8	10
Munch	3	5	1	1
Dali	1	3	5	3

Colour the bars as follows:

Picasso: red, Munch: green, Dali: yellow

5   Save the presentation as **art debate1**.

6   Print the slides as handouts to fit on one page.

Note: These are only practice tasks. Successful completion does not imply certification of the module by the ECDL Foundation.

Module 7

Information and Communication

In this section you will practise and learn how to:

- use Internet terms: Internet, World Wide Web, HTTP, URL, ISP, FTP
- appreciate security issues
- open a web browsing application
- understand the make-up and structure of a web address
- use application Help functions
- display a given web page

- change the web browser home page
- save a web page/picture as a file
- download files and software
- close the web browsing application
- change view/display modes
- modify toolbar display
- display/hide images on a web page

Note: Much of the theory content of this module is covered in Module 1. Please refer back for revision purposes.

1.1 The Internet and the World Wide Web

The *Internet* is made up of interconnected computer networks all over the world that send, receive and store information. An individual with a computer and the relevant communications equipment can gain access to this network by subscribing to an *Internet Service Provider* (*ISP*) so that he or she can connect to the Internet as often or as seldom as he or she likes (or can afford). Large companies, educational establishments and government offices have their own arrangements and are usually connected to the Internet all the time.

When connected to the Internet, all calls are charged at local telephone rates. The agreement you have with your ISP will determine how much your time online will cost. Some ISPs offer some hours free but technical support, when you need it, could be expensive. They all have their individual deals (these are changing all the time) so it is worth shopping around for the best to suit your particular needs. Instead of using a telephone line to connect, you may be able to use a high-speed digital connection. Your ISP will be able to advise you on the various connection methods available.

If you pay for your calls, it is worth waiting for the times of day when it is cheap rate, or weekends. Some phone companies have a minimum three-minute charge so it is better to be connected for the full three minutes than make three one-minute connections. Keep a note of how long you are spending *online* (connected). Read web pages *offline* (when not connected) and compose and read e-mails offline too. Once you have learnt the basics, use shortcut keys to save time. If you plan to use the Internet a lot, ensure that you add the Internet number to your low-cost options with your telephone provider.

The *World Wide Web* (*WWW* or *web* for short) is one of the services run on the Internet. It contains millions of *websites* – linked pages of words that usually include pictures, sounds and graphics. All these sites can be explored using a web browser (see below). Web pages contain *hyperlinks* to other web pages and other websites so that users can plot their route through depending on their area of interest.

The number of websites is growing at a phenomenal rate. Each website is created and managed by an organisation or individual and each have their own unique addresses so that you can locate them. Websites are stored on computers connected to the Internet. In fact, with a little know-how, anyone can create a website and ISPs usually provide the facility and storage space to host one. Websites come and go and are constantly being updated. As a result, what you see on a site one day could be quite different from what you see the following week.

Note: The web addresses and screenshots of sites used in this book were correct at the time of writing but may have changed by the time you access them.

Websites are usually presented in an interesting and attractive way to encourage people to spend time exploring them. There are websites covering almost every subject imaginable. Some websites are protected, ie they cannot be displayed without a user name and password. Such sites contain sensitive or confidential information, eg sites for ECDL tutors that cannot be accessed by learners; pages on websites that contain your personal information, eg account details. Large companies have *firewalls* (special software and hardware) in place that guard against unauthorised entry or tampering with their sites, eg sites with confidential information for their personnel only. Many people are concerned about security issues associated with online purchasing. Although there is a risk of credit card fraud, most e-commerce websites now implement a range of secure purchasing procedures. *Digital certificates* are used to ensure identities and secure sites use encryption – all the details that you enter are turned into a code that is meaningless other than to the computers involved. A digital certificate is a statement signed by an independent and trustworthy third party. It typically contains subject name, public key information and a certifying authority (CA) signature. Digital certificates are available from various suppliers. Using these techniques, your personal information cannot be tampered with whilst being transmitted.

Computer viruses (unwanted, destructive computer coding) are often spread through computer communications, eg by downloading infected files. Always use an *antivirus utility program* to alert you to a virus and remove it. Remember that antivirus utility programs must be updated on a regular basis to be able to cope with new viruses.

1.2 What is a web browser?

A web browser is software that allows you to view, navigate and interact with the World Wide Web. Currently the two most commonly used browsers are Internet Explorer and Netscape Navigator. In this module the examples use Internet Explorer. You will need to check which browser your ECDL test centre uses. If your test centre uses Netscape Navigator (for practising), this can be downloaded free from the Internet. There are some differences between the two browsers. Check that you know how to transfer the skills practised in Internet Explorer.

1.3 Loading Internet Explorer

Exercise 1

Load Internet Explorer.

Method

From the **Start** menu, select: **Internet**, **Internet Explorer** *or* click on: the **Internet Explorer** icon on the desktop.

Info

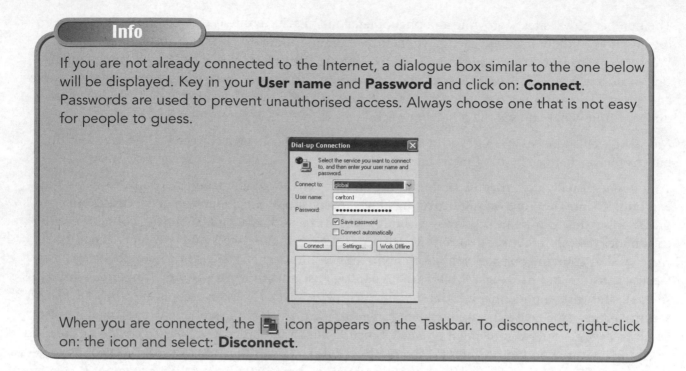

If you are not already connected to the Internet, a dialogue box similar to the one below will be displayed. Key in your **User name** and **Password** and click on: **Connect**. Passwords are used to prevent unauthorised access. Always choose one that is not easy for people to guess.

When you are connected, the ⊞ icon appears on the Taskbar. To disconnect, right-click on: the icon and select: **Disconnect**.

Either method will result in the Internet Explorer window being displayed (Figure 7.1).

Note: The first web page displayed when you open Internet Explorer is determined by the setup of your computer. Toolbar buttons are labelled in Figure 7.2.

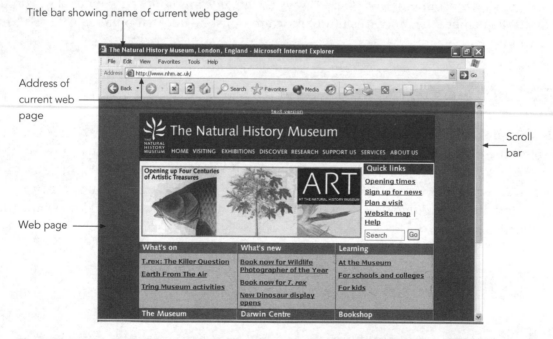

Figure 7.1 Internet Explorer window displaying the Natural History Museum website home page

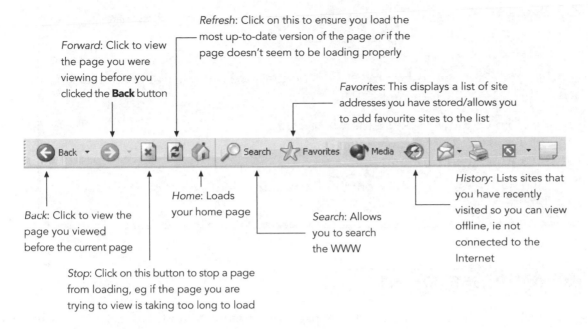

Forward: Click to view the page you were viewing before you clicked the **Back** button

Refresh: Click on this to ensure you load the most up-to-date version of the page *or* if the page doesn't seem to be loading properly

Favorites: This displays a list of site addresses you have stored/allows you to add favourite sites to the list

Back: Click to view the page you viewed before the current page

Home: Loads your home page

Search: Allows you to search the WWW

History: Lists sites that you have recently visited so you can view offline, ie not connected to the Internet

Stop: Click on this button to stop a page from loading, eg if the page you are trying to view is taking too long to load

Figure 7.2 Internet Explorer toolbar buttons

Info

Scrolling

Web pages vary in length. If some of the web page is out of view, use the scroll bar to reveal the remainder.

Getting help

Get help when using Internet Explorer by making a selection from the **Help** menu, eg **Contents** and **Index**. *or* press: **F1**.

Figure 7.3 Internet Explorer Help

Help

You can select:

- The **Contents** tab for a list of help topics. By double-clicking on a topic, a display of that topic will appear.
- The **Index** tab. This allows you to enter key words or scroll through the alphabetical list and then click on: **Display**. The topic will then be highlighted in the contents list and the topic displayed as above.

- The **Search** tab. This allows you to key in key words and click on **Search**. Again, the topic will be highlighted and displayed as above.
- The **Favorites** tab. With this tab selected, the topic displayed in the right-hand pane can be added to a customised list by clicking on the **Add** button. To open a chosen favorites topic, select the topic in the left-hand pane.

  To close the Help window, click on: the **Close** button.

Accessing Help in a dialogue box

To access Help in a dialogue box, click on: the **Help** button in the dialogue box and then click on the item you want help about.

1.4 What is a web address?

The first page of a website is the *home page*. Every web page has a unique address. This is known as an **URL** (**U**niform **R**esource **L**ocator). It usually begins with 'http://www.' (http stands for *HyperText Transfer Protocol* and tells the web browser that it is looking for a web page). Most modern browsers have 'http://' stored so you can start keying in the website address from 'www'. Here are some sample URLs:

http://www.bbc.co.uk
http://www.bargainholidays.com
http://www.nhm.ac.uk

The text after the 'www' shows:

- The domain name – the organisation or site's name, eg BBC, bargainholidays and nhm (Natural History Museum).
- The type of site, eg .co and .com are commercial companies; .ac is an academic community.
- The country, eg uk for United Kingdom. (Often there is no country name.)

Note: The dots are important in a web address and the address must be spelt correctly. Sometimes URLs are longer because they include the pathname to the web page, eg:

www.bbc.co.uk/weather/worldweather/europe/index.shtml

Folders where the information is stored   Name of the page document

1.5 Displaying a given web page

Exercise 2

Display the following web page:

www.itn.co.uk

Method

1 Key in the web address in the **Address** box; press: **Enter** *or* click on: the [⟳ Go] **Go** button.
2 The home page of the ITN website is displayed.

Exercise 3

Change your web browser's home page so that it is the home page of 'This is London'. The address is **http://www.thisislondon.co.uk**

Info

Notice that I have used the words *Home page* twice in the exercise above. A home page can mean the page that your browser displays when it first starts up or it can mean the first page of a website. The home page of the 'This is London' website is the first page you see when you enter its address.

Method

1 Go to the **This is London** home page by keying in the web address.
2 The **This is London** home page is displayed.
3 From the Tools menu, select: **Internet Options**. The Internet options box is displayed (Figure 7.4).
4 With the **General** tab selected, in the **Home page** section, click on: **Use Current**.
5 Click on: **Apply** and then on: **OK**.

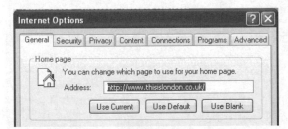

Figure 7.4 Setting a browser's home page

1.7 **Displaying/hiding images**

Info

It is quicker to load a web page when you do not load the images contained in it since image files are quite large. You are able to set up your browser so that it does not display images.

Exercise 4

Load the Natural History Museum home page without images. The address is:

http://www.nhm.ac.uk

Then change the settings back to load the page with images.

1 From the **Tools** menu, select: **Internet Options**.
2 Click on: the **Advanced** tab.
3 In the **Multimedia** section, click in: the boxes next to **Show pictures**, **Play videos**, **Play Animations** so that there are no ticks.
4 Click on: **Apply** and then on: **OK**.
5 Key in the Natural History Museum address.
6 The Natural History Museum home page is displayed without images.

Re-loading with images

7 Follow steps 1–5 again, this time placing ticks where they were removed.
8 Click on: the **Refresh** button to redisplay the page with images.

1.8 Changing view/display

You may find that you want to change the look of web pages to suit your needs, ie colours, fonts etc that you find easier to read. To change settings:

1 From the **Tools** menu select: **Internet Options**.
2 With the **General** tab selected, click on: **Colors** and make your choices. Similarly, click on: **Fonts** to set your preferences.
3 Click on: **Apply** and then on: **OK**.

Changing text size

From the **View** menu, select: **Text Size**. Select the size you prefer.

Displaying/hiding toolbars

From the **View** menu, select: **Toolbars**. Ticks appear next to the toolbars currently displayed. Click on: the toolbar name to add/remove the tick.

1.9 Saving and duplicating web content

Save one of the web pages you have visited as a file.

1 Load the web page by keying in the address in the **Address** box.
2 From the **File** menu, select: **Save As**.
3 The Save As dialogue box is displayed.
4 Select the location where you want to save the web page and key in a filename.
5 In the **Save as type** section, select from the list (Figure 7.5).
6 Click on: **Save**.

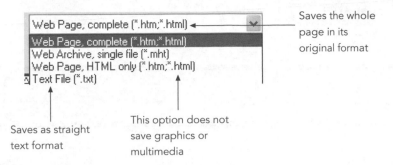

Saves the whole page in its original format

Saves as straight text format

This option does not save graphics or multimedia

Figure 7.5 Saving a web page

If you want to save only a picture from the web page, right-click on: the picture to save and select: **Save Picture As** from the pop-up menu. The Save Picture dialogue box is displayed. Select the location where you want to save the picture and key in a filename. Note that the picture type is usually JPEG. Click on: **Save**.

Duplicating text, images, URLs to your own documents

1 Select the item to duplicate.
2 Right-click on the selection.
3 From the pop-up menu, select: **Copy** (or press: **Ctrl + C**).
4 Open the document to copy to and position the cursor where you want to copy to.
5 Click on: the **Paste** button (or press: **Ctrl + V**).

Note: Select text to copy using normal selection procedures. To save all text from the web page, from the **Edit** menu, select: **Select All**.

Duplicating web address hyperlinks

1 Right-click on the hyperlink web address.
2 Select: **Copy**.

1.10   Downloading files

In addition to saving web pages, it is possible to download files (text, image, sound and video) and software from the web. *FTP (File Transfer Protocol)* is used for transferring large files over the Internet. Instructions on how to download the file/software are usually given on the web page. If not, right-click on the file and make a selection from the pop-up menu. Save the file to your own storage medium, eg hard drive C.

1.11 Closing Internet Explorer

Exercise 6

Close Internet Explorer.

Method

From the **File** menu, select: **Close**.

Practice 1

1 Open a web browser.

2 Display one of the following website home pages:

   http://www.cnn.com
   http://www.channel4.co.uk

3 Set one of the site home pages as your web browser home page.

4 Save the web page as a file.

5 Save one of the images only from the web pages.

6 Change the browser's settings so that images are not loaded.

7 Display the following website home page:

   http://www.information-britain.co.uk

8 Change the browser's settings so that images are displayed.

9 Open a new document in Word and copy the *information-britain* web address to the document and save as **web addresses**.

10 Exit Word.

In this section you will practise and learn how to:

- navigate using hyperlinks
- work with favorites

- display previously visited pages
- use the terms cookie and cache

2.1 Using hyperlinks

Web pages have links (called *hyperlinks*) that you can click on to take you to other places within the current site or to other websites. Links can take the form of underlined text, text in a different colour or they can be image links. When you hover over a link the pointer usually turns into a hand symbol. The home page of the British National Space Centre (www.bnsc.gov.uk) site has text and image links (Figure 7.6).

Text link

Image link

The mouse pointer changes to a hand symbol when hovering over a hyperlink

© Crown copyright

Figure 7.6 Text and image links

Exercise 1

Follow one of the links on the British National Space Centre home page to find out specific information.

Method

1 Click on the link. The linked page is displayed. Notice that the **Address** and **Title** bar have changed to reflect that you are viewing another page.
2 Collect the information you are looking for.
3 Return to the original page by clicking on: the ⬅ Back **Back** button.

   Note: Clicking on the **Back** button arrow
   displays recently visited pages. Click on the page to redisplay it.

Exercise 2

Display a web page in a new window.

When you have clicked on a hyperlink, the original displayed page is usually replaced in the window by the new one. If you want to keep the original page displayed so that it is easier to switch back to the original page, eg there may be more than one interesting hyperlink that you want to explore, it is useful to display the new page in a separate window.

1 Right-click on: the hyperlink.
2 From the pop-up menu, select: **Open in New Window**.

2.2 Saving a list of your favourite websites

Info

When you find a site that you would like to visit again, or a site that you visit often, it is a good idea to save the address of the site to make it easier to revisit in the future. These sites are then known as *Favorites* or *Bookmarks*.

Exercise 3

Save the Natural History Museum site in your **Favorites** list.

Method

1 With the home page of the site displayed, from the **Favorites** menu, select: **Add to Favorites**.
2 The Add Favorite dialogue box is displayed.
3 A default name already appears in the **Name** box. Change the name if you want to.
4 Click on: **OK**.

Accessing Favorites

Method

From the **Favorites** menu, click on: the website name.

Deleting Favorites

Method

1 From the **Favorites** menu, right-click on: the website name.
2 From the pop-up menu, select: **Delete**.

Organising favorites

So that your list of favorites does not become unmanageable, you can organise it by creating folders to store similar content pages.

Method

1 From the **Favorites** menu, select: **Organize Favorites**.
2 The Organize Favorites dialogue box is displayed (Figure 7.7).
3 Click on: the **Create Folder** button.
4 Key in a name for the new folder and press: **Enter**.
5 Drag the relevant favorites into the folder.
6 Click on: **Close**.

Note: Use the **Move to Folder** button when moving multiple favorites.

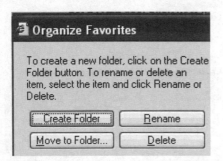

Figure 7.7 Organising Favorites

2.4 **Displaying previously visited web pages**

In addition to using the **Back** button and accessing **Favorites**, there are other ways to display previously visited web pages. These include using the browser **Address** bar and using **History**.

Using the Address bar

1 Click on: the **Address** bar down arrow.

2 A list of previously visited sites is displayed (Figure 7.8).

Figure 7.8 Address bar list

3 Click on: the address to redisplay its page.

Using History

1 Click on: the **History** button.

2 **History** is shown to the left of the current page displayed (Figure 7.9).

Figure 7.9 Displaying History

3 Clicking on a folder in the list displays the pages that were visited on that site.

4 Click on: the relevant page to revisit.

Note: By clicking on the **View** button in Figure 7.9, you can select from the options shown in Figure 7.10.

Figure 7.10 History Options

2.5 Deleting browser history

Method

1 From the **Tools** menu, select: **Internet Options**.
2 The Internet Options dialogue box is displayed.
3 In the **History** section, select: **Clear History** (Figure 7.11).

Note: Use the up/down arrows to select: **Days to keep pages in history**.

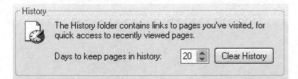

Figure 7.11 Clearing History

2.6 About the Internet cache and cookies

You may have noticed that the web pages that you have already visited are now taking less time to display. This is because when you visit web pages, copies of the information are automatically saved to your local disk. When you request to redisplay a page, the browser first looks to retrieve it from the local drive's *cache*. This is usually quicker than downloading it again from the web. It is worth emptying the browser's cache from time to time, since having numerous files stored means that the browser may slow down as it has to look through the stored files before finding the relevant one to display. (To empty the cache: **Tools** menu, **Internet Options**, **General** tab, **Temporary Internet Files** section, click on: the **Delete Files** button.)

Be aware that web content changes regularly and you may therefore need to click on: the **Refresh** button to ensure that you are viewing the most up-to-date page.

Sometimes you may notice that websites are already set to your preferences when you view them. This is because they have created a small file (*cookie*) about you/your preferences on your computer's hard disk. Once you revisit the associated site the cookie is activated, thus saving you time and effort.

Practice 2

1 Access a few of the sites listed below:

The Louvre	**www.louvre.fr**
British Space Centre	**www.bnsc.gov.uk**
The Guardian	**www.newsunlimited.co.uk**
ITN Online	**www.itn.co.uk**
Football365	**www.football365.com**
Cinema Guide	**www.scoot.co.uk/cinemafinder**
The Mirror	**www.mirror.co.uk**
The Times	**www.the-times.co.uk**

2 Using hyperlinks, find out some information that is not available on the home page.

3 Practise navigating backwards and forwards between pages.

4 Add the home page of a couple of the websites above that you find interesting to your favorites in a folder with the name **ECDL practice**.

5 Delete the browser history.

Section 3 / Searching

In this section you will practise and learn how to:

- use search engines
- modify page setup options
- print a web page
- complete a web-based form

3.1) Searching the web

There are many ways that you can find information on the web:

- If you know the web address of the site where you can find the information, go straight to the site by keying in the address and using hyperlinks to navigate through the site or use the site's search box if it has one.

- Using Internet Explorer's **Search** button enables you to key in a word(s) (known as a **key** word) or a phrase. It then uses a search engine that will look for the key word(s) on a database of websites. A search engine looks like a normal web page with a box or boxes to enter key words that you are looking for. The search engine runs a program that searches its own database (an up-to-date list of websites that have been registered with it) for sites containing the key word(s) and, after a short time, displays a list of 'hits', ie sites that contain the key word(s). Usually the list contains the first ten most appropriate sites (according to the search engine).

- Using a chosen search engine. You may find that a particular search engine usually finds what you are looking for and/or you find it easy to use. Common search engines include:

  http://www.google.co.uk
  http://www.altavista.com
  http://www.ask.co.uk

- Using a search directory. A search directory sets out information in subject categories. This is useful if you are conducting a broad search. Currently, the most common search directory is Yahoo (**http://www.yahoo.com**). Other common search directories include:

Lycos	**http://www.lycos.com**
LookSmart	**http://www.looksmart.com**
UK Online	**http://www.ukonline.com**

Exercise 1

Find the addresses of ECDL test centres using the different search methods. Compare the different methods as you progress; ie time taken, usefulness of results, ease of use.

3.2) Using the Search button

Method

1 Click on: the **Search** button.
2 Key in: **ECDL** into the **Search** box and enter it by clicking on: **Go**.
3 Follow the links for information (Figure 7.12).

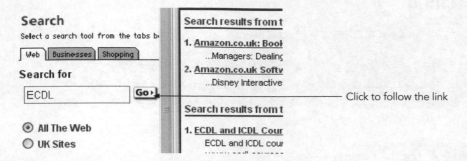

Click to follow the link

Figure 7.12 Finding information using Search

3.3   Using a search engine

Method

1 Access the AltaVista website.
2 Key **ECDL** into the **Search** box (Figure 7.13) and enter it by clicking on: **Find**.
3 Follow the links to find test centres in your area.

Figure 7.13 Using a search engine

Reproduced with the permission of AltaVista

3.4   Using a search directory

Method

1 Access the Yahoo site. Figure 7.14 shows some of the site's categories.

Reproduced with permission of Yahoo! Inc.
© 2003 by Yahoo! Inc. YAHOO! is a trademark of
Yahoo! Inc.

Figure 7.14 Using Yahoo

2 Click on links in the directory that you think are appropriate for your search.

Using logical operators

You can refine your searches by keying in more than one word and using logical operators: AND, NOT (or their equivalents AND, +, &; NOT, -) and OR. Different search engines have slightly different rules about how you enter searches with logical operators.

Using AND

Use AND or one of the symbols when searching for more than one word. Results will list sites that contain all the search words. Examples:

- You are interested in finding information on football and in particular Everton. In the Search box, key in **Football + Everton**.
- You are interested in finding information about Oscars and Disney. In the Search box, key in **Oscars + Disney**.

Using NOT

Use NOT or the minus sign when searching for information but omitting certain information. Examples:

- You are interested in finding information on football but not on Everton. In the Search box, key in **Football – Everton**.
- You are interested in finding information about Oscars but not Disney. In the Search box, key in **Oscars – Disney**.

Using OR

You are interested in finding information about cameras. You could key in **Camera OR photography**, since both of these might find useful information.

> **Info**
>
> For some search engines, quotation marks can be used to group words together, eg "motor racing" may find more confined results than motor racing.

Try out some other searches with logical operators. Note the different search format requirements and which methods give the most relevant results.

3.6 **Modifying page setup ready for printing**

> **Method**

1 From the **File** menu, select: **Page Setup** (Figure 7.15).
2 Change the paper size, orientation and margins.
3 Use Internet Explorer Help if you want to set headers and footers.
4 Click on: **OK**.

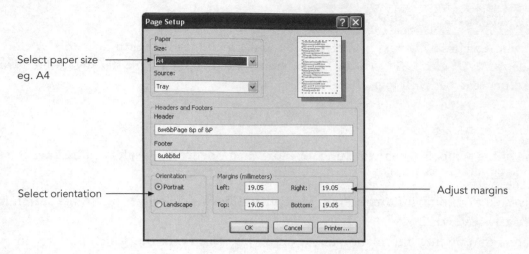

Figure 7.15 Page Setup

Printing a web page

Method

1 From the **File** menu, select: **Print**.
2 The Print dialogue box is displayed (Figure 7.16).

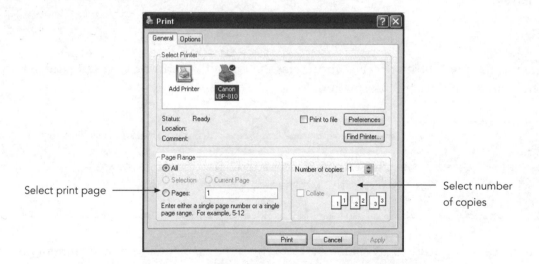

Figure 7.16 Printing

3 Make selections as appropriate.
4 If the web page is divided into frames, click on: the **Options** tab and enter your choices in the **Print Frames** section.
5 Click on: **OK**.

Info

You can also choose to print a table of links. This is useful for reference. Click on: the **Options** tab to access this. If your browser has a **Print Preview**, it will usually be found in the **File** menu.

Section 3 / Searching

In this section you will practise and learn how to:

- use search engines
- modify page setup options

- print a web page
- complete a web-based form

3.1) Searching the web

There are many ways that you can find information on the web:

- If you know the web address of the site where you can find the information, go straight to the site by keying in the address and using hyperlinks to navigate through the site or use the site's search box if it has one.

- Using Internet Explorer's **Search** button enables you to key in a word(s) (known as a **key** word) or a phrase. It then uses a search engine that will look for the key word(s) on a database of websites. A search engine looks like a normal web page with a box or boxes to enter key words that you are looking for. The search engine runs a program that searches its own database (an up-to-date list of websites that have been registered with it) for sites containing the key word(s) and, after a short time, displays a list of 'hits', ie sites that contain the key word(s). Usually the list contains the first ten most appropriate sites (according to the search engine).

- Using a chosen search engine. You may find that a particular search engine usually finds what you are looking for and/or you find it easy to use. Common search engines include:

  http://www.google.co.uk
  http://www.altavista.com
  http://www.ask.co.uk

- Using a search directory. A search directory sets out information in subject categories. This is useful if you are conducting a broad search. Currently, the most common search directory is Yahoo (**http://www.yahoo.com**). Other common search directories include:

Lycos	**http://www.lycos.com**
LookSmart	**http://www.looksmart.com**
UK Online	**http://www.ukonline.com**

Exercise 1

Find the addresses of ECDL test centres using the different search methods. Compare the different methods as you progress; ie time taken, usefulness of results, ease of use.

3.2) Using the Search button

Method

1 Click on: the **Search** button.
2 Key in: **ECDL** into the **Search** box and enter it by clicking on: **Go**.
3 Follow the links for information (Figure 7.12).

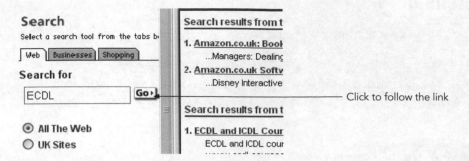

Click to follow the link

Figure 7.12 Finding information using Search

3.3   Using a search engine

Method

1   Access the AltaVista website.
2   Key **ECDL** into the **Search** box (Figure 7.13) and enter it by clicking on: **Find**.
3   Follow the links to find test centres in your area.

Figure 7.13 Using a search engine

3.4   Using a search directory

Method

1   Access the Yahoo site. Figure 7.14 shows some of the site's categories.

Figure 7.14 Using Yahoo

2   Click on links in the directory that you think are appropriate for your search.

Warning: Remember, anyone can set up a website and information may not always be correct or may therefore be misleading. Always check that information is from a reliable source.

3.8 Completing a web-based form

When using the web, you will sometimes be asked to complete a web-based form, eg to order an item or to request further information that relates to your specific requirements. Web-based forms usually look like printed forms; they have boxes in which to enter the relevant information. Clicking in a box will allow you to key in information. As with a printed form, always check the information you enter carefully. You can move from box to box either by using the **Tab** key or pressing: **Enter**. Some boxes may be optional and you should be advised of this (a * symbol may denote optional entries). When you have finished filling in the boxes, you will usually need to click on a button, eg **Submit**, to continue. You should then be advised that your data has been sent successfully. If errors have been noticed, you are usually advised and an opportunity is given to repeat an entry or entries.

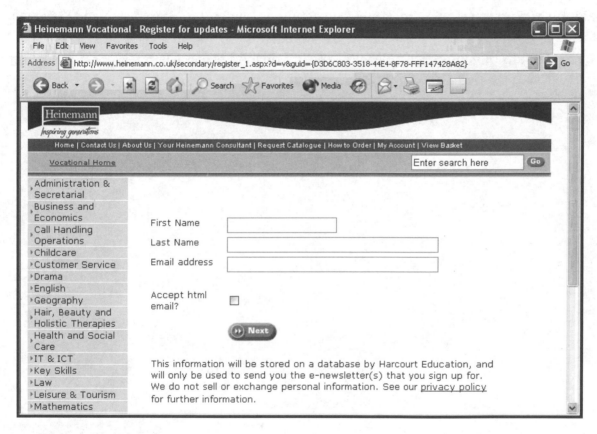

Figure 7.17 A web form

3.9 Exit Internet Explorer

Practice 3

1 Using a search engine or a search directory, find answers to some of the following questions:

- What is on BBC1 and Channel 4 at 7 pm this evening?
- What is the population of Wales?
- What time do trains depart from Chester tomorrow morning (leaving at approx 10.30 am), destination London? Are there any changes en route?
- What is the current line-up of the Bristol City football team?
- What is the current most popular choice of first name for girls/boys?
- Which driver won the Grand Prix title in 2000? Was the winner the same as in 1999? Who won the Belgian Grand Prix in 1998?
- Did John McEnroe ever win the Wimbledon Tennis championship? If so, when and how many times?

2 Print out the results of your searches detailing the information requested.

Section 4 — Getting started with e-mail

In this section you will practise and learn how to:

- open an e-mail application
- use Help functions
- change display modes
- modify toolbar display
- create a new message
- use a spellchecking tool (if available)

- send a message with low/high priority
- copy/blind copy a message to another address
- receive messages
- add an auto-signature to a message
- close the e-mail application

Note: The following sections focus on sending and receiving e-mail using Microsoft Outlook Express 5. By demonstrating the methods used by Outlook Express you will gain an insight into the procedures involved, even though you may be using a different e-mail system. It should be relatively easy to apply what you learn here to your own e-mail system.

Since Outlook Express can be configured to suit your needs, the Outlook Express settings used in the examples may differ slightly from your settings. This could result in some of the methods given not conforming exactly to those that you may see on your computer.

4.1 — About e-mail

E-mail is a method of sending messages between connected computers. You can send and receive the electronic equivalent of letters, faxes, pictures, video and sound. It is a quick and efficient means of communication. It has the advantage that you can send and receive your messages when you choose, unlike 'live' telephone communication, and is cheaper because calls are charged at local rates (and sometimes even free!). (*Note*: If you have a web e-mail account, eg Hotmail, then you can send and receive messages from most computers wherever they are, eg in a cybercafe in another country.) You may send messages to many addresses at the same time. In addition, you will usually be informed if your message has failed to reach its destination(s). E-mail messages (and any files transmitted with them) can be saved and edited by the recipient, whether text or graphics. For security purposes, encryption techniques can be used to ensure that a digitally transmitted document originated with the person signing it and that it was not modified after signature. This is known as a *digital signature*.

When working with e-mail it is important to follow *netiquette* (network etiquette). This includes being polite, brief and to the point and not shouting (using capital letters in e-mails is considered to be shouting). Try to use accurate descriptions for message subjects. It is a good idea to use the spellchecking facility before sending your e-mails.

You should be aware that (as with junk mail) you may well receive unsolicited e-mail (known as *spam*). Unfortunately, for most regular e-mail users this is becoming ever more frequent and annoying. It is now an offence for a British firm to send unsolicited junk mail or text messages to personal email accounts, unless the recipient has given their permission. Be cautious when opening any unfamiliar e-mails or attachments that could pose the potential hazard of infecting your computer with a virus. In most circumstances it is best not to open but to delete any suspicious mail and attachments. Keep your virus checker up to date and set it to check incoming messages.

4.2 — Opening Outlook Express

Exercise 1

Open Outlook Express.

From the **Start** menu, select: **E-mail**, **Outlook Express** *or* click on: the 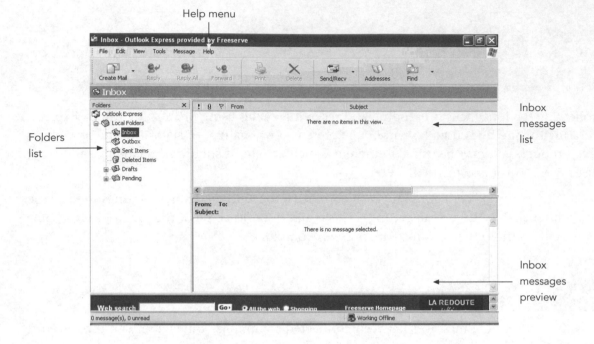 **Outlook Express** icon on the desktop.

Either method will result in the Outlook Express window being displayed on screen (Figure 7.18).

Figure 7.18 Outlook Express 5 window

The Folders list includes:

- Inbox folder – where incoming messages are stored.
- Outbox folder – where outgoing messages are stored.
- Sent Items folder – where sent messages are stored.
- Deleted Items folder – where deleted items are stored.
- Drafts folder – where draft messages are stored.

Info

To get help, use the **Help** menu or press: **F1**. You can change the layout and modify the toolbar to suit your needs by selecting: **Layout** from the **View** menu. The Window Layout Properties box is displayed as shown below:

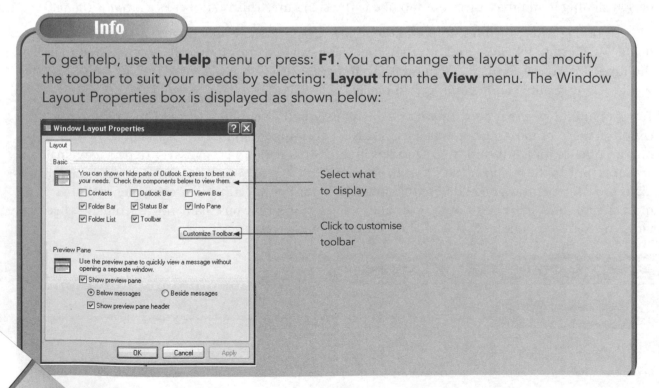

Help

You can select:

- The **Contents** tab for a list of help topics. By double-clicking on a topic, a display of that topic will appear.
- The **Index** tab. This allows you to enter key words or scroll through the alphabetical list and then click on: **Display**. The topic will then be highlighted in the contents list and the topic displayed as above.
- The **Search** tab. This allows you to key in key words and click on **Search**. Again, the topic will be highlighted and displayed as above.

To close the Help window, click on: the **Close** button.

Accessing Help in a dialogue box

To access Help in a dialogue box, click on: the **Help** button in the dialogue box and then click on the item you want help about.

4.3 Creating messages

Exercise 2

Create the message (shown below) and send it to someone you know who has an e-mail address.

Note: If you do not have anyone to send it to, then send it to your own e-mail address.

Hello [insert person's name]

How are you? I am learning how to use e-mail. Please let me know if you have received this message.

Thanks

[Insert your name]

Method

1   Click on: the  **Write Message** button.
2   The New Message window appears (Figure 7.19).
3   Click in the **To:** box and key in the e-mail address of the person you are sending the message to. Check that you have keyed in the address correctly.

Header section: Click in the boxes and key in the e-mail address(es) of recipient(s) and subject here

Message section: Click in this area and key in your message here

Figure 7.19 Creating a message

It is very important that the address is keyed in correctly, otherwise it will not reach its destination. Each dot (full stop) is important. If you have made an error, you can delete it and key it in again.

E-mail addresses are made up of the user's name, followed by the @ symbol, followed by the address of the user's service provider. This includes the domain category (in this example co, meaning a company or commercial organisation in the UK, followed by the country, in this example uk, meaning United Kingdom). For example:

asmith@somewhere.co.uk

Common domain categories include the following:

- ac = academic community (in the UK)
- co = company or commercial organisation (in the UK)
- com = company or commercial organisation
- edu = educational institution
- org = non-profit organisation

Each country has its own unique code, eg fr = France, ca = Canada, se = Sweden.

4   Click in: the subject line of the header section, and key in: **First mail test**.

5   Click in: the message section below and key in the message.

Note: The subject of your message 'First mail test' has replaced 'New Document' on the Title bar.

At this stage you can use:

- The 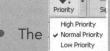 **Spelling** button to check spelling. The spelling dialogue box displays words that are not in the dictionary. Click on: **Change** or **Ignore**. Repeated words are also highlighted. Click on: **Delete** where appropriate.

- The **Set Priority** button to determine the priority of the message. The default is **Normal Priority**. A **High Priority** message has a red exclamation mark and a **Low Priority** message has a down arrow.

6   Click on: the **Send** button.

Note: This will not send the message at this stage but will transfer it to your **Outbox** folder.

7   You are returned to the original Outlook Express window with the **Outbox** folder contents displayed (Figure 7.20).

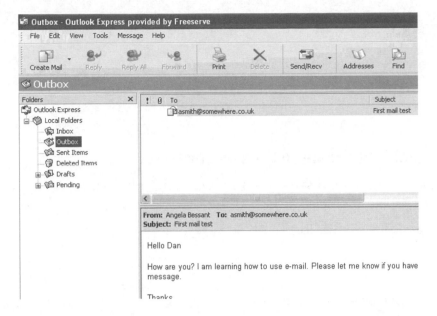

Figure 7.20 Outbox contents are displayed

4.4 Transmitting and receiving messages

Exercise 3

Transmit the message that you have prepared.

Method

1 Click on: the ![Send/Recv] **Send and Receive All** button.
2 Outlook Express will send the message automatically and will display that it is sending the message.
3 When it has been transmitted, it is placed in the **Sent Items** folder. Click on the folder to check.

4.5 Copying messages

The same message can be sent to more than one address at a time.

Method

Sending the message on equal terms to more than one address

In the **To:** box, key in the e-mail addresses and separate them with semicolons, eg
asmith@somewhere.co.uk;jjones@somewhereelse.ac.uk

Note: You don't need a space after the semi-colon.

Sending 'carbon copies'

1   In the **To:** box, key in the first person's e-mail address.
2   In the **Cc:** box, key in the second person's e-mail address.

The main recipient(s) is the person in the **To:** box, with a 'carbon copy' sent to the second addressee(s).

Sending blind copies

Sometimes you may want to send a copy of the e-mail to an addressee(s) without other recipients' knowledge.

1   From the **View** menu, select: **All Headers**.
2   A **Bcc:** box appears where you can enter the recipient's address(es).

Note: With all the above, the message is again placed in your **Sent Items** folder and is still treated as one message, even though it has been transmitted to more than one e-mail address.

Info

If the Cc or Bcc boxes are not displayed, from the **View** menu, select: **All Headers**.

4.6 Close Outlook Express

Method

From the **File** menu, select: **Exit** *or* click on: the **Close** button.

Practice 4

1   Open an electronic mail application.

2   Send the following message with high priority to someone you know and a copy to someone else. Give the message the title **Attendance of conference**.

Hello (recipient's name)

Are you aware that there is a two-day conference 'Organic Farming' coming up soon? Do you think that it would be worthwhile attending? If so, are there any funds available to cover costs?

Thanks

Regards

(your name)

In this section you will practise and learn how to:

- open a mail message
- open a mail inbox for a specified user
- attach a file to a message
- delete text in a message
- delete a file attachment from a message
- open and save an attachment
- use reply to sender/reply to all
- reply with/without original message insertion

- forward a message
- use cut/copy and paste/delete
- create a new mail folder
- delete a message
- sort messages by name, subject, date etc
- move messages to a new mail folder
- flag a message in a mail folder
- search for a message
- mark a message as unread/read

5.1 Opening received mail messages

Exercise 1

Open messages received.

Note: If you have not yet received replies to your e-mails then you will need to send an e-mail to your own e-mail address so that there is a message received.

Method

1 Load Outlook Express as in section 4.2 (if not already loaded).
2 You will notice that there is a number next to your **Inbox** folder – in this example, 2, indicating that two messages have been received (Figure 7.21).

Folders
- Outlook Express
  - Local Folders
    - **Inbox** (2)

Figure 7.21 Messages have been received

3 The messages are displayed in the right-hand pane.
4 Click once on a message to see it in the Preview window (Figure 7.22), or double-click on it to see it in a separate window.

Info

When a message has been read, it displays an open envelope next to it. If this does not happen, use the **Tools** menu, **Options**, **Read** tab and set to your preferences.

5 Close the message by clicking on: the **Close** button.

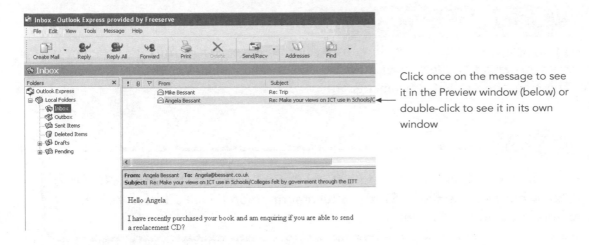

Click once on the message to see it in the Preview window (below) or double-click to see it in its own window

Figure 7.22 Viewing a received message

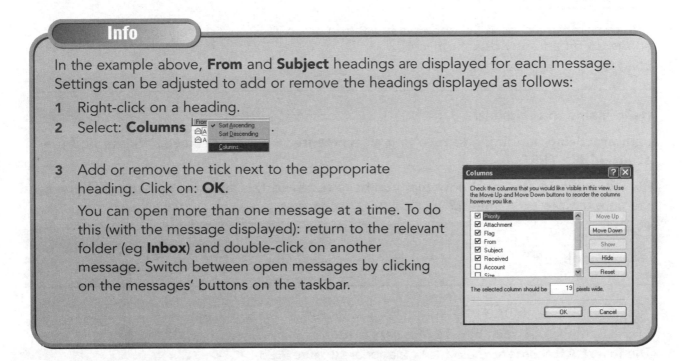
5.2   Opening another user's Inbox messages

Creating folders for other users

There may be several people accessing mail on the same account. If this is the case, you can add new identities for the other users as follows:

1   From the **File** menu, select: **Identities** then: **Add New Identity**.

2   Key in the name of the new user.

3   Enter a password if you want to use one for this user.

4   Repeat these steps until all users have been entered.

Opening user's inboxes

If another user wants you to check his or her mail, look to see if he or she has a number next to his or her folder. If so, click on the folder so that his or her messages appear in the right-hand window. Access as in section 5.1.

5.3   Attaching files to messages

Sometimes you may want to enclose something with your message, eg a picture or a different type of file. In such cases you can add a file to your message. This is called an *attachment*. You can add more than one file. These are then called attachments.

Exercise 2

Create or recall a simple Excel or a Word file. Save the file with the filename **TEST**. Send a message, together with the file **TEST** (the attachment) to an e-mail address. Ask the recipient to send you an attachment.

Method

1 Create or recall a simple file and save it with the name **TEST** in a place you will know where to find it (eg on a floppy disk in drive A).

2 Load Outlook Express and key in the following new message:

Hello [name of recipient]

I am practising sending and receiving attachments to e-mail messages. Please find the attached file TEST.

Please could you let me know that you have received this and also please could you send me an example attachment?

Thanks

[Your name]

NB DO NOT CLICK SEND YET

3 Click on: the 📎 **Attach File To Message** button.

4 The **Insert Attachment** dialogue box appears (Figure 7.23).

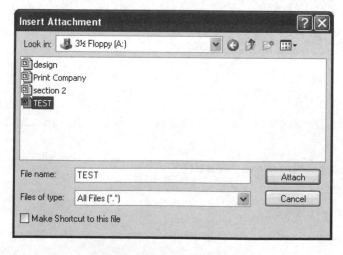

Figure 7.23 Insert Attachment dialogue box

5 Select the drive where the file is located, eg Drive A. Click on the file so that it appears in the **File name** box (or key in the filename).

6 Click on: **Attach**.

7 You will notice that your attachment is now shown in the **Header** section (Figure 7.24).

Subject:

Attach: TEST.doc (28.0 KB) ◄──────── Attachment shown here

Hello Jim

Figure 7.24 E-mail with an attachment

8   You can now send the file in the normal way.

Info

You can attach more than one file to a message by repeating steps 3–6 for each extra file.

5.4   Viewing attachments

Exercise 3

View an attachment you have received.

Method

When you receive a message with an attachment, the message has a paperclip icon next to it (Figure 7.25).

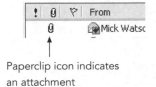

Paperclip icon indicates
an attachment

Figure 7.25 Receiving attachments

1   Double-click on: the message to view it in a separate window.
2   In the **Attach** box, double-click on: the attached file (Figure 7.26). The file will appear in its own program window.

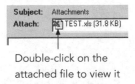

Double-click on the
attached file to view it

Figure 7.26 Viewing an attachment

3   When you have finished viewing the file, close its window in the normal way. You are returned to Outlook Express.

5.5 Saving a file attachment

Method

1 Double-click on the message with the attachment so that it appears in its own window.
2 From the **File** menu, select: **Save Attachments**.
3 The Save Attachments dialogue box is displayed (Figure 7.27).

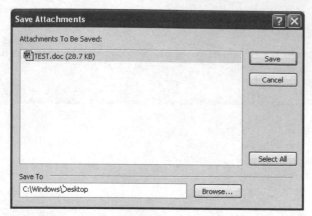

Figure 7.27 Saving attachments

4 Click on: **Browse** to choose where to save it.
5 Click on: **Save**.

or

Right-click on the attachment and select: **Save As** (Figure 7.28).

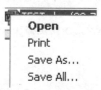

Figure 7.28 Saving the attachments by right-clicking

5.6 Deleting a file attachment from a message

When sending attachments, if you have chosen the wrong one or need to delete one for any other reason, select the attachment by clicking on it. Press: **Delete**.

5.7 Replying to a message

Method

1 With the message open in its own window, click on: the [Reply] **Reply to Sender** button. The address and subject are already entered.
2 Key in your reply directly under the Header section.
   Note: You will see that there is a message separator between your reply and the original message.
3 If you want to delete the original message, select the text and press: **Delete**.
4 Send the message in the usual way.

Click on: the **Reply All** **Reply to All** button if you want to reply to multiple e-mail addresses that were on the original message.

Click on: the **Forward** **Forward** button to forward the message on to another e-mail address(es). Key in the e-mail address of the recipient(s). You can also add your own personal message to the new recipient(s) by clicking in the message window and keying in the text.

Note: When using the **Reply** button, your message subject automatically has **Re:** added to the Subject. When using the **Forward** button, your message subject has **Fw:** added to the Subject.

5.8 Using cut/copy and paste/delete

You can use the **Cut/Copy** and **Paste** from the **Edit** menu, as in other Office applications, to move and duplicate text within a message or to another active message. Switch between open messages by selecting from the Taskbar. You can also cut text using normal deleting procedures.

You can also **Cut/Copy** and **Paste** to insert text from another source, eg a Word document or web page.

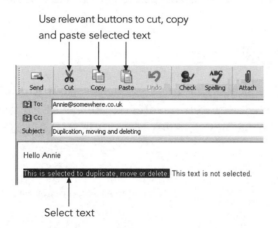

Figure 7.29 Moving text

Duplicating text within a message, between messages

1 Select the text and click on: the **Copy** button.
2 (Open the destination message and) position the cursor where the text is to be placed.
3 Click on: the **Paste** button.

Moving text within a message, between messages

1 Select the text and click on: the **Cut** button.
2 (Open the destination message and) position the cursor where the text is to be placed.
3 Click on: the **Paste** button.

Duplicating text from another source into a message

1 Open the source file in its own application, eg Word, Notepad.

2 Select the text and click on: the **Copy** button.

3 Open the message and position the cursor where the text is to be placed.

4 Click on: the **Paste** button.

Deleting text

Select the text to delete. Press: **Delete**.

5.9) Deleting a mail message

In the main window, select the message to delete. Press: **Delete**. To select adjacent messages, hold down: **Shift** when selecting. To select non-adjacent messages, hold down: **Ctrl** when selecting.

Info

Deleted messages are sent to the **Deleted Items** folder. It is a good idea to empty this folder from time to time. To do this, right-click on the folder and select: **Empty 'Deleted Items' Folder**. Messages can be restored from the **Deleted Items** folder by right-clicking on the message and selecting: **Move to Folder**.

5.10) Sorting messages

When you have numerous messages, you may want to sort them so that they are easier to locate. To sort by name, subject or date, click on the relevant heading at the top of the messages window (Figure 7.30). In Figure 7.30 there is a down arrow next to **Sent** indicating that the messages are sorted in descending date order.

Figure 7.30 Sorting messages

For a more comprehensive sort, from the **View** menu, select: **Sort By**. Options available are shown in Figure 7.31.

Figure 7.31 Sorting messages using the View menu

5.11 Moving/copying messages to a new mail folder

To move messages

Method

1 Select the message(s) to move.
2 From the **Edit** menu, select: **Move to Folder** or **Copy to Folder**.
3 The Move or Copy dialogue box is displayed (Figure 7.32).

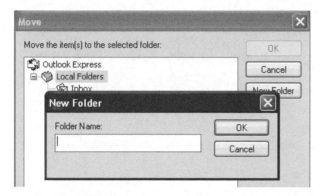

Figure 7.32 Moving messages to a new folder

4 Click on: **New Folder** and key in a name for the folder.
5 Click on: **OK**.
6 The message(s) is moved or copied to the new folder.

Note: You can also create new folders as follows:

1 In the **Folders** pane, right-click on a folder.
2 Select: **New Folder**.
3 The Create Folder dialogue box is displayed.
4 Key in the Folder name.
5 Click on: **OK**.

5.12 Searching for a message

Method

1 Select the folder where you think the message is saved.
2 From the **Edit** menu, select: **Find**, **Message** or click on: the **Find** button.
3 The Find Message dialogue box appears (Figure 7.33).

Info

In this example, I have selected the **Inbox folder** at step 1. This method searches the **Inbox** folder and its subfolders when the **Include subfolders** box is ticked. If you do not find your message in a particular folder, click on: **Browse** to select other possible locations.

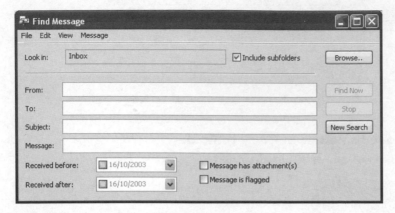

Figure 7.33 Finding messages

4   Key in details of your message in the appropriate boxes and then click on: **Find Now**.

5.13   Flagging messages

To save having to search for a message, it can be a good idea to flag it so that it is easy to locate.

Method

1   Select the message.
2   From the **Message** menu, select: **Flag Message**.
3   A flag symbol is now displayed next to the message (Figure 7.34).

To remove a flag

From the **Message** menu, select: **Flag Message** so that the tick is removed.

Figure 7.34   Message is flagged

5.14   Marking a message as read/unread

Method

In the **Inbox** folder, right-click on the message and select: **Mark as Unread** or **Mark as Read**.

5.15   Printing messages

Method

1   With the message displayed in its own window, click on: the 🖨 **Print** button.
2   The Print dialogue box is displayed (Figure 7.35).

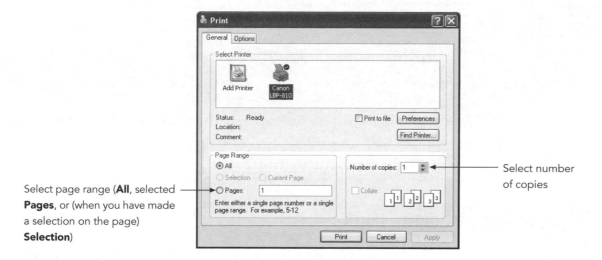

Select page range (**All**, selected **Pages**, or (when you have made a selection on the page) **Selection**)

Select number of copies

Figure 7.35 Print dialogue box

3 Make selections as appropriate and click on: **Print**.

> **Info**
>
> Use **Print Preview** if your e-mail application has this facility (usually found in the **File** menu).

5.16 Close Outlook Express

Section 5 Information and communication practice

Note: For the following exercise you will need the file **visitors**.

Practice 5

1 Access any received message and forward it to someone.

2 Copy one sentence from a received message to a new e-mail message.

3 Title the new message **Attachments**.

4 Send it to someone and send a blind copy to someone else.

5 Send the word file **visitors** as an attachment with the e-mail.

6 Save any received e-mail to a folder named **ECDL**.

7 Save a received attachment onto your own work area.

8 Look for all messages from a particular person using Find, Message.

9 Sort your emails into date order.

10 Delete an old message that you don't need to keep.

11 Flag one of your messages.

In this section you will practise and learn how to:

- add a mail address to an address list
- update an address book for incoming mail
- delete a mail address from an address list
- create a new address list/distribution list
- send a message using a distribution list

6.1 About the Address Book

The Outlook Address Book enables you to store addresses that you use often. Using the Address Book means that you do not have to remember all those cumbersome e-mail addresses and saves having to key in addresses each time you send messages.

6.2 Adding an address to the Address Book

Method

1 Click on: the [Addresses] **Address Book** button.
2 The Address Book dialogue box is displayed (Figure 7.36).

Figure 7.36 **Displaying the Address Book**

3 Click on: the **New** button and then on: **New Contact**.
4 The Properties dialogue box is displayed (Figure 7.37).

Figure 7.37 Properties dialogue box awaiting new contact details

5   With the **Name** tab selected, key in the details of your contact.

Note: By selecting other tabs you can enter further details of your contact as appropriate.

6   Click on: **OK**. The new contact is added to your Address Book list.

> **Info**
>
> Outlook Express can automatically add addresses to your Address Book when you send e-mail. To set this option:
>
> 1   From the **Tools** menu, select: **Options**.
> 2   Click on: the **Send** tab.
> 3   Click next to **Automatically put people I reply to in my address book**.
>
> Outlook Express can add addresses to your Address Book by the following method:
>
> 1   Open the mail message from the contact.
> 2   From the **Tools** menu, select: **Add to Address Book** and click on: the contact name.
> 3   Click on: **OK**.

6.3 Deleting an address

Method

1   Open the Address Book as in 6.2.
2   Select the address to delete.
3   Press: **Delete**.
4   You will be asked to confirm the delete. Click on: **Yes**.

6.4 Creating an address list

If you want to send a message to people who belong to a certain group, you can create a group address list. When you have set up the group list you will only need to key in the name of the group to send the message to all members.

Method

1 Click on: the **Address Book** button.
2 Click on: the **New** button, then on **New Group**. The Properties dialogue box is displayed (Figure 7.38).

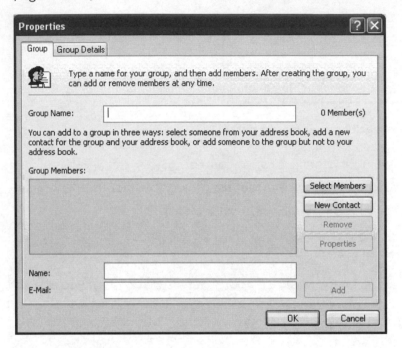

Figure 7.38 Adding a group

3 In the **Group Name** box, key in the name of the new group.
4 Click on: **Select Members** to add addresses already in your Address Book.
5 Click on: **New Contact** to add new addresses to both the list and your address book.

   Note: If you want to add an address to the group list only, enter the name and e-mail address in the boxes at the bottom of the Properties dialogue box.

6 When you have completed the group entries, click on: **OK**.

6.5 Sending messages using the Address Book

Method

1 Click on: the **New Message** button.
2 In the **Header** section, click on: the **To:** section button.
3 The Select Recipients dialogue box is displayed.
4 Click on: the recipient's name or the group name and click on: the To: -> button.
5 Click on: **OK**.

6.6   Close Outlook Express

Section 6   Information and communication practice

Practice 6

1   Add the following contact to the Address Book:

Jason Burgess
j.k.burgess@someplace.com

2   Delete one of the names in your Address Book.

3   Set up a new group called **Football**. Include the following in the group:

Jason Burgess and two other contacts in your address book.

4   Send a message to the **Football** mailing list with the title **Fixtures** as follows:

News just in…
Fixtures announced
Manchester United to play Aston Villa at Old Trafford on October 12th.
Your name

5   Close the electronic mail application.

Using the web quick reference

(The following is a list of generally useful tasks associated with this module. For more information on specific items, refer to the module content.)

Action	Keyboard	Mouse	Right–mouse menu	Menu
Access a website	Key in the web address (URL) in the address box. Press: **Enter**			
Change view/ display				**Tools, Internet Options, General** and Make selections from **View**
Exit Internet Explorer		Click: the ❌ **Close** button		**File, Close**
Favorites, adding to		Click: the ⭐ Favorites **Favorites** button, click: the ▣ Add... **Add** button	**Add to Favorites**	**Favorites, Add to Favorites**
opening		Double-click: the ⭐ Favorites **Favorites** button. Select from the list		
Folder, create favorites folder		Click: the ⭐ Favorites **Favorites** button, click: the 📁 Organize... **Organize** button		**Favorites, Organize Favorites**
Help	**F1**			**Help, Contents and Index**
History		Click: the 🔄 **History** button		
clearing				**Tools, Internet Options, General, Clear History**
Home page, setting				**Tools, Internet Options, General, Home page**
Hyperlink, following		Click: the hyperlink		
Images, displaying/not displaying				**Tools, Internet Options, Multimedia, Show Pictures**

Action	Keyboard	Mouse	Right–mouse menu	Menu
Open Internet Explorer	In Windows desktop			
		Click: the 🌐 **Internet Explorer** icon on the desktop		**Start, Internet, Internet Explorer**
Page setup				**File, Page Setup**
Print	**Ctrl + P**	Click: the 🖨 **Print** button	**Print**	**File, Print**
Return to original page		Click: the **Back** button		
Save, web page, graphic				**File, Save As**
			Save Picture As	
Searching, using common logical operators	Use **Search** button *or* a Search Engine Use AND, +, &, or NOT, -, or use OR			
Toolbar, customizing				**View, Toolbars**

Electronic mail quick reference

(The following is a list of generally useful tasks associated with this module. For more information on specific items, refer to the chapter content.)

Action	Keyboard	Mouse	Right–mouse menu	Menu
Access received messages		Click: **Inbox** in left-hand window Click: the message (to view in Preview) *or* Double-click: the message (to view in own window)		
Address Book, open		Click: the **Addresses** **Address Book** button		**Tools**, **Address Book**
Add address	Open Address Book			
		Click: the **New** **New** button		**File**, **New Contact**
	Click: the **Name** tab. Enter details. Click: **OK**			
Delete address	Open Address Book			
	Delete	Click: the **Delete** **Delete** button		**File**, **Delete**
Create address/ distribution list	Open Address Book			
		Click: the **New** **New** button		**File**, **New Group**
	Click: the **Group** tab. Enter Group Name **Select Members** to add addresses already in the Address Book **New Contact** to add new addresses Click: **OK**			
Attach a file(s) to a message		Click: the **Attach** **Attach File** button		**Insert**, **File Attachment**
Attachment, delete	Double-click the message with the attachment so that it appears in its own window. Select attachment			
	Delete	Click: the **Delete** **Delete** button		
Attachments, save	Select the attachment			
			Save **As**	**File**, **Save Attachments**

Action	Keyboard	Mouse	Right-mouse menu	Menu
Copy/ paste	**Ctrl + C** **Ctrl + V**			**Edit, Copy** **Edit, Paste**
Copy/move messages to folders			**Copy to Folder** **Move to Folder**	**Edit, Move to Folder** **Copy to Folder**
Create message		Click: the **Write Message** button		
Delete, message	Select message				
	Delete	Click: the [Delete icon] **Delete** button	**Delete**	**Edit, Delete**
Delete, text	Select text			
	Delete			
Display mode				**View, Layout**
Exit Outlook Express		Click: the [X] **Close** button		**File, Exit**
Flag a message	Select the message				
				Message, Flag Message
Folders, create new				**File, New, Folder**
Forward a message	**Ctrl + F**	Click: the [Forward icon] **Forward** button	**Forward**	**Message, Forward**
Help	**F1**			**Help, Contents and Index**
Highlight message				**Tools, Message Rules, Mail**
Load Outlook Express	In Windows desktop				
		Click: the [Outlook Express icon] **Outlook Express** icon on the desktop		**Start, E-mail, Outlook Express**
Print messages	(With transaction details and message visible in its own window)				
	Ctrl + P	Click: the [Print icon] **Print** button		**File, Print**
Prioritise messages		With the message displayed, click: the [Priority icon] **Set Priority** button arrow		

Action	Keyboard	Mouse	Right–mouse menu	Menu
Reply to all	**Ctrl + Shift + R**	Click: the **Reply to All** button	**Reply to <u>A</u>ll**	
Reply to sender	**Ctrl + R**	Click: the **Reply to Sender** button	**Reply to <u>S</u>ender**	
Route/address messages *Multiple recipients*	Key in the address in the **To:** box Separate addresses with semicolons (;) Use **Cc** box to send a 'carbon copy'. Use **Bcc** box to send a 'blind copy'			
Search for a message		Click: the **Find** button		**<u>E</u>dit, <u>F</u>ind, <u>M</u>essage**
Sort messages	Click on the relevant heading at the top of the messages window			
Spellcheck	**F7**			**<u>T</u>ools, <u>S</u>pelling**
Transmit/ receive messages		Click: the **Send and Receive All** button		**<u>T</u>ools, <u>S</u>end and Receive**
View, attachments	(With message in its own window – attachment visible)			
		Double-click: the attachment		

Message icons

Icon	Denotes
📎	Message has file attachment(s)
✉	Message has been replied to
✉	Message has been forwarded
✉	Message has not been read
✉	Message has been read
⚑	Message is flagged
↓	Message has been marked low priority
!	Message has been marked high priority

Answers to the following questions can be found in the Module 7 or Module 1 text.

Note: For these exercises you will need the file **meeting info**.

1   What is a web browser?

2   Explain what a hyperlink is.

3   Give an example of a web address (real or made up). Explain how each part is derived. What is another name for a web address?

4   *Home page* can have two different meanings. Explain.

5   What methods are employed to help ensure credit card transactions are not subject to fraud?

6   When carrying out a search, what is a *key* word?

7   Explain how a *search engine* would help you find something on the web.

8   Why are passwords used when accessing the Internet?

9   What is an e-mail attachment?

10   How do you send e-mail messages to more than one person at the same time?

11   In e-mail, what is an Address Book and why is it useful?

12   What is a group address list?

13   Explain what is meant by the browser's cache.

14   What is meant by *netiquette*? What does using capital letters in e-mail denote?

15   What can you do to help prevent virus attacks?

Practical tasks

You work as a PA to the Marketing Manager at a small publishing company. The Manager has a meeting in Paris next month and you have been asked to sort out travel arrangements for this overnight trip. He wants to fly from Luton early on Monday morning to arrive in Paris by 10.30 am and to return on Tuesday after lunch (departing Paris before 3.30 pm if possible). You also need to find accommodation details within easy reach of the airport in Paris.

You also need to find out what the current exchange rate is for the UK £ against the euro.

1   Delete the *History* from the browser.

2   Search the Internet to find out what airlines fly from Luton to Paris Charles de Gaulle airport.

3   Send an e-mail to your manager, and cc it to another colleague, with web addresses of suitable airline sites and details of the times that might suit.

4   Search the Internet for hotels close to the Paris airport.

5   Print the home page of the hotel that you would choose as the most appropriate.

6   Save a photo of the hotel (if there is one) to your work area.

7   Look for a map of directions to the hotel (if available) or a map of Paris (if not), save it to your work area and print.

8   Send an e-mail to your manager with the Word file **meeting info** as an attachment.

9   Search the Internet for currency conversion rates (UK £ against the euro) and make a note of today's rates.

10   Save the web address in step 9 in your favorites folder.

Note: These are only practice tasks. Successful completion does not imply certification of the module by the ECDL Foundation.

Using IT

This chapter brings together many general issues related to using computers. Most of these have been covered in previous modules so you will need to refer back as necessary.

1.1 Legal issues

There are numerous legal issues that relate to working with computers. Many of these have been addressed in Module 1. When working in an organisation, there are set rules that govern computer usage. These are taken very seriously and it is normal to sign an agreement that sets out rules tailored for the particular working environment. These rules would incorporate the issues below.

Understand the rights of an individual to be informed of, and to access, data held about them by an organisation (Data Protection Act).

The UK Data Protection Act was first passed in 1984 and has been updated (1998) to give full effect to the European Directives on Data Protection. Individuals have the right to know that information is being held about them, eg by tax offices, banks, doctors. Individuals are also able to see information that is held on them if they request to do so. There are a few exceptions to this, eg data held by the police. If an individual feels that information is not being properly used, he or she can contact the Data Protection Commissioner who will investigate the claim. Individuals can seek compensation for damages or distress caused by inaccuracy, unauthorised destruction or wrongful disclosure of data. (*Module 1, section 4*)

Understand the legal issues when gathering data, and the need for consent to hold such data. Understand the need for confidentiality of information (employee and client). Know management responsibility for honesty and accuracy in recording, manipulating and presenting data.

Every individual or organisation that processes and stores personal information should register as a data controller with the Data Protection Commissioner. Management should ensure that staff are suitably trained to adhere to the Data Protection Act principles (listed below) to ensure that information is handled properly. It is most important that any information collected is checked for accuracy, honestly recorded and kept up to date (individual's circumstances change, eg you may have paid off that million pound loan that is blocking you being able to take out a further loan!). There are strict penalties (unlimited fines) for anyone who does not comply with the rules. The data controller should also check that security measures are in place to ensure unauthorised access to data does not occur, and to prevent accidental loss or damage to personal data.

The main eight Data Protection Act principles relating to personal data are that data shall be:

1   Fairly and lawfully processed.
2   Obtained only for specified purposes and not disclosed in any way incompatible with those purposes.
3   Adequate, relevant and not excessive.
4   Accurate and, where necessary, kept up to date.
5   Not kept for longer than necessary.
6   Processed in line with the rights of data subjects.
7   Kept secure.
8   Not transferred to countries outside the European Economic Area without adequate protection.

Note: Point eight above has implications for personal data displayed on the World Wide Web and the individual would need to give permission for this.
(*Module 1, section 4*)

Understand the rules associated with computer misuse/inappropriate use.

The Computer Misuse Act (1990) was introduced to deal with problems related to unauthorised access or modification of computer-held information (commonly known as 'hacking'). This activity is now a criminal offence and can lead to imprisonment. The Act specifies three offences:

1   *Unauthorised access*: Examples of this include: using someone's password to access data; sending e-mails or posting to the web using another person's name.

2   *Unauthorised access with intent*: This offence builds on the one above. Examples include using someone's password to access data and then using this in a fraudulent manner, eg transferring money from one account to another, accessing examination questions.

3   *Unauthorised modification of data*: Examples of this include creating or infecting computers with viruses; deleting another user's files; changing exam results.

Understand problems regarding the creation, transmission, storage, downloading or display of any offensive, obscene, indecent, or menacing images, data or other material.

Types of inappropriate material and rules relating to such material are usually set out quite clearly in an organisation's policy documents. These rules should be strictly adhered to since being in breach of such rules could not only have dire consequences for the individual and the organisation but may also be illegal resulting in severe punishment. Some examples of illegal breaching are creating, downloading, transmitting, storing or displaying child pornography; adult material that breaches the Obscene Publications Act; and criminally racist material.

Understand the issue of copyrights over published electronic data belonging to individuals and organisations.

Copyright means that the original work cannot be used without the author's permission, the author being an individual or an organisation. We are used to seeing the copyright symbol © on printed documents to remind people of this. (*Note*: Even when this symbol is not displayed, the work may still belong to its originator.) However, copyright also applies to electronic data. For example, when working with files or browsing the Web, be aware that you should not make copies or print out multiple copies (without permission).
(*Module 1, section 4*)

Know the concepts of the need to ensure data security, backup systems, data recovery. Use a computer's system software to safely and securely create and manage files and folders.

It is very important that you keep data as secure as possible. You should never divulge your passwords to anyone or leave your computer unattended with the possibility of enabling unauthorised access. Ensure that you run up-to-date virus-checking software to protect your files. Data should be backed up at regular intervals (organisations usually do this automatically but you would need to check if it is your responsibility) in case your data should be lost or damaged. Data can often be recovered using specialised software. When deleting files, you should be aware that using normal deletion methods will delete only a file's location reference and not the actual file itself. This will still exist on your computer and so could (for someone with the know-how) be accessible. Secure deletion software is available. Remember that backups of data need to be kept safe and secure (in a separate location, eg offsite so that if an accident occurs at the workplace, eg a fire or flood, the backups will not be damaged).(*Module 1, section 4*)

1.2   Health and Safety

For this module you need to be aware of the issues below. Refer back to Module 1, section 3 to remind yourself of the importance of creating a comfortable and safe working environment, disposing of computer equipment and consumables, and environmental concerns.

Know the correct procedures for working with IT equipment, including ergonomic arrangements, safety of individuals and equipment.

Understand the causes of Repetitive Strain Injury (RSI), and how the risk of RSI can be minimised.

Understand implications when disposing of computer equipment and consumables with respect to environmental issues, eg print consumables – recycling or disposing of used equipment, safe disposal of hardware.

Recognise some of the ways that energy efficiency can be improved – energy-saving software, use of screen savers, use of environmentally friendly monitors.

Most computers have energy-saving features such as power management that powers down the screen and/or the hard disk(s) after it has not been used for a set elapse of time. Powering down the screen is preferable to using 'screen savers' – these do not save power but were originally used to prevent damage to the screen. (Access and adjust the power saver features in Windows from the **Start** menu, **Control Panel**, **Performance and Maintenance, Power Options**.) The following points will help you be more energy efficient, which is better for the environment and saves money:

- Turn off your computer when you are not using it for a few hours, and at night. (Note that this does not apply to servers.)
- Turn on the power management for your monitor or turn your monitor off when you are not going to be using it for a quarter of an hour or longer.
- Flat screen (LCD) monitors use less power than other monitors.
- Remember that laptops with their integrated flat screens use only about a quarter of the energy of a desktop computer.

Understand the importance of print preview to minimise paper wastage and improve output.

A Print Preview display is available in most applications. Remember to use it before printing to save discarding copies that do not appear on paper as you had expected.

1.3 Integration

Work with data files to select and import data across applications.

Understand the capability to link information between packages – eg mail merge using spreadsheet or database file.

Understand the mechanism used to combine information from one application into another – eg use a spreadsheet chart in a word processed document.

Distinguish between the storing and displaying of information in different Office applications.

One of the useful things when working with computer files is the ability to use data created in one application, for example a chart in Excel, and paste it into another application, for example into a Word document. This can be done using a 'copy and paste' method or using the **Insert** menu. Information can also be linked between applications. For example when creating a mail-merged document in Word, the data for the merge can be sourced from an Excel spreadsheet or from an Access database file.

Understand how to resize linked data as appropriate.

When data is linked it will often not display in its original format (eg entries may be displayed incomplete, columns might be inconsistent). Such data will need to be resized as appropriate. Resizing can be done using a variety of methods, eg selecting the linked object and using its sizing handles, selecting columns and dragging the borders to display content in full.

Know the major vehicles for cross-platform transfer of information (rtf, txt, dif, csv etc).

Applications allow for files to be saved in a number of file formats. Module 2, section 3 gives examples of common file types. When transferring files to different (non-Microsoft Office) applications to ensure that the data can be interchanged, the files can be saved in generic formats as follows:

- txt – This is a file format that contains data made up of ACSII (American Standard Code for Information Interchange) characters. It is a basic text file that contains no formatting.
- rtf – This is a Rich Text File format. It contains formatting such as font styles, sizes and so on.
- dif – This is a Data Interchange format. This is used for spreadsheet data that is structured in rows and columns.
- csv – This is Comma Separated Value format, sometimes called comma delimited. This is used for database records that separate fields with commas. The field data usually has quotation marks.

Understand how to open/import data from generic files and appreciate limitations of these formats.

Files in generic file formats can be opened in many applications (by selecting the file type when opening) or can be imported into applications (usually using the **Insert** menu options). Generic files usually have very basic formatting (if they have any).

Understand the procedures for transferring data between files when using the clipboard.

When copying/cutting and pasting between applications, data is stored in an area of memory called the clipboard. This memory is cleared when the computer is turned off. In Office XP applications, to view the clipboard's contents, select: **Office**, **Clipboard** from the **Edit** menu.

Know the limitations when copying data to another document (the need to update).

When data has been copied to another document, it will not be automatically updated each time the original document is updated. In order for this to happen the original document would need to be linked to the new document. When producing documents for the Web, since these will not be linked to your computer, you would need to update and repost them.

1.4 Good practice

Understand the importance of maintaining integrity of imported data.

When importing data it can sometimes not reproduce exactly as it should, eg numeric data may be chopped or may be in the wrong format. Always ensure that data is imported in its entirety, eg the final part of a paragraph is not omitted in the process, thus reducing the meaning and value of the imported text.

Understand common generic methods for accessing files and folders.

Using Windows Explorer (Module 2) the files and folders stored on your computer (and accessible networked drives) can be displayed. To access a folder, double-click on it. The contents of the folder will be displayed. To access a file, double-click on it and it will open in its own application. Files can also be opened by loading an application and selecting **Open** from the **File** menu.

Understand how to create, name and rename folders and sub-folders.
(*Module 2, section 3*)

Understand the advantages of using the search and replace functions over manual methods to find and replace specific data.

Most Office applications have a search and replace facility. It is always preferable to use this option over manual methods since it is much quicker and less prone to error. For example, when replacing a word or phrase in a document it would be easy to miss an occurrence of it and thus leave it unaltered. Using manual methods it would also be easy to replace occurrences of a word with inconsistency of spelling.

Understand the purpose of copy/move/delete files.

As with any filing system, good housekeeping of files is important so that they can easily be accessed and recalled. Copying and moving files so that they reside in folders that are ordered and named in a meaningful way can save time and effort. Copying and moving are also a useful function when wanting to share files. Deleting old or obsolete files should be carried out from time to time. This will not only ensure that you open and work on the latest version of the file but will also free up space on your computer storage area and reduce access time.

Identify and access appropriate software for the task.

The preceding modules have given information and instructions on a number of applications. Have a glance back through to remind yourself of the various applications covered and review Module 1, section 1 for information on other applications.

Distinguish between documents/files and executable applications and appreciate the function of file extensions.

When a document is saved it has a three-character file extension. This enables you and the computer to determine what file type it is. An executable application has the file extension .exe. When you double-click on an exe file, the application is then loaded ready for use.
(*Module 2, section 3*)

Understand how to access existing files (text, database, spreadsheet, image, chart).

Files can be accessed by opening a corresponding application and selecting **Open** from the **File** menu. Image files (depending on their file type) can be opened in various applications, or they can be imported into documents. Charts can also be imported into documents. Charts created in Excel are saved together with the spreadsheet they are derived from, so you would need to switch to the chart sheet to access the chart.

Understand the need for accurate data entry in documents.

It is extremely important to ensure accurate data entry. There is a saying, 'garbage in garbage out'. For example, if you enter an invoice total incorrectly, then the customer will receive an incorrect bill. Using computers, this incorrect entry may be automatically replicated elsewhere and the computer will not always be able to flag it up (unlike a person who may have spotted and questioned an erroneous entry). Always check and proofread your entries carefully.

Understand the need for using appropriate date and time formats.

Since data is now global, it is important to check that the date and time formats are clear and accurate. Unlike the UK, where dates have a DD/MM/YY format, in the US dates have a MM/DD/YY format. For instance a date of 10/5/02 in the UK is 10 May 02. In the US this would be October 5 02. Since the millennium, dates now often have YYYY formats so that 20th and 21st century dates are accommodated. Time formats can be 24 hour or 12 hour. When using 12-hour formats, remember to state whether am or pm. Regional settings can also be set using the **Start** menu, **Control Panel**, **Date**, **Time**, **Language and Regional Options**.

Understand the use and purpose of using codes for data entry.

When entering data it is a good idea to use codes for entries. For example, if you were to create a database of stock, you could create codes for suppliers' delivery times, ie supplier Hinchcliffe Paper Products could be coded HPP; delivery times could be coded A, B, C ... where A represents 1–2 days, B 3–5 days and C 1–2 weeks. Coding data makes for less effort when entering, and saves space and time. It is also less error prone since there is less to key in.

Understand the importance of maintaining the original proportions of images and charts.

Maintaining the original proportions of images is important so that the image is not distorted by looking too wide or too tall (imagine a wide giraffe!). Logo images are distinctive and would not look quite right if distorted. Charts should maintain their original proportions to ensure that the data that they are representing is clearly recognisable. All text should remain legible and easy on the eye.

Understand the concept of good spreadsheet design – refer to data already entered in cells rather than re-entering; enter formulas from left to right, top to bottom, where appropriate.

Good spreadsheet design minimises the need to re-enter data, thus reducing data entry errors. For example, formulae should be generated from existing cells. Formulae should be entered from left to right and top to bottom so that they are/can be replicated.
(*Module 4*)

Understand the use and purpose of not replicating zero values over blank cells.

When working with data always ensure that zero values display only when they should display, ie as a result of a calculation using real data. In Excel, when replicating formulae, zero values will often display as a result of using 'blank' data. If this is not noticed, results of functions such as Average, Min and Count will be incorrect since the zero cell entries will have been included by mistake.
(*Module 4, section 3*)

Understand how amendments to data may affect dependent formulae and appreciate the uses of this in the efficient modelling and projection of data.

When using spreadsheets it is very efficient and easy to model and project data. For instance, say that you have entered an interest rate of 6% in a cell and have based projections on this. Changing the cell entry up to 6.5% or down to 5.5% will automatically update all entries in the spreadsheet that relate to this cell. One simple change would also update any charts that are linked to the data. With the minimum of effort, several alternative 'what if' scenarios can quickly be viewed.

Understand how to minimise the risk of attack by viruses.

Minimising the risk of a virus attack has been covered in Module 1, section 4 and in Module 7, sections 1 and 4.

Know the importance of backups, and different methods to create and maintain records (full/incremental backups, rotation of files, grandfather/father/son).

Backups of important data should always be made for security reasons, in case the data is lost or corrupted. You can create backups yourself or various backup programs are available that allow you to make a full backup or record only changes that have been made since the last backup was made (incremental backup). Large organisations use the grandfather, father, son method for storing previous versions of data that is continually changing, eg bank and building society accounts. In this method the son is the current file, the father is from the previous backup and the grandfather from the backup before that.
(*Module 1, section 4, Module 2, section 3*)

1.5   International aspects

Understand how to insert special characters particularly where relevant to foreign languages.

Special characters, such as ©, ✂ and ☎, and foreign characters, such as é (as in café) or ñ (as in mañana) can be inserted into documents. In Word select: **Symbol** from the **Insert** menu or use **Character Map** (from the **Start** menu, select: **All Programs, Accessories, System Tools, Character Map**).
(*Module 3, section 2*)

Understand how to spell-check using a foreign language.

When working in applications, eg Word, the language can be set by selecting **Language** from the **Tools** menu. The appropriate foreign language spellchecker can then be used. Regional settings can also be set using the **Start** menu, **Control Panel, Date, Time, Language and Regional Options**. This ensures that time and date formats are correct.

Have a knowledge of international computer qualifications.

Holding up-to-date international computer qualifications denotes that you have the computer skills and capability to use computer technology within or outside your home country. An employer, college or university in a foreign country will be able to recognise and accredit you with your achievements. Not all computer qualifications are internationally recognised, so you should always check with the awarding body or with your training provider if you are considering working abroad. ECDL/ICDL is a leading and recognised worldwide qualification.

Understand how to sort data maintaining the integrity of corresponding data. Know the limitations of packages in doing this.

Understand the limitations of spreadsheets when used as a database (sorting doesn't maintain record integrity; all data is held in memory, maximum 3 levels of sort).

Some applications provide superior sort facilities to others. For example, when sorting data in Excel, it is vital that data in corresponding rows/columns is also selected before sorting. If only one column or row is selected, then only the data in that row is sorted; the corresponding rows will then not match up with the sorted row. Excel can be used as a database but using Access can be preferable since its sorting facilities are better – it maintains record integrity, sorts can be saved and the level of sorting is greater than three (the limit for Excel).

Understand the use and purpose of various field types (text, number, date/time, currency, auto number).

Fields can be set to different types that can be formatted so that data entry errors are minimised. For example, number field type entries would not accept text, date/time field type entries must contain a genuine date/time, eg not 41st June 20004. Setting field type formats is efficient and entries are neat and easy to read.
(Module 5, section 1)

Understand the use of OR between two fields and within a field.

Understand the use and purpose of using combined logical and range operators when defining search criteria (Boolean Logic).

The above topics have been covered in Module 5, section 3 and Module 7, section 3.

Understand the use of wild cards when searching for data.

Wild cards can be used as follows:

The wildcard *

The * is a wildcard that stands for any number and type of character, eg if you were unsure how to spell a name (in this example SMITHSON), you could enter SM*THSON or SM*SON. You can place the * wildcard before, after and between characters and you can use it more than once in a single field, eg SM*TH*.

The wildcard ?

The ? wildcard is an alternative to the * wildcard but acts as a placeholder for one character only, eg SM?THSON.

Understand the use and purpose of calculated fields.

Calculated fields can be useful when you want to find out, for instance, the average grade for an exam, the number of hours worked by an employee, subtotals and final totals. This saves having to count or calculate manually and is less error-prone.
(Module 5, section 4)

Understand the effects on data of different types of sorting (alphabetical, numeric, chronological).

Data can be presented dependent on the reason for your sort. For instance, it is normal when sorting lists of names to sort in ascending alphabetical order of surname and then alphabetical order of first name. This generates a list where a name is not preferentially listed at the top or bottom. When producing charts or graphs, sorting data in date (chronological) order can make for a more coherent representation. Sorting numeric data can, for instance, display your best customer at the top of the list.

Understand the purpose and effect of formatting numeric data (percentage, date, time, negative, currency, general).

Formatting numeric data is more efficient and entries are neat and easy to read. If numeric data was presented irregularly, eg some as percentages and some as actual numbers, it would be difficult to determine the relationship between them making the data difficult to compare.

Understand the use and purpose of headers and footers.

Many of the applications in this book provide the facility to create headers and footers on documents. Headers and footers can be included at the top and bottom of pages so that they display common text about the document, eg page numbers, date created, filename. This is a very useful feature, especially when creating multi-page documents or when working in teams.

Understand the concept of standard documents and use of styles to create uniform documents.

Understand the use and importance of style sheets for consistent formatting of text (typeface, size, weight etc).

Most organisations have standard documents with set styles, eg layout, font type and size, logo positioning. This gives their documents a standard look that can easily be recognised and understood. Using uniform documents and letterheads can make production of correspondence more efficient.

Distinguish between exploding pie charts, bar/column charts, line-column graphs and XY scatter graphs and understand when to use them.

Understand the importance of emphasising particular data.

Understand the need for a legend to correctly identify the data series displayed on chart.

Charting was covered in Module 4, section 6 so it is worth revisiting this.

Exploding pie charts display the pie segments pulled apart. A single particular segment could be pulled out to emphasise it (Figure 8.1).

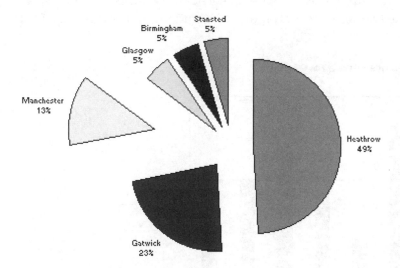

Figure 8.1 Exploded pie chart with the Manchester segment emphasised

An XY scatter graph shows if there is a relationship between two sets of data and identifies trends. Like a normal graph, it has *x* and *y* axes. If the points plotted are scattered randomly, there is no correlation (link) between the two sets of data (Figure 8.2).

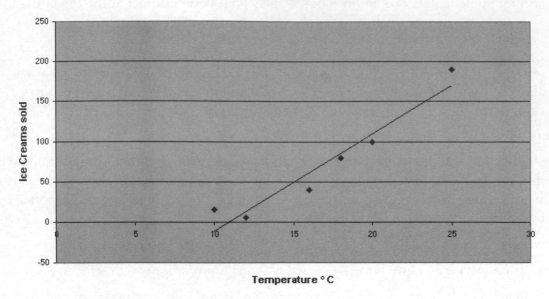

Ice Cream Sales/Temperature

Figure 8.2 Scatter graph

A typical line-column graph looks like Figure 8.3. It has columnar bars to represent one data series. This is plotted with another data series, represented by a line, on the same axis. The columns can be compared against the line. In this example, the columns represent actual grades achieved by students (students are labelled A, B, C and so on) and the line represents the average grade achieved by all the students in this sample. From this, we can easily see that seven students achieved the average grade or above and only four were below the average grade.

In this example the line is straight because it is plotting an average. However, in some graphs the line will not be a straight (Figure 8.4). The graph in Figure 8.3 has just one columnar data set but it is also possible to plot more than one data set in columns, as in Figure 8.4. The line on this graph is not a straight line because the average is of the two tests for each individual student, not the average for the whole group.

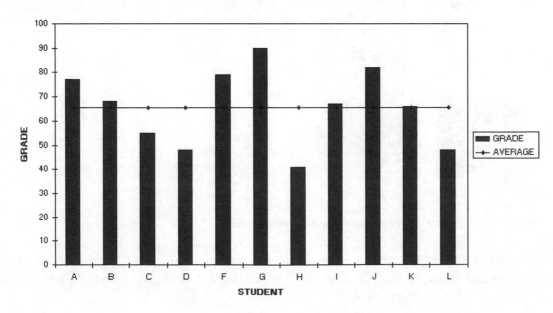

Figure 8.3 Line-column graph with one set of columnar data

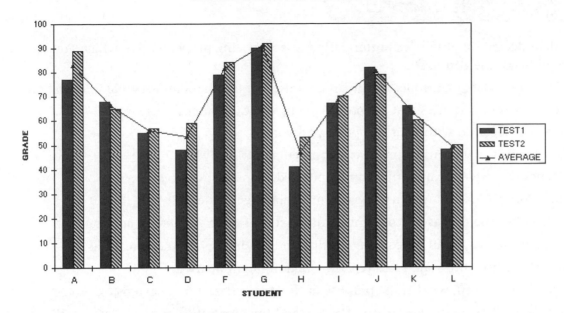

STUDENT GRADES FOR TWO TESTS

Figure 8.4 Line-column graph with two sets of columnar data

When there is more than one set of data, it is important to display a legend so that data sets can be determined. Legends are often used with pie charts, thus eliminating the need to label each segment.

1   If an individual decided that personal information was not being properly used, which government agency should he or she contact?

2   Explain the role of a Data Controller within an organisation that handles personal information.

3   Give three examples of activities that are prohibited by the Computer Misuse Act.

4   What should you never do with your computer password?

5   Why are flat screen (LCD) monitors more environmentally friendly?

6   Name the Windows display feature that can help to reduce paper waste.

7   Which application is most likely to use the Comma Separated Value (CSV) file format?

8   What term describes the process of combining information from a number of applications?

9   Name the area of memory used for copying/cutting and pasting between applications.

10 Give an example of how the search and replace function might be used.

11 When a document is saved, what is the purpose of the three-character file extension?

12 Explain the difference between the UK and US date and time formats.

13 What are the advantages of using codes for data entry?

14 Why should you try to minimise the need to re-enter data when designing a spreadsheet?

15 Name the three family members used to describe a method of storing backup files.

16 In which type of document/s might you need to insert special characters?

17 When would you find it advantageous to hold an international qualification?

18 Compared with Access, give one example of an Excel limitation when used as a database.

19 Why would you need to use Boolean Logic functions?

20 Explain how a wildcard might be used when searching for information.

21 List three types of data sorting.

22 Give two reasons why organisations often adopt standard document styles and layouts.

23 What type of chart/s would normally be used to identify trends?

24 What type of chart would normally be used to show percentages?

Note: These are only practice tasks. Successful completion does not imply certification of the module by the ECDL Foundation.

Appendix

Copying a file from the CD-ROM

1 Press the button on the CD-ROM drive to access the CD tray.

2 Place the CD in the tray with the label uppermost (ie showing).

3 Push the tray in to close it.

4 On the Windows XP desktop, from the **Start** menu, select: **Run**. The Run dialogue box is displayed.

5 In the **Run** box, key in the name of the CD drive. *Note*: This is usually drive D or E so key in **D:** (or **E:**).

6 Click on: **OK**.

7 The contents of the CD-ROM are displayed.

8 Locate the relevant file. (If the file is contained in a folder, you will need to open the folder by double-clicking on it to display the filename.) See below if you want to select multiple files or the entire contents of the CD-ROM.

9 Select: **Copy this file** from the **File and Folder Tasks** list.

10 In the **Copy Items** box, click on: the destination drive.

11 Click on: **Copy**.

Copying more than one file from the CD-ROM

Follow the steps above except:

At step 8, select multiple files by holding down the **Shift** key (selects adjacent files) or the **Ctrl** key (selects non-adjacent files).

At step 9, select: **Copy the selected items**.

Copying entire contents

Follow the steps above except:

At step 8, from the **Edit** menu, select: **Select All**.

Copying Access database files

1 Copy the files onto your hard disk (as above).

2 Before you open each file, in *My Computer* or *Windows Explorer*, right-click on the file and select: **Properties** at the bottom of the drop-down list.

3 With the **General** tab selected, in the **Attributes** section, click in: the **Read-only** box to remove the tick.

4 Click on: **Apply**, then on: **OK**.

Office Assistant

To hide the Office Assistant:

Right-click: over the Office Assistant; select: **Options** and set them to your preferences; click on: **OK**.

To turn the Office Assistant on:

From the **Help** menu, select: **Show the Office Assistant**.

Checking spelling and grammar

There are many options available. Throughout the book, I have chosen not to check on an ongoing basis but after keying in entire documents. Should you wish to choose other options:

From the **Tools** menu, select: **Options**. Click on: the **Spelling & Grammar** tab. Select your preferences and click on: **OK**.

Changing the unit of measure

To change the unit of measure from inches to cms or vice versa:

1   From the **Tools** menu, select: **Options**, and then click on the **General** tab.
2   In the **Measurement units** box, click on the down arrow and then on the option you want.
3   Click on: **OK**.

File maintenance within programs

In addition to using Windows Explorer and My Computer, you can carry out file maintenance within programs. When opening or saving a file, you are able to gain access to your files within the window (shown below). This is common to most Office programs. This window was opened in Word and displays only Word documents (by default). If you want to see other documents, click on: the down arrow next to **Files of Type** and make your selection. Click on: the **History** button to see recently opened files.

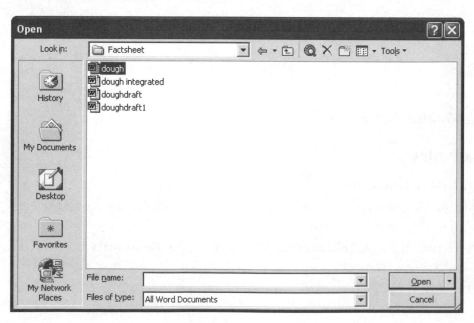

The main shortcut buttons that you will find useful are shown below. Using these will enable you to create folders and find out details of your files.

Up one level ──────────────┐   ┌────── Views
                           │   │
Create new folder ─────────┘

Clicking on: the down arrow next to the **Views** button produces a menu where you can select what detail you want to see in the **Open** window. The choices are: **List** (the default), **Details**, **Properties** and **Preview**.

Right-clicking on a file/folder will bring up the pop-up menu shown. This allows you to carry out any of the tasks on the menu.

A quicker way to delete a file or folder is by selecting it and pressing: **Delete**.

Note: You cannot carry out file maintenance on a file when the file is open.

A guide to document layout

When you have edited text or moved text within an exercise, remember adjustment of line spacing is often necessary. When proofreading pay particular attention to line spacing between paragraphs.

When inserting a sentence within a paragraph, make sure the spacing after any punctuation marks remains consistent. Make the necessary adjustments if required.

Use the Spellchecker but do realise its limitations.

Line spacing between paragraphs

Press: the **Return** key twice to leave one clear line space between paragraphs.

Underlining/underscoring

Underlining should not extend beyond the word. For example:

<u>word</u> is correct   <u>word </u>is incorrect

Punctuation

Be consistent with your spacing after punctuation marks. Use the following as a guide:

Punctuation	Mark	Number of spaces before/after
Comma	,	No space before – 1 space after
Semicolon	;	No space before – 1 space after
Colon	:	No space before – 1 or 2 spaces after
Full stop	.	No space before – 1 or 2 spaces after
Exclamation mark	!	No space before – 1 or 2 spaces after
Question mark	?	No space before – 1 or 2 spaces after

Hyphen

No space is left before or after a hyphen – eg dry-clean.

Dash

One space precedes and follows a dash – never place a dash at the left-hand margin when it is in the middle of a word or a sentence, always place it at the end of the previous line.

Brackets

No spaces are left between brackets and the word enclosed within them, eg (solely for the purposes of assignments).

Keyboard shortcuts that work (almost) everywhere

Keyboard	Menu	Keyboard	Menu
F1	Help	Alt + F4	File, Exit
F7	Tools, Spelling and Grammar	Ctrl + X	Edit, Cut
Ctrl + N	File, New	Ctrl + C	Edit, Copy
Ctrl + O	File, Open	Ctrl + V	Edit, Paste
Ctrl + S	File, Save	Ctrl + Z	Edit, Undo
F12	File, Save As	Ctrl + A	Edit, Select All
Ctrl + W	File, Close	Esc	Cancels items
Ctrl + P	File, Print		

Don't forget

Right-clicking over objects displays pop-up menus.